The Decline and Fall of Public Service Broadcasting

D0217603

The Decline and Fall of Public Service Broadcasting

Michael Tracey

BOWLING GREEN STATE UNIVERSITY LIBRARY DISCARDED

OXFORD UNIVERSITY PRESS

1998

BOWLING GREEN STATE
UNIVERSITY LIBRARY

Oxford University Press, Great Clarendon Street, Oxford OX2 6DP

Oxford New York

Athens Auckland Bangkok Bogota Bombay Buenos Aires
Calcutta Cape Town Dar es Salaam Delhi Florence Hong Kong
Istanbul Karachi Kuala Lumpur Madras Madrid Melbourne
Mexico City Nairobi Paris Singapore Taipei Tokyo Toronto Warsaw

and associated companies in
Berlin Ibadan

Oxford is a registered trade mark of Oxford University Press

Published in the United States
by Oxford University Press Inc., New York

© Michael Tracey 1998

First published 1998

All rights reserved. No part of this publication may be reproduced,
stored in a retrieval system, or transmitted, in any form or by any means,
without the prior permission in writing of Oxford University Press.
Within the UK, exceptions are allowed in respect of any fair dealing for the
purpose of research or private study, or criticism or review, as permitted
under the Copyright, Designs and Patents Act, 1988, or in the case of
reprographic reproduction in accordance with the terms of the licences
issued by the Copyright Licensing Agency. Enquiries concerning
reproduction outside these terms and in other countries should be
sent to the Rights Department, Oxford University Press,
at the address above

This book is sold subject to the condition that it shall not, by way
of trade or otherwise, be lent, re-sold, hired out or otherwise circulated
without the publisher's prior consent in any form of binding or cover
other than that in which it is published and without a similar condition
including this condition being imposed on the subsequent purchaser

British Library Cataloguing in Publication Data
Data available

Library of Congress Cataloging-in-Publication Data
Tracey, Michael.
The decline and fall of public service broadcasting / Michael
Tracey.
Includes bibliographical references.
1. Public broadcasting—Case studies.   I. Title.
HE8689.7.P82T7   1997
384.55'4'09—dc21   97–11243
ISBN 0–19–815925–0
ISBN 0–19–815924–2 (pbk.)

1 3 5 7 9 10 8 6 4 2

Typeset by Graphicraft Typesetters Ltd., Hong Kong
Printed in Great Britain
on acid-free paper by
Biddles Ltd., Guildford and King's Lynn

I dedicate this book to my children Jash, Kashia, and Zoshia, who have brought more joy, love, and warmth to my life than I probably deserve, and certainly more than I ever expected. I dedicate it in the hope that some day they will read this work and understand something of that in which their daddy believed.

A Personal Prologue

In December 1991 I happened to be in London and went with a friend, David Mills, to the Granada Christmas party at the company's headquarters in Golden Square. Apparently there is always a theme to these events and that year it was 'the casino'. Guests could gamble mock money on such games as roulette and win prizes contributed by the company. The atmosphere was ostensibly festive, but beneath the surface there was a current of anxiety, a real fear of what the future held. In attendance and surrounded by his new wannabees was the recently appointed chief executive of the Granada group, Gerry Robinson, who had been brought in to restore the organization's health. He had come from a catering company and was an accountant by training. It is easy to be sniffy about this, and that needs to be avoided. But clearly there was something peculiar about such a figure taking over, among other things, a company in the shape of Granada Television which was regarded quite simply as one of the greatest TV organizations in Britain and, therefore, the world. Gerry Robinson's lack of affection for *Brideshead Revisited* was well known, on a par with Mark Fowler's description of television as a toaster with pictures,[1] and Michael Green's that there was no difference between a TV programme and a cigarette lighter.[2]

Robinson's mission inevitably would bring him into conflict with the traditions and practices which had garnered Granada Television's reputation, and in particular with the man who more than any other represented the qualities which had riveted the world of public service television for so long, David Plowright. Plowright was not at the party. Indeed, there seemed to be few telly types, presumably because one does not voluntarily sup from the poisoned chalice.

[1] Fowler was Ronald Reagan's first chairman of the Federal Communications Commission and very much the architect of the deregulatory policies that were to characterize that agency's policies in the 1980s.
[2] Green now owns the largest commercial franchise in Britain.

There was, however, someone else there, a man who even at first glance seemed out of place. He was small and quiet, and sat alone. He looked to be in his late fifties, though he wore an air of sadness which suggested a greater burden than age. He had on what we used to call 'Sunday best', the kind of off-the-peg, smart but sensible grey suit that once upon a time one could get from Burton the Tailor. His knotted tie was slightly askew and spoke of someone not familiar with such garb. David Mills and I spoke with him briefly. His name was Don Lomax, his job to take the office mail around Granada's headquarters. And just before Christmas 1991 the new Granada regime had arrived at one of their first decisions. Brought in to 'sort out' Granada, Don sacked the mailman. He had the reputation of being the shyest man in the company. This was his last office Christmas party. And even though his time was past, and he certainly did not fit in with all the corporate types who flocked around Robinson like gulls off the stern of a tramp steamer, he had come to take part in what was for him a time-honoured tradition. As we chatted he told us that he had been a bit nervous of attending, but added with quiet dignity, 'I thought I ought to come.' I remember one tragi-comic aspect. He was drinking beer, though the free bar was stocked with all kinds of spirits and wines. It emerged that he would like a whisky, but felt a little ill at ease asking the bartender. We got him a large one, and then drifted away, as did he.

Several months later I heard that David Plowright had also been driven from Granada. The battle with Robinson had come to a head. He wanted to squeeze more profit out of the television side of the group, and Plowright refused on the grounds that to do so would irreparably damage its programme-making abilities. The subsequent carnage is a matter of public record.

When I heard that news of Plowright, the image of Don Lomax and the Christmas party was very much on my mind. From the lowest to the highest rung, both men victims, and in the process something which had been important, perhaps even wonderful, facing possible debasement. And then I thought of all those others who had once been involved in British public service broadcasting, possibly the greatest single system of diverse, quality communication the world has ever seen. No jingoism here—I do not especially like Britain anymore—rather, a simple truth recognized by everyone, at home and abroad. The 1980s were the Passchendaele of public broadcasting: a whole officer class of talent and conviction destroyed by idiotic decisions from above and the short-sighted acquiescence of a population troubled by other things. And with them went the likes of our friend from the mailroom. David Plowright and Don Lomax suffering the same fate at the same hands.

With the demise of Plowright in Granada and the rise of John Birt as Director-General at the BBC yet again the bell seemed to toll for public service broadcasting. The demise was certainly being drawn out; indeed here was a death so lingering as to have become a new form of life.

A number of influences had led me to think about organizations such as the BBC and Granada. My family background was very much centre left Labour Party which took as given the importance of the public sector in providing for those things in life which the private could not or would not. I was enormously influenced by the thinking and writing of Tony Smith, now of Magdalen College, Oxford, and Jim Halloran of the University of Leicester. Both were seminal figures in their own right, both had powerful personalities that inevitably influenced me in ways which they have perhaps never quite understood. Theirs was scholarship informed by moral purpose, by commitments to fairness, justice, and democratic practice. Since I came to see the arguments about public broadcasting as essentially points of entry to more fundamental arguments about the condition of society, it would be only fair to say that it is there that their influences are most apparent. Perhaps even more significant in shaping my view about public broadcasting was my involvement with Hugh Greene, Director-General of the BBC from 1960 to 1969. I first met Greene when writing my doctoral thesis, which included a chapter on the circumstances of his retirement from the BBC, in effect arguing that he had slowly been forced out.

Hugh Greene was a great Director-General in a way in which those who came after him were not. This is not to say that they were not good men, indeed were probably almost certainly better men as friends, fathers, spouses. Greene was neither a good father nor husband, and had few close friends. What he had was an extraordinary potency to articulate values which one might reasonably suggest are crucial to the general well-being of this democracy. Whatever we mean by charisma, he had it with some to spare.

In the course of my research for the book I came to see that while the political Establishment and its gofers—in the press, Parliament, the Board of Governors, the Churches—found Greene troublesome, and while others saw in him a certain moral laxity, many held him in affection. I remember one occasion in 1979 in the George pub, just round the corner from Broadcasting House. I was there with Greene after a party for the launch of Asa Briggs's *Governing the BBC*. The champagne had been good, but Greene liked beer and the odour of smoke and flesh that constitutes the English pub. At one point a gentleman approached us. He had, it emerged, worked as a journalist in the BBC during the 1960s. On this evening he was a tad under the weather, his portly frame swayed as if his body were, leaf-like, touched by a gentle breeze. His nose was stubby and criss-crossed by reddish markings that suggested he had lived well and drunk even better. Under his eyes the flesh hung like the crenulated curtains one sees in the cinema. The fact that I was writing a biography of Greene became known to him and he launched a stubby finger at my face and said in a demanding tone, 'tell them what he did'—and here his stubby finger altered course and veered toward Greene—'tell them that *he* was DG, that then we could *do* things, that then it was something, it was exciting to be in the BBC'. The next time I heard a sentiment put in a similar way was when I spoke with those who had been close to David Plowright, former Chairman of Granada, whom I have come to know well in recent years. He reminds me of Greene, though there are some profound personal differences. Plowright was clearly tough and abrasive but he was also charming and kind. Most of all though he had principles, believed in the creative freedoms and responsibilities of his programme-makers, and saw in Granada not commerce but a means to the end of serving and thus nurturing a better society. It is *there* that he and Greene touched.

Greene was progressive, iconoclastic, liberal, and naughty. He was emotionally and intellectually in tune with the mood of the country and of those, relatively young, people who had moved into the BBC in the 1950s, though he was never emotionally in tune with his own young people, his children thus perhaps affirming Yeats's observation that 'the intellect of man is forced to choose Perfection of the life, or of the work'. One cannot suggest that Greene chose work over life; childhood circumstances did the choosing. His work seems nevertheless to support George Steiner's proposition that 'There are men and women who in addition to having special gifts, seem to embody the times in which they live. Somehow their biographies take on and make more visible to the rest of us the shape and meaning of the age.'

It occurs to me that, viewed from this perspective, John Birt, who became the Director-General of the BBC in 1992, is as interesting a figure as John Reith (Managing Director of the British Broadcasting Company 1922–6, Director-General 1927–38) and Hugh Greene, precisely because of the way in which each was, is, metaphor to a larger reality: in Reith austere Christian and patrician certainties; in Greene the trinity of wit, secular humanism, and liberal democracy; in Birt the rationalizing efficiency, pragmatism, and authoritarianism of a creaking political economy which neither welcomed nor even recognized the need for the provision of a public space for public communication. In each was the moment: the lingering paternalism of Victorian capitalism; the populist democratizing of the 1950s and 1960s; the struggles of late twentieth-century capitalism.

In Rome in 1965 Greene told his audience:

historically the greatest risks have attached to the maintenance of what is right and honourable and true. Truth for ever on the scaffold, wrong for ever on the throne. Honourable men who venture to be different, to move ahead of—or even against—the general trend of public feeling, with sincere conviction and with the intention of enlarging the understanding of our society and its problems, may well feel the scourge of public hostility many times over before their worth is recognized. I see it as the clear duty of a public service broadcasting organization to stand firm against attempts to decry sincerity and vision—we have a duty to take account of the changes in society, to be ahead of public opinion, rather than always to wait upon it. I believe that great broadcasting organizations, with their immense powers of patronage of writers and artisans, should not neglect to cultivate young writers who may, by any, be considered 'too advanced' or 'shocking'.

What he did essentially was to give his producers their head; they appreciated that this was his role and responded with one of the great creative explosions in the history of broadcasting. Grace Wyndham Goldie, the legendary doyenne of BBC current affairs television, noted: 'I must admit that I'm prejudiced about Hugh Greene. I like him. A lot of people didn't and a lot of people didn't get on very well with him, and I quite often disagreed with him. But he was easily the most congenial DG with whom I've ever had to work. Because largely we recognized him, we, the production staff I mean, as one of us.' One of the most influential producers in the history of British television, Donald Baverstock, argued that what emerged during the latter part of the 1950s and the early part of the 1960s was a kind of self-managing bureaucracy. He felt that there were two ideas of how to run the BBC:

either that it was managed or that it was up to each person in his job to do as responsible a job as possible bearing in mind the overall necessity to enable the BBC to survive. It was the difference between, if you like, the idea of management which was based on a notion of power and the idea of self-control, not control, which really necessitates trust. Unless people trust each other they can't talk honestly to each other. If they're taking orders they are not expected to take the right initiatives of their own accord.

The difference that Baverstock was suggesting was the difference between the managed society and the self-governing society: 'if you have a system of trust you must trust your superiors but your superiors must trust you.' Clearly they trusted Greene. What is interesting about this view is that it suggests that what happened in those years depended not so much on the sudden, miraculous appearance of lots of creative and clever people, but rather on the way in which the BBC was managed: 'you can't order people to have good ideas. You can order people not to have dangerous ideas quite easily and they all go off and do things that nobody could possibly object to . . . the BBC should not see itself as being managed but see itself as a series of groups all managing themselves, and you must trust them to employ the true principles of the BBC as they see them, as best they can.'

What was carried on the spittle of the drunken journalist in the George and the comments of Goldie and Baverstock was a profound feeling that the BBC had changed, intellectually and managerially. Much has been made in recent times of the impact of John Birt on the BBC, and that certainly needs to be explored. Birt, however, was the culmination of a process not its originator, though one suspects that he would very much prefer to be seen as the latter. One of the best books ever written about the Corporation, Tom Burns's *The*

BBC: Public Institution and Private World (1977), is based on a series of interviews which he undertook in 1963 and then in 1973. What is utterly clear from the account is the way in which even in those years one could see the rise of a new professionalism and managerialism in which the commitment of programme-making was more to the activity itself than to any sense of a larger meaning of the place of the broadcaster in society. At one point he refers to 'the surprising absence, in so exceptionally articulate a working community, of discussion about the social purpose or the social consequences of broadcasting'.[3]

This was a conclusion which gelled very much with what was then my own youthful sense of what was happening to the BBC. It was clear that Greene had been forced out in 1969 for reasons that were to do with the increasing nervousness of the British political and social establishment about 'everything' and the increasingly parlous state of the public treasury and the household purse. The real travails, when Burns published and I had first written about Greene, were yet to come. But tilt the head upward and it was not difficult to get the first scent of winter on the wind.

This book, however, is not about Granada or the BBC alone, or even just about public broadcasting. It is, I hope, more than that. It is about the larger condition of society refracted through the experience of one, key, institution: public broadcasting. The book is, I recognize, personal, since much of what I have come to understand about public broadcasting and its larger significance was fashioned by the marvellous experience of having come to know those who made it happen, who created a quite extraordinary culture of broadcasting, animated by principles and a sense of relationship to society, now replaced by the hungry eyes of the monied classes, the quick fix of organization theory and the techno-babble of overpaid management consultants. There were many such figures, too many names to list. Some, such as Hugh Greene, Grace Wyndham Goldie, Ian Jacob, Arthur fforde, are no longer with us. Others exist in a kind of twilight zone to which they were dispatched in the 1980s and the early 1990s.

My curriculum vitae is dotted with the dates of talks given in many different countries, sometimes in an academic setting, but often among broadcasters. The pretext was usually my research but the real reason for being there—as with the real reason for writing this book—was political not analytical, to make the case for public broadcasting as a means to making the case against a global order which danced with ever greater fervour to the tune of the market.

At some point, however, in the relatively recent past the exercise suddenly felt slightly foolish and closed-minded. This is not meant to suggest that in

---

[3] T. Burns, *The BBC: Public Institution and Private World* (London: Macmillan, 1977), 132.

principle the arguments put forward were foolish, but rather that the fervour with which I pursued them had seriously impaired my judgement analytically. Perhaps the feeling was born of living since 1988 in the United States—most commentators and theorists of public broadcasting did not—which for all its wonders and promise does have some very heavy-duty negatives.

I came to see that I had drifted away from positions which spoke of the need to maintain public broadcasting but nowhere explored that desire as a historically realizable ambition. In a commentary on a draft manuscript of this book I was told:

My sense living in Britain is that the forces attacking the principles of public service broadcasting are starting to receive their come-uppance. Birt's 'reforms' at the BBC are being seen as poverty stricken. The 1990 Broadcasting Act which gave Michael Green and others the go-ahead has revealed them as being incapable of producing new programming of any quality and, increasingly, even ITV's popularity is now coming into question. Most grievous of all, I do not think Tracey has taken on board the sense (which I believe to be prevalent in the US) that the cable television challenge has now been met. In short, then, I find the manuscript a little too defensive and I think it would be necessary to have it revised and updated; much of the most recent work on the theory of the public sphere which I would have thought would have been of considerable grist to his mill and would anyway have grounded his defense of the principles of public service broadcasting in a somewhat less polemical way. I say this as one who firmly believes that it is only by recourse to the idea of the public sphere that public service broadcasting can be defended.

There was much that was forcefully interesting in this critique of the position which I had begun to adopt. However, I have to say that I think it is utterly wrong. In order to explain this more clearly I need to make a general point, and this flows from the well-established proposition that how we 'see' depends to a considerable extent on where we stand. The reviewer stands and thus sees from within a British, academic debate that has been powerful and insightful but which now has shifted over into a certain wistful prescriptiveness. This is most telling in the argument that I should deal more with the public sphere literature since in such theorizing lies the real defence of public service broad-casting. That seems to me to misunderstand the power of theory, but it also does not seem to recognize that one of my central arguments is that the realm of 'the public' is severely damaged, and that one does not need Mr Habermas to understand that. I am not saying that literature on the public sphere is un-interesting, nor that it did not have important things to say about the decline of a public realm. I am saying that that body of theory has insufficiently dealt with the concrete impacts of new corporate and technological architectures. That it has not done so is I believe because theory became anchored within a sentimental desire for the comforts of a more collectivist ethic and sociology.

There is a phrase from E. P. Thompson which is useful in this context. In a critique of bankrupt left theorizing he observes that much of its problem has been its avoidance of what he calls 'the collisions of evidence and the awkward confrontations of experience'. There is too much theorizing which is more sentimental than analytical, and far too much with no dirt under its fingernails.

This disposition translates into a habit, very much alive in Britain, of declaring the merits of public service broadcasting as if that will be enough to preserve and protect. God knows I have tried over the years to make the case, as have many others in Britain. But there comes a time when one should recognize that the game is up, at least in any way which we would recognize, and that the objective circumstances within which the institutions of public service broadcasting find themselves, not just in Britain but everywhere, are antithetical to the basic principles and will continue to be so into any foreseeable future.

Inevitably I now 'see' the relationship between public broadcasting and more broadly based developments in the infrastructure and social practice of communications from within the United States. What I see is troubling and disturbing, and nothing has led me to believe that the critiques of the crassness of much of American popular culture which we all engaged in during the 1980s were wrong. What we probably did not see, or refused to see, was the sheer extent to which that popular culture was articulated through structural and ideological developments throughout the industrial democracies. We can espouse the virtues of public service broadcasting as much as we like but that will not inhibit the continuing development of market-based systems employing digital technologies. That is why it is difficult to agree with the argument that in Britain the forces attacking the principles of PSB 'are starting to receive their come-uppance'. Equally, while Birt's 'reforms' may well, from one perspective, be seen to be 'poverty stricken' it is only a sliver of the community which does so see them. At a conference of the EBU in 1993, with Birt in the front row, I noted that all was not well inside the BBC if one viewed that organization according to the classical standards of public service broadcasting. He hated my doing so and accused me of withering away in Colorado and being out of touch. The fact remains, however, and we have to recognize this: John Birt won the battle for the Corporation. I wish he had not but he did, just as Gerry Robinson won at Granada and David Plowright was ousted. I wish he had not but he did. I can see no circumstances in which the *status quo ante bellum* will be restored. Even with a Blair administration, or its equivalent elsewhere, there is absolutely no going back to a 1960s public service model, no way of disinventing cable and satellite. There is more chance of Blair renationalizing steel—and there is no chance of that. Broadband/digital interactive/compression technologies, satellite, virtual reality systems, will not go away. Like broken hearts, nuclear weapons, and Oprah Winfrey, unfortunate but there. In fact, and perhaps perversely, they will be further encouraged.

And the more that happens the more the problems will mount up for public broadcasting.

One more ill-explored assumption within the commentary on my manuscript was that any book such as this should 'include the failures of market place solutions'. From within the terms of the 1980s and 1990s, the marketplace has been fantastically successful. From within the terms of the debate about public service broadcasting, the market-place has been a disaster—but a disaster initiated by the success of the market. I might add here that one of the problems with the defence of public broadcasting in recent times has been precisely that there appeared to be a feeling that simply by articulating the brilliance and benignity of PSB, as it had traditionally been, one would necessarily win the war of words which was being waged, by the 1980s, over the whole future of communications, and in particular of television. It is interesting for example that, if one ranges across the titles of numerous articles, books, monographs, and conferences about PSB, terms such as 'preserve', 'defend', 'save', 'uphold' figure prominently. There is nothing wrong in this, indeed there is much that is praiseworthy since such debates tended to be part of a dialogue about the future of society. There is, however, something naïve about the position, since the challenges to public service broadcasting lie not in the whimsical play of politics, but in very basic changes in the whole economic, technological, and philosophical organization of the planet. This is by no means to suggest that the debate over language is unimportant. Any institution is inscribed with discourse fashioned by particular ideologies. The fate of any institution is always—though rarely overtly—determined by the character of that discourse. There has to be a conceptual proximity between 'the idea' which informs the institution and the philosophical, sociological, and cultural terms which provide the context within which it rests and by which it is formed. Nowhere more so than in the realm of broadcasting. If, however, we conclude that there is disjunction between 'the idea' and the context then all the declarations about preserving, in this case, public broadcasting will be for naught. That is why, for example, the increasing use of the term 'customer' by BBC executives in their public statements is so revealing. What it reveals is a corporation which is increasingly in lock-step with a larger *Zeitgeist*, but more and more out of step with any meaningful concept of public service broadcasting. The thought which informs my work more than any other is that the fundamental problem which public broadcasters face lies in the shakiness of the very idea of a 'public good' and 'public interest', that history has passed it by, leaving political rhetoric, institutional weakness, and nostalgic chatter.

Indeed, there is within the public broadcasting community, one senses, a certain wistfulness nestling alongside a kind of fear and foreboding. It is a mood that was well captured by a programme on British television in 1994, an interview between the writer and broadcaster Melvyn Bragg and the television playwright Dennis Potter. Threaded throughout the talk was an argument about what constitutes great television and what provides the crucible within which the alchemy of creation happens. The wistfulness was born of a feeling that something was being lost, carried within the metaphor of life ebbing away, because Potter was dying of cancer and punctuated the conversation with sips from a flask of liquid morphine. Within it lurked stubborn optimism, that if only we can maintain the licence fee, get the right kind of person in as DG—Potter mentioned that intelligent populist Michael Grade, who now runs Channel Four—demand more of ITV, encourage more independent production, if only . . . then the glory that was British television will once more be. The backward glance to a past and better age of television was powerful. It was, however, just that: a backward glance.

It is possible that those who have argued that the public sphere in broadcasting will finally triumph over the forces of the market will in the long term be shown to be correct. They have more optimism, more sunshine in their hearts than I am able to summon since while I hope they are correct I seriously doubt it.

The more this book has brewed, the longer I remain in the USA, but watch the rise of Clintonism in Britain and elsewhere, the more that all I can summon up is a certain dimming of the spirit and a conclusion that what is in danger is not public broadcasting, but democracy itself. That paradoxically the years of the Cold War forced at least a rhetorical commitment to principles of democratic practice. Their passing has left the field clear for the assertion of the values of capital, with consumers consumed with consumption, a politics of pragmatic power and the occasional savagery of imaginations which are not modern or post-modern but feudal.

In this book I very much wanted to explain to new and younger audiences why the argument around public service broadcasting was about so much more than broadcasting. It was about the whole character of our lives, about principles and values and moral systems that the market was marginalizing. At the same time, however, I did not want to pretend that every problem has a solution, nor that a difficult situation is always retrievable. Sometimes, the more one studies the more one grieves.

I begin to sense a certain innocence in the very ambition of supporting public broadcasting. It is probably over, for many reasons that will preoccupy the following pages. It is not an innocence of which one should be ashamed or which one should deny. My favourite description of Hugh Greene is that he was an *enfant terrible*, sometimes more *enfant* than *terrible*. That was said by Glanmor Williams and the tone was warm and caring not cynical, understanding of the fact that in Greene were qualities to be cherished. I think of Greene and these others often, and know that their spirit has animated me, more than anything else other than possibly close family and a few friends. But what they stood for is probably over, and we are the lesser for it. Yet whatever the shabby cynicism of the modern era, grasping and uninspired, as an age it can never destroy the conviction that, in the words of Robert James Waller, "The old dreams were good dreams; they didn't work out, but I'm glad I had them.'

M.T.

Boulder, Colo.
Summer 1996

Acknowledgements

I should like to thank a number of people who have supported my work over the years. Michael Traber of the World Association for Christian Communication did a marvellous job of editing an early version of the manuscript. The Hoso Bunka Foundation of Tokyo, and in particular Mr Shinichi Shimizu, gave invalubale support to me on a number of occasions. The University of Colorado, and Wick Rowland, Dean of the School of Journalism, not only provided resources but a wonderful environment in which to write. Pat Hatfield, Judy Jensen, Kristin Koida, Diane William all worked diligently on producing the manuscript. Finally, I want to thank Andrew Lockett, my editor at OUP. Not only was he a delight to work with but he revived a writing project that I had thought dead and instilled the confidence that it could indeed be completed. I will always be enormously grateful for that.

Contents

Part IV. The Ceremony of Innocence

I cannot help wondering whether from this great money-eyed industry anything of value to the human spirit can ever emerge.

(Graham Greene on Hollywood, June 1936)

Now it is the beginning of a fantastic story. Let us take a journey to the cave of monsters.

(Preamble to the video game Babble, Bobble)

PART I

—

Theories

1 Public Service Broadcasting in the Post-war World

History is on fast forward. It seems that each day, each moment, something momentous is happening. This regime dies, that country is born, tribes and economies collide. *Change* is the call sign of the age. And at the heart of that process of change lies electronic communication, down wires, through the ether, from the heavens. Cable, earth-based transmitters, and satellites have become the dominant technologies of our time. The instruments of the modern age seem no longer to be just weapons of war, but forms of conversation, exchange, dialogue, understandings (and confusions) of a kind we have never experienced before. The globe never sleeps because global communications systems need never sleep. Where governments once addressed each other through the diplomatic pouch, the discreet whispers in a corner at formal meetings, through 'the proper channels', now they are made to speak to each other through global news distribution systems. Consider that during the Gulf War of 1991 the common source of information for the three principals, George Bush, Saddam Hussein, and King Fahd, was the Cable News Network (CNN), and that the American Secretary of Defense Dick Cheney was heard to mutter, 'like the rest of you I'm receiving my news from CNN'. While there may have been a touch of disingenuousness about this—Cheney would after all have had intelligence and analysis from the vast array of American intelligence agencies—the fact and nature of the comment suggested something significant, that the transnational propagation of news had come of age and was now an important part of the infrastructure of global life. The solemnity of the development was symbolized perfectly when the founder of CNN, Ted Turner, was canonized in that peculiarly American way by being anointed as *Time*'s Man of the Year. And there is so much more in what is truly, risking cliché, the Age of Communication.

Telecommunications and computers, some argue, are the altar at which the future prays. Personal communications systems grow, and by the end of the decade low-orbit satellites will ensure that every square inch of the planet's surface will be made available to the mobile phone. The cheap home computer provides access to distant databases, teleworking, electronic noticeboards, a portal to places that are not real but imagined, an avenue, depending on one's perspective, to a new Cyberia, chip-based gulags or new communities within which the Jeffersonian ideal is finally established. High-definition television, digitalization, video, broadband networks, are the gizmos which seem to define the age with increasing force, reminding me of a comment by Carlyle on locomotives in the nineteenth century: 'they are our poems.' New communications empires rise, matched by the apparent terminal decline of the old. Deregulation and commerce, multiplication of services, more of what we know and promises of lots that we do not, provide the lexicon of the modern era.

In short we live at an extraordinary moment in history which to a considerable extent is defined not only by the technological and institutional capacity to communicate but by the amplified human propensity to do so. Collectively we travel more, desire more things to watch, yearn for more things—especially music—to listen to; collect more and more television channels and videocassettes in the manner of small boys in a simpler time collecting baseball cards and toy soldiers.

Television, in particular, lies at the heart of political, social, and cultural life. Our pleasure, our information, our enlightenment, our grasp of world and local affairs, much of our leisure time begin with and are absorbed by the medium. To say such is almost clichéd, and yet it is an obvious, unassailable, potent, and portentous truth. It is, therefore, an obvious conclusion to draw that, if television is such an important institution at the national and global level, what happens to it is of some considerable significance.

There are two ways to study television. One is to see the medium as consisting of a series of institutions with their own interior life, surrounded by a set of political and economic imperatives. A second way, however, is to see television as expressive, as articulating the symbolic character and substantive ambitions of society—writ small as a nation-state, or large as global life. From this perspective the institution of television is a keyhole through which to survey a larger room in which lie the real choices society is making about itself and for itself. *How* we inform, amuse, and educate ourselves through television tells us much about how we wish to be informed, amused, and educated as a society. If there lies mediocrity or excellence in the doing of television, it is possible that mediocrity or excellence will dominate the wider terrain.

This is not to suggest some simple process of causality, that 'poor' television creates an impoverished culture. Rather it is to suggest that through this primary medium can be seen oozing to the surface of public life the subterranean ambitions, philosophies, and deep character of this or that nation-state, or more contemporaneously the global structures of cultural trade which are laying waste the very idea of national culture.

It follows that if television is representational of the play of values within society, to ask questions about the character of the drama, or children's, or news, current affairs, or documentary programming offered; to ask about the *purpose* of the institution in terms which require something more than a simple pointing to fiscal effectiveness; to ask what values prevail within the medium is necessarily to ask about the character and values which prevail outside its walls.

If, for example, a programme is made, not because it might educate, amuse, move, even shock us to our greater enrichment, but simply because it might make money, then that suggests a profound, but different, choice for this potentially most wonderful of media. Consider American local television news—with its orthodontically perfect, immaculately coiffed, oozing with bonhomie anchor persons; its trivia, its factoids masquerading as journalism, its mock seriousness in the face of real pain and suffering, its sheer superficiality; its manipulativeness of its audience, its crass, brutal commercialism, and the screaming absence of much that is truly excellent. If one cares to look closely at this it is at least plausible to suggest that one can see the real soul of the machine, the crass commercialism, superficiality, and sheer mediocrity of too much of American life. Laid bare in local television are very much the choices America has made for itself.

If one takes a very broad historical perspective it is as if at the geopolitical level we have been living for forty years in a time-warp. It is a fact of biological life that when the temperature of the body is lowered it starts to function at a slower and slower rate until it ceases to function at all. So one might now look at the post-1945 world, defined by the appropriate phrase the Cold War, as one in which history was slowed down to the point of being frozen into a terrified immobility. What was frozen was a set of cultural and national relationships which had been formed over millennia and which had provided the swirl of global life until 1914, when began the cold dark age which reached its nadir in the rise of fascism, the years of Stalin, the 1962 Cuban missile crisis, and the near disastrous collision between the United States and the Soviet Union in the deserts of the Middle East in the early 1970s.

With the thaw provided by the initiatives pursued by Gorbachev in the first instance, the freeing of the states of Central Europe, and then the collapse in

August 1991 of the Soviet Union, came old life in new form. That is why one looks at events in Europe, in the Far East, in the Balkans with a fearful sense of *déjà vu*. There is, however, an important difference between the late 1980s and pre-1914: in the years of the Cold War, capitalism, the dominant form of economic activity, re-formed and restructured itself into a system of truly global activity. No longer did the largest companies define themselves as belonging to this or that country. Now they belonged to all. And paralleling this was the emergence of colossal new arrangements—economic and political—between nation-states. The European Economic Community and the North American Free Trade Agreement between the United States, Canada, and Mexico are only the most obvious examples of this process. What we can in effect see happening is a metaphorical shifting in the very concept of national boundary to accommodate the evolved structures of global markets.

A somewhat more Panglossian view of the meaning of this, one which anti-cipated the changes just described, and one of the most overworked phrases of the modern era, is probably McLuhan's 'the global village'. The very phrase is transparent and seductive in its meaning: we are all linked in a single global, nurturing, and comfortable community, what has been called a tribal oneness. And what has made it possible is communication. The problem with this is that wherever one looks the villagers are killing each other, or perhaps one might say the members of one village are killing those from another. The age in which we live has in part become defined not by uniformities but by an extraordinary array of divergencies, sometimes brutal and deadly. The world is far from uniform, nor is it unified by a global culture. Human society remains a mosaic of differences and multiple singularities. It is a totally plaus-ible thesis to suggest that contemporary history at street level is the aggressive assertion of national and cultural difference. How else does one explain the rise of Islam in slums from Tehran to Cairo to Algiers; resurgent fascism in various parts of Europe; deadly ethnic strife throughout Central and southern Europe; urban riots in Britain and race riots in Los Angeles; insurrections in Peru, Mexico, northern Spain, Northern Ireland; the remarkable Catalanization of the 1992 Olympics; nascent separatist movements in French Canada, the south-western United States, northern Italy; the slow-motion revolution of the street that we label urban violence; collisions between people of different moral and sexual persuasions; bitter conflicts over political correctness?

There may be powerful attempts to create a global culture through the col-onization of world-wide systems of communication, but that is very different from any easy conclusion that such attempts have been successful. It is one thing to point to the ubiquity of MTV culture, CNN, blue jeans, and the Sony Walkman. It is quite another to assume that new cultural orders are being formed.

The view expressed here is not necessarily one which is widely shared. One writer observed that:

the Japanese have contributed, if not to world peace, at least to the reduction of social restiveness, by providing the world with high-quality, relatively affordable and technically ingenious items, many of which are aimed primarily to make ordinary daily life just a little more enjoyable. There is an aspect of this fact that has come to intrigue me of late, namely, that Japanese products, almost all of them, are what might best be described as 'Uni-cultural'. There is nothing 'Japanese' about them. They are not the kinds of things like, say, airplanes, ocean liners, zeppelins, or even haute couture which can be hyped into some kind of symbol of national grandeur. Whether we speak of cameras, automobiles, TVs and VCRs or the vast array of audio devices made so readily available the world over, the purpose of the item is to give a boost to someone's daily life. . . . The goods are generic, universal, only the inputs vary. Japanese products, in effect, since they are primarily instruments of communication, are the common carriers driving us all more deeply into a world-wide Uni-culture.[1]

Sherwood seems here to be broadly welcoming this culture of unification for what I take to be an interesting, even important, but contestable reason. He feels that the basic problem which confronts us as a species is the problem of social order, of how we keep the demons safely in the cave. If the production of cultural products, particularly ones that provide for pleasure—this music, that programme, this movie—achieves this then so be it. Passivity through the creation of the consuming society.

Other writers have however castigated this process, seeing in the spread of a single global culture the destruction of indigenous cultures, those unique to and formed by a particular place, and the submersion of national sovereignties and basic democratic freedoms beneath a structure of political control through cultural distribution. With the idea of the global village and uniculture therefore goes a parallel but very different discourse of cultural imperialism and assaulted cultural identity. Neither should one imagine that these are somewhat abstract academic debates. No, these debates touch major political nerve centres. Jack Lang, the former French Minister of Culture, made his reputation calling for the protection of French culture from the corrosive influences of imported American culture. The vote by the Danish electorate in June 1992 to refuse to accept the Maastricht Treaty, which would have continued the march to a federalized Europe, was widely and correctly interpreted as a rejection of any further loss of their national and cultural independence.

Indeed the whole construction of the new Europe is very much premised on the need to nurture the continent through a substantial level of protection of its cultures, all the better to pursue the doomed ambition of a larger, coherent Euro-culture. In here is the reason why, at the end of 1993, European negotiators, and in particular the French, were willing to threaten the successful outcome of the GATT talks in order to have audio-visual culture exempted from

---

[1] John Sherwood, unpublished MS (1993).

free trade. The rationale was wrapped in the language of cultural identity and national cultural sovereignty, implicitly recognizing that nations and cultures and social orders live primarily within the imagination. Everything else is artifice, consequence, metaphor.

The debate about the place of communications in national and global life is wide and controversial and highly political. To understand why is not difficult. We ascribe to the media, particularly to television, something which we always ascribe to the dominant medium of the age: power; the power to shape our forms of thought, our patterns of behaviour, the power to feed the imagination, to give it credence and legitimacy; but most of all the power to create extraordinary wealth. The American FCC estimates that the world-wide communications sector generates approximately $3.8 trillion in revenue; mass media (including publishing) $1.4 trillion; telecommunications $1.2 trillion; computers $800 billion; consumer electronics $400 billion.[2] Every day there are billions of hours of television viewing on the planet, and the assumption is that more and more of that viewing is defined by a content which is uniform, the product of vast transnational corporations which impose their character on the global mind like a seal on hot wax.

Imagine if you will that you are the Minister of Culture and Communications for India as the 1990s gather pace. You are a Cabinet Minister in one of the world's poorest countries; you also know what is available to the television audience. Every day, all day, you can watch not only India's national broadcaster, Doordarshan, but also BBC World Service Television, MTV, a sports channel, and two entertainment channels coming in from Hong Kong. Your neighbourhood cable operator offers you these services for an installation fee of $50, and $10 a month rental. You can sit at home and watch Australian rugby, a British talk show, or Indian opera. Perhaps most significantly you are sitting within the 'footprint' of the new Star Television service, provided by the Hong Kong-based Hutchvision, run by Rupert Murdoch. Star TV's five channels are transmitted by Asiasat-2, a venture initiated by the British company Cable & Wireless, the Chinese government's overseas investment corporation (China International Trust and Investment Corp.), and Hutchison Whampoa of Hong Kong, and launched in April 1990, with a signal that stretches from Turkey to Tokyo, over 38 countries with 2.5 billion people. You know that by 1995 there are 2,000 TV channels technically available in Asia.

You also know that CNN is developing its Asian operations, having just opened a bureau in Delhi, with all kinds of plans for further development in Asia. As Minister you are worried that events may pass you by as the world is reconstructed according to the whims and needs of the 'megamachinery', that Atlanta, Georgia, is becoming singularly significant in the development of

---

[2] *Satellite News*, 20 Apr. 1992.

a society 8,000 miles away. And almost inevitably the BBC is plying its wares with new-found aggression and ambition.

The correspondent for the Australian Broadcasting Corporation, writing in a memo to the Sydney headquarters of ABC in 1992, pin-pointed the issue accurately:

India is a crucible for studying the evolving pattern of control. The country's history and culture incline it towards attempting heavy controls. But the government has appeared paralysed by the speed of developments. In wiring up whole suburbs of Delhi and Bombay the cable operators have simply ignored the law, which prohibits the laying of cables across public roads. The government obviously fears a backlash if it attempts to crack down now, and I think they're right. The satellite TV horse in India has bolted. When the ABC house here was wired I found I could connect the staff quarters at virtually no additional cost. I told our driver Joseph it was available, but said he should think carefully about the effects on his young family before deciding. He did, decided in favour and the extension was done. Now, like millions of Indians, the Madans are amazed and very impressed by the world that has been opened up to them. No government is going to take that away.

The Indian government, however, worried that satellite news services in particular would carry stories that would not be conducive to the public good or social order, did decide to build a monitoring station at Jalna to keep tabs on satellite television. But all it could do was watch with a certain helplessness as the viewing of Doordarshan in homes with cable was decimated, and wait in horror for the start of Star TV's Hindi service.

The Singaporean Minister of Information and the Arts, George Yeo, observed: 'It is increasingly difficult to insulate the domestic market from foreign broadcasts. As satellite dishes get smaller with higher power satellites and [more clever] signal processing, it will become impossible to stop television signals from being received.'[3] In an attempt to address this problem the Singaporean government has banned the private use of satellite dishes. And the Malaysian Information Minister Mohamed Rahmat said: 'On the question of having an open sky, the position of the government today is . . . no, for various reasons. These include questions of security and content of programmes.'[4] Malaysia is a largely Muslim country which bans screen nudity and anything that might offend Islamic sensibilities. It has therefore banned satellite dishes capable of receiving DBS signals—except for government officials and the royal family. The Japanese Ministry of Posts and Telegraph, which has regulatory authority for broadcasting, has launched an investigation into the implications of the fact that the Star footprint now takes in Japan.

Elsewhere in Asia Indonesia launched its Palapa satellite, but insists that it will not be used to transmit foreign programmes into the country, even though

[3] George Yeo, quoted in Sherwood MS.   [4] Mohamed Rahmat, quoted ibid.

Perumtel, the state-owned consortium which manages the satellite, made a three-year $6.5 million deal with CNN. Thailand's Shinawatra Computer and Communications company launched that country's first commercial satellite in 1993 with a footprint that will cover Thailand, Malaysia, Singapore, and Hong Kong. TV Zealand and the Australian Broadcasting Corporation are upgrading their services to the Pacific Islands, at the same time as a consortium of INTELSAT, Asiasat, and the US-based Orbix, better known as PanAmSat, are planning to launch a series of satellites to cover the whole of the Asia–Pacific region.

There is, in short, a blizzard of activity across the whole face of the planet. As we shall see in much more detail later the context for all these activities has two elements. National governments want to encourage economic growth, and assume that no economy can grow if it does not stimulate new markets with high-tech. communications equipment. The second element is the presence of several enormous companies on the international stage, offering high-tech. satellite systems, for whom national boundaries are an irrelevance or a nuisance. For example, a senior executive of the satellite consortium PanAmSat observed that technological and political trends 'need to be accelerated and joined together for a goal of open market competition on a level playing field. If artificial barriers are placed in front of either technology use or political reform, the entire industry will suffer. Growth will be slowed down and costs will rise. That is not in the public interest any place in the world.' And Don O'Neal of Hughes Aircraft's Space and Communications Group, commenting on the increasing numbers of direct broadcast satellites, observed, 'All of this will be good for the consumer, who will have more choices as we come closer to the global village envisioned by Marshall McLuhan in 1967.'[5]

Here then in clear tones are the lyrics of the age in which we now live. They reveal an orientation which is equally clear: that the market—with all its logics and language—lies at the heart of human affairs at every level. One may dispute the precise extent to which the idea of the market has spread. Clearly there remain areas of human activity which still hum a different tune. It would, however, be markedly myopic to suggest that the market does not preoccupy the waking moments of a considerable proportion of humankind. Its institutions, intellectual preoccupations, and suppositions are dominant. By necessity then other beliefs, other ways of being, are diminished. Therein lies the fate of public service broadcasting, an institution born in one age, seeking to survive in one which is utterly different.

At its simplest, then, the various chapters in this book contain a proposition that within the whole of broadcasting there is a basic conflict. It is a conflict familiar to many people in different places, within different societies,

---

[5] *Satellite News*, 23 Dec. 1991.

and is essentially one of ideological direction and institutional challenge and decay.

The debate is between two opposed models of how choices should be made for the development of the audio-visual media and the kinds of programmes they will make available to the public-as-audience. The models invoke different conceptions of democratic rights and freedoms, different views of the relationship between culture and economics. One model suggests that to sustain the general well-being of this society and its culture the state (perhaps 'the body politic' is a better phrase) has not just a right but a duty to make strategic decisions and interventions through its nominated institutions. In broadcasting those interventions are to guarantee a range, depth, quality, and independence of programme output which other arrangements would simply not supply. Those arrangements have been carried out in many countries through the model of public service broadcasting.

Against this is set a very different model in which 'regulation' through public policy is held to be neither right nor necessary. The theory defining this alternative model suggests that in a democratic society the state has no right to make choices for its citizens in the audio-visual area any more than it has a right to tell them which books to write or read. To use a by now well-worn phrase, what matters is 'consumer sovereignty'. Democratic rights, moreover, are now made more feasible by enormous advances in the physical capacity to communicate through broadband cable systems and satellite communications. The difference is between the individual as part of the collective, and the individual as just that, an individual.

Here then are two models between which the audience-as-citizen is being asked to choose: policy guided by the hand of 'public' regulation, employing 'public' values, serving the 'public' interest; and policy as the *ad hoc* result of a myriad individual choices with the collective good and interest in effect being what the public, using economic judgements, say they are. In country after country one can see a collision between a 'cultural' or civic model for the development of broadcasting and the 'economic' or circus model for the larger construction of a culture of communications of which television and radio are one part.

Two broadcasting camps glare at each other. The 'friends of public service broadcasting'—I borrow the phrase from a Canadian grouping—essentially honour the throne on which once sat people such as John Reith in Britain, Hans Bredow in Germany, James Shelley in New Zealand, Hartford Gunn in the United States, and all those other founding figures of a substantial section of world broadcasting. Yes, I know, that is a gross oversimplification, but it contains sufficient truth for one not to baulk at making the point. Theirs was a view which had within it seeds of élitism, maybe even, as Raymond Williams put it, 'an authoritarian system with a conscience', but which created the possibility for programmes of excellence, high standards, creativity, range, honesty, delight. For these figures and the legislators who gave them their power the limitations of the radio spectrum were not a prison but an excuse to shape the future of their societies' cultures. On the other hand, there are now those who clamour for change, or at least declare change to be 'inevitable', and who honour consumer choice, the market, a populist interpretation of culture, the rights of 'ordinary' people over those of metropolitan élites, and so on. In the multiple channels of cable and satellite they see the necessary vehicles to realize that ambition. Those two concepts, world views, ideologies, whatever one calls them, provide the bookends within which this series of chapters rests.

It has to be said, even at such an early stage in this book, that while one can really define the two models analytically, and while there remain powerful allegiances to both models within most broadcasting cultures, the public debate about the future of audio-visual communications has become severely unbalanced. The imbalance is simply a result of political developments which in many countries favour the economic over the cultural model. As revealing of the dominance of the economic model have been the occasional throwaway words of key figures. Michael Green, the Chairman of Carlton Communications and very much a major mover in the emergent British television scene, observed: 'I think of television as a manufacturing process. What is the difference between a television programme and this lighter?'[6] Inside this comment lies a whole world of discourse about broadcasting and society, about culture and industry, and about the relationships which exist between them.

It has also to be said that, whatever the complexities, not to say contentiousness, of this discourse, the philosophical assumptions in which Michael Green is steeped are in the ascendancy. What we do not yet finally know is if they are triumphant.

The debates within the public service fraternity have been distinctly nervous, defensive, and often confused as it has singularly failed to define, or redefine, the idea of the public good, the public interest, the common weal in communications at the moment when technology is seen, rightly or wrongly, to be acting on, rather than being guided by, social development and social needs. It seems to have been, and to remain, inordinately difficult to examine the social worth and purpose of public service broadcasting without foundering on the rocks of 'tradition', a code word for something which is not quite relevant, devoid of contemporary use and purpose, arcane.

In response to their failure to articulate an argument for the continuing validity of public service values in the face of the materialism and individualism of the economic model, public service broadcasters have looked to the defence of the city walls, to more aggressive and competitive scheduling, to

---

[6] *Independent*, 30 Mar. 1988.

the slow attrition of core commitments, for example to the single play, to the use of marketing nostrums, and a hungering for co-productions and co-financing. The net result has been the slow smoothing out of the texture of the output, its gradual creative impoverishment. Organizational 'efficiency', 'cost-effectiveness', 'value for money', 'markets and marketing' are catchwords which blended together have all the nutritional worth of hemlock.

Missing from almost all public and policy debates about public broadcasting is a language that consumed much academic deliberation of late. This is the idea that, one author explains, as modern society evolved it fell 'to the mass media system to provide the informational and cultural resources that would underwrite the rights and responsibilities of citizenship'.[7] In other words the media become both potent expression and nurturing agent of democratic practice within a public sphere: 'The concept of the public sphere here refers to the arena of civic discourse, in which the mass media are said to play a central role in providing social mechanisms for public dialogue on the common concerns of society.'[8] The classic western European model of public service broadcasting is seen as a deliberate expression for, and an understanding of, this role: 'the tradition of Western European democratic theory and practice situates modes of public communication at the heart of the democratic process, within the very core of the notion of civil society.'[9] The obvious logical point is that if such is the function of a public/civil sphere anything that happens to alter, affect, damage, dilute that sphere by *definition* alters, affects, damages, and dilutes democratic practice and culture. It is equally obvious that *everything* that has been happening within the realm of communications is having those consequences, not however by any process of random change or happenstance but as deliberate acts of governmental policy in every major industrial democracy, and most which are not so major.

The process of stimulating such change is universally defined by an essential characteristic, that the consequences for democratic practice were rarely if ever explored. In so far as there was any consideration of the political consequences it was either driven by concern about moral values or it was assumed that the public broadcasting sector would survive intact and thus able to fulfil its democratic function. Indeed, it seems impressionistically that those individuals who did seriously question, who suggested that the calculative power of 'the economic' was not the only, or even the most important, consideration in defining the place of communications in the late twentieth century,

---

[7] Graham Murdock, 'The New Mogul Empires: Media Concentration and Control in the Age of Convergence', *Media Development*, 4 (1994), 3–6.

[8] Shalini Venturelli, 'The Imagined Transnational Public Sphere in the European Community's Broadcast Philosophy: Implications for Democracy', *European Journal of Communication*, 8 (1993), 491–518.

[9] Ibid. 495.

were routinely marginalized, scoffed at, and in increasingly numerous cases removed from office.

The various chapters of this book should be seen as different ways of gnawing away at these bones of argument which exist within and about a form of broadcasting we call public service broadcasting. I would not claim that the parts of this book slot into each other like some perfectly tooled piece of engineering. The whole is, however, linked by three questions: what is public service broadcasting; how is it evolving; what is its fate? These questions pointed me in two particular directions: a close look at some of the history of the ideas and institutions of public broadcasting; and an examination of the contemporary state of those ideas and institutions, particularly in light of the alleged implications of recent and future developments in cable and satellite television.

In addressing these issues one is open to the accusation of picking over the embers of a fire which is almost out. Speaking to the Royal Television Society, John Davey, who, as a senior official in the British Home Office Broadcasting Department, was the man immediately responsible for the development of cable TV in Britain and subsequently became the first Director-General of the Cable Television Authority, said: 'I do not wish to suggest that I am not a strong believer in the good that public service broadcasting has achieved for us. But one message that I feel I must emphasize is that sticking to what we know and love and has served us well in the past is simply not an option for the future.'[10]

Note how the debate about the nature of communications—for that in essence is what this is—has been transformed. Principles and ideals are transmuted into practicalities. Mute technologies are endowed with a kind of transcendent force, a power and inevitability separate from human reason or volition. Public service broadcasters must adjust or die. There is, however, a certain potency in Davey's nostrum. Hans Kimmel of ZDF in Germany captured it well when he said, 'public service broadcasting will not be kept alive by the imminent proclamation of its eternal truths: the Catholic Church had to accept Luther, Galileo and Marx as reality.'[11] The problem is, adjust to being what: communicators with a wider social purpose, or simply the efficient providers of information and entertainment which is meant to have no purpose other than to fill the television screens of the nation and the coffers of the new moguls? There is a very profound sense in which the question of public service broadcasting is no longer one in which what is at issue is how it can adjust to changed circumstance, but rather whether adjustment, as opposed to terminal decline, is any longer an option.

The reader, then, will find in the following pages an examination of the ideas which constitute public service broadcasting, detailed history about very

---

[10] *Guardian*, 16 July 1984.   [11] Transcript of personal interview.

precise moments in the post-war history of public service broadcasting, along with a more general assessment of events in recent years. Within the histories there are key moments of three of the most powerful and established public service broadcasting organizations—the BBC in Britain, NHK in Japan, and what was Nordwestdeutscher Rundfunk, part of the federally structured but institutionally linked public service ARD in Germany. What I have tried to describe are moments at which one could see with real clarity the construction of the intellectual and institutional edifice of public broadcasting organizations. I begin, however, with the presumption that it is futile to try and isolate historical events from wider canvases on which they are no more than a detail. In looking at broadcasting in Germany and Japan, for example, I wanted also to paint in the background, the streams of political, economic, and social thought which are a vital part of the fortunes of any creative activity such as broadcasting. The re-establishment of broadcasting in these two countries, for example, took place as part of the total reconstruction of their societies by an occupying power. As I approached more recent events such as the implications of the 'cable revolution', it became more difficult to widen the lens sufficiently to have that same breadth of vision. Nevertheless, I did try to have some sense of the relationships between developments in the new media, public service broadcasting, and the wider socio-political context. One can no more understand the character of broadcasting systems outside that context than one can understand the development of a topography separate from its underlying geology.

Informing this study, I hope, is a deeply held personal conviction that public service broadcasting has historically been a major benefit to the cultures within which it has existed. This does not mean that I feel no criticism of the practice of public broadcasters. They are fallible and flawed, but I would borrow the theological adage of damn the sin, but not the sinner. That belief is wrapped around another, which is that the debate about broadcasting is but one part of a wider debate about public culture in private worlds. It is because of that debate that one cannot avoid the monetarist orthodoxies which now form the financial heartblood of the leading western economies. Every developed industrial society within the capitalist economies is undergoing a profound shift in its nature: from societies of industrial production and manufacture to those of service and the use of 'information'. Whether there has been a direct evolution into the information society—the so-called 'long march' through the sectors from an agrarian to an industrial to an information order—or whether the shift is much less tidy, matters little. Equally, after the oil crisis of the 1970s and the brutal 'stagflation' of that decade, new economic imperatives and agenda seemed essential. The swell from this sea-change washed over public service broadcasting as it did over every other social outcrop.

If public broadcasting *is* under threat and even if the nature of the threat has shifted and become more complex, that is merely a continuation of the permanent state of its existence since the idea was first dreamed up by those stiff-upper-lipped gentlemen who conceived of the BBC in the middle years of the 1920s. To develop a public service system which would be devoid of another interest—commercial or political—and would have as its sole purpose the offering of a 'service', flowed to a considerable extent from the Victorian idealism and paternalism which animated such men as John Reith, the BBC's first Director-General. They did manage though to create a mould which others could use, but which remained fragile and easily breakable. The whole history of public broadcasting has been about efforts to break that mould, to cast a new one from the clay of political ideology or commercial need. Public broadcasting is not about technology. It is about an idea, which happens to employ a technology, of how one creates and feeds a society and its culture.

A key assumption behind public service broadcasting, only rarely made explicit, is that broadcasting entails important moral and intellectual questions and ambitions which are separate from any technological or financial considerations. Take away those questions and ambitions and one prepares the ground for that famous 'vast wasteland'. A broadcasting service, indeed any cultural activity divorced from such inner forces, becomes just another television service, the audio-visual version of the proposition that when men cease to believe in God, they do not cease to believe but start to believe in anything. One of the most powerful articulators of the social purpose of broadcasting was someone who spent his whole life in the belly of the beast, the American commercial television system. Speaking to the annual conference of the Radio and TV News Directors in 1958, Edward R. Murrow observed:

To a very considerable extent the media of mass communication in a given society reflect the political, economic and social climate in which they flourish. . . . We are currently wealthy, fat, comfortable and complacent. We have currently a built-in allergy to unpleasant or disturbing information . . . our mass media reflect this. . . . I would like to see it reflect occasionally the hard unyielding realities of the world in which we live. . . . This instrument can teach; it can illuminate; yes, it can even inspire. But it can only do so to the extent that humans are determined to use it to those ends. Otherwise, it is merely wires and lights in a box.[12]

What then is the character of these challenges to a set of public service broadcasting institutions which for most of their history seemed impregnable? A number can be identified:

- the structural challenge born on the one hand by the desire to shift the 'burden' of funding away from the public purse, with the inevitable call

---

[12] In F. W. Friendly, *Due to Circumstances beyond our Control* (New York: Random House, 1967), 122.

for even greater reliance on commercial sources of revenue, and on the other by the desire to develop high-tech. cable and satellite systems with all the consequent implications for a multi-channel environment;

- the ideological challenge from the new right to the very idea of public culture, and the articulation of the proposition that social good flows not from collective activity organized from the top down, but from a myriad individual decisions organized from the bottom up, rooted in the right of the individual to choose. The obvious implications of the structural challenge to this ideological use lie in the definitive destruction by the multi-channel environment of the notion that audio-visual communication *has* to be treated as a social good because it employs in the radio spectrum a physically scarce resource with important social potentialities. If that core theology is undermined, then so are the cathedrals built to espouse it;

- the development and character of new technologies, which offer plentiful, interactive communications, which emphasize the visual, immediate, and sensual at the expense of the deliberative and cerebral;

- the continuing impact of rationalizing forces within the western industrial order with an attendant re-engineering of any language which is abstract and narrative, as opposed to concrete and instrumental;

- social practices which are ever more homebound, which put distance between the individual and the 'public' character of the institution. Social scientists refer to this as the privatization of leisure, a termite-like process eating away at the foundations of the collective and the communal.

Because we have no real idea of the precise weight and configuration of these challenges it is difficult to gauge exactly what might happen in the next five to ten years. What seems certain is that none of these challenges will simply go away and that the *status quo ante bellum* is no longer an option for the future. Herein lies the cruel dilemma. If the public service broadcasting organizations are shifted in a more commercial direction then there follows, at least from one perspective, the deconstruction of their very purpose for being, with a consequent avalanche of unfortunate consequences: increased competition, decline of programme standards, and the general impoverishment of the nation's culture and spirit. But even if an attempt is made to tinker with the design, to reconstruct the idea and the institution of public service broadcasting, the attempt may well fail dismally. It is rather like Newton's wooden bridge, held together not by the artificial force of nails and bolts but by the genius of its design, but which once dismantled to see how it worked could not be put back together again.

2 Principles of Public Service Broadcasting

In a public system, television producers acquire money to make programmes. In a commercial system they make programmes to acquire money. However simple, this little epigram articulates the divergence of basic principles, the different philosophical assumptions, on which broadcasting is built. History and experience fashioned inside public broadcasting a definable canon, a set of principles and practices which constitute its purpose. They are the core theses around which the institution has been formed and shaped, which have guided its performance, and which powerfully suggest its potential worth.

There is no suggestion here that these principles exist perfectly formed in some divine fashion. What is being suggested is that to the unprejudiced eye they are clearly to be seen as the intellectual and creative lattice-work which has informed a good deal of public broadcasting. The institutional structures and forms of funding may vary, but public broadcasting is above all else a structure of ambition, a belief that the sheer presence of broadcasting within all our lives can and must be used to nurture society, to proffer the opportunity for society and its inhabitants to be better served than by systems which primarily seek consumers for advertisers. By looking at the issue of public broadcasting in this way—by positioning it concretely in relation to its past— one can illuminate its potential for the future, not as pie-in-the-sky idealism but as a vital part of the whole cultural ecology of society as it moves towards the twenty-first century.

This chapter has in reality many fingerprints on its intellectual evolution—in particular the members of the Broadcasting Research Unit in London 1981–8, and my colleague in Boulder, Wick Rowland.

Any understanding of culture and society must begin with a sense of the history which has given birth to the particular moment. This is especially true of broadcasting, which lies at the crossroads of many forces. Some of the most powerful visions of the purpose of broadcasting emerged within unusual and trying circumstances. Consider, for instance, the cultural histories of the occupations of Germany and Japan in the late 1940s and the formulation of Allied policy for broadcasting in the rebuilding of those societies. There one can see powerful testament to the idea of broadcasting as primarily a social rather than an economic process, as something with moral, cultural, intellectual, and creative purpose and not just a source of mild comment and moderate pleasure. The charters of NHK and the ARD, dictated to a great extent by foreign military governments in Japan and Germany, were replete with the public service ideal. If broadcasting was to comment, it should do so with a flourish. If it was to amuse, it should do so with *élan*. If it was to educate, it should do so with real professionalism. It was simply understood by the American and Allied leadership that the life of the mind of a society was far too precious and important to be left to the vagaries of a commercial system.

It could be argued that such policies were creatures of the moment, as massive destruction demanded enormous reconstruction, of which communications would inevitably be part. But what was required was the restoration not just of highways, buildings, plants, but also of the shattered imaginative lives of whole populations. The architects of post-war Germany and Japan sensed correctly that healthy, diverse cultural institutions were a prerequisite to a functioning liberal democracy. Broadcasting was thus to be used as a key part of the cultural and social regeneration of those societies. In that lies the real clue to the nature and purpose of great broadcasting: that it makes best sense when it represents a national and moral optimism within a society, when it suggests—through the diversity and quality of its programmes—that we can be better than we are: better served, better amused, better informed, and, thus, better citizens.

Let me return to a period which is widely regarded within the advanced industrial societies as a high-water mark of public service broadcasting, the BBC in the early 1960s. A key figure from those years was Sir Arthur fforde, possibly the greatest of the chairmen of the BBC. In 1963 he wrote: 'By its nature broadcasting must be in a constant and sensitive relationship with the moral condition of society.'[1] He felt that the moral establishment had failed modern society and that broadcasting was a way in which that failure could be rectified. He added that it 'is of cardinal importance that everyone in a position of responsibility should be ready to set himself or herself the duty of assuring, to those creative members of staff . . . that measure of freedom, independence and elan without which the arts do not flourish'.[2]

---

[1] Arthur fforde, 'What is Broadcasting About?' (privately printed, 1963).
[2] Quoted in M. Tracey, *A Variety of Lives: A Biography of Sir Hugh Greene* (London: Bodley Head, 1983), 235.

That idea of providing a protective layer within which the imaginative spirit might create lay at the heart of the BBC version of public service broadcasting which flourished in the post-war years. Ian Jacob, Director-General of the BBC from 1952 to 1959, refined the notion. In 1958, in an internal document called 'Basic Propositions', he described public service broadcasting as:

a compound of a system of control, an attitude of mind, and an aim, which if successfully achieved results in a service which cannot be given by any other means. The system of control is full independence, or the maximum degree of independence that Parliament will accord. The attitude of mind is an intelligent one capable of attracting to the service the highest quality of character and intellect. The aim is to give the best and the most comprehensive service of broadcasting to the public that is possible. The motive that underlies the whole operation is a vital factor; it must not be vitiated by political or commercial consideration.

This is one of the best attempts to capture in words a concept and view of broadcasting which continues to slosh around the world of cultural politics. Yet even here the vision, the articulation, is limited. Jacob's words imply that we understand the nature of public service broadcasting not by defining it, but by recognizing its results, rather as one plots the presence of a hidden planet or a subatomic particle not by 'seeing' it, but by measuring the effects of its presence. The Pilkington Committee said as much in 1962 when it observed: 'though its standards exist and are recognizable, broadcasting is more nearly an art than an exact science. It deals in tastes and values and is not precisely definable.'[3]

Such canons were also seen as a way of protecting 'standards', one more difficult concept to define and yet one which lay and lies at the very heart of the idea of public service broadcasting. On the one hand, the word 'standards' has come to mean somewhat traditional notions of culture, no longer relevant in the modern world; on the other, it invokes a commitment to quality, to a refusal to pander to dull and barren mass taste, to preserving a sense of value and moral purpose. It is the rejection of a debilitating mass culture which is, in the words of Richard Hoggart, 'too damned nice, a bland, muted, processed, institutionalised decency, a suburban limbo in which nothing ever happens and the grit has gone out of life'.[4] From these perspectives, the idea of public service broadcasting rests on the mighty and worthy ambition that we can, collectively, be *better* than we are.

In constitutional terms, the definitions of public service broadcasting are in Britain clear if not extensive. The Broadcasting Act, 1981, required that commercial broadcasting should be conducted as a public service by a public

---

[3] Postmaster-General, *Report of the Committee on Broadcasting, 1960*, Cmnd. 1753 (London: HMSO, 1962) (Pilkington Report), 13, para. 34.

[4] Richard Hoggart, *Only Connect: On Culture and Communication* (London: Chatto & Windus, 1972).

authority set up for the purpose to disseminate programmes of information, education, and entertainment, of a high technical standard with a proper balance and range in their subject-matter. Programmes must, the Act states, 'maintain a high general standard in all respects, and in particular in respect of their content and quality'. Through the preamble to its charter and in an annexe to the licence and agreement the BBC, through its Governors, recognizes the same obligations.

The articulation of a commitment to balance, range, standards in entertainment, education, and information is useful and important. It does not, however, tell one *how* to achieve those ends, any more than their simple reiteration explains *why* it is important that broadcasting functions in this way. It is a bit like the difference between saying that the rules of soccer lay down the basic structure of the game and explaining the art of a star player. The difficulty with these prescriptions is that they do not amount to a definition, though they do constitute an attempt to provide some of the elements which might go into such a definition.

In Britain the high-water mark of public and official acclaim for the definition of public broadcasting as understood by the BBC was the Report of the Pilkington Committee inquiry into the future of broadcasting, published in 1962. The Report stated:

The duty of providing a service of broadcasting, and the responsibility for what is broadcast, are vested in public corporations—the BBC and the ITA—since the purposes and effects of broadcasting are such that the duty and responsibility should not be left to the ordinary processes of commercial enterprise, and because there are compelling objections to their being undertaken by the State.[5]

It suggested that the products of these bodies should be a service which fully realizes the purpose of broadcasting, which it later defined as:

one which will use the medium with an acute awareness of its power to influence values and moral standards; will respect the public right to choose from amongst the widest possible range of subject-matter, purposefully treated; will at the same time be aware of and care about public tastes and attitudes in all their variety; and will constantly be on the watch for and ready to try the new and unusual.[6]

Others have suggested that public service broadcasting is broadcasting in the public interest in as many ways as the public may in effect demand. The definition assumed that in each case the public interest can be defined and then acted upon. The classic aphorism, oft heard in the BBC, was that the essence of public service broadcasting is to make popular programmes good, and good programmes popular.

[5] Pilkington Report, 121, para. 402.   [6] Ibid.

An excellent, if more formal, stab at a definition is contained in the introductory section of the Broadcasting Research Unit's *Report of the Working Party on New Technologies*. The chairman of the working party, Robin Scott, himself a former senior BBC executive, reiterates the prescriptive commitment to balance, range, and high standards, accountability to Parliament, and the benefits that flow from the fact that the BBC and the independent television companies (ITV) do not compete for the same source of revenue. He then adds:

Were it possible to define good broadcasting in legally enforceable terms, it might be possible to abandon as irrelevant the question of institutional forms and methods of providing finance. The insuperable difficulty remains, however, that, because judgments of broadcasting are made by reference to tastes and opinions which themselves change and evolve, the necessary criteria cannot be prescribed. In a free society any attempt to prescribe them would be bitterly resented and fiercely resisted: rightly so, for that road leads straight to cultural imprisonment. So relevance of institutional form and method of finance is inescapable: if the country wants good broadcasting, then there must be custodians to establish in practice what that is. They may be told that the necessary characteristics are choice and quality, and that they must try to be fair and impartial. Thereafter, good or bad broadcasting can be described by the broadcasters by reference to evolving practice; and it can be recognised, and checked, by opinion.[7]

As with so much of the discussion about public service broadcasting there is here an elegant vagueness that is studied and deliberate. The text was actually written in a memo to Robin Scott by another member of the working party, John Lawrence, who had been secretary to the Pilkington Committee and much involved in the drafting of that Report. He had also been a senior adviser within the Home Office, the government department then responsible for broadcasting policy. Lawrence's real insight was that the one thing that could be understood about defining public service broadcasting was that in any abstract sense it cannot be done. Hence to point to the studied vagueness is not to be snide but rather to point the finger at an objectively real condition.

The bent that lurks in the shrubbery of those discussions is that, whatever the definitional uncertainties, public service broadcasting can be experienced and recognized but never properly captured by language; someone has to decide on what is 'good' and 'bad'. It was totally axiomatic to a thinker and policy-maker such as Lawrence that broadcasting should only do good, and that that would require a guiding hand. So dangling inside the Scott/Lawrence statement is a word imbued with extraordinary meaning, 'custodians'. The term is used not in its janitorial sense but in that of 'the caretakers' of culture. The whole logic of the concept presupposed two things: that the idea of

---

[7] Robin Scott, in *The Working Party on New Technologies* (London: Broadcasting Research Unit, 1983), 6–7.

custodianship was totally unproblematic, and that it was clear just who the custodians were, the characteristics they would possess, and the locations in which they would be found. Such presuppositions appeared only natural throughout the history of broadcasting because that history was embedded within a social order in which hierarchy was also assumed: hierarchies of social status and cultural judgement. And in a curious kind of way the point of hierarchy is to reproduce itself since the fundamental belief of the hierarchical is, and has to be, that such arrangements have worth and merit. The plausibility of such a thesis becomes very much dependent on delivering evidence that attests to both worthiness and meritoriousness in such a way as to drown out the noise of any emergent countervailing thesis.

What then were the early public broadcasters, such as John Reith, and their political supporters in the ruling classes trying to achieve and was it a hopeless mission? Tom Burns in his study of the BBC points to a certain antagonism towards the low culture of film and the national press:

The film industry by the early twenties was proving itself extravagantly successful and profitable. And in the view of people like Reith and the Conservative Party politicians and civil servants who made the decisions, the products of the industry represented the consequences of 'giving the public what it wants' and were consequently silly and vulgar and false. Broadcasting, if they were to have anything to do with it, had somehow to be developed in the completely opposite direction.[8]

He adds:

Mass circulation newspapers, popular weeklies, children's comics and pulp fiction had, by the 1920s, subverted the role of the printed word as an instrument of religion, cultural, and social and political enlightenment. . . . Films and the popular press together form the backcloth, the negative reasons, which have to be added to the positive reason of Reith's missionary zeal, his energy and his ability, to understand that in undertaking the task of ensuring that broadcasting would not go the same way—as it already was going in America—he had the backing of the powerful from Baldwin, the Prime Minister on down, as well as the good and the godly. More importantly, younger people, of much the same social class, and with the same sort of outlook, were available for recruiting into a public broadcasting service and ready to accept the principles he had formulated—if they did not have them.[9]

Such considerations and worries lay behind much of the support for the BBC being created as a public service broadcasting organization. The Pilkington Committee noted that since 'the frequency space available to broadcasting is limited, it is essential that what is available should be used to the best advantage'.[10] The cultural geology of this decision had however a deeper level to it, based on nineteenth-century assumptions about the ways in which the arts and

---

[8] Burns, *The BBC*, 42.   [9] Ibid.   [10] Pilkington Report, 12, para. 33.

humanities could elevate the human condition. In an essay on the formation of modern literary analysis Steiner wrote that behind the study of literature in the nineteenth century lay:

a kind of rational and moral optimism . . . a large hope, a great positivism. . . . The study of literature was assumed to carry an almost necessary implication of moral force. It was thought self-evident that the teaching and reading of the great poets and prose writers would enrich not only taste or style but moral feeling: that it would cultivate human judgment and act against barbarism.[11]

Steiner then quotes Henry Sedgwick who saw in the study of English literature an enlargement and expansion of our sympathies 'by apprehending noble, subtle and profound thoughts, refined and lofty feelings' and a 'source and essence of a truly humanizing culture'.[12]

Reading this account one could quite properly substitute the word 'broadcasting' for 'literature' and have a powerful explanation of what the creation of the BBC model of public service broadcasting was all about: a relocation of a nineteenth-century humanistic dream. And the fear that drove that dream was of 'the mob'. The pervasive belief among cultural, religious, and political élites that there was indeed a dark side to the human soul that was, when let loose, dangerous and devastating to the flesh as well as the spirit. And who is to say that they were wrong, nestling as they did between the first great war and a looming second? There remained, however, a residual faith, tied to the whole condition of the Enlightenment, humanism, and belief in progress, that popular culture need not be debauched but could in fact transcend itself. Consider these key passages from the Pilkington Report:

no-one argued against any departure from 'giving the public what it wants' on the grounds that it implied a measure, however small, of 'paternalism' and was for reasons of democratic doctrine inadmissible. On the contrary, all accepted that there was a responsibility to help towards a broadening and deepening of public taste. To sum up: from our preliminary study of the representations put to us, it seemed to us that there was ground for supposing that in television the purposes of broadcasting were to a material extent not being realised. This conclusion pointed in turn to a need to consider the nature of the responsibility of the two broadcasting authorities. This we look at from two angles; first, from a consideration of the effect that television will have on the character of our society; and second, from a consideration of the need to use the potential of the medium to give people the best possible chance of enlarging worthwhile experience.

Television has been called a mirror of society: but the metaphor, though striking, wholly misses the major issue of the responsibility of the two broadcasting authorities.

[11] Quoted in George Steiner, 'To Civilize our Gentlemen', in *Language and Silence* (London: Faber, 1985), 77–8.
[12] Ibid. 78.

For, if we consider the first aspect of this responsibility, what is the mirror to reflect? Is it to reflect the best or the worst in us? One cannot escape the question by saying that it must do both; one must ask then whether it is to present the best and the worst with complete indifference and without comment. And if the answer is that such passivity is unthinkable, that in showing the best and the worst television must show them for what they are, then an active choice has been made. This is not only to show the best in our society, but to show also the worst so that it will be recognised for what it is. That this choice must be made emphasises the main flaw in the comparison. Television does not, and cannot, merely reflect the moral standards of society. It must affect them, either by changing or by reinforcing them.

Finally, and of special importance: because the range of experience is not finite but constantly growing, and because the growing points are usually most significant, it is on these that challenges to existing assumptions and beliefs are made, where the claims to new knowledge and new awareness are stated. If our society is to respond to the challenges and judge the claims, they must be put before it. All broadcasting, and television especially, must be ready and anxious to experiment, to show the new and unusual, to give a hearing to dissent. Here, broadcasting must be most willing to make mistakes; for if it does not, it will make no discoveries.[13]

The suggestion here is not that public broadcasters are all hoping and dreaming that their programmes will transform people from cultural and intellectual slobs into something of which one can more readily approve, but rather that objectively some such argument must be the public broadcaster's last line of defence. The language is of standards, quality, excellence, range. The logic is of social enrichment, that in however indefinable a manner this society is 'better' for having programmes produced from within the framework of those social arrangements termed public service broadcasting, compared to those programmes produced within an environment in which commerce or politics prevail.

One cannot, however, escape the charge that those sentiments rest on a set of ill-explored assumptions about the sociological organization of modern culture. *How* are we better? What are the mechanics? And, vitally, where is the evidence? Indeed, what would such evidence even look like? All the evidence we have of, say, the effect of television in the much rehearsed area of violence is that it is of marginal relevance. Other forces shape social reality. So we must consider the example of modern Britain an interesting and troubling paradox. It is widely recognized by peers around the world that British broadcasting from the 1960s on was more consistently and broadly creative and powerful than any other system. This is not to say that everything was brilliant, but there was much that was. So much is relatively unproblematic. However, it is equally clear to many people that while we may have been triumphant in our

---

[13] Pilkington Report, 19–20, paras. 50–3.

television we have been much less triumphant in making the larger society. The sense of decline, the decayed infrastructure, the anger and rage, the fear of crime, and the deep sense of personal insecurity are, by the 1990s, palpable. The only way out of this conundrum is to recognize that the principles of public service broadcasting can only properly be understood as expressively metaphorical rather than literal.

The Public Service Idea: Eight Principles

A number of colleagues in the UK and the USA set about the task of defining precisely what we understand public broadcasting to be about. Eight principles were identified which suggest that, more than any other part of the electronic media system, public broadcasting can lay true claim to being something other than mere wires and lights, to being a vital part of the culture and society of the nations in which it is present, well able to teach, to illuminate, to inspire.

This section has many fingerprints on its intellectual evolution—in particular the members of the Broadcasting Research Unit in London 1981–8, and my colleague here in Boulder, Wick Rowland.[14]

1. Universality of availability

Public broadcasting has historically sought to ensure that its signals are available to all. It is axiomatic to the public broadcasting community that no one should be disenfranchised by distance or by accident of geography. The imperative which guides this principle is not that of maximizing customers in a market but of serving citizens in a democracy. It is an imperative which then recognizes that if one defines one's audience as the citizens of a country, then logically one has to reach them all. To a remarkable extent in country after country this principle has been made real.

2. Universality of appeal

Public broadcasting seeks to provide programmes which cater to the many different tastes and interests which constitute a society's life. The public broadcasting community understands that each of us, at different moments, is part of a majority and a minority. In seeking to provide programmes for a wide range of tastes and interests, public broadcasting does so with an eye cocked to the need to ensure that whether the programme is pitched at the many or

---

[14] The model of this exercise was a publication of the Broadcasting Research Unit in London, of which I was director 1981–8, *The Public Service Idea in British Broadcasting*. The inspiration for the exercise came from Stephen Hearst, Kenneth Lamb, and Richard Hoggart.

the few it is done so with real quality. Public broadcasting does not expect that it can please all the people all of the time—indeed it sees in that approach precisely the kind of populism which nurtures cultural mediocrity, as quality is sacrificed on the altar of maximizing the audience size. Public broadcasting does, however, believe that well-produced programmes can please a lot of the people a lot of the time, and everybody some of the time. Public broadcasting is thus driven by the desire to make good programmes popular and popular programmes good; it understands that serving the national diversity of a society is not the same as 'giving people what they want'.

The principle of serving the diverse interests of the public is the basis then for the presence in the schedule of programmes which serve the young as well as the elderly, those interested in local affairs as well as the national political canvas, members of diverse subcultures as well as those in the mainstream. There are numerous examples of programmes dealing with the history, geology, and ecology of particular regions, just as there are programmes whose focus is the whole planet. There is programming for those who love opera, as well as those who follow country and western. The person who is an avid gardener is served as well as the dog fanatic. There is news in nature, as well as regional, national, and global coverage of political events. Programmes on consumer affairs rub shoulders with those dealing with the world of business. Those with a taste for the wit of comedy are provided for, but so is the person who seeks classical drama.

It is an important element of this principle that public broadcasting serves not only tastes and interests which are readily apparent, but also those which are dormant and latent—which may be part of the potential we all possess but which circumstance may not have allowed us to develop. Public broadcasting understands that television must go beyond just catering to existing tastes; that it should open us up to the new—to new tastes, new interests, new potentialities. The late Michael Rice put this idea well when he observed that public television's greatest value exists for those 'who may not ever know what they are missing until they discover it, perhaps just stumble on it, in broadcasts, that reach them in the least intimidating way'.[15] There are innumerable examples in most public systems of significant success in this goal.

3. Provision for minorities, especially those disadvantaged by physical or social circumstance

It is commonplace to characterize the medium of television as essentially serving 'the masses'. Certainly public broadcasting understands the vast capability

---

[15] Michael Rice, 'Public Television: Issues of Purpose and Governance', Wye Papers (Aspen Institute, NY), 10.

of one medium to reach enormous numbers of people. It sets its face, however, against the logic of commercial systems to see people as no more than statistics in skins, with a definable value captured in the most desirable rates, demographic buys, and cost per thousand. As suggested in Principle No. 2, public broadcasting views the public as a rich tapestry of tastes and interests each of which, in so far as possible, should be served.

There are whole subcultures of minority social experiences crying out for attention. People of different colour, language groups, and religious preferences all have vital needs for expression in the political and social discourse of the nation. Public broadcasting is dedicated to a dual role here—on the one hand to give access to such groups, to provide them with the opportunities to speak to one another and to voice the issues as they see them, and on the other to provide coverage of their histories, interests, and concerns for the public at large.

In this third principle, which partly overlaps with the second, public broadcasting speaks to its recognition that some audiences have other specific characteristics, and specific needs. The point has been eloquently put by Richard Hoggart:

There are [some minorities] who do not necessarily have either great purchasing power or much political clout. They [are] minorities not of taste but of the accidents of nature: the disabled, the blind, the deaf, the immigrants, the very old and very young, the indigent. To broadcasters whose eyes are on maximizing profits such people and groups will not seem worth the wooing. Yet manifestly their needs are at least as great, and the comfort they may draw from broadcasting even greater, than those of the hale and prosperous. Public service broadcasting recognizes them as special cases with special needs.[16]

4. Serving the public sphere

Some television programmes are successful because they get a fair-sized audience, make some money, and sometimes even exemplify the craft of popular television. Other programmes are successful because they reach out and touch a small, particular, but powerful audience. Some programmes are successful because the craft of the programme-maker is used to speak to us all. They touch us, move us, make us laugh and cry and cheer. They speak to us because they speak for us. Like all great art, they help us to make sense out of life, to see and understand things with a fresh eye, and give us a burning sense of the collective, of belonging to the nation-as-community. In the United States, *The Civil War* was one such experience. It flooded the attic of the nation's mind with new, brilliant light. These programmes are powerful not just because they

---

[16] Richard Hoggart, 'The Public Service Idea', in *British Broadcasting: Main Principles* (Broadcasting Research Unit, London, 1983), 5.

are wonderful examples of their art, but because they bind us together, however momentarily.

Richard Hoggart observed about public broadcasting that one of its benefits 'is exactly that it allows a nation to speak to itself'.[17] It is an increasingly vital principle of the work of public broadcasting that it recognizes its special relationship to a sense of national identity and broad community. Any nation is a patchwork of localities and regions, but it is also a nation, heterogeneous and homogeneous to a remarkable degree at one and the same time. The brilliance of *The Civil War* lay not just in its artistic creativity, its attention to detail while never losing sight of the wider canvas. Its real genius lay in its speaking to an extraordinary range of Americans, of saying to them and for them, this is how you as a nation were formed. In the United Kingdom, out of numerous examples I could point to, the mid-1980s drama series *Boys from the Blackstuff* was one example of programming which spoke to a whole society, which said in a painfully brilliant and moving way, this is who we are today. And that is an important, even vital function of television, because the health of any society lies in its understanding of individual impulses and its formation as a community with a collective character. Public broadcasting's very nature is then to nurture the public sphere as a means of serving the public good. It understands that while within civil society individuals pursue their own private self-interests, it is within the public sphere that they function as citizens. It is a fundamental principle then that *public* broadcasting must motivate the viewers as citizens possessing duties as well as rights, rather than as individual consumers possessing wallets and credit cards.

One way of interpreting the demise of the old single or dual systems is to see this as a necessary corollary of the 'modernizing' dynamism of the 'new media'. As more channels become available so the audience fragments. Erik Svendsen's research in Denmark and much similar research elsewhere points to the remarkable persistence of attention to the national broadcasting system. There are, however, implications of a multi-channel environment which need to be considered. For example, a way of interpreting the decline of the US networks, whose executives are now looking to never again holding more than a 50 per cent share of the viewing audience, is to point to the proliferation of cable channels, their presence in 60 per cent of American homes, the growth of small independent stations, the establishment of direct broadcast satellite services each offering well over 100 channels. From within such a context, it is not unreasonable to conclude that, whatever the merits or otherwise of the programming, what we are witnessing as both cause and effect is the increasing balkanization of the national mind alongside, and, somewhat paradoxically, its immersion in, an emergent global culture.

---

[17] Ibid.

The very logic of television economics makes this inevitable. On the one hand is the creation of niche audiences which can be profitably served. On the other are the increasing fiscal difficulties leading television companies to seek and produce for ever-wider audiences defined not by national boundary and therefore culture, but by the exigencies of economics and certain universalities in popular television. Anyone who reads the trade press will see a tale of structural globalization, the making of 'product' which will sell in more than one market, the increasing importance of co-production and co-financing.

There is a great temptation for public broadcasting to participate in this process of transnational production and distribution. And from certain standpoints of economic efficiency and the recognition of common, globally appealing topics, there is a need for such activity. But, as with the commercial world, the tendency can be over-extended, undercutting a public broadcasting service rising out of and speaking for a particular national culture. Only a well-funded public service system can resist the full force of this temptation and thereby stand against its consequences, as a voice for a public as against a private good.

5. A commitment to the education of the public

The most outstanding example of public broadcasting's commitment to the audience-as-citizen is the long-time provision in almost all systems of educational programming at every level. Public broadcasting knows that political and social literacy, as well as of course literal literacy, is an essential prerequisite to the healthy working of a democratic order. Above all else, the commitment to this principle requires that it treat its audience as mature, rational beings capable of learning and growing in many ways. Thus much of public broadcasting has retained its commitment to institutional services. Daytime school broadcasting and formal learning services of all kinds continue to play a role in most national services.

Meanwhile, however, major challenges to that role have appeared from other, more commercial sectors. If the United States is any model for the future, what is clear is that the new commercial sector based in cable and satellite will, as it matures, seek to purchase a level of respectability by offering educational services which were previously solely within the domain of the public broadcasting community. The Whittle experiment with advertising-based Channel One, the Jones efforts through Mind Extension University, and the work of the Cable Alliance for Education (CAFE) all reflect tendencies to provide instructional services through new technologies and funding mechanisms.

6. Public broadcasting should be distanced from all vested interests

It is a simple but key principle of public broadcasting that its programmes can best serve the public with excellence and diversity when they are produced from within a structure of independence. Programmes funded by advertising necessarily have their character influenced in some shape or form by the demand to maximize the garnering of consumers. Programmes directly funded by the government, and with no intervening structural heat shield, inevitably tend to utter the tones of their master's voice.

The whole history of public broadcasting has been dominated by the commitment to the idea that it can best serve the nation when it remains distanced from any particular commitment to any particular power structure inside the nation. Of particular importance to this principle is the ability of public broadcasting to support a cadre of independent-minded programme-makers, who are thus well able to speak with authentic tones and to offer that singularity of vision allied to creativity and passion which has traditionally produced some of public television's finest moments. It follows that the political and economic architecture of this principle is such as to support the making of programmes which are good in their own terms, whatever their intended audience. In the making of programmes for public broadcasting, there should be no ulterior purpose or motive. It is axiomatic to this principle that the funding of public broadcasting should be such, in total amount and in the absence of any strings attached, as to encourage rather than negate the independence enjoyed.

7. *Broadcasting should be so structured as to encourage competition in good programming rather than competition for numbers*

This principle is central to public service broadcasting and essentially involves a commitment to making programmes which, whatever their intended audience, are of high quality. The overwhelming mass of the evidence leads to the conclusion that the most important aspect of such structuring relates to the forms of finance. Where commercial sources of revenue are dominant, or even present, or where there is direct subvention from government, the programme-maker's eye is almost inevitably diverted away from what should be the main focus, the inherent quality of the programme he or she is making.

8. *The rules of broadcasting should liberate rather than restrict the programme-maker*

While all broadcasting will inevitably be governed by certain prescriptions —'educate', 'inform', 'entertain', 'balance', 'fairness'—and certain broadly drawn restrictions—obscenity, national security—the essence of the legislative foundation by which it is empowered should sustain a liberal function for the programme-maker. The legislation should 'create secure living space, arena for action, for broadcasters with all kinds of interests in possible programmes and possible varieties of audience, rather than leaving the field to those who are interested chiefly in delivering maximum audiences most of the time'. The legislation should also ensure that the higher echelons of broadcasting contain executives and governors who understand its potential and who themselves care for the importance of the creative work of their staff, such as Hugh Greene of the BBC, who once observed that there should always be a place for the dissenting radical. Part of that understanding would be the need for experiment and innovation in broadcasting, the need to provide a focus for a society's quarrel with itself, the recognition that mistakes will be made but as such may signify the health of the system.

Perhaps above all else, such leadership should be helped to understand that experiment, innovation, quarrel, and mistake are likely to come from the younger programme-maker, without whom the system is in danger of institutional arteriosclerosis.

Afterword

It could be argued that these various principles were created within a particular historical epoch, but today are *passé*. If that is the case, then we do have some very serious questions to ask about the general evolution of our social and cultural order. If, however, these are not *passé* sentiments but real and necessary commitments for the future, as they have been for the past, then the pre-eminent question is how to provide for the necessary architecture to ensure their realization not just in the life of public institutions but more importantly in the lives of all our people.

3 The Deconstruction of Public Service Broadcasting

Preamble

One senses that there is out there—in the common rooms of the academy, the better gentlemen's clubs of London, Amsterdam, New York, and Tokyo, the smoke-filled bars still visited by the remnants of the left, the opinion columns of more traditional newspapers—a feeling, a charming nostalgia that a formula can be found that will protect, support, preserve the institution of public service broadcasting into the twenty-first century. My own reluctant conclusion is that the process will be more akin to the preservation of primeval bugs in amber than the continuance of any vibrant cultural species.

Public service broadcasting was very much an idea constructed within one moment in time, the early part of the twentieth century; on patrician and governmental principles from another, the nineteenth century. As we approach the twenty-first century, it becomes clear that the sets of principles through which the idea of public service broadcasting was articulated have a precarious social, political, economic, and cultural anchorage.

One can in fact begin to suggest what now constitutes basic truisms about the future of audio-visual culture:

- there will be more—much more—of it;
- it will be produced in response to the most basic desires and wishes, but not needs, of the audience, rather than those of traditional élites;
- some of that television will be domestically produced, but much of it will originate elsewhere;
- the notion of paying for television from the public treasury will become increasingly rare, replaced by commercial funding and direct payment;
- audiences will continue to fragment with, as a consequence, an accelerated deconstruction of concepts of a public citizenry;
- the ability of governments to regulate the content of audio-visual culture will be diminished, partly because the implicit patricianism has come to be seen as *passé* and partly as an act of self-withdrawal in the interest of encouraging new communication technologies;
- the ability of broadcasters to reach large audiences with informative and educational material, as well as entertainment, will be hugely diminished.
- while it is overwhelmingly clear that a market model now dominates, the language which is associated with that—for example the term 'choice' as in 'increased choice'—fundamentally misconstrues the character of culture constructed by the market. If we take the United States as the location of the most profound articulation of the market model, it is totally clear that the operation of the market tends to produce a culture that is crass, trivial, shallow, exploitative, and fundamentally distorting of the long-established human desire to construct cultural, social, and political practices which are rational, informed, and enriching of the human experience. One must therefore conclude, at the prescriptive level, that if the USA is the model for a market system for producing culture then a health warning should be placed against that model.
- at the analytical level, however, one must conclude and recognize that the market model is triumphant, is the future.
- that triumph—a term that I use in the same way in which one might have said that the Wehrmacht, the German army, was triumphant in 1940 in Europe, i.e. something which I recognize, but do not applaud—translates into a set of consequences which are widespread and profound. Translated specifically into societal terms it is likely that the greater use of the market principle will inevitably have deleterious, i.e. negative, impacts on the prevailing character of culture traditional and modern. The dilemma which traditional and developing societies will face is that the felt need to continue to be modern and economically successful will force the rejection of those values and sentiments which are felt in the heart. The social, psychological, and emotional consequences will be substantial and disturbing. In short, in importing the US economic model they will also import the social neuroses which lurk in that deeply troubled society. That I think is sad.

In the early summer of 1990, the (London) *Observer* carried a profile of Anthony Simmons-Gooding, Chief Executive of British Satellite Broadcasting, which was accompanied by a photo of him beaming and holding his famous 'squarial'.[1] His bumptious optimism was somewhat premature, reminding one of Theodore Adorno's comment that 'The smile on the model is the grin of the victim.' It was not difficult to foresee that such models for the future of television as BSB would inevitably have a troubled birth. And yet Simmons-Gooding and others of his ilk, such as Messrs Murdoch, Maxwell, Berlusconi, Bond, Seydoux, and Turner, seemed to bestride the world of television in that decade like, in Ben Bagdikian's memorable phrase, the Lords of the Global Village. Theirs was the present, and so theirs also was to be the future.

In the cold light of the 1990s, BSB and Simmons-Gooding are no more (though the latter walked away with a pay-off), News International teetered on the edge of bankruptcy, Bond was bankrupted, Maxwell was dead, Turner was bailed out by TCI and other US cable companies, and was subject to the influence of John Malone. Of the others, we shall see. But what is clear is that the birth of the new age was always going to be troubled, with a not inconsiderable infant mortality rate. The true consequence of the grand ambition of the new age to which the 1980s were allegedly giving birth, however, would inevitably lie in the ravages wrought on the old and, in particular, on the structure of public culture which historically had found such a powerful incarnation in public service broadcasting. To be blunt, a combination of ideological and fiscal pressures, a failure of nerve, inside and out, have left most public broadcasting systems changed, nervous, bullied, uncertain.

In this chapter I want to examine a number of things: (1) the ideological and structural challenges of the 1980s to most public broadcasting organizations around the globe; (2) the consequences of those challenges for the place of broadcasting and, most especially, television in all our lives; (3) what was being challenged, to whit, what is this thing which we so easily term 'public service broadcasting'? The purpose of this question is, however, not to wallow in nostalgia, to paint the past in beautiful pastels and the present in various shades of grey. The point is to understand something of the condition of what continue to be important cultural institutions, and to ask about the appropriate institutional and intellectual architecture for them in the twenty-first century.

These are questions which I believe are not only, or even primarily, of academic importance. They touch upon some of the most profound issues of how our societies are being formed, as information systems, as cultural systems, as moral systems. To ask questions about public broadcasting is to ask questions about the character of our societies. That is why one might reasonably be concerned with the health of public broadcasting, because if it is less than well then this is possibly suggestive of a much wider and troubling pathology.

---

[1] The 'squarial' was a square dish able—at least in theory—to pick up direct signals from a satellite.

When we think about broadcasting we tend to think about this or that organization or occasionally we look in a comparative way at a collection of organizations. To understand in detail the innards of organizations is of course important, for how can we know the condition of the body if we do not occasionally examine its vital organs? It is, however, important to pull back from the particular observation of a particular institution to find a view of the whole body politic. Indeed, I would go so far as to argue that one cannot possibly hope to understand broadcasting in the modern age without that wider perspective. If we do broaden the perspective, the questions that emerge are not just about the individual, national TV systems, but about the whole evolution of global culture, about the relationship between culture and society, about what Raymond Williams called the 'felt quality of life'.

In 1991, Elmer Johnson—a former General Counsel to and director of General Motors—in a rather spectacular example of biting the hand that fed him rather well, asked: 'Have we so successfully inculcated a culture of economic individualism that we are losing our capacity for the ethics of citizenship?'[2] He adds, borrowing from the writer Louis Auchincloss, that 'we've fabricated a society of wolves and coyotes' and that 'the commercialism of the last ten years has turned many more of us into full-time consumers. Everything is for sale, including human companionship and conversation.'

Arthur Miller drew the parallels between America today and yesterday. He observed that America in the late 1920s was 'on some kind of obscene trip, looking to get rich at any cost to the spirit, and had elevated into power the men who could most easily lead that kind of quest. . . . They were sharks leading not only the economy but the spiritual side of the country. And there's a bit of that today, not only here but all over the world. There's never been a more materialist moment since I've been around.' He also adds that 'genuine social concern and a yearning for shared human values' have been thoroughly evacuated from American public policy.[3] I would go further and say that this is not a specifically American phenomenon, it is global.

With that evacuation of the language of 'shared human values' has been abandoned much of the vocabulary of moral discourse, of engagement with our humanity, of any sense of spirituality, of notions of moral enrichment through cultural experience. Consider some of the traditional arguments about public service broadcasting, not the substance but the sentiments, the mood, the self-conscious virtuousness. Consider something like this:

The broadcaster opens a window on the world and for many, especially for the young, it is a window opened for the first time. If those who look out, with the eyes we have

---

[2] Elmer Johnson, 'Can We Keep the Market in the Proper Place?', *Aspen Institute Quarterly*, 3/1 (winter 1991), 134.

[3] *Guardian*, 4 Aug. 1986.

given them, see only the familiar, the comfortable, the reassuring, then surely we have failed, for the world is not like that. If we ensure that only the ugly, the bestial, the violent and the tawdry appear before them, then just as surely we have failed, for the world is not like that either.[4]

Or try this: 'the BBC can best contribute to the preservation of freedom in the human situation today, by preserving within itself freedom for the creativity of those people who constitute its real and living assets.'[5]

Take those words, put them in the mouths of modern senior broadcasting executives, and try not to laugh. This is not to say that modern broadcasting executives are not mostly honourable people. They are, but the whole tone of these words, let alone the ideas, would simply seem unreal, out of time, even bizarre, such is the narrowness of the contemporary debate about broadcasting, which is now more truly defined as the culture of accountants. That it is so is partly a consequence of the formal demands posed by governments everywhere with their constant chanting of such questions as: can we get rid of the licence fees or government subsidy? what about subscription, sponsorship, selling spectrum space, sacking staff? how much advertising is there, how do we balance the books? The poverty of the debate is also a reflection of the general narrowness of moral vision which has overtaken the western liberal democracies, the stark decline of humanistic values and ambition.

Mao Tse-tung was once asked what he thought the legacy of the French Revolution was: 'too early to tell,' he replied. Maybe we are too close to the movement of history which so conditions who and what we are as communicators. One must confess, however, that, writing from within the memory of the wreckage of the 1980s, the temptation is to ask what a decade of conservative hegemony has left us with. In the film *Wall Street* Gordon Gecko, the corrupted spirit at the heart of Stone's bleak tale of the Reagan years, stands up at a shareholders' meeting of a company he wants to buy and then slice up for sale. He makes a speech—a kind of ode to the values of the 1980s—in which he mouths the words which were uttered by the real-life Gecko, the felonious financier Ivan Boesky: 'Greed is good.' In a rather stark way, while that evoked the moral bankruptcy of the decade, at the same time it captured its primary commitments: the acquisition of wealth at the expense of all else, and the necessarily concomitant deification of the individual as consumer.

In real time, we have allegedly dealt with the excesses of the Boeskys, the Milkins, and their various kith and kin in different cultures. What we have not done, however, is dismantle the ideological and institutional architecture which housed them. In fact it remains intact, which is why the parallel dismantling

---

[4] Hugh Greene, Director-General of the BBC, speaking in 1981. Quoted in Tracey, *A Variety of Lives*, 195.

[5] Arthur fforde, Chairman of the BBC 1957–64. Quoted ibid. 235.

of public broadcasting continues apace. In so far as the ascendancy of these gentlemen entailed the glorification of the market and the necessarily consequent dismantling of public culture, we are left with the problem of how to reassert the more communitarian, caring, and non-material commitments which the architecture of public culture was meant to house, of how to breathe fresh life into the ethic of citizenship. A fascinating aspect of studying broadcasting is that by asking questions such as 'whither the BBC?', 'whither Danmarks Radio?' one is asking about the condition and fate of institutions which are inherently important and which, allowed to follow their original and primary purpose—public service—have served us on a daily basis, and as viewers-as-citizens, rather well.

There is, however, another question raised by studying broadcasting that attaches to the symbolic function which historically has lain at the heart of public service broadcasting. Because public service broadcasting always represented the aspirations of societies to be properly served—journalistically, culturally, and, more recently, in the creation of quality popular culture—its demise necessarily entails the potential abandonment of such ambitions. There may be some good programmes produced by commercial systems, but they are incidental to the real activity of the organization, the acquisition of wealth. They are not produced as a matter of course nor as a function of the core thesis of the institution. As I understand it, the pursuit of excellence—viewed at different levels—lies at the heart of the project of public broadcasting. This is not to say that all, or even most, programmes produced by such organizations are excellent, merely that the pursuit of the ambition is the only way in which they can realize their intrinsic purpose.

The symbolism of this, nationally and globally, seems to me to be crucial. I understand all the arguments about hierarchies of values, the philosophical issue of how can one say that A is 'better than' B? I cannot however but still conclude: if there is a poverty of imagination at the heart of the central mental experience of all modern societies, the viewing of television, how can one properly expect that there will not be an impoverishment within the more general imaginative life of the society?

If there is, because of fiscal pressure and ambition, a squeezing out of programme elements unique to a particular national culture, a smoothing out of difference, and its replacement with a rather bland, undifferentiated pan-national culture—what Jeremy Isaacs once, memorably, called 'Europudding' —how can one feed off and thus reproduce and nurture the vibrancy and creativity which is what national culture at its best is all about?

If power is used to put the survival of the organization ahead of the purpose for which it was created, if all these conditions pertain, if all these signals are sent, then we face a very profound problem about the real character of what it is we have been creating in our societies—a problem which stretches from the ability to do great, or even good, journalism, to use television as an art—in both a narrow and a more general sense—to have television which entertains us well, right up to the most profound issue of the social and cultural health of the society. If the organization of the dominant means of communication in our society is such as to suggest, through its very character, 'that joy lies in goods', then one might reasonably argue that no good can lie there.

The United States, in many ways, represents this process; look at it and you are, maybe, peering into the future. I once shocked, even appalled, a class of graduate students when I told them that I thought there was a relationship between the condition of the vast bulk of US television and the fact that the Hubble telescope was launched and then was found not to work. The linkage, I suggested, was not causal, more evocative of the mediocrity and absence of a commitment to quality which now define much of US society (with, possibly, the interesting exception of its military hardware).

It seems fairly clear that the development of the policies which have afflicted broadcasting was not the result of some impossible-to-divine processes deep within modern civilization; or the result of free-market cosmic dust floating across the galaxy to alight by random chance on the third planet from the sun. What happened to broadcasting, and so much else, in the 1980s was to a considerable extent a result of the self-conscious structuring in power of a certain ideology with the clear understanding that this would serve very particular interests. It was Emerson who said that 'there is properly no history, only biography'.

There was in effect in most major western societies—and certainly within the USA and the UK—a kind of silent *coup d'état* around the time that the 1970s became the 1980s. The 1990s are the result. The use of the market to serve the 'public interest' translated into a continuing act of betrayal of the public in the broad sense in order to sustain the interests of the few. Thus we can see how a public broadcaster is placed in such a position that it can only proceed and survive by changing itself, and that it must do so in order to make way for the new 'Lords of the Global Village'. If the BBC, or NHK, or DR are stable, and able to fulfil their original mandates, to work within the confines of a distinct cultural context, and can treat its audience as real people rather than statistics in skins, then not only would the 'new' in the shape of Murdoch be stillborn by the national broadcaster's continuing ability to hold its audience, but its survival would constitute a constant affront to an ideological orthodoxy which loathes public culture.

If there is a point I wish to stress in these pages, it is that the definition of policies for national broadcasting systems is necessarily suggestive of a definition of policies for the character of a whole society. They capture the sets of choices and preferences which colour all the imperatives, ambitions, and institutions which constitute in the most literal sense a social order. Two hundred years ago, when Poland was going through one of its periods of political reform, the leadership called on Rousseau to advise them. As to the economic system, he observed:

[The choice] to be adopted by Poland depends on the purposes she has in view in reforming her constitution. If your only wish is to become noisy, brilliant and fearsome, and to influence the other peoples of Europe, their example lies before you; devote yourselves to following it. . . . Try to make money very necessary, in order to keep the people in a condition of great dependence; and with that end in view, encourage national luxury, and the luxury of spirit which is inseparable from it. In this way, you will create a scheming, ardent, avid, ambitious, servile and knavish people, like all the rest; one goes to the two extremes of opulence and misery, or license and slavery, with nothing in between. I know that men can only be made to act in terms of their own interests; but pecuniary interest is the worst, the basest and most corrupting of all, and even, as I confidently repeat and shall always maintain, the least and weakest in the eyes of those who really know the human heart. In all hearts there is naturally a reserve of grand passions; when greed for gold alone remain, it is because all the rest, which should have been stimulated and developed, have been enervated and stifled.[6]

Challenges

Public broadcasting is everywhere being forced to re-examine its purpose, its nature, its mission. The past decade has seen a widespread assault on the importance, even legitimacy, of public service broadcasting in the major industrialized democracies. From the close of the Second World War until the late 1970s, public broadcasting organizations had stood in powerful, resilient opposition to commercial systems, and they dominated the cultural geology of the societies from which they had been formed. (The only major exception to this pattern was in the United States, where public broadcasting had been much slower to develop and had far fewer resources.) Political problems faced even the strongest of these institutions, but as an intellectual, cultural, and creative construction, the edifice of public service broadcasting seemed permanent and inherently stable.

By the closing years of the 1980s that edifice was widely seen to be crumbling. In the shift from the 1970s to the 1990s, broadcasting became a potent symbol of a collision of ideas over how western society should be organized, not just economically, but also culturally, creatively, morally.

---

[6] J. J. Rousseau, 'Considerations on the Government of Poland', in J. J. Rousseau, *Political Writings* (Madison: University of Wisconsin Press, 1986), 182.

The whole landscape of public broadcasting is dotted with statements that things have changed, things are worse, but might get better if only we batten down the financial hatches, become more competitive, and so on. We do not, however, need the weatherman to tell us too many times that it is winter. We need merely to look out of the window. Two powerful forces have nurtured an intellectual bleakness, or have at least demanded a reappraisal of how to respond to events which all too often are taken to be irresistible.

The first force is the remarkably rapid growth in major television societies of a multi-channel environment, either as something which is real, extant, or as something which gestates as fetal policy in the minds of politicians and their *apparatchiks*: the second is ideological, the near abandonment by political élites of the idea of public culture which fed the idea of public broadcasting.

The New Communication Environment

The key fact of life for those concerned with broadcasting policy in the twenty-first century will lie in the increasing inability to make such policy. The most obvious characteristic of broadcasting in the twentieth century was the willingness, even desire, of governments to regulate it. The manner in which this was done, the forms of regulation and funding of broadcasting, varied from place to place, but there was a general consensus that actively shaping the output of broadcasting in pursuit of publicly defined goals was a 'good thing'. More cynically, it was often argued that such regulation was a 'necessary' thing in that it was a particularly effective instrument of social and political control.

The latter part of the century saw a series of developments, ideological, technological, and structural, which taken together undermine the very ability of governments to have the same hands-on influence over the direction of broadcasting. There is, in fact, a powerful symmetry and synergy between a market system that views the audience as consumers, and technologies which are 'narrow' in their casting. There is in many countries, particularly noticeable in Asia, a deep contradiction between the desire to employ new technologies of communication as part of a broad-based effort at modernization and a residual desire to maintain certain traditional values and moral systems. This will be a key issue for the next century, with the likelihood that the modernizing tendency will marginalize the traditionalist tendency.

The most immediate fact of life for the public sector, and a major source of its compromised condition, is the sheer growth of the commercial communication industrial sector. By the beginning of this decade there were 354 national broadcasting organizations in the leading (i.e. economically) developed 100 countries in the world. The number of national *channels* increased by 46 per cent between 1987 and 1991, from 354 to 521. In addition, there were at least 650 local and regional channels—and these figures did not include the USA. Of all these organizations, 47 per cent still have a licence fee; 32 per cent have some direct government financing; 27 per cent rely wholly on advertising. In addition, 125 new television services started around the world—outside North America—in the decade after 1981, and were still in operation in 1991. These new services offered 145 new channels. Of the 125, 229 operate 24 hours a day; 62 are advertising-supported; 39 are wholly subscription-based—and 33 are aimed at international markets.[7] Seventy-five per cent of these new services rely on imports to fill at least half of their screen time. By 1995 there were something like 2,000 satellite-delivered TV channels available in Asia. In Europe in 1995 33 new satellite-delivered channels were launched, bringing the total to 186, delivered by 28 satellites. On the evening of 9 April 1996, SES, the Luxembourg-based company which operates the Astra-system of satellites, launched its second all-digital satellite. With a third launched in 1997 SES has available 56 digital transponders with the capacity to broadcast 500–60 channels over Europe. Entersat, which is owned by Europe's main telecommunications operators, has plans to offer 800–1,000 channels by the end of the century. In Britain, BSkyB launched a 200-channel digital satellite service in 1997. Pay-TV revenues in Europe in 1995 were $3.8 billion, with projections of $9.3 billion in 2000 and $14.8 billion in 2005. In 1995, $18.9 billion was spent on TV advertising, with almost $30 billion predicted for 2005. Against this one must place the revenue realities of European public broadcasters, in which public funding is stagnant or in decline, and which had revenues from advertising fall from 44 per cent to 28 per cent between 1990 and 1994.[8]

Perhaps, however, the most powerful figures on the growth of the commercial communication industrial sector come from the United States. In 1995 cable industries' revenues were $22 billion; video purchase and rental $16.8 billion; TV advertising $27 billion; movie tickets $5 billion. The purchase in 1995 and 1996 of dishes to receive signals from the new direct-broadcast satellite services such as Direct TV was such as to make them the fastest ever selling consumer product—of any kind. Perhaps, however, the most important statistics are those for the telephone industry, whose total gross revenues in 1994 were in the region of $180 billion, considerably larger than the economies of most countries.

The recent telecommunications law in the United States, passed by Congress and signed into law by President Clinton on 8 February 1996, by deregulating the communication industries even further, unlocks a huge amount of capital. It appears inevitable that not only will the communication sector in the United States be considerably reconfigured, that sector will have, because it has to have, even more aggressive global ambitions.

---

[7] *Screen Digest*, Feb. 1992.   [8] *TV in Europe to 2005* (London: Zenith Media, 1996), 10.

I quote these figures not only because they describe the evolution of the world's largest broadcast markets but also because they are taken by many, inside and outside broadcasting, to be a portent. Throughout Europe—whether that be defined as the 152-member EU, the 22 countries of the Council of Europe, or the 32 countries of the European Broadcasting Union—we have seen in the past decade an astonishing series of policy developments which transformed the structure, and, therefore purpose, of broadcasting. Those policies encouraged the development of new systems of distribution, based on cable and satellite technologies, and the privatization of existing, and the creation of new, terrestrial systems.

In fact, the 1980s saw country after country begin to change, or at least question, their public systems. In Canada for example in May 1985 Marcel Masse, the Minister of Communications, announced the formation of a task force 'to examine the current environment and future trends and to analyze the various broadcasting policy options available to the government'. The specific terms of reference were for the task force to make recommendations

on an industrial and cultural strategy to govern the future evolution of the Canadian Broadcasting System through the remainder of this century recognizing the importance of broadcasting to Canadian life. The strategy will take full account of the overall social and economic goals of the government, of government policies and priorities, including the need for fiscal restraint, increased reliance on private sector initiatives and federal-provincial cooperation, and of the policies of the government in other related economic and cultural sectors. It will also take full account of the challenges and opportunities in the increasingly competitive broadcasting environment presented by ongoing technological developments.

In New Zealand in January 1986 the Minister of Broadcasting, Jonathan Hunt, released details of a royal commission on broadcasting and related telecommunications. The brief of the Commission was to

inquire into the institutions, operations, financing and control of New Zealand broadcasting and related telecommunications and to report on what changes are necessary or desirable to use in an economically efficient manner those advances in technology which fit New Zealand's circumstances and resources, to widen the choice, and improve the quality of programmes to secure independence, depth and impartiality in news and current affairs programmes, and to reflect New Zealand's cultural and social variety so that the structure and resources of broadcasting may be better organized to serve all New Zealanders.

The subsequent creation of the commercial station TV3 was a direct consequence of this process of change. In Australia the Labour government engaged, and continues to engage, in a wide-ranging examination of the ABC's financial arrangements and, in particular, the issue of the Corporation being made to take some form of commercial funding.

In Ireland, government-appointed consultants recommended radical changes in the structure and output of Radio Telefis Eireann. The Spanish government decided to break up the public broadcasting monopoly and to create three new national and five regional channels. On the basis of a government report the Swedish government decided to centralize production in one centre in an attempt to retain broadcasting within the public sector. And in December 1985 Sweden, Norway, Finland, and Ireland announced plans for a two-channel DBS satellite, Tele-X, in 1987.

The Benelux nations (Belgium, the Netherlands, and Luxembourg) are not only the most densely cabled countries in Europe but, because of their location, are washed over by the terrestrial programming of several major countries. The Dutch courts in 1986 set a precedent by accepting private-ownership bids for state-controlled operations. New media laws were also being prepared, along with a review of proposals to extend commercial airtime. Private interests developed a Dutch subscriber-supported film channel, Film Net, with backing from the Swedish conglomerate Esselte, Dutch publishing interests, and the US distributor United International Pictures.

The Belgian group Bruxelles-Lambert, the principal shareholder in Radio-Tele Luxembourg (RTL), became a major mover in new media developments in Europe, working closely for example with Rupert Murdoch. Luxembourg had its own ambitious DBS plans with its sixteen-channel satellite, Astra, and the imminent launch of new satellites. The German publisher Bertelsmann developed a 40 per cent interest in the German-language satellite channel RTL-plus and the German federal government planned its own direct-broadcast satellite. Denmark developed its own plans for a second television service, organized at least in part on a commercial basis.

Perhaps the classic case of the growth of private television was Italy, with the property magnate Silvio Berlusconi central to events there. The rewards of piracy and the deregulation of broadcasting by the Constitutional Court in the mid-1970s led to the creation of hundreds of private television companies in Italy. These slowly coalesced into loosely organized networks, with Berlusconi's Canale Cinque the largest. Berlusconi also developed ambitions in Spain, Canada, and France, including playing a key role in French DBS plans.

In Austria Gerhard Weiss of Oesterreichischer Rundfunk spoke of his fear that 'a mounting tide of international media offerings will sweep over the national media scenes of the industrial countries'.[9] In Switzerland the Société Suisse de Radiofussion et Télévision (SSR), a monopoly for fifty years, suddenly faced stiff competition with new radio licences; a pay-TV trial; and more than 50 per cent of TV homes subscribing to cable systems which bring such

---

[9] Quoted in 'Cable Programmers Scan the Globe for New Opportunities', *Broadcasting Abroad* (Nov. 1989), 30–1.

services as Sky Channel. Leo Schürmann, Director-General of SSR, argued that in terms of political and technological choice Switzerland 'is at the crossroads'. In an attempt to adjust to the new environment, SSR diversified its services into new radio channels, for local radio; teletext; pay TV; and involvement in French- and German-language service satellite transmissions by ECS.

In the UK the Thatcher government encouraged wholesale rethinking of the position and purpose of the BBC; stimulated the growth of cable and satellite; prepared the ground for a fifth channel; and changed the whole character of ITV by auctioning the franchises and making Channel Four sell its own air-time.

In France, the 1980s saw the creation of extensive plans for cable television and DBS, as well as a continual restructuring of the public service system. The emergence of Canal Plus in 1984 was a straw in the wind: an example of an over-the-air TV system, owned and controlled by a mixture of state and private interests, with revenue from a mixture of a small amount of public service material and a large amount of subscription. One prominent figure in French broadcasting, Jean Autin, observed of this development that 'thanks to this experiment a new type of television is emerging similar to the public service, yet wholly separate from it'.[10] In 1985 Mitterrand decided to liberalize French broadcasting further and authorized, amid a great deal of political controversy, the start of La Cinq, a general entertainment channel showing mainly films and imported programmes, and supported by advertising. Particular controversy attached to the fact that ownership of the channel was handed to Silvio Berlusconi and a French businessman and supporter of President Mitterrand, Jérôme Seydoux. A music channel, TV6, was also started, aimed at the youth market and again supported by advertising.

In 1986 the newly elected conservative government of Jacques Chirac cancelled the previous decisions on La Cinq and TV6, put them up for sale, and decided to privatize TF1 and the new DBS systems. The new communications law of July 1986 formally abolished the Haute Autorité and replaced it with the Commission Nationale de la Communication et des Libertés, as well as laying the groundwork for the privatization of TF1. In February 1987 the La Cinq franchise was awarded to a consortium headed by Robert Hersant, but including the former operators Berlusconi and Seydoux. TV6 went to a consortium led by La Lyonnaise des Eaux and Compagnie Luxembourgeoise de Télédiffusion (CLT). In April 1987 the CNCL announced that TF1 had been sold to a group led by François Bouygues, and with Robert Maxwell as the second largest shareholder, for 3 billion francs. The key element in the structure of public service broadcasting had thus been finally privatized.

In Japan there is a long tradition of examining the development of broadcasting, and particularly of NHK, within the context of a wider strategic plan to

---

[10] Ibid.

create the infrastructure of the information society based on broadband cable and satellite technology. Numerous scenarios have been developed for the future of broadcasting. They tend to begin, however, with the basic assumption that by the turn of the century there will be more satellite communication, more cable penetration, and a vastly enhanced telecommunications network characterized not only by the transmission of digitalized data but also by audio-visual images.

There is another element here which needs to be at least pointed to, the development of what might be called structural globalism. The increasing need of corporate capitalism to expand markets outside any national context in order to maximize the opportunity for capital formation is by now a clear and powerful aspect of global economic life. At least half of the top 500 US corporations now see themselves as in effect belonging to no single nation. Their boards of directors have, as it were, declared the nation-state *passé*.

Inevitably, the pattern of globalization is now taken as given. The head of what was Robert Maxwell's Entertainment Group observed:

If you're not global, you're not going to be a player. That's the bottom line. You're not going to be able to compete. The level field will no longer be domestic markets. The level playing field will be the global markets. You will be disadvantaged in terms of buying power, distribution, clout, etc. if you don't have your hands in the media business worldwide.

And Andrew Brilliant, Vice-President of ESPN, commented: 'I'd like to think that it's all one business. It's not inconceivable that everything becomes international, one market. The U.S. may be most important, but only as one part of the mix.'[11]

An edition of *Broadcasting Abroad*, an American trade magazine, in November 1990 had a map of the globe spread across two pages. Underneath the text read:

Europe's 320 million viewers and the TV advertising growth potential in a rapidly deregulating market make American programmers' and marketers' mouths water. Eastern Europe is opening its doors to the west. Opportunities loom in Asia—the launch of PanAmSat, with its powerful reach into Latin America has prompted several programmes to focus on that region, and some are looking hard at the commercial opportunities in the highly competitive, deregulating Australia–New Zealand markets.

Accompanying this is the formation of all kinds of global corporate alliances, co-productions, co-finance deals. For example, at the Monte Carlo TV market in 1990 alliances were sprouting like mushrooms after a rain storm—between

---

[11] *Broadcasting*, 19 Dec. 1988.

Canal Plus and the German Bertelsmann and Kirch Group; between Berlusconi, TF1, and the Kirch Group; between Canal Plus, the French company Chrysalide, and the LA financial consortium the Moore Group; between Bristol Telco International (the distribution arm of TVS), Nickelodeon, Disney, TBS, Showtime, Discovery, and HBO; and between Berlusconi and Canal Plus and, again, the Kirch Group. In November 1989, the Association of Commercial TV in Europe was formed by TF1; CLT in Luxembourg; the UK's ITVA; the German SAT1; and, of course, Berlusconi. CNN is now seen in over 100 countries; MTV is in 14 European countries, and shortly Eastern Europe, and in Australia, Japan, Latin America; ESPN is in Europe, Asia, and Latin America; Discovery is in Europe and Japan. American cable and telephone companies such as TCI, US West, Pactel, and Jones Intercable are in the process of spending, during the 1990s, £10 billion on wiring Britain. If we simply take a look at developments in 1994 and early 1995, we see a continuation in the almost frenetic growth of the amount of television available around the planet. The message is clear: a colossal and massively funded attempt that multiplies the amount of television and in effect begins to smooth out the political geography of nations, placing the need of corporations ahead of any public or national interest.

The New Ideological Environment

The profundity of the question raised by the rise of the new media and the private, terrestrial systems was conceived and sustained by another force which again was beyond the ability of the public broadcasting community to control but which it clearly must confront. That is the ideological prominence of *the market* in broadcasting, which has spread across the globe not so much as a ripple, more like a tsunami. During the past two decades the challenge to the very idea of public culture, or in its minimalist form the public interest, has become widespread and strident.

The roots of this emergent ideological orthodoxy lie in the radical conservative political hegemony in the 1980s, itself a creation of a public unbalanced by the decay of the collectivist orthodoxies of the post-war era which were buried beneath the painful stagflation of the 1970s, a shrewd use of such populist sentiments by an assertive corporate capitalism and the utopian tease of a technologically determined post-industrial age.

The character of the assault is best evidenced in the very language of the dialogue about the future of television. For example, late in the decade, Charles Jonscher, a prominent adviser to the Thatcher government on communications policy, attacked what he described as 'the myths of broadcasting' that 'used to shape the thinking of governments on all public services from the railways to the national health, and which still survives in this field of broadcasting. The chief myth is that because an activity fulfils a public service it is not subject to basic laws of economics . . . the principles of supply and demand.'[12]

While Jonscher recognizes in passing that programmes imply, indeed require, social judgements, the leitmotif of his whole piece is a reiteration of the decade's emergent orthodoxy: that television is primarily an economic and industrial process and should be treated as such.

Another echo sounds in the thoughts and words of Mark Fowler, Chairman of the US Federal Communications Commission from May 1981 to April 1987 and perhaps the single most influential figure in the ideological assault on broadcasting as a publicly regulated process. In an address to the International Radio and Television Society in 1981, Fowler summed up this whole philosophy in one sentence: 'From here onward, the public's interests must determine the public interest.' In November 1988, the US Department of Commerce's National Telecommunications Information Agency, in its report, *Telecom 2000*, commented: 'There is no basis for assuming that any risks to the public's interests are so great, or that alternative remedies are so ineffective, or any harms will materialize so quickly or irremediably, that perpetuating the current regulatory scheme is warranted.'

Margaret Thatcher crystallized this position when she told an interviewer that 'there is no such thing as society'. Former senior Conservative Cabinet member and Eurocrat Leon Brittan elaborated on her view: 'This vision is not a plan: indeed it depends on the rejection of planning. It requires a system in which the customer rather than the philosopher is king.'[13] The Thatcher-appointed Peacock inquiry into the future financing of the BBC concluded: 'British broadcasting should move towards a sophisticated market system based on consumer sovereignty. That is a system which recognizes that viewers and listeners are the best ultimate judges of their own interests, which they can best satisfy if they have the option of purchasing the broadcasting service they require from as many alternative sources of supply as possible.'[14] The subsequent publication of the Thatcher government's policy document *Broadcasting in the 90s: Competition, Choice and Quality* showed definitively that the message had been heeded. These sentiments would not have been surprising as an expression of the Fowler position and US neo-conservative philosophy, but as a reflection of the new orthodoxy in Britain—the chief bastion of a rich notion of public culture—they were telling. And they were sentiments which, as I have already suggested, underpinned the development of numerous national policies on broadcasting.

---

[12] *Sunday Times*, 1 May 1988.   [13] *Guardian*, 7 Dec. 1984.
[14] Home Office, *Report of the Committee on Financing the BBC*, Cmnd. 9824 (London: HMSO, 1986) (Peacock Report), para. 711.

The Decline of Tradition

These various statements were the surface appearances of far more fundamental shifts in the socio-political geology of industrial capitalism. Traditionally,
the public regulation of broadcasting rested on a central logic: a paternalistic
or patrician relationship with the audience. I do not mean paternalistic in a
Reithian sense, in which the ambition of the cultural élite is to elevate the
'masses' to a higher level of attainment, but rather in the sense that the very
nature of 'old' communication technologies effectively disenfranchised the
audience, preventing them from having a significant say in what would be
produced for them. In no way do I want to suggest that this was a necessarily patronizing relationship, though there were and are moments that are a
kind of priestly offering of the host to the congregation.

The emerging logic of communication fundamentally deconstructs this traditional way of doing things. In the first instance the logic is about consumers
in the market-place, not citizens in the nation. The development which is key,
technologically and conceptually, is that of *interactivity*. The ability of the audience member to interact with the TV set and the multiplicity of offerings which
are made available is not just some new gizmo, but a profound shift in how one
thinks about the relationship between the communicator and the audience.

The brute truth is that in an interactive communications system, the construction of which necessarily presupposes a significant increase in the amount
of potential communications that are available, it is difficult, probably impossible, to have a patrician relationship with the audience. The relationship becomes
one of providing the market with whatever the consumer might decide he or
she needs. From the standpoint of democratic rhetoric there is much which is
compelling within this argument; who, after all, wants to be seen to be paternalistic in an egalitarian age? The reality, of course, is that there is a hidden
paternalism in market-dominated systems as commercial providers offer what
they interpret as the things that the public wants/needs. The result is, on the
whole, a populism without intelligence.

The development of communication technology is, however, part of an
inevitable strategy by all major industrial societies to alter radically the means
by which they produce wealth. There is no way in the medium to long term
that any economy of any size or with any ambition will be able to avoid the
further development of communications technologies. The pursuit of the information society, based on an architecture of broadband cable, non-wired
technology, satellite, and computers, thus becomes not just a likely but an
inevitable part of economic strategy and at the heart of that will lie interactive
communications, since *it is inevitable that it will be seen as being in the national,
regional, and local economic interests that such developments should continue to be
encouraged.*

The Techno-ideology of Change

Any developed understanding of the future of television in the twenty-first century has to begin with a sense of the political, social, cultural, technical, and economic geography of the later twentieth and early twenty-first centuries. How did we come to be where we are? In answering that question we will begin to have a much better sense of where we might be going since events in the latter part of the twentieth century are highly determinative of the intellectual and institutional character of communications in the twenty-first.

The post-war 'settlement', to use Hall and Jacques's phrase,[15] of western industrial society was based on a conception of the world being a place of full employment, stable currencies, perpetual growth, coherent nation-states, a fearful global stability based on the nuclear terror of the Cold War, and a commitment to the provision of welfare services to working populations. It was an order which from within the confines of the nation necessarily presupposed a significant sense of the collective, the shared, the group. Labour unions had been an important part of the construction of that collectivist ethic by their persistent argument that everyone should share in the fruits of a surging capitalism. One-nation, benignly paternalistic conservative parties easily shared the same legislative chambers with mildly reformist social democratic parties. Long before the end of history was declared the end of ideology was declaimed. And nestling easily within this post-world war order were the mixed systems of communication: the public broadcasting institutions, the obvious and most efficient articulators of the national order paid for out of a public purse which could afford the indulgence; the commercial broadcasters plying their advertising-supported goods; the world of print and the largely publicly controlled telephone companies.

The 1970s were to see erupting to the surface tensions within the settlement which would inevitably challenge its contours, shifting the landscape of the time. Stagflation, oil crises, under-investment, competition from the Third World, a working class which enjoyed its new-found pleasures and wanted, if anything, more of the same, all these and more were forces which shook the structure of post-war life and cracked a façade which had seemed so solid. The settlement no longer was able to work in its own terms and capital had to seek new ways to guarantee its continued well-being, even if that meant dismantling the key institutions of the post-war settlement.

Something else had, however, been taking place, flowing from earlier humiliations of the political right. This was the construction of an ideological order which would provide the language to justify the process of deconstruction of

---

[15] Stuart Hall and Martin Jacques (eds.), *New Times: The Changing Face of Politics in the 1990s* (New York: Jeno, 1990).

the post-war order. There is always a danger in attempting an overly precise pin-pointing of moments of historical change, particularly at the level of the mental reconstruction of a given order. However, ideas do not just happen, nor are they deposited on earth by some celestial wind like so much galactic dust. Ideas, beliefs, intellect, ideology, all are made and sometimes the process of manufacture is opaque, sometimes remarkably clear. The ideas which came to replace the post-war settlement are one such example of the latter. Two moments stand out: 1964 and the humiliation of Barry Goldwater in the presidential election won by LBJ; 1974 and the humiliation and downfall of the British Conservative Party and the Prime Minister Edward Heath. Both events were followed by the cold determination of a number of well-placed and well-financed 'rightists' to reverse what they took to be these historic wrongs and errors. Sidney Blumenthal's *The Rise of the Counterestablishment* brilliantly portrays the intellectual creation of what became known as Reaganism. And any examination of the rise of Thatcherism would need to disinter the flow of influence from the likes of Airey Neave, Keith Joseph, and Alfred Sherman. From both camps flowed a key argument, drawing succour from the economics of Friedman and his Chicago Valkyries that the crisis of economy and society which bedevilled the 1970s lay not in the structural contradictions of capital but in the collectivist and statist orthodoxy of a post-war settlement which crowded and smothered the inherent potential of 'the individual' and 'the market'.

The challenge posed to the very idea of public culture, or in its minimalist form the public interest, became widespread and strident, emanating from the proposition that social good flows not so much from collective activity organized from the top down, but from myriad individual decisions organized from the bottom up. There were two opposed models of social and political order involving different conceptions of democratic rights and freedoms, different ideas of the relationship between culture and economics. Applied to broadcasting, one model suggested that to sustain the general well-being of society the body politic had not just a right but a duty to make strategic interventions and decisions through nominated institutions. Public broadcasting had historically been one such institution. Those interventions were to guarantee a range, depth, quality, and independence of programme output which other arrangements would simply not support.

Here was also an institution which could be adopted, for example by left intellectuals of various hues, as a bulwark against the immanent inadequacies and inanities of Kapital. One had only to point the finger at the condition of American television, or so it seemed, to render mute any counter-argument to the virtues of public service broadcasting.

This was, to say the least, a curious alliance. An institution founded in the image and likeness of a patrician class reared on a sentiment of obligation to those less fortunate than oneself, and intellectuals to whom class was anathema. The profound irony then was that the public broadcasting sector could only be served by encouraging the caring, bourgeois democratic element within capitalism. What was to become clear as the 1980s unfolded was that there is no contest as between the need to reorganize radically a tottering economic order and a lingering *noblesse oblige*.

Against the idea of public service broadcasting was the theory which had come to underpin the growth of the multi-channel environment, that such 'public' interventions and regulated culture are neither necessary nor proper. In this model what matters is consumer sovereignty, the marriage of the individual as economic actor *and* the possessor of basic democratic rights. From the late 1970s the new technologies provided the rationale, the argument that while there once may have been a case for regulating the spectrum as a scarce national resource in the public interest, developments in the technical capacity to communicate obviated that position.

No institution of the old settlement could remain untouched. There could be no geological remnants on this new terrain, and if the winds of change did not reduce them to rubble then political dynamite would do the job, destroying careers, changing the nature of organizations as an act of political will, privileging the commercial, supporting accommodatory neo-fascist and authoritarian regimes, smashing organized labour, spawning a new breed of econo-bureaucrats through a kind of colossal social *in vitro* programme. Once these intellectual constructs had taken hold, sanctified by the election of numerous right-wing governments, then on the political dais could be placed the individual-as-consumer and the needs and interests of 'the corporation'. And buried deep beneath the rubble of the old order were such concepts as public good, public interest, community, public culture, citizenship, governance, and, increasingly, the nation-state. The decay of the latter in particular suggested the real extent of the triumph of the corporatist ethic. There remained few if any national markets that could satisfy the needs of companies. The terms 'global markets' and 'globalization' were chanted with incessant fervour and ever greater volume, and nothing was to be more globalized than communications. Indeed, the very nature of evolving communication technologies—with their sheer capacity to allow the individual to construct his or her own communications—placed them in powerful lock-step with the new and dominant discourse of the late twentieth century, that of the culture of the market, an enclosing system of values, assumptions, and social practices from which it is difficult, even impossible, to escape.

The challenge to public broadcasting from new media and new ideologies is relatively easy to grasp. There are, however, other changes afoot—in some way linked to these—profound in their implications for the whole organization of audio-visual culture. It is characteristic of the new television, suggesting a redefinition of its place in our lives, that there is a shift to the audience *possessing*, but barely *using*, television.

Historically public service broadcasting rested on a useful myth that took credence from the limitations of technology. The radio spectrum was limited, it was suggested, and therefore this natural resource had to be carefully guarded lest it be over-exploited and made useless. The national interest required nothing less. So was established a means whereby the most powerful form of communications to date could be constructed towards a particular agenda which in many cases was, and remains, that of a narrow membership of established political, social, and cultural clubs. In many instances, out of such conditions of control emerged, like flowers from a parched land, individuals who worked the system and its rhetoric. These were men and women who called the bluff of the political establishment and who saw the potentiality of a form of communication uncompromised by the values of commerce or state control, and were determined to serve what they understood to be the public good.

The growth of cable and satellite television inevitably made this idea redundant. Where once there had been technological scarcity now there is abundance, and the provision of multiple forms of pleasure to gasping audiences seemed to many governments a fine, cheap, and quick way of financing the construction of a new communications infrastructure for the twenty-first century. No longer, it was argued, need broadcasting be 'nannied' for the people. Individuals were sovereign, and technology provided the infrastructural wherewithal finally to allow them to choose for themselves. The market for books and magazines became the analogy.

That analogy in itself is interesting. I suspect that a dominant characteristic of 'the book' in modern times is that it is purchased more than it is read. Some reading takes place, of course, but much is bought that is not read as the idea of cultural forms—high and low—becomes more significant than their actual use. Time, motivation, intellect all fall into step and lead us to a place in which *we have* but do not *do*. So the culture of communication of the twenty-first century will be about its possession rather than its use, a fetishist and fragmented medium, which is however only possible *now*.

There is something else which has to be allowed for in examining the evolving relationship between 'the public' and 'communications'. This is a change in the fundamental nature of communication, and in our relationship with, and use of, the technology.

Matsuhisa Takashima tells a fascinating story of television and a small boy in Tokyo suffering from muscular dystrophy.[16] The boy, who cannot move his limbs, remained optimistic and courageous despite a prognosis which was not favourable. He was fond of telling his doctors and counsellors at the hospital

[16] Matsuhisa Takashima, speech at meeting of Prix Jeunesse (Munich, 1993).

of his memories of visiting Tokyo's Ueno Zoo. Clearly he wanted to relive the experience. A member of the Educational Board and a local production company heard of his plight and determined to recreate the experience for him using the power of high-definition television and computer technology. A camera crew went to the zoo and put themselves at the eye level of the boy. The cameraman then moved around the zoo, glancing here, glancing there, visiting the lions and the monkeys and the bears. The recorded material was then transferred to a disk. A device that detects the eye-movement of the boy was attached to a computer and, synchronized with the boy's eye movement, the images of the animals were displayed on the screen. If the boy opened his eyes wider to gaze at a particular portion, that portion of the image automatically enlarged. If the boy lingered, so did the image. The excitement of the young boy was, apparently, wonderful to behold.

The hardware of technology and the 'intelligence' of computer software came together to help a small boy realize a dream. An immediate reaction might be, why didn't they just take the boy to the zoo? But let us assume that his medical condition was such that this was not possible or advisable. What is fascinating about the story, which is a true one, is the nature of the communication which is enabled by the technology. The experience is fundamentally about the senses and the emotions and forms of pleasure. It constitutes an experience which is personal, and for the provision of which one does not need public service broadcasting. The experience spoke to his needs and in that sense the technology was liberating.

This story reminded me of a comment by a GTE engineer involved in that company's development of an interactive communications system in Cerritos, California. He observed that among the possibilities offered by the technology 'the video signals can be sent from a video camera in one home to a television set in another, thus users can create their own picture telephones. This would allow a grandmother on one side of town to watch a grandchild's birthday party on the other'. There is only one screamingly obvious question in response to this; why wasn't granny invited to the party? The issue for the future, as the experiential and sensory nature of the social uses of technological capacity becomes ever more apparent, and as we retreat as societies into an inner realm of the domicile and the psyche, is: will we have constructed a world in which the technology is not liberating, but rather gets in the way of our humanity by technologizing our being and desocializing our life? There is no way of knowing, but it does not look hopeful.

A conclusion then can be drawn about *the new television*. Its very nature constitutes a fundamental taking apart of that sense of the collective, the public, the shared which is a precondition for the continuity of public service broadcasting. But we delude ourselves if we do not acknowledge that such a process could not happen if the individuals who constitute 'the public' were not complicitous. Power and institutional dynamic come into play in shaping culture, but two hands must work at shaping the clay and the other is provided by what Adorno called 'the congealed results of public preference'.

The American sociologist George Ritzer describes what he calls 'the McDonaldization of society'.[17] There is a certain clumsiness to the phrase but the significance of the observation should not be underestimated. It suggests the way in which more and more institutions have taken on board the characteristics of the McDonald's corporation: efficiency, particularly as that affects the speed with which things can be done; the quantification of goods and services by the customer with the intended effect of creating the feeling that one is getting value for money; predictability, so that there is a very good sense beforehand of what is going on, no surprises; control of process especially by the substitution of non-human technology for human activity or highly developed administrative procedures for those which were previously relatively informal.

The most profound articulation of the implication of the impacts of rationalization in human affairs is to be found in the work of the nineteenth-century social theorist Max Weber. For Weber the central defining characteristic of western capitalism is the possibility, indeed necessity, of rational calculation of profit and loss. The implications are profound: 'The spread of bureaucracy in modern capitalism is both cause and consequence of the rationalisation of law, politics and industry. Bureaucratisation is the concrete, administrative manifestation of the rationalisation of action which has concentrated into all phases of western culture, including art, music and architecture.'[18] According to Weber 'the further advance of bureaucratic mechanisation'[19] is inevitably increasingly revealing the

tension between the demand for technical efficiency of administration on the one hand, and the human values of spontaneity and autonomy on the other. The bureaucratic division of labour constitutes the 'cage' in which modern Berntsmenschen are compelled to live. 'The Puritan wanted to work in a calling; we are forced to do so.' The Faustian 'universal man' has to be renounced in favour of the specialisation of labour which is the condition of the efficiency of modern production—'specialists without spirit, sensualists without heart'.[20]

For Weber the most important question is not how the process of rationalization and bureaucratization can be reversed. It cannot. The *only* question is 'what we can set against the mechanization to preserve a certain section of humanity from the fragmentation of the soul, this complete ascendancy of the bureaucratic ideal of life'.[21]

[17] George Ritzer, (1993).   [18] A. Giddens, (1971), 183.   [19] Ibid. 235.
[20] Ibid. 235–6.   [21] Ibid. 183.

Even the most limited vision of the recent history of public broadcasting will see the significance of such Weberian analysis. Almost every major public broadcasting institution, for example, has, throughout the 1980s, been engaged in making itself more efficient, leaner, constructed around process rather than human performance. One of the more frustrating aspects of this is that, viewed superficially, who would argue with being more efficient, particularly in the context of spending scarce public resources? The danger, a word carefully chosen and employed as Weber might have used it, is that the pursuit of efficiency becomes an end in itself, in which organizational process begins to substitute for organizational purpose. Means become ends.

Here lies the source of the rise to power in the 1980s of a generation of senior public broadcasters whose purpose for being appeared to be a commitment not to public service principles but to technocratic procedure. Their response is that there simply is no alternative and that by invoking new procedures, organizational practices, and forms of accountancy, and burying the misty-eyed amateurism of earlier times, they will be well placed to protect and preserve public service broadcasting. At the level of *realpolitik*, of broadcasting as the art of the possible, there is real potency to this argument. One cannot, however, escape another perception that dances across the mind's eye, that rather than the midwife to a new golden age, the late twentieth-century technocracy of public service broadcasting is mortician to an age now past, the elegantly turned out incarnation of the real triumph of the modern era, that of unprincipled technique, an amoral spectre, all mind and no heart, evacuated of conviction and therefore necessarily the obsequious servant of larger and more powerful interests. The modern senior executive of the world's leading public service broadcasting organizations has, possibly, become iconic, not just of a particular organization, or of an institution, public broadcasting. In him (it is invariably a him) is an image of the age: clever, pragmatically rational, internally coherent and consistent, but somehow devoid of passion for any principle other than the perpetuation of the organization. What bedevils public service broadcasting is, then, not just the culture of the market but also the cult of applied reason. The phrase 'specialists without spirit, sensualists without heart' immediately conjures up an image of a number of key figures in the world's major broadcasting organizations. One could not help but see a more brutish version in a speech by Dennis Potter at the Edinburgh Television Festival in 1994 in which he described John Birt and Marmaduke Hussey, Chairman of the BBC and Birt's sponsor, as 'Daleks', inhuman programmed machines made famous in the cult programme *Dr Who*.

The point, however, is far more important than mere personal abuse. The grave danger of techno-rationality lies in its capacity to smother both spontaneous creativity and the exercise of freedoms, independence of thought and decision. Since the historic purpose of public broadcasting, broadly drawn, was precisely to provide a location for the creative and the democratic in society, to embody and articulate those ideas which had constituted the elements of democratic culture, any diminution of that capacity within this particular institution would have disproportionate, deleterious consequences.

The implications of these assaults are clear and serious: (1) the potential slicing up and fragmenting of the audience; (2) the offering through new outlets of 'cultural', 'informational', 'educational', and 'quality' programming which historically had been the special claim to fame of public broadcasting and radio; and (3) the increasing representation of the 'audience' as 'consumers' rather than citizens, whose needs are representative of transnational rather than national tastes, who can therefore best be served only by transnational distribution systems.

Each of these raises a question mark against some of the core theses of public broadcasting: its command of an audience; its provision of programmes of quality, range, and distribution not offered by the commercial systems; its national orientation.

The answers from public broadcasters to the questions posed by these challenges—in admittedly strained circumstances—were not what one might have hoped, or even anticipated. In the 1970s the demands for new services, the rising costs of production and operations, and increasing political—and in some instances public—resistance to tax increases forced public broadcasters to begin negotiating with governments over their funding arrangements much more frequently than before. Such negotiations always carried the potential for extensive review of fundamental purposes and structural assumptions. By the early 1980s the funding squeeze, combined with the enthusiasm about new technologies and privatization, had made parliamentary review of public broadcasting a regular event in nearly every country, regardless of the party or coalition in power. Accustomed to several years of grace between formal reviews, public broadcasters now found themselves subject to frequent and formal government reports and inquiries, and often drastic legislative proposals. Such reviews were in one respect a wholly appropriate process of accountability associated with democratic governance, but they were also useful to those interested in undermining public broadcasting for any cause. Public broadcasters have been forced to spend considerable energy on managing political defences, which diverts them from programme planning and production and leaves them in constant turmoil.

The seriousness of the crisis in public service broadcasting is measured by the apparent difficulty the public broadcasting community has had in country after country in finding its own new voice. More effort has been expended in developing corporate strategies which all too often have nothing other than the air of survival. Such strategies, for example, have been to apply more aggressive and competitive scheduling, to erode traditional programme commitments, to use ratings-based marketing nostrums, to pursue co-productions and co-financing in a revenue-driven belief in international sales potential, to adopt commercial financial community attitudes toward generating capital, to achieve organizational 'efficiency', cost-effectiveness, zero-based budgeting, shed staff, restructure. In short, the strategy is to respond to all the technocratic catchwords and commitments of the modern era by adopting them. The consequence of this process has too frequently been to incarnate the mundane, the middlebrow, the safe, the uncreative, the mildly pleasurable as the measure of achievement. In other words, to adopt much of the ethos and values of those commercial systems against which historically public broadcasting had been established as a counterpoint.

This is not to say that such systems are totally dire, akin to watching TV Tirana in Albania, or that there are not real moments of creativity. It is, however, reasonable to suggest that the character of most of what one sees in more 'consumer'-oriented systems is just mediocre. Now the beauty of being mediocre is that you are always at your best, and that is the point—no real risk, formulaic, maximizing audiences, playing to the obvious. What that tends to leave out, however, is real talent and creativity, the insightful and innovative, that which can stir the imagination rather than dull the senses, that can elevate the level of pleasure to be found in a drama, a comedy, a children's programme. What it ignores is the recognition that what define us are the divergences of taste as much as commonalities of culture.

In fact the whole point about, for example, defining structural globalism is to underscore the fact that the inherent logics of such systems literally cannot afford to recognize divergence and difference, the rich mosaic of human culture. In Australia, I heard the Minister of Communication say that whatever the Australian government did, they would 'maintain support for Australian content'. It is a familiar, yet ironic refrain from governments who have encouraged industrial strategies which nurtured the globalization of cultural industries.

Indeed, debates about broadcasting, particularly the collision between publicly regulated and market-driven systems, and between nationalism and globalism, illustrate the schizophrenic social pathology of the modern polity. On the one hand, governments feel the need to be efficient, fiscally responsible, generators of even more wealth, members of the colossal trading blocs which are emerging. On the other hand, societies seem to want—increasingly—to be caring, equal, emotionally mature, responsive to pain and hardship, peaceful, avoiders of conspicuous wealth and greed, true to their national identity and cultural heritage. In some ways the most interesting and telling examples of the consequences of the twin assault of ideology and structural change lie not with the likes of the BBC—which like a great ocean liner is neither easily nor quickly turned around—but with smaller, more vulnerable, less stately organizations. TVNZ is one such and its story in the past ten years illuminates the process with, to my eye at least, a shocking clarity.

Broadcasting in New Zealand had two fathers, James Shelley who saw it as a 'sacred trust' held on behalf of the people of New Zealand, and Colin Scrimgeour for whom it was to be used to reach out to the 'common man'. Shelley in particular insisted that what was broadcast had to be the best available. By the mid-1970s the key ethos of what was then the NZBC was the centrality of programme-making. According to one recent and exhaustive study, 1974–6 'was the period which saw programme makers rise to dominate the television system'.[22] It was a time of discovery, excitement, and innovation among programme-makers. One commentator concluded, 'there quickly emerged a consensus among broadcasters that they were now relishing an atmosphere of creative purpose such as they had not previously experienced'.[23] The subsequent two years, 1977–9, saw increasing political and social threats, financial pressures, and 'fresh claims from administrators to manage where they argued professionals had failed'.[24] In the NZ Broadcasting Act of February 1977, the government in effect advanced the claim of the need for accountability, principally to Parliament, centralization, and tighter financial management, 'allied to an insistence on loosely-defined moral standards'.[25] Increasingly such concerns were translated into two key ambitions: financial accountability and socio-political responsibility, which

in turn meant the management and control of what were perceived to be unruly broadcasters. Invariably, this management turned on judgments about what constituted acceptable public expression and also the consequences of exceeding those boundaries in terms of the response of broadcasting's political patron, the National Party. What also becomes clear throughout this period is that the reconstitution of the Board membership . . . shifted the Board's ideological leanings away from programme makers and towards the managerial views of administrators and the newly arrived business contingent on the Board.[26]

Interestingly, even curiously, the first Executive Chairman of the new TVNZ, Ian Cross, was cast very much in the old mould. He once commented that TV was important to New Zealanders 'because it is virtually the only means of our achieving any sense of community as a country'.[27] He was also a firm believer in the role of the producer, while still acknowledging the need for a wider system of accountability:

Broadcasters cannot be their own judges and juries on what they do; they must be under a controlling body which ensures that they serve the public interest and their own best standards . . . If, however, broadcasters are made to feel that they are sub-

---

[22] John Farnsworth, 'Two-Channel New Zealand Television: Ambiguities of Organization, Profession and Culture' (Ph.D. thesis, University of Canterbury, 1989).
[23] Ibid. 79.   [24] Ibid. 133.   [25] Ibid.
[26] Farnsworth, 'Two-Channel New Zealand Television', 126.
[27] Ian Cross, then Executive Chairman TV New Zealand quoted ibid. 134.

servient to an administrative class which exercises only negative control over their activities, their present morale and drive will fade away.[28]

Ian Cross resigned in 1986 following a period of increasing pressure for a closely managed, centralized control of TVNZ's monopoly. With his departure came a whole new perspective 'more openly exploiting and articulating commercial priorities within a limited form of decentralized competition between channels, and predicated on the anticipation of a deregulated media industry'.[29]

By 1988 the new Director-General of TVNZ, Julian Mounter, had heralded a much more commercial orientation in the coming years. In an address to advertisers in September 1989, Mounter quipped: 'If I can introduce myself to you again now, I'd say "Hello, I'm Julian Mounter, Chief Executive of a private company with a balance sheet of around $300 million. Healthy profits, which pay shareholders excellent dividends." '[30] He had already defined in an interview in 1988 TVNZ's four objectives as '(1) beat the hell out of the opposition, (2) hack back even further on production costs, (3) exploit new markets for what is bound to be an increasingly fragmented market, and (4) look for coproductions and facilities sharing deals'.[31] And in an interview with the magazine *Broadcasting*, he discussed his response to the establishment of the private, commercial TV3:

We have geared up and radically changed the company in an effort to have something that is aggressively commercial and will deal with [TV3] . . . We are going to attack and we are going to be like them. The difference [will be] that if we are doing a drama, we know it's got to rate, and it's got to sell. What's wrong with that? Our whole philosophy is that it's no good for a public service organization, as deregulation comes along, to be elitist. You have to stop saying we are making the best, and start asking 'what is it they [the public] want?' We'll make it! That's what we've done, and I think it helped.[32]

I relate this account of the developments in New Zealand because they are a capsule statement of so many similar processes around the globe. And perhaps the most telling aspect is that TVNZ was not so much mugged and robbed of its public service values, rather it committed a kind of ideological hara-kiri on the pretext, largely, that competition from TV3 would force it to change anyhow. And what happened to TV3? It went into receivership.

There is, I accept, an implication within this examination of the consequences of the challenges to public broadcasting that the shifting intellectual

---

[28] Ian Cross, then Executive Chairman TV New Zealand quoted ibid. 136.   [29] Ibid. 203.

[30] Julian Mounter, *Televiews*, 12 Sept. 1989, p. 13.

[31] Quoted in *Broadcasting Abroad* (Nov. 1989), 30–1.

[32] *Broadcasting*, 18 Dec. 1989, pp. 84–7.

environment in which it finds itself, the fear of loss of audience in a more competitive situation, and the rise to power of a new managerial class have had an impact on the character of programming. What is made, how is it made, for whom is it made, what is *not* made, and why? These are the kinds of questions with which we are left. Perhaps the most difficult, even tragic, question of all is, how can we ever pose such questions without being utterly out of step with a *Zeitgeist* that will not countenance them? For we live in a secular and relativist age in which it has become fashionable, on both left and right, to decry the idea of a hierarchy of values in human creative affairs—even if these various apostles of post-modernism cannot utter their claims without logically asserting the superiority of their own views over those of others. Nevertheless, to say therefore that one can and should make judgements about the merits and worth of programmes is derided as hopelessly *passé*, as being riddled with nostalgia for a more élitist age. Yet behind such accusations lies a spurious and corrupting populism that drips with a wider, contemporary pessimism about the human capacity to be other than a consuming being.

PART II

Histories

4 Reinventing the BBC in the 1950s

Public service broadcasting has lost a history without yet finding a future. Behind this book, which is first and foremost an attempt to understand public broadcasting, lies an admittedly battered faith: that, somehow, the idea of public service broadcasting must find new life, difficult though that increasingly is. That is accompanied by another theme: that the weight of influence is increasingly with new communication industries and an attendant ideology which articulates the virtues of the market. The intellectual response to the call for deregulation, privatization, and consumer choice has been, to say the least, less than adequate.

The reasons for this intellectual vacuum remain unclear, but possibly have something to do with the more general decline of the concept of public culture, the ability of technological possibility to freeze the mind of even the most ardent would-be critic. Ideologies on the rise can only succeed institutionally if they are embedded in the world views of those who are in power inside the institution. One of the most significant changes in public broadcasting around the planet has been the rise to positions of influence of executives who are functional and pragmatic.

While the scale of current events may be unprecedented, they are far from unique. Step back thirty years and consider how the BBC responded to new circumstances, to those shifts in ideology and technology which respect not regulations and traditions and which mean that either the institution evolves or it perishes. This chapter sets its sights firmly on broadcasting in Britain in the 1950s and 1960s. Implicitly it is about the strong parallels with events and conditions today: the ideological challenge of commercial television, the antagonisms implicit in the breaking of the monopoly and a forcing of a re-examination of the BBC's cultural leadership; the potential economic problems caused by a declining audience share threatening the integrity of the licence fee; and the rise of a new technology, television.

The Last Paternalist: William Haley and the BBC

On 8 April 1957 the Director-General of the BBC, Sir Ian Jacob, was inter-viewed on the current affairs television programme *Panorama* about recently announced changes in BBC radio. These he described as 'readjustments of out-put' to satisfy the multiplicity of tastes and values within the community. In a key phrase he said that 'a wind of change' had been flowing through the Corporation. That change had several origins: the rise after 1955 of commer-cial television; the sharp decline of the BBC's audience share and the obvious need to restore it to at least parity with ITV; the rise of television and decline of radio; the promise of a whole new generation of producers within the BBC, who were inventive and imaginative and looking to do new things in new ways in a society which was demanding just that, something new. The cumu-lative effect of these forces was a challenge to, and eventual destruction of, the idea that the BBC had a specific cultural mission to elevate, and the forcing of a redefinition of the idea of public service broadcasting.

To understand what happened in those years one must step back into the mind of Jacob's predecessor as Director-General, the strange, paradoxical, neo-Reithian figure of William Haley. He was a self-taught man, from what was then regarded as a 'lowly' social background. His admirers took enormous pleasure in the fact that, as Director-General, he would often be found in the BBC's library, tucked away in some quiet corner, reading a book. It was indeed a gentler age. He was, however, a clever man—at least in those ways of clever-ness interpreted as such by the British Establishment.

In December 1950 Haley wrote that broadcasting 'should play its part in bringing about the reign of Truth. . . . "Beauty is truth, truth beauty—that is all ye know on earth, and all ye need to know." ' This was for him a 'Living Law' against which broadcasters must measure and judge their work. Truth is a noble quality to seek to attain, but it depends on what truth we are talk-ing about, and for Haley truth was fashioned very much in his own image and likeness. When it came to deciding what truth was, he saw only one set of possible arbiters, those of intellectual and cultural standing. In a revealing comment Haley, arguing that one cannot leave broadcasting to a *laissez-faire* system because of a cultural Gresham's Law, bad driving out good, placed the responsibility for this fairly and squarely on the intellectual poverty of the bulk of the masses: 'So long as general free education remains in its present early state, that is for at least another generation, the good in almost every sphere is in danger of being driven out by the bad.'[1]

The central problem of broadcasting, Haley argued, is the problem of the relationship between freedom and standards. His analysis of the state of society, his assessment of the potential of broadcasting, and his almost missionary-like zeal led him to define the medium as a transformational force: 'Broadcasting, despite all its diversity, must be regarded primarily as an educational medium, with a cumulative effect and a progressive aim.'[2]

In a speech in 1946 he had referred to the 'valuable missionary work' of the BBC for which the highest calibre of person must be attracted, animated by 'a faith in the things that matter', always bound though to the absolute truth of 'the ancient moral values [that] derive from Greece, Rome and the Holy Land' and which form 'the basis of our civilisation', and pursuing a duty to 'the classical repertory' and 'the great masters' in drama, music, literature, and other arts.[3]

Haley's values were those of the Christian middle class, which had, in its Reithian version, colonized the BBC. It was a philosophy and way of life strengthened by a belief in its own superiority and worth, and a desire not to be swamped by the vulgar mass appeal of television. There was also, however, nuance and optimism. Haley argued that the BBC's 'highest duty is to the disinterested search for Truth' and that 'it should be frankly stated that to raise standards is one of the purposes for which the BBC counts', but it must do this 'within the broad contract that the listener must be entertained . . . [but] while giving him the best of what he wants, it tries to lead him to want something better. Broadcasting should not fear to assume leadership.'[4] The less people watched or listened, he argued, the more successful the BBC could claim to be, since his was a vision of the active, animated society in which citizens partook of pleasures and intellectual pursuits rather than being the passive recipients of the products of broadcasting. He told a conference in 1949 that 'it cannot be repeated too often that broadcasting, whether it be by means of sound, or television, is no substitute for the satisfaction that comes from taking part in everyday life, its contrived excitements and gregarious pleasures. We are only a means to an end and that end is an educated community, each member of which is taking an active part in a full and intensely interesting existence.'[5] Broadcasting would, therefore, be successful if it led people to the theatre and the concert hall—concert hall, mind, not music-hall: 'Its aim

[1] Internal memo, 19 Dec. 1950.   [2] Ibid.

[3] W. Haley, 'Broadcasting and British Life', address to the Radio Wholesalers' Federation, 21 Sept. 1946.

[4] Haley, 'The Place of Broadcasting', talk on the Home Service, 14 Nov. 1947.

[5] Haley, speech to Radio Wholesalers' Federation, 18 May 1949.

must be to make people active, not passive, both in the fields of recreation and public affairs. . . . The wireless set or the TV receiver are only signposts on the way to a full life. That must finally lie in a sense of beauty and joy in all things, and in the experience of participating in life as a whole.'[6]

There was in Haley something which to the jaundiced eye of the late twentieth century is either obviously patrician or charmingly naïve. He once observed that historically the function of the BBC had been to introduce a contemplative element within national life:

It is not far fetched to suggest that many a man and woman after hearing Shakespeare and Aeschylus, Beethoven or Mozart, have returned to the contemplation of the great affairs of the hour, or even the dull frustration of the daily round with serenity and sanity refreshed. And on altogether another plane such ageless examples as Mrs. Dale's and her family have been companions to many and sustained them in the task of decent and sensible living.[7]

Reading the speeches of Haley one sees his roots in traditional Arnoldian middle-class values about culture and leisure, combined with a rigid view of different cultural levels, good to bad, with the 'classical repertory', as he calls it, comprising the good and light entertainment the bad. It was the very narrowness of Haley's social and cultural vision, and of his interpretation of public service broadcasting, which threatened the long-term development and even existence of the BBC as an institution. That may seem harsh, but the BBC in the 1950s was faced with major threats; at one level in the emergence of ITV, at another in a shift in the whole character of British society. The traditions which Haley represented were, if continued with, likely to lead to institutional death, if only because in their curious blend of complacency and certainty, created behind the barrier of the monopoly, they had fed a body of resentment to the whole position of the BBC and to what appeared increasingly to be its cultural irrelevance.

One consequence of Haley's ruminations on the role of the BBC in society had been the creation of the Third Programme, a radio service devoted to talks and music for 'the serious minded, for the educated and those who had wished to be so'.[8] It began on 29 September 1946 and in his inaugural speech Haley argued that the BBC's broadcasting pattern was now complete, both in the sense that it was able to serve a section of the audience which had previously been ignored, and also in the sense that it matched its own original intentions as defined by the Crawford Committee in 1926. The broadcaster Harman Grisewood described those intentions as that 'broadcasting in Britain

    [6] Haley, 'The Place of Broadcasting'.
    [7] Haley, 'The Public Influence of Broadcasting and the Press', Clayton Memorial Lecture, 15 Mar. 1954.
    [8] Ibid.

should be content with nothing less than the provision for the people of the best of all that can be communicated by sound, the best in literature, in music and in all that words can tell of human affairs and of man's highest achievements. This spirit of public service was, as we all know, the high ideal of the Corporation's first Director General, now Lord Reith.'[9]

Grisewood illustrated the essential difference between the Third Programme and the more 'middlebrow' Home Service. In the various Goethe celebrations which were due to take place in 1946, Grisewood explained, the Home Service would offer extracts from *Faust* while the Third would broadcast the whole of the play with 'a substantial portion' of it in the original German. And where the Home Service might have a general talk about the poet, the Third would have a whole series which together would constitute a 'real contribution to Goethe studies', the standard of which 'will be that of, say, the *Cambridge Journal* or the *Journal of Classical Studies*'. This view allowed not the slightest tinge of populism: 'you cannot count on popularizing the best. You can make it available but you can have no dilution of it.'[10]

Populism, however, was hammering on the door and the problem that perplexed the Haleys and Grisewoods was how one prevented the mob from getting their grimy, coarse hands on it: 'How are we to ensure the continuity of our culture in an age of mass participation? An age which rejects the notion of privilege and distrusts the principle of private patronage and yet an age which insists on the results of refinement in every branch of human activity.'[11] It is important to recognize that Grisewood was not just preserving culture but using an instrument such as the Third Programme to restore a theological view of man, 'some central concepts of the human being' drawn from the Judaeo-Christian tradition. Grisewood's finale was a quote from Matthew Arnold:

The mass of mankind will never have any ardent zeal for seeing things as they are; very inadequate ideas will always satisfy them. On these inadequate ideas repose, and must repose, the general practice of the world. That is as much as saying that whoever sets himself to see things as they are will find himself one of a very small circle; but it is only by this very small circle resolutely doing its own work that adequate ideas will ever get current at all.[12]

One must not imagine that the Third Programme was merely the cave into which a small clique of unrepentant élitists retreated, biding their time till retirement. To a more populist eye the Third Programme was an aural formaldehyde in which were preserved the values of a disappearing culture. To its adherents the Third Programme was alive and capable of growth, the very sperm bank of western culture.

[9] Harman Grisewood, 'The Third Programme and its Audience', *World Review* (Dec. 1949), 33–6.
[10] Ibid.   [11] Ibid.
[12] Ibid. See also Grisewood's autobiography *One Thing at a Time* (London: Hutchinson, 1968).

Leadership of any broadcasting organization necessarily entails a series of intellectual and moral choices about the relationship between the organization and the moral culture of the community. This may not be so readily understood, let alone articulated, today but there was in the BBC of the 1950s a far more profound engagement with the social, cultural, and moral purpose of broadcasting. It was a debate founded on a sense of the relationship between the broadcaster and the public but with a real wariness on the part of the former about the worth and potential of the latter. Haley observed that the 'secret of leadership in broadcasting is that of always being ahead of the public yet not so far as to be out of touch'.[13] He added that the BBC is 'a public service whose only interest is the greatest common good'. The problem was that in the new age it had become less than certain what that common good looked like or who would define it.

Haley's values, and his whole way of life, simply did not contain the answers to the serious questions which, as he came towards the end of his career in the BBC in 1952, were to be posed about the future of public broadcasting in Britain. The solution would lie in the creation of a linkage between preserving the heart of the idea behind the BBC—that is programmes unsullied by either commercial or political partialities, crafted rather than merely made—and the provision of programmes which began to have not just quality and creativity but some semblance of contemporary relevance to the lives of people who made up the bulk of the audience for television and radio. When he said dismissively that 'we shall safeguard broadcasting from becoming a glorified jukebox',[14] he displayed a remarkable ignorance of the rhythms and moods which were beginning to flow through western society as well as of the fact that, though the BBC may have had a mission to preserve excellence, it had no right to be anachronistic. The task then for the BBC in the 1950s was to shake off its élitist, even arrogant traditions and to come to grips with the difficult relationship between its public service nature and its relevance to the society around it. There was inevitably an element of a Faustian bargain about this since it was not necessarily clear that they would be able, over an extended period, to balance public service and relevance. This may seem somewhat paradoxical since it might be argued that public service is a simile for relevance. Within the definition of public service broadcasting as understood by the BBC was an idea of 'excellence' in programming which slept uneasily with the new populism. Haley's departure was in retrospect inevitable and, it has to be said, self-conscious. Reith wrote in his diary the day Haley called to tell him that he would be leaving the BBC to take up the editorship of *The Times*: 'He had much to say about the BBC and himself. He thought though

---

[13] W. Haley, internal memo, Dec. 1950.   [14] Ibid.

he might in time have brought the BBC back to what it was in my time without TV, TV would beat him.'[15]

The key to the future of the BBC lay with the former soldier Sir Ian Jacob, who became Director-General in December 1952. Jacob is one of the most remarkable figures in the history of the BBC, less well known than others such as John Reith and Hugh Greene but hugely influential nevertheless. This rather stiff, shy soldier who had worked with and idolized Churchill during the war was a significant modernizing influence on the BBC in the 1950s, and provided the ladder up which climbed the icon of the new BBC, Hugh Greene. His great contribution was to encourage a debate within the Corporation about the relationship between élitism and populism, and thus to provide the basis for a moment when creativity and imagination had a moral context that was not traditionalist, but modern and humanistic. Jacob's task was to plot a new course for the BBC between rampant competition on the one side and an archaic Reithian version of its cultural mission on the other. The whole of Jacob's period as Director-General was taken up with the continuing question of the future of broadcasting in Britain and the place of the BBC within it.

Jacob was a member of the tightly defined, amazingly self-aware group of the middle class that did not go into business, but rather exerted energy in 'service', in furthering the administrative and military needs of the nation and the Empire. In this sense the BBC was one more part of an imperial social order. Such young men, and the occasional woman, emerged from the nurseries of the political and social establishment, the preparatory and public school, equipped with habits of heart and mind which invoked mission and authority and nurtured a self-confidence that controlled, with remarkably little force. There was effortless ease in the demeanour, certitude and rectitude in great dollops. There was, however, a blindedness, a *naïveté* which would become all too telling and destructive two decades or so later as, amidst a shrunken and shrivelled traditional order, the BBC was further assaulted by a new fiscal establishment. Jacob was temperamentally of the old order, but intellectually very much a modernizer. At the time of his appointment he was back in Whitehall, on leave from the BBC where he had been working since the war, as Chief Staff Officer at the Ministry of Defence, deputy secretary to the Cabinet, and fixture to satisfy Churchill's desire to be surrounded by his wartime staff.

The press broadly mentioned his appointment, describing him as 'a super efficient worker', 'a great mixer', 'a wisely analytical unemotional brain', 'a no-nonsense chief who hates carefree inefficiency, loathes red-tape, is outspoken to the point of rudeness if a job is bungled'. On the eve of his taking office he received editorial advice from the *Star*, 'Be human . . . Be bold . . .

---

[15] *The Reith Diaries*, ed. Charles Stuart (London: Collins, 1975), 481, 29 May 1952.

Look ten years ahead.'[16] Sir Ian Jacob already had a good sense of where the main problems of the BBC lay as he took up his new office: 'The thing that struck me, which I had been conscious of for some time, was that TV was being starved of money. Haley had a curious outlook on this. He had the view that the country ought not to lock up more than a certain number of people in totally unproductive work and he was therefore rather against the BBC getting any bigger. . . . I don't think he really understood, in the early 1950s, the tremendous steps that TV was going to take.'[17] He recalled one revealing incident when, as the new Controller of the Overseas Service, he went to Haley to ask for funds to develop the studio of the BBC's Paris office. 'We haven't got an office in Paris,' was Haley's reply, even though the BBC did in fact have one, along with a correspondent. Jacob was determined to adopt a somewhat more engaged posture, for the BBC to be more expansive and assertive, partly because of the imminent emergence of commercial broad-casting but principally because of a more diffuse feeling that all was not well with the Corporation.

On 23 June 1953 Jacob announced at a press conference that the BBC was embarking on a ten-year development plan involving the building of new trans-mitters, new studios, and a television centre; the provision of an alternative television service and the development of a colour system; and the expansion of television output from five to seven hours a day. He also pointed out that the Corporation needed more money through an increase in the licence fee, plus a move to give the BBC the full benefit of the licence, since at that time it only received 85 per cent of the revenue. He told the press conference 'that we have got to develop in television a news service of the same quality and standard as we have in sound'. *He was, in effect, outlining almost every important development that would shape the BBC for years to come.*

The strengths and weaknesses of the BBC at this time were interrelated. A strong organization, experience, established standards, high reputation of a sort, good staff, bumped up against inflexibility and complexity of opera-tion, a cloying arrogance resting on the kudos gained in the war years and guarded by nostalgic old men whose rheumy eyes were largely blind to the problems of a future which anyhow lay with the 'young turks' of television. Jacob optimistically called upon the different parts of the BBC to 'look upon themselves—to use a military phrase—as a force of all arms engaged on a single campaign'.[18]

The obligations of public service remained: inform, educate, entertain, be impartial, provide a balanced service, and so on. The immediate problem, however, was practical, not intellectual, and concerned the way that new

[16] *Star*, 28 Nov. 1952.   [17] Ian Jacob, interview with author.
[18] Ian Jacob, Minutes of BBC General Liaison Meeting, 23 June 1953.

programme choices would shift the audience away from the BBC. In a paper to the Board of Governors, Jacob reflected on this problem:

It will be very difficult for the Corporation to continue to do something which is not being done by our rivals if in doing so we sacrifice a large part of our audience. It does not matter very much from a Corporation viewpoint if audiences are increasingly drawn from the Home Service to the Light Programme. It is within our power to adjust matters if we think it desirable to do so. It is quite another matter if the audience for BBC television is drawn away by competitors who offer little but popular fare. Our aim cannot be fulfilled unless we retain the attention of the mass audience as well as of the important minorities. The justification for the existence of the Corporation, supported by a universal licence, largely disappears if the mass audience is lost.[19]

All the competition had to do was to employ the catechistic logic of the BBC which demanded a national, mass audience, and destroy it by undermining its claim to universality. This would in turn undermine its philosophical foundations of being all things to all men, as well as its ability to raise revenues on the basis of being the national instrument of broadcasting. The nightmare of the BBC was precisely that at one and the same time its intellectual and financial foundations would be shaken. Jacob proposed that they confront this problem in three ways: some of their programmes should aim specifically at attracting a mass audience; the range of programmes attempting this should be greatly broadened so long as they retained 'the highest possible standard of excellence in their own field'; and, finally, 'the second television channel must be realised as quickly as possible so as to ease the burden thrown on the Service by having to satisfy the Corporation's obligations within so small an output'.[20]

The Governors echoed Jacob's thoughts in 1954, when they argued that 'It is obviously not possible to provide in a single programme the full range of broadcasting which the Charter enjoins . . . a second television programme is thus a necessity if the responsibilities of the Corporation are to be carried out.'[21] They were clear, however, that part of creating that vital relationship between institutional interest and cultural integrity lay in establishing a television channel on which they would be more likely to satisfy that sense of integrity while leaving them on the main channel to get on with the serious business of preventing commercial television from decimating their audience.

There was, therefore, no question of Jacob's BBC trying to side-step or ignore the new commercial competition, and he made it clear that the BBC

---

[19] Ian Jacob, 'The Corporation's Attitude to Competition', Note by the Director-General, 20 Aug. 1953.
[20] Ibid.   [21] 'Aide Memoire: On the Future of Broadcasting', G 10/54, 15 Jan. 1954.

needed 'to retain the attention of the mass audience' and therefore must pre-vent any competition capturing it. It was therefore 'bound to compete'.

To meet the challenge, Jacob asked the Governors to develop the televi-sion service by introducing television news, expanding the hours to include an earlier start and more on Sunday, improving afternoon programmes and developing the facilities for experiment and training; protecting the BBC's sports coverage as well as its famous parlour games; guaranteeing the fees and work of the best scriptwriters, artists, and commentators; improving the salaries of the best staff producers to avoid poaching by rivals; introducing flexibility into recruitment to ensure that the BBC got 'the best people from the open market'.

The idea of 'the best' tolls out through all his words. It was perhaps the key moment in the post-war history of the BBC since he was setting the pat-tern for the next two decades. He offered a hope that they would not, need not, be ravished by the competition, though he also constantly warned of the dangers, 'the Corporation can never afford to let the people of the country feel that they have no incentive to buy a licence'.[22] He was establishing a new balancing act for the BBC in which the objective need to hold the mass of the audience for at least some of the time had to be achieved without departing from a conception of 'the best' whether that be a talk about humanism on radio or a light entertainment programme on television. Self-interest and integrity were delicately tied together and the trick would be in ensuring that they remained in a creative tension without snapping. But something else was also happening under Jacob, something more fundamental than tactical adjust-ment: the idea of what could be considered 'the best' was slowly redefined as he and many of his colleagues came to understand that quality and popular-ity were not necessarily antagonistic and that if the BBC was to survive at all it had to begin to reflect that truth.

It was not just the threat of ITV which was prompting this rethinking with-in the BBC, but a sense that it had begun to drift. The germ of that aware-ness was dependent not only on the growth of commercial television but also on the social awareness of an intelligent man. Quite simply, Jacob was the first Director-General of the BBC who did not believe in its paternalistic role, and told the Governors bluntly that its efforts to elevate the public taste had given the public indigestion. He later recalled a meeting he had with Reith, shortly after becoming Director-General: 'he argued that the BBC ought to lead the country and have a policy which would be for improving the education of the country. I said to him, "well what you are suggesting is that I should run the BBC the same way that Beaverbrook runs *The Daily Express*, with a pro-prietorial policy." I said "the moment you offer a choice that goes out the

<hr>

[22] 'Aide Memoire: On the Future of Broadcasting', G 10/54, 15 Jan. 1954.

window. A choice should be a real choice. If a person wants jazz, its not up to you to say well you shouldn't have jazz today." [23]

Jacob's main task was to continue to articulate this shift in basic philosophy. In the now defunct *BBC Quarterly* which was circulated to staff, he reviewed what was called the 'tasks before the BBC today'. One central statistic stood out, he said: there had been 7,000 television licences in 1946, in 1954 there were 350,000. He told the Corporation's employees that in furthering the cause of public service broadcasting they must 'develop to the maximum the potentialities of the medium as a means of communication . . . Secondly, the Corporation must try to satisfy the needs and tastes of the full range of listeners and viewers. It is often said that "the public" wants this, or doesn't want that. In broadcasting terms there is no such thing as the public as some kind of solid block. There are 50 million people with an immense variety of interests, capabilities, tastes and perceptions.' He then added, significantly, that public service broadcasting

must set as its aim the best available in every field. This does not mean what is often foolishly stated, namely that the Corporation decides what is good for people and gives that in place of what people want. It means that in covering the whole range of broad-casting the opportunity should be given to each individual to choose between the best of the one kind of programme with which he is familiar, and the best of another kind of programme with which he may be less familiar. In this way a constant opportun-ity is offered for the widening of experience and the increasing of enjoyment. There should be no lack of light entertainment and triviality alongside the more serious and informative, but it should be of a kind which avoids indecency and does not exploit vulgarity, violence or tawdriness. [24]

If there had been any lingering doubts as to the extent to which Jacob was abandoning Reith and paving the way for a more democratized relationship with the audience, after this there could be none. This shift in the relationship with, and sense of, the audience, which was to provide one of the principal reasons for the success of the BBC in the 1960s, was the key intellectual ele-ment of that whole package of measures which Jacob had outlined. The vital difference between Jacob and Reith was that he was fundamentally optimistic about the public's ability to choose, whereas Reith had a profound pessimism. There was a certain necessity in Jacob's confidence in the wisdom of common folk since without it the reformation of the BBC would have been impossible. There was no choice, other than to trust the public, which was not élitist in intent, in a Reithian sense, but which did not betray the lingering sense of professional and moral integrity without which public service broadcasting was meaningless. The intellectual shift was both a response to, and a stimulation of, a whole raft of other developments: the rise of television; the shifting role

---

[23] Interview with the author.   [24] *BBC Quarterly* (autumn 1954).

of radio; the establishment of competition from commercial broadcasting; technical developments; development of infrastructure, such as the new TV Centre at White City; experiments in colour; the laying down of plans for a second television channel; the projection of a decade-long development of a comprehensive, balanced, and technically efficient BBC. There was much then that was incubating within Jacob's BBC of the 1950s just as there was within the guts of the wider society. The question that was slowly unfolding was whether one could change the BBC from an élitist, Arnoldian tradition to one which was more populist, egalitarian, and intelligent. The only way of achieving this was to balance 'appeal' with 'standards', while never quite being clear just what the latter term meant. The answer could only lie in practice in programming which after the event would be recognized as having achieved the alchemy of appealing to the audience and satisfying the residual hunger for professional standards.

In the summer of 1958 a new offensive appeared on the horizon, a likely government-sponsored investigation into the future of broadcasting. In August of that year Jacob drafted a paper of what he called 'basic propositions' about the BBC and circulated it to all those members of the BBC who might usefully take part in 'the task of getting the truth of these propositions accepted', particularly by those who 'guide public opinion and by those who will ultimately have to decide the future development of broadcasting in this country'.

That notion of 'truth', almost brazen in its self-confidence, explains something of the sheer psychological toughness which the BBC retained. The first of these truths was that the BBC was the founder of the concept of public service broadcasting. In essence, he observed, it is broadcasting by an independent organization 'which is free from the necessity of bowing to outside pressures and can pursue the single aim of giving the best and most comprehensive programme service to the public'.[25] The two great threats to that service, he argued, were political and commercial pressures and only by maintaining a strong and independent service could the BBC fend off pressures of that nature. Precisely because commercial broadcasting was an affront to that almost metaphysical notion of broadcasting the BBC had to respond to ITV's existence.[26]

On the eve of his retirement Jacob felt that he had succeeded in maintaining the integrity of the BBC in the face of competition. His parting comments to the Governors warned of the massed ranks of financial interests in the lobbying of the forthcoming committee of inquiry. The requirements for the successful continuity of the BBC, he argued, would be no change in the unitary system binding television, radio, and the External Services together; adequate finance derived from the licence fee; the continuation of the BBC's

---

[25] Ian Jacob, memo, 5 Aug. 1958.   [26] Ibid.

independence; a second television channel; the continuation of the radio broadcasting monopoly; and the maintenance of a reasonable share of the viewing audience.

Holding to a politically viable share of audience involved a difficult balancing act between having mass appeal and maintaining the 'best' and 'most comprehensive' service. Throughout the middle years of the decade Jacob was telling his staff that the way to defeat ITV, or at least prevent them from defeating the BBC, was to continue to develop its competence and, while recognizing the plural nature of the population, to maintain standards. Lurking within Jacob, and some of those around him, was a nagging concern that while the BBC necessarily and properly moved towards a more populist orientation, it should never be too popular. As he was about to retire in 1959, when he felt that the BBC's integrity had been maintained, the BBC's audience share for television was only 35 per cent. Jacob was content with this and felt that they 'would be in grave danger . . . if we had secured a 50 : 50 average because in doing so we would have made our output indistinguishable from that of ITV'.[27] He had fallen into the very trap which in many ways he had done more than anyone to attempt to destroy, that there was a necessarily inverse relationship between quality and mass viewership. He had, however, set in motion changes which would utterly transform the BBC and, in the longer term, pose profound questions about the essential nature of public service broadcasting and its continued intellectual and institutional plausibility in the decades to come.

The Reinvention of Public Service Broadcasting

Deep within the recesses of the BBC in the 1950s were a number of programme developments which in their blend of populism and creativity allowed the BBC, during the first years of the 1960s, to combine an equal share of the viewing audience with the maintenance of creative excellence. In particular, developments in radio and news provide fascinating and revealing case histories not only of the impact of Jacob on programme-making, but also of the first shock waves in the intellectual revolution in programme-making which was to reach fruition in the 1960s. Jacob intuitively felt this, though he hardly understood its true dimensions:

To allow broadcasting to consist of output which is merely good enough to attract people in their unthinking mood, and to limit its horizons to proved successes would be a grave failure. The full exploitation of the medium, the new capabilities, the insistence on quality, in all forms of programme, and the setting of the high standard throughout—these are the marks of a first class broadcasting service.[28]

[27] Ian Jacob, 'The BBC: Past and Future', memo from the Director-General, G 122/59, 1 Dec. 1959.
[28] Ibid.

That the process of redefinition of public service broadcasting was as much about general intellectual inquiry as it was about institutional survival is highlighted by the fact that while competition was for the television service, the most interesting and revealing debates took place about the future of sound broadcasting. The first murmurs of new thinking can be seen in a note by Rooney Pelletier, the Controller, Light Programme, to the Director of Sound Broadcasting, Lindsay Wellington.[29] Pelletier suggested that the BBC could respond to ITV in two ways: by adopting an ivory tower attitude such as 'we will do nothing but the best and sooner or later we will be recognised', or by engaging in a 'skirmish; i.e. recognition of the terrible nature of the enemy tactics and the clear-sighted decision to fight him on his own grounds *in order to retain the attention of the masses*' (the words are underlined in Pelletier's original document). Pelletier left no doubt that he was in favour of the skirmish: 'We *must* have the audience otherwise we waste our increasing sweetness on progressively more desert air.' He added: 'Failure to retain audience has almost immediate consequences i.e. failure to pay licence fees and consequent disappearance of our revenue . . . when the public ceases to support us by paying licences, we might continue to exist for a bit as one of the agencies of a national bad conscience (the Arts Council is a pathetic example), but we must sooner or later be swept out of existence by a strong public opinion thoroughly conditioned (when the moment arrives) to a totally philistine view'.[30] He reminded Wellington that Haley, with the arrival of commercial television, had observed, with 'phenomenal' foresight, 'The robots are on the march.'[31] Noting that commercial television was a reality, it was nevertheless the BBC's duty 'to fight the revolution in rational manner and thought, which commercial television by its very nature must seek to impose upon the public'.[32]

The way to win the skirmish, he suggested, lay in thinking 'progressively about programme content', in acting as 'a mirror of what is going on', in being topical, in extensively publicizing their activities (in the years of monopoly there had been no real need to publicize the BBC), in keeping 'vitally intact' and encouraging 'more and more water to flow freely from the spring of imagination and healthy enterprise . . . and by keeping "the masses" within our camp'. He ended with a rather dramatic analogy which only a BBC man would—without blushing—make. It was an analogy between the condition and future of his organization and the fate of the Church in 1054. In *The Times* he had read a review of Stephen Runciman's *The Eastern Schism* and was struck by a sentence which seemed to him to capture the essence of the major policy problems facing the BBC. It is to say the least an interesting use of a quote. He prefaced his usage with the comment: 'I use this apparently far

[29] Rooney Pelletier to Lindsay Wellington, 28 Sept. 1955.   [30] Ibid.   [31] Ibid.
[32] Ibid.

removed analogy because I am deeply conscious that the Corporation is a major guardian of the nation's culture and the British way of life.' Discussing Runciman's views on the Great Schism of 1054 the reviewer had written: 'While Latin Christendom was absorbing the barbarians at the cost of being temporarily barbarised, Greek Christendom was holding them at bay at the cost of being permanently sterilised.' He was, Pelletier said, 'pleading for a measure of temporary barbarism because I believe that in the other direction lies inevitable, ivory tower, frustrated audience-less sterility.'[33]

Wellington agreed and a month later wrote a paper in which he asked whether earlier definitions of the role of the BBC were still valid in 1955, to whit, what did its being the 'trustee of the public interest' actually mean? He described this as 'a phrase and a concept which were dear to Lord Reith and which he planted in the minds of important people of many kinds—Ministers, Archbishops, elder statesmen in or out of power, eminent people in all walks of life. It is a concept which is entirely acceptable to what Henry Fairley in the *Spectator* has recently called the Establishment.'

The monopoly, he continued, protected that view of the BBC until the war forced an ever-greater demand for light entertainment. Britain, he believed, was changing in its 'nature, climate and values. . . . It is true to say that as the idea of Establishment weakened, it is not surprising that the support of the Establishment was not enough to preserve us from commercial TV.' The old concepts, he argued, were in effect inadequate, no longer 'vital and contemporary'. His condemnation of the ethos which had prevailed within the BBC was really quite brutal:

The other side of the 'on the side of the angels' medal may read 'holier than thou.' Silence in the face of attack may read 'too proud to fight.' Insistence on being responsible and careful and reputable in all we do may be made to appear to be timid or stuffy or avuncular as if we are too proud to fight.

He ends on what is to be the key theme of the coming years, a liberal and humanist view of the relationship between the BBC and the audience. Could the BBC, he asked, recognize a new role for itself 'which is more apt for 1955 in a society which is enduring a silent revolution, a society in which fully employed people enjoy a sense of their own independence and dislike being dragooned or got at for their own good'?

In the latter part of the 1950s there was a debate taking place at different levels in the BBC in which senior figures were trying to come to grips not just with the implications of the rise of TV and commercial television, but with a whole new social reality, part of which was the stark fact that public service radio was declining at the same time as there were vast changes in social

[33] Ibid.

values and conventions. Another radio executive, George Camacho, wrote to Pelletier about the fact that Luxembourg was the one radio service available in the UK which had not lost its audience from the encroachment of television and suggesting that this was in part due to its popularity among National Service conscripts: 'There can be little doubt of the influence of 200,000 young men each year being called up and subject for two years to Luxembourg conditioning.' He went on:

Corporation standards of taste and culture are of very great importance; but not perhaps as important as its standards of responsibility as the main instrument of broadcasting. To lose a substantial part of the Corporation's mass audience is at once to betray this responsibility and to spell the doom of responsible public service sound broadcasting.[34]

The BBC—or at least its more reflective and perceptive employees—was waking up to the fact that the social divisions within British society had created a mass, collective rejection of 'intellect and culture' as represented by the BBC. 'The mass', Camacho observed, 'prefers the frank commercialism of the *Daily Express* and the spectacular sensationalism of the *Daily Mirror* . . . The Corporation in the eyes of many is suspect of both institutionalism and "do goodism." . . . Does in fact the Corporation know enough about what the public wants? . . . Could Listener Research be used more positively to discover public tastes and habits?'

He was right in his rhetorical question: the BBC had never known what its audience wanted, partly because the fact of the monopoly had never created the need to know, and partly because the catechism of faith derived from Reith made knowing what the audience wanted not only unnecessary but positively dangerous. The changed circumstances of competition, however, made it very clear that if they did not begin to create that more meaningful relationship with the audience then they would be in serious trouble. As Camacho concluded: 'a rigid maintenance of rising standards of taste and culture is simply to fill the moat and raise the drawbridge of an ivory tower.'[35]

At the end of October 1956 Wellington established a working party to look into the future policy of the Sound Broadcasting Service, and to assess how that policy might be implemented with fewer and fewer resources. He sent the three men given the task—Marriott, Standing, and Gillard—a note expressing his confidence: 'I feel quite sure that we can vivify Sound Broadcasting; tighten it up and improve it and make it more contemporary and more realistically responsive to contemporary needs.'[36]

[34] George Camacho to Rooney Pelletier, Home Service Policy File, 24 Oct. 1955.   [35] Ibid.
[36] L. Wellington, 'Sound Broadcasting: Future Policy and Practice', statement by Director of Sound Broadcasting, 30 Oct. 1956.

Since the previous major review of sound broadcasting eleven years before two big events had taken place: the development of television at the expense of sound and the introduction of commercial television. In fact in 1956 the number of combined licences for sound and television equalled the number of sound-only licences for the first time. It was estimated that whereas there were 7.3 million combined and 7.2 million sound-only licences in 1957, by 1962 there would be 12.3 million and 2.7 million respectively. It was also expected that in the same five years the number of adults with access to television at home would rise from 18.3 million to 30.7 million and that that figure would therefore include a cross-section of the whole community.

The working party argued, however, that decline in sound was only partly due to television, and that 20 per cent of the decline of BBC Sound had taken place before either television or Radio Luxembourg were an effective influence. They agreed that the

loss of its monopoly in broadcasting has very much reduced the BBC's power to manipulate programme policy in the interest of social and cultural aims. It is instead engaged in a battle for its position as the nation's home entertainer, a position it must retain if it is to continue as the mirror of the nation's great events and a cultural and educational influence of social importance.[37]

Programme policy in the sound services, they observed, had been based not only on the idea of different cultural strands, but also on what Haley had described as 'the conception of the community as a broadly based cultural pyramid slowly aspiring upwards' with the 'pyramid being served by three main programmes, differentiated but broadly overlapping in levels and interests, each Programme leading on to the other, the listener being induced through the years increasingly to discriminate in favour of things that are more worthwhile'.[38] Each of the programmes was given an audience target—60 per cent for Light, 30 per cent for Home, 10 per cent for Third—and each was expected to compete with the others in order to get 10 per cent above this quota, with the hope that increasing numbers would be attracted from the Light, to the Home, to the Third.

It was this whole edifice of broadcasting theory which the working party challenged. They challenged, and wished to see modified, among other things, the BBC's strong sense of 'cultural and educational mission',[39] which 'led to the force of monopoly being harnessed to the support of a programme policy aimed to lever up the level of popular culture by reducing the volume of easy entertainment and edging up that of fare held to be more estimable'.[40] In the eyes of the members of the working party even if there had been merit in this

---

[37] M. F. C. Standing et al., *Working Party Report on the Future of Sound Broadcasting in the Domestic Services* (Dec. 1957), para. 15.

[38] Ibid., para. 21.   [39] Ibid., para. 24.   [40] Ibid., para. 25.

position—which they doubted—it was no longer practicable strategy in the wake of the loss of monopoly and the changing mood of the country since 1945. They added:

we hold that this use of the power of monopoly was not a justifiable one, and that so dominating a sense of cultural mission is not an inevitable or indeed a natural characteristic of public service broadcasting. It does not derive from the Charter. In indicating that the BBC should disseminate information, education and entertainment, the Charter does not suggest that differing values should be attached to each element, nor that each element should appear in each Programme service. All it says is that the three elements should be provided.[41]

In the place of a cultural mission they proposed a new policy in which programmes reflected both what people wanted and the circumstances in which they would receive them; that the familiar trilogy of education, information, and entertainment should be retained, but that there should be no *open or concealed value judgments being made between each element*. Professional standards of production and impartiality should be maintained, but should exist within a context defined by 'prevailing outside trends of taste and behaviour. Lowering of standards should not be confused with popularisation.' And they encouraged the BBC to 'end the paternalism of the present policy. For the future we would sort BBC programmes in two qualities—the excellence of the material offered in every category and the skill in adjusting its range for the listeners' free choice. We would substitute "At your service" for "This will do you good." '[42] In effect, listeners' preferences were to prevail at the same time as the audience was being divided up into blocks of different people with different tastes, different abilities, different interests. *The BBC mission to 'elevate' and 'better' the large bulk of the population was over.* The working party counselled that 'for all programmes, stricter attention should be paid to the question "What would the listener like to have on the radio?" and less weight to such questions as "ought the BBC to cover this subject?" ' They were in effect proposing a system in which people could exercise a choice, rather than having choices made for them.

The ideas and proposals of the working party were rapidly circulated throughout the BBC. Wellington passed them on in a statement to his senior staff in which he told them that they must 'be better attuned to the public need', that the presence of ITV had created 'a different atmosphere', that the BBC must satisfy 'its many audiences more as it finds them than as it would wish them to be'. They were, he said, under siege, fighting for the 'continuance of public service broadcasting and all it stands for. And fight we will, whatever

[41] M. F. C. Standing *et al.*, *Working Party Report on the Future of Sound Broadcasting in the Domestic Services* (Dec. 1957), para. 26.
[42] Ibid., para. 28.

that may call for in the ways of hard work, fresh thinking, the breaking of old habits of thought if we see them to be wrong or out of date, and the need to be economical and purposeful in the spending of our money.'[43]

There was, almost inevitably, a moment when fear entered the soul, a fear that they were totally debasing the value of their coinage by moving away too fast and too far from those traditions which had nourished the Corporation in decades past. The Board of Management felt ill at ease with the Report and they choked on the question of what on earth to do with it. They decided to add their own qualification to it before it was sent off to the Governors for their approval. Where the Report had said that the Corporation's concern with its cultural mission was wrong in principle and impracticable in a competitive world, the Board of Management insisted on adding: 'In short, while not losing its traditional sense of mission in the cultural and educational fields the BBC must keep this sense of mission within bounds, and seek to satisfy its many audiences more as it finds them than it would wish them to be.' It was no more than a very thin smokescreen and the balance of the argument still lay with those, like Lindsay Wellington and the authors of the Report, who could argue that the BBC no longer believed it 'right or sensible to try to dragoon taste, or compel it by refraining from offering a straightforward programme of simple entertainment for those listeners—the majority of the community at any given time—who like and prefer it'.[44]

At a stroke the authors of the Report, and all those senior managers who were endorsing their conclusion, were casting aside the whole philosophical structure on which the previous thirty years of the BBC's history had rested. Their reasoning was simple: there was no alternative but to recognize the rise of a new medium, television, a new institution, commercial television, and a new social order, post-war Britain.

The sentiments of those who would transform the BBC's radio services found powerful backing throughout the increasingly central and confident television service. In 1958 Gerald Beadle, the BBC's Director of TV Broadcasting, said: 'I want, if I may, to debunk one of the most pernicious of modern heresies. The heresy postulates that really good things can never hope to be popular; good things can only be appreciated by a small élite. Those things that are popular on the other hand must inevitably be frivolous or worthless. . . . Anyone who is frightened by the word "popular", who feels that there is something derogatory about it, has no place in Television.' Where Grisewood had identified the spread of mass education as a bacillus, eating away at public taste and the power of appreciation, Beadle and his colleagues wanted fundamentally to re-examine the relationship between television and its public: 'Let me speak for BBC TV and its development so far as I can foresee

---

[43] Note by Lindsay Wellington, 9 Apr. 1957.   [44] Ibid.

it. We have to reflect the people, their lives, their perplexities, their humour and their spiritual needs. The current situation of the nation is something we shall fully involve ourselves in. Television, especially non-commercial television, will be very much alive and up to date, not living in an escapist world of old-fashioned thought. It will try to avoid the false and trashy values which have in all ages tended to attach themselves to some kinds of popular entertainment.' And then, in a clear snub to earlier traditions, he added: 'Above all I hope that we in the BBC will never fall into the error of taking ourselves too seriously. We shall always take our work seriously, but not ourselves. Surely it is one of our more important functions in television to help the human race see the funny side of itself.'[45]

In his statement to the Governors, Jacob issued the death notice on the Reith–Haley tradition when he argued that though there may be various reasons why radio listening had declined—television, changing social habits, Luxembourg—'we feel sure that one of the causes is that the effort to improve public tastes has been made in such a way that the public have been given indigestion and have turned away. We feel that the policy under which the losses have been sustained should now be modified.'[46]

The changes were announced at a press conference on 8 April 1957. The BBC was changed forever. The changes anticipated an inquiry which would prove to be the final phase in the fermentation of change and the high-water mark in the classic articulation of public service broadcasting.

On 23 June 1958 Ian Jacob informed the Board of Management of the BBC 'that there was a likelihood that the Government would in the near future set on foot an inquiry into certain specific aspects of broadcasting on which it was considered that early decisions were called for. Amongst these would be the question of a third service of TV. It would be necessary for the BBC to be ready with its own up to date policy and proposals on this matter.' A month later he told them that he anticipated that the question which the inquiry would pose would be 'What are the essential characteristics of public service broadcasting and how do they differ from those of a commercial broadcast system?' Indeed it was his own efforts to answer those questions which led Jacob to prepare his document 'Basic Propositions'.[47] By the time that the Postmaster-General announced in the House of Commons on 13 July 1960 that the government had decided to set up a committee of inquiry into the future of sound and TV broadcasting under the chairmanship of Sir Harry Pilkington, the BBC had for months been attuning itself psychologically for the coming fight as well as preparing the basic papers in which its case would

[45] G. Beadle, speech to the Bristol Diocesan Conference, Chippenham, 1958.

[46] 'The Future of Sound Broadcasting in the Domestic Service', Note by the Director-General, G 23/57, 7 Mar. 1957.

[47] Board of Management, Min. 385, 27 July 1959.

be contained. Indeed preparation had begun in May on a paper which would outline how the BBC had developed since the last such inquiry in 1952: outlining the present nature and state of the BBC, and indicating its plans for the future of sound and TV. By June drafts began to appear of the basic paper which became known as BBC Memo No. 1, which was to be the essential document from which everything else stemmed.

Hugh Greene, the new Director-General, outlined his ideas to senior management at the General Liaison Meeting, a regular gathering of the Corporation's senior figures. He described the next four years as ones in which, though there would be no major changes in the pattern of broadcasting, the BBC would be constantly under the sharp eye of sharp men. He had, he said, spent

a lot of time recently with various committees of the Conservative and Labour Parties who were doing their own work in preparation for a Committee of Inquiry, and had also talked to individual MPs and other interested people. One could see a certain political atmosphere beginning to form, and one of the main features was the feeling particularly strong on the Conservative side, that the commercial monopoly must be broken. However cynical we might be about the breaking of the monopoly, it was a political reality that we had to face that this feeling existed, even amongst those who were leading exponents of commercial TV a few years ago. In his talks with Labour MPs DG said it was apparent that, although starting from an entirely different point, they were converging on this one central point, the need to break the commercial monopoly.[48]

The immediate danger of this, he argued, was that the BBC would itself be expected to help break the commercial monopoly by taking adverts.

'If we once went in for advertising, the more successful we were in the commercial field the more dangerous it would be.' He thought that from a severely practical point of view our independence must be based on the rock of the licence revenue, and that once we were driven off that rock, we would be in a very dangerous position. 'If we were successful in the commercial field there would be inevitable political pressure to deprive us of our licence revenue, gradually but in the end totally, and we would be reduced to the level of ITV.' He 'stressed that in all our public relations we should maintain our absolutely firm front on this point of our finance, and that we should set as the first objective for the Inquiry the maintenance of the other present method of financing the BBC'. The second subject for the inquiry to consider was television, and in particular who would get the unallocated Band III. The BBC's view was that ideally this should be used to improve the national coverage of TV by reaching those homes for which at present reception was difficult. Should, however, the decision be made to allocate the wavelength to a new channel he expressed the BBC's eagerness to have a means of providing a

[48] General Liaison Meeting, Minutes, 30 Mar. 1960.

'planned alternative service to our own serious programmes, although some of the attractions of this had inevitably been lost through the existence of commercial TV'. The other possibility which had been put forward about the third channel was that it should be awarded to a new authority, possibly concentrating on educational TV. It was an idea which the BBC was eager to strangle at birth on the grounds that it 'would seem to be a vote of no confidence in the BBC by providing another authority to do what we had shown we could do extremely well. It would shake our national position as leaders in the broadcasting world and thereby do a great deal to lessen the authority of the BBC in the outside world on which the success of our External Services was based'.[49]

The third major issue he described as facing the Committee was the future of sound broadcasting 'and in particular whether or not we should have to provide commercial radio in various cities', if only because a number of what Greene termed 'the robber Barons' were dividing up the country. They were, Greene suggested, 'anxious to create the impression that the coming of commercial radio in this country was inevitable. DG said he did not believe it was inevitable, and we should do everything we could to repeat that we did not believe it was inevitable and indeed thought it extremely doubtful.' His basic assumption was that the political atmosphere was not there to support the idea of commercial radio as it had been to support the idea of commercial TV a few years before. Whatever his feeling about the likelihood of a commercial radio system developing he was eager to cover his bets by announcing that the BBC would be starting its own local radio service.[50]

It was inevitable that the inquiry would force the BBC to think in the abstract about its nature and purpose: in short, force it to consider the virtues of the public service system of broadcast. This was partly a direct result of the questions posed by the Committee; and indeed the very first question put by the Committee to Hugh Greene when he appeared before them was, what was the purpose of the BBC? He gave what he himself describes as a faltering reply. Sir Harry Pilkington observed that the BBC's first submission 'Memo No. 1' took too much for granted by crediting the members of the Committee with more knowledge than they in fact had, as well as by postulating certain assumptions, 'for example, that the licence revenue was the only satisfactory way of financing PSB, which the Committee would want to examine carefully'.[51] Another example though of how the process induced a considerable reflectiveness on the part of the BBC is contained in discussions between Hugh Greene and the head of television programmes, Kenneth Adam, about the preparation of a paper on further education:

[49] General Liaison Meeting, Minutes, 30 Mar. 1960.
[50] Board of Management, Minutes, 23.1.C1 (1979).
[51] Minutes of meeting between the BBC and the Pilkington Committee, 7 Oct. 1960.

(1) I think it is very important that the main stream of serious broadcasting, which is educational in the widest sense of the word, should remain within the control of the TV service. Otherwise I am sure we shall get confused as to our intentions and responsibilities. I believe that the world of adult education is most likely to be won over to support the BBC, if we make it clear that we intend to maintain our high standards of outlook and approach over the whole range of our programmes. . . . In a very real sense all serious programmes and many programmes conceived as entertainment only, are in fact educational in the most profound sense. Nothing is more educational, for example, than being brought closely in contact with people of great quality. Such programmes as 'Face to Face,' 'the Brains Trust' and 'Press Conference' are in themselves a process of education which only TV can provide for the millions. In the same way education is not merely a matter of instruction or information, but a matter of conveying attitudes to life and a sense of values. I quote 'Zoo Quest' as being of special value in this respect, not just because they show unknown lands and interesting creatures, but because in every attitude and inflection of David Attenborough there is implied an affection and reverence for the animal creation which is educationally all the more important because it is unconsciously conveyed.[52]

Greene's first major speech addressing the issues facing the Pilkington Committee was in June 1960 when he addressed the St Antony's Society on 'Broadcasting as a Public Service'. It was a key speech and many of the arguments within it were to recur over the next few months as he worked to drive home one basic point, that the only kind of broadcasting system that civilized, cultured, and democratic society should aspire to was the public service one. A society, he implied, was like an organism which needed to be sustained, to be cultivated, and allowed to develop: thus, if its people needed health, then they would be given health; if they needed to develop the mind, then they would be given education; if they needed culture, then they would be given the BBC. As Greene described it:

the history of broadcasting is part of our social and institutional growth. . . . Now broadcasting can safely boast that it is the most public of all services. The essence of it, as its very name implies, is to convey to the public material which would otherwise be restricted. The ideal of using broadcasting for the benefit of the whole community—rather than for the interest of any group or class—appealed strongly to those who established broadcasting in this country. The ideal was pursued with great energy and imagination by the man who shaped the broadcasting service in its early years—the present Lord Reith. He was helped by general support and indeed an enthusiasm for this ideal as the reality began to show itself and to achieve results. The conception was perfected by entrusting the broadcasting service to one organization, by freeing that organization from any motive except the service of the public and by giving the organization what seemed a daringly large measure of independence for the government of the day.

[52] Kenneth Adam to Hugh Greene, 13 Oct. 1960.

He then asked the key question, upon what principles had the BBC developed its public service of broadcasting? He argued:

I think there were two: first, the fullest possible development of the potentialities of the medium, and second the provision of the best available in each category of broadcastable material. These two ideals become progressively far harder to fulfil after the pioneer state has been passed; the stage when maturity has been reached and when those who have laboured longest and hardest begin to believe that there are no more discoveries to make—the state when the potentialities have been thoroughly explored, and when the programmes are well used to being fed on the best that money can buy. Middle age has its dangers not only for husbands but for institutions.

One can see here his feeling that the BBC's problems lay in the fact that it had become flabby, self-satisfied, uninspired. He continued:

But to develop the potentialities of the medium and to insist upon the best available as your standard, requires know-how on the one hand and single mindedness on the other. The profit motive—the mere desire to attract attention—innovation for its own sake—salesmanship—all that is merely meretricious—these characteristics will not take you far, judged by the high standards the public have set for the service that they expect. . . . I believe a profit-servicing system is defective. Its interests can never be towards providing the best in every category—its concern is fundamentally with sales and its categories of broadcasting are categories of salesmanship. . . . Salesmanship and broadcasting can show similarities, of course, but they are not identical, and from the standpoint of public service a broadcasting system tied to salesmanship is bound to be restrictive and its popularity is bound to be a deceptive and specious one—measured by the requirements of a public service. These requirements are as manifold and diverse as are the individuals who compose the public. A Library considered as a public service could hardly be correctly evaluated merely in terms of the number of books borrowed. If this were the standard of measurement, the Libraries would have a very easy road to success and we could easily guess at what the contents of this library would be. But a public service of broadcasting, like the library, must provide so far as possible for every taste and for every sort of entertainment, for information upon every worthwhile topic, and for education wherever it is needed. Broadcasting in Britain was developed with these diverse requirements in mind. And it may claim I think to have anticipated some of the needs which broadcasting has supplied, to have educated the appetite and to have enlarged the field of experience and appreciation far beyond what was foreseen at the time broadcasting began.

The implications of this statement are considerable. He is, in effect, suggesting that the BBC should be all things to all people: if they want music, then it shall be provided whether it be light or serious; if they want information, drama, light entertainment, discussion, emotion, to be stretched intellectually, to enjoy sport, anything that one can think of, then the BBC is, literally, constituted to offer it; not just to offer, but to offer *the best*. Here is perhaps the single most important notion developed in the 1950s and 1960s. It is also the one most difficult to understand especially by public broadcasters in countries which hold to a much more restricted definition of 'best', in which the notion is interpreted to mean programming which is 'worthy', reflective of the values of a middle class which despises popular culture and lauds its own. The idea which emerged in the BBC during these years was that one could take popular culture—for example, drama or comedy—and do it in such a way, with such intelligence, professionalism and sheer *élan*—that it rose from the mediocre and took its audience with it. I never fail to be baffled by the profound inability of public broadcasters elsewhere—most notably North America—to get their mind around this notion. The programmes which exemplified the Corporation's approach bordered on the eccentric sometimes, but were quite brilliantly captivating in their execution. Greene consistently and forcefully challenged the idea put forward by his counterpart in the Independent Television Authority, Sir Robert Fraser, that the BBC was indifferent to the likes and dislikes of 'ordinary' people.

He told a Canadian audience that the BBC 'has to concern itself with the whole of life in Britain; with the popular and the unpopular. It must be in the best sense, all things to all men. People must turn to the BBC to find what they want, whatever it is.'[53]

Individual people do not only make up majorities; they also form part of innumerable minorities—and perhaps this is truer in this country than of any other in the world. People are gardeners, or enjoy cricket, or breed whippets, or like listening to 17th century music, or are amateur archaeologists, or collect old detective stories, or want to learn a foreign language. It seems to me that if the ideas put forward by Sir Robert Fraser in his speech to you were accepted as valid, these minorities would have a poor deal because they would be consistently out-voted—a curious interpretation of democracy.

His attack on the *commercial* nature of ITV went on relentlessly—it is in this context useful to point out that he always refused to use the title *Independent* TV and always insisted that the opposition be described as the *commercial* broadcasting system. He spent much of a speech to the National Liberal Club attacking the influence of advertising on ITV's programmes, and on how the companies were becoming no more than parts of sprawling business and entertainment empires which would inevitably guide their development not with the public good in mind but with private profit as the sole criterion of success. He outlined in great detail, for example, the various other interests of the people who ran Associated TV and asked rhetorically:

Is it in the public interest that a group of men answerable only to their shareholders . . . should exercise such influence over TV, commercial radio, films, music halls, the

---

[53] Hugh Greene, speech to the Canadian Club of Ottawa, 24 Nov. 1961.

booking of artists, wireless and TV relay services, gramophone records and music publishing . . . ought such power to repose in the same hands, however well intentioned
they may be?

What he was challenging, or rather trying to implant in the mind of those
who could influence the future of broadcasting in this country, was a doubt
about the very logic of commercial broadcasting:

Entertainment reassures. The consumer needs to be reassured and relaxed in order to
receive the advertiser's message in the right frame of mind. Since commercial broadcasting lives by the services which it renders to advertisers, it must put a premium on
material which does not in any way disturb the viewer. It must put a premium on the
familiar and the unadventurous, on the intellectually unchallenging. . . . The spread of
commercial broadcasting would be the biggest influence in the commercialisation of
our whole society. The values to which commercial broadcasting must be tied are
inadequate and ultimately false and disastrous. . . . They give a deceptive comfort in a
world where there is very little real comfort to be had.

Wherever he was going, from civic reception to political meeting, he was
addressing the same points: the need to stop the spread of commercial broadcasting and to support public broadcasting. Running within that key theme
were the arguments for a new channel, for radio, and for colour: all means
towards the end of good, and therefore public service, broadcasting. It was
a role, moreover, which he was clearly enjoying and he told a meeting of
Conservative MPs in a revealing moment: 'Perhaps a certain spice has been
added to life; perhaps I am enjoying making this speech more because I have
got something to attack.'[54] The more that attack could succeed the more likely
he was to be able to convince opinion inside and outside the Committee that
the BBC was worth defending. He was not suggesting that it be defended
simply because it existed but because only that particular form of broadcasting organization with that particular set of principles could offer something
far more valuable than all the stocks and shares so carefully accumulated by
all those gentlemen who formed his opposition. The BBC could offer *Truth*,
a quality which the old journalist in him treasured above all else. The finest
exposition of this, however, did not take place on his home shores, but in the
lions' den itself. In November 1961 he addressed an anniversary dinner of NBC
in New York. It was an invitation which had filled NBC executives with some
fear and trepidation at what he might say to the assembled body of the
American great and good. The BBC's New York representative described them
as 'extremely apprehensive. The broadcasters fear that any speech by you
putting up a good case for public service broadcasting will only serve to
strengthen the hands of those who are pressing for increased control of the

---

[54] Hugh Greene, talk to the United and Cecil Club Dinner, 12 July 1961.

networks.'[55] He described the 'true purpose of the BBC' as being 'concerned with the whole of life'.[56]

He continued:

The new age of broadcasting which lies before us should not stand in the service of governments, political parties, big business or sectional interests. It should stand to my mind in the service of truth or the nearest to the truth one can get, and it is import- ant to remember that there is artistic truth as well as the hard factual truth with which events should be presented.[57]

The period of the inquiry was in fact the only period in Hugh Greene's life when he had consistently to define his view of broadcasting. He had never been an especially reflective person in any manifest sense, but he did have a number of sharply defined beliefs in the nature of culture, and the kinds of values which should prevail. He was now having to articulate those values in a way which in effect reflected his conception of the relationship between the BBC and the rest of society. To the National Institute of Adult Education Annual Conference he talked about 'Adult Education and the Common Good':

The national culture is diverse; it has its regional characteristics and inflections, its class differences, its sectional pursuits. It is the business of the BBC to reflect that diver- sity. It does not stand outside and apart from society. It has simply to respond as sens- itively as it can to all the main currents of the national life. That does not mean that we have no firm values to go by. I do not regard 'paternalism' as a dirty word and I hope I shall not sound 'undemocratic' if I say that by and large it is fairly well agreed in our society that knowledge is better than ignorance, tolerance than intolerance, an active concern for the arts or public affairs better than indifference, and that wide inter- ests are better than narrow.

This was a time, as was seen with the debate about radio, when the spectre of mass society, created by TV and a simile for 'mob', still haunted the minds of some observers and practitioners of broadcasting. They feared at best that, somehow, the ubiquity of the TV would paint the whole of the culture the same rather dull colour, at worst the hobgoblins of an impoverished public imagination. Richard Hoggart, author of the much vaunted *Uses of Literacy*, would hold that the Pilkington Report described the danger of a mass culture which is 'too damned nice, a bland, muted, processed, institutionalised decency, a suburban limbo in which nothing ever happens and the grit has gone out of life'. There was something of a left-puritanism in a view that life had to be a struggle in order to be meaningful. There was also something of a paradox since the idea of social struggle was to enable the working class to overcome the 'grit' which capitalism had a nasty habit of putting into their lives.

---

[55] M. Russell to Hugh Greene, 13 July 1961.
[56] Hugh Greene, quoted in Tracey, *A Variety of Lives*, 195.   [57] Ibid.

Wonderbread television was, though, a widespread fear, and for Hugh Greene the problem was how to persuade the Pilkington Committee that not only was the BBC endeavouring to avoid the quicksands of mass taste, and put some of the 'grit' back into the national life, he was also in effect saying that *only* the BBC could do that. In knocking on the head the idea, which he was associating with ITV, that the broadcaster should only give the people what they wanted he went right back to the Founding Father himself: 'As John Reith put it in his evidence to the Crawford Committee in 1925, "He who prides himself on giving what he thinks the people want is often creating a fictitious demand for lower standards which he will then satisfy." ' At the heart of Reith's view of society and broadcasting lay a paternalism whereas at the heart of Greene's view lay a certain faith in all those individuals who possessed a wide range of different interests, but who from time to time may exhibit mass taste. He quoted with pride the 1 million people who had listened to a Bach Promenade Concert and the 4 million who had watched Sir Mortimer Wheeler's series on archaeology.

Greene had become the principal articulator of the process of the transforming of the BBC, begun under Jacob, from an élitist channel to one which was closer to the people: 'Democracy rests in the last resort on faith in the plain man. The cynicism that provides a flow of trivial entertainment for the masses while despising it and them'—and here he had in mind Norman Collins—'is very close to the political cynicism which regards them as dupes to be manipulated or fooled.' He was in effect trying to establish a balance: the need to maintain a certain cultural dignity and eminence within broadcasting without becoming distanced from the bulk of society. Television, he argued, must 'make a common culture part of the common good'. He invoked Matthew Arnold's 'men of culture' as 'the true apostles of equality. The great men of culture are those who have had a passion for diffusing, for making prevail, for carrying from one end of society to the other the best knowledge, the best ideas of their time, who have laboured to divest knowledge of all that was harsh, uncouth, difficult, abstract, professional, exclusive; to humanise it, to make it efficient outside the clique of the cultivated and learned, yet still remaining the best knowledge and thought of the time, and a true source therefore of sweetness and light.' It was a new view of an old idea, a democratized and humanized version of the missionary role of the BBC to bring that 'sweetness and light' to a people not because they needed it but because they in effect wanted it without quite having so realized[58]—hence his rhetorical question: 'How many of the British public would have asked in 1945 for programmes on archaeology?'

[58] Hugh Greene, 'Adult Education and the Common Good', speech to the National Institute of Adult Education annual conference, 22 Sept. 1961.

The Pilkington Committee's Report, published on 17 June 1962, was a huge vindication of broadcasting as seen by the BBC. Public service values were praised, commercial values seriously questioned. The BBC had gained almost everything it wanted: a new channel, colour, a switch to 625 lines, maintenance of the licence fee as the source of revenue, the development of sound broadcasting, confirmation that it remained the main instrument of broadcasting in the country, all were recommended by the Committee in a package of structural and psychological developments which left the BBC probably stronger and more prestigious than at any time in its history, before or since.

The Strange Case of Tahu Hole and the Battle for News

There is one story which captures the essence of this process of change and that is the story of the battle for news. (It is a story which I promised Hugh Greene that one day I would tell.) News is always a key part of any broadcasting organization, if only because perhaps more than any other form of broadcasting it touches the lives of the population by relaying the maxima and minima of their world.

In this instance, the debate was given a particular edge by the fact that during the 1950s the BBC's head of the News Division, Tahu Hole, was widely and intensely disliked as an autocrat who had no more idea about the nature and role of news in the modern world than he had tact and consideration towards his brow-beaten employees whom he variously abused and appalled. Tahu Ronald Pearce Hole lingers in the mind's eye of many of those who knew him as a terrible figure, attracting a quite extraordinary level of loathing. Hugh Greene relates how Hole bullied his staff; how he ignored routine procedures such as reading to staff the contents of their annual reports; how he actively broke BBC regulations by refusing to allow his foreign correspondents to apply for other positions within the BBC; not to mention his highly restrictive attitude towards news. What seems to have really offended Hugh Greene, however, was the impression that Hole debased and degraded the dignity of those people who had to work with him. 'Tahu Hole had an appallingly corrupting effect on the characters of otherwise good people.'[59] Greene recalled how he was told that staff would sometimes bring in presents to give to Hole in the hope of gaining his favour 'rather as natives would place gifts before an idol in order to forestall its wrath'. It was that debasement of their humanity and self-respect which made Greene seethe at the very mention of Hole's name.

To be blunt, Tahu Ronald Pearce Hole is a man accused: a man who hindered the whole development of the BBC news from the day he took over in

---

[59] Hugh Greene, interview with author.

October 1948 with his obsessive commitment to outmoded and restrictive practices of broadcasting news. Stephen Bonarjee, who in January 1957 became
assistant head of TV news, recalls Hole's 'extremely rigid concepts of what
was news', of how he enforced them rigidly, of how the only stories which
would be used were 'important' stories, of how there was no place for human
interest but plenty of place for 'Establishment stuff'. Bonarjee added: 'People
were afraid of him in a kind of way. He ruled his empire with a rod of iron.'[60]
Hole refused to allow 'scoops' and would carry no story unless it had been
checked with more than one other source, such as a news agency.

More important than these difficult personal problems was the feeling
among Hole's opponents that the News Division was an empire within an
empire, which refused to co-operate with, to switch the metaphor slightly,
all the other barons. It was probably Hole's refusal to co-operate with other
departments, and in particular with the television service, that led to his downfall, and why it offers a useful, if idiosyncratically brutal, symbol of a changing BBC.

It was indicative of Hole's attitude towards television news that he refused
to allow any reporters to work specifically for TV. For a long time, too, Hole
refused to name his newsreaders, even though the commercial Independent
Television News had done so with great success from the very beginning, with
Robin Day and Chris Chataway having become national names. It was not
until Hole was directly instructed by the Governors to name them that newsreaders such as Robert Dougal became more than anonymous figures.

Hole infuriated the BBC's TV service. He clung, with a certain bulldog
tenacity, to the control of news, thus denying TV, bursting forth with youthful energy, its own news service. What was worse this left the definition of
news to people who the young turks of television news and current affairs,
such as Donald Baverstock, felt had no understanding of either the medium
or the nature of news. A popular joke was that Hole's idea of a lead story on
TV news would begin with the opening line 'The Queen Mother yesterday
. . .', it was the Queen Mother because he fawned over her, it was yesterday
because they did not know how to process film any faster.

Hole described his own view of news in broadcasting in a letter to *The Times*
in 1978. He said that the editorial philosophy which he employed

often in the face of internal opposition enabled the Home and Overseas news bulletins
to establish themselves universally as examples of journalism 'proper and unique to
broadcasting' and won for the BBC its reputation for integrity and reliability. The aims
were accuracy, objectivity and impartiality—to guard against any form of editorialis-
ing, just to tell the unvarnished facts as far as they could be ascertained, to reflect
opinion, comments and judgments of others, including those of the press.[61]

---

[60] Hugh Greene, interview with author.   [61] *The Times*, 29 Aug. 1978.

Despite emergent opposition from the TV service Jacob was determined that the News Division retain control of the whole of the BBC's news output. At a press conference in June 1955 Jacob announced that as of 5 July the BBC would start a TV news service which would go out at 7.30 p.m. and would consist of news and newsreel. It is extraordinary to recall that before this time the BBC had had no 'illustrated' news service.

He told the assembled press that the time had come for new ideas:

It is in the realm of news and current affairs and of actuality that the potentialities of TV are the greatest. . . . We hope to give the public not only a comprehensive illustrated News Service of a scope and quality equivalent to the service that they have been receiving for many years in Sound radio, but also the latest moving pictures of current events as soon as they can be obtained.

Jacob had decided that while Hole formally retained overall control of news he would take direct control of it himself, and create within News Division a distinct TV news department. The impact of commercial broadcasting in such areas as news had made it far too dangerous to allow the continuation of a personal, anachronistic, and demoralizing fiefdom of Tahu Hole. At the same time the sheer speed with which TV was emerging, and the manifest silliness of Hole's attitude to TV news, his apparent total incomprehension of the visual medium, sowed important seeds of doubt in Jacob's mind. Those doubts fused with the minds of a rising generation of TV personnel which challenged not only the particular empire of Hole, but the whole hegemony of Broadcasting House within the BBC. In this they were led by their presiding genius, Cecil McGivern, Controller of Programmes in the Television Service.

As the BBC had changed in radio, so it was now changing in TV, as new talents emerged, with fresh ideas. But for the final victory one had to see the body of the ancien régime in its coffin. That is why the demise of Hole took on such importance because, if one might extend the metaphor, not until they could watch the body being buried, could they really feel that the new BBC was being born.

Greene, when he became Director-General in 1960, saw as his first major test ridding the BBC of Hole. He knew that many eyes would be on him to see if his resolve to change the Corporation was really firm. He had the support of Sir Arthur fforde, the Chairman, and Sir Philip Morris, the Vice-Chairman, but had 'some very sticky meetings with the Board of Governors when I recommended that Tahu Hole should be required to leave. I remember Lord McDonald, the National Governor for Wales, saying that it was all very well for a new broom, but not for a new broom who was sweeping in that sort of ruthless way. But fforde and Morris remained absolutely steady, and it was finally decided that he should be asked for his resignation and given a golden handshake and I put my name to a statement, an entirely false statement, about his service to the BBC and so on.'[62] There was a special board meeting on 14 March 1960 with the fate of Hole as the only agenda item. There was no minute and one imagines that this was the day that Hole's departure was finalized. He formally left on 18 March.

Organizational changes and victims were inevitable, but the crucial development in these debates had been an intellectual one. Not only had the cultural mission been abandoned but in its place was offered a new argument. This held that it had been misguided to assume that good broadcasting always equated with 'serious' broadcasting, that one could in fact still search for a quality which would not necessarily be defined by earnestness or pomposity but by standards of integrity and impartiality, by avoiding degrading material, and most of all by always being professional within programmes of whatever kind. Down that path lay the possibility of establishing a relationship with a diverse audience which enlightened, informed, amused, but did not patronize. That was the new meaning of public service broadcasting.

It was a meaning which had been made inevitable by *the* key institutional developments of the 1950s: the shift from the dominance of radio to the dominance of TV, from the word to the image, and the rise of commercial competition. This inevitably meant that attitudes of and to broadcasting were also changing and that the old beliefs rooted in a traditional view of culture and society, of the difference between high and low, were being reshaped by the increasing popularity of television.

I am not here idly writing narrative history, rather suggesting relevance to the debates which are taking place about the future of the BBC today. That relevance is not just of the particular character of a creative moment or the kind of political and economic pressures which can build up. Those are the parallels. The real relevance has to do with the intellectual seeds which were sown by Jacob in particular and lay dormant. Those seeds contained what might be described as the democratization of popular choice. That process itself reflected deep changes within British society which had, to borrow Elizabeth Eisenstein's phrase, been incubating for several decades. The age itself was more socially secular, reformist, less forgiving of hierarchies of status and value. An institution as central to Britain inevitably became a metaphor for the change, though the freshness which emerged for a time was less the first swallow of summer and more a canary down the shaft.

The character and extent of the change was not lost on its founder. In his diaries Reith wrote: 'The BBC has lost its dignity and respect; in the upper reaches of intellectual and ethical and social leadership it has absconded its responsibilities and its privilege. Its influence is disruptive and subversive; it is no longer "on the Lord's side." I am sorry I ever had anything to do with

---

[62] Hugh Greene, interview with author.

it.'[63] He felt 'immensely sad (and more than that) at the eclipse, or rather complete overthrow and destruction, of all my work in the BBC. It was my being prepared to lead, and to withstand modern laxities and vulgarities and irreligion and all. No one was ever in such a position as I; I did what my father and mother would have wished—to universal amazement. All gone. Feeling most melancholy.'[64]

On first blush it would seem that the message from those years to the present day is that the response to new competition need not necessarily have an adverse consequence, and indeed may well lead to new energy and ideas. Unfortunately, it is not quite that simple. What emerged from the debate in the 1950s was a compromise between a commitment to the best and a desire to please, not elevate, the audience: the character of the BBC had shifted to one which allowed for choices made by the audience. It had had to make that shift in order to survive. In doing so, however, it was instigating the logic which is proffered today by proponents of new television services, that they also, and even more so, can be all things to all people willing to make choices. It would be wry irony if the shift which saved the BBC in the 1950s and 1960s was really the seed which would ultimately destroy it.

---

[63] *Reith Diaries*, 18 May 1964.   [64] Ibid. 30 Mar. 1964.

5 The BBC and Funding

On 3 November 1972 the BBC celebrated its fiftieth anniversary. It did so in grand style with an impressive dinner at the Guildhall. Dress was white tie and tails and the assembly was a classic gathering of the great and good of the land. The main speaker was the Prime Minister, Edward Heath. *The Times* wrote a glowing editorial. Ten years later, on the sixtieth anniversary, the Corporation, or rather its Chairman, George Howard, decided it would be appropriate if they marked the occasion by providing a moment for the great and good to thank the Lord for bestowing this mighty institution on them and the common folk. The place was St Paul's Cathedral. The royal family were represented, but the Prime Minister, Mrs Thatcher, was not. On the morning of the service she sent a message apologizing for not being able to attend.

The agony of the BBC was only just beginning, a slow but relentless assault on the political and fiscal integrity of the Corporation by a Conservative government bent on changing the BBC—even if the 'to what' remained unclear. The then Home Secretary, Douglas Hurd, declaimed that the licence fee was not 'eternal'. Apparently the government was considering establishing—as part of its examination of renewal of the BBC royal charter—a Public Service Broadcasting Council, partly funded by the licence fees which had hitherto gone only to the BBC. In a manner which some saw as a wimpish grovelling and others as a necessary and new pragmatism the BBC began to shed staff and services. The context in which this was taking place was clear: the rise of the 'new media' of cable and satellite; the effective privatizing of the ITV system which in effect shed public service obligations, despite an alleged commitment to 'quality'; and a consistent policy of squeezing the real value of the licence fee.

The absence of the Prime Minister at the cathedral service thus might reasonably be viewed as signalling a new age in which the significance and importance of the BBC would be utterly diminished.

In the years that followed a combination of ideological and technological forces developed a momentum that weakened, and possibly fractured, the political, moral, and cultural consensus within Britain on which the BBC had always depended. The most immediate, though symbolically revealing, challenge to the BBC was also the most prosaic: the placing of a rather large question mark over the continuing validity of funding the Corporation by means of a universal licence fee. Almost all debates about the BBC tend to come down to debates about the licence fee, payment by every owner of a television set of a fee to be allowed to receive the broadcast signals. The fee is not only a useful way of funding broadcasting, but carries a statement of principle and purpose—the financial and, therefore, political and, therefore, creative independence of the broadcaster. At least, that is the theory. Tamper with the licence fee and you tamper with the soul of the institution. Destroy the licence fee and you destroy the BBC.

The roots and significance of the licence fee lie within the origins of the BBC as a constitutional creation. When the British Broadcasting Company was founded in 1922 it was as the creation of a group of companies selling wireless sets. The notion was a neat one: the BBC would broadcast programmes which would then lead to the sale of more sets. The Post Office charged 10 shillings from anyone who owned a 'BBC' receiver, half of the fee going to the Company to pay for the making of programmes. The various manufacturing companies involved were also to receive a royalty from each set sold which was to bear the stamp of the BBC.

One way some listeners found to avoid this was to assemble their own wireless sets, claiming that as they were not official sets the licence fee did not apply to them. In 1923 the Sykes Committee, which was looking into the development of broadcasting, recommended a blanket licence of 10 shillings for anyone with any wireless receiver. The fee remained unchanged for twenty years.

Various forces pointed in the direction of unified control of broadcasting and the licence to pay for programming. In the 1920s there emerged in Europe, a crowded Europe, a strong feeling of the need to ensure that signals in one nation did not interfere with those in another. The official historian of the BBC, Asa Briggs, places considerable emphasis on the consequences of a visit by a Post Office official to the United States and the chaos he discovered there in the use of the airwaves. On his return he emphasized the need for such chaos to be avoided in Britain. At the same time, newspaper interests were eager to ensure that the BBC not be allowed to compete with them for advertising. Political parties were equally anxious to make sure that broadcasting was not run by the government, if only because they feared it might be used against them when they were in opposition. These pressures prompted much thought about what could be the appropriate institutional form for the BBC. In July 1925 the Postmaster-General, Mitchell-Thomson, announced a committee of inquiry under the 27th Earl of Crawford and Balcarres to examine that question.

The first head of the BBC, John Reith, had already spelled out his own view of how the BBC should be developed in his book *Broadcast over Britain*, published in the autumn of 1924. In it he spoke of how broadcasting properly used could help create 'a more intelligent and enlightened electorate'; of how it could bind together the whole of society: 'the Parliamentary system divides the nation geographically, the press system divides them on the basis of opinions and prejudices . . . what is lacking is some integrating element . . . a national broadcasting system will become that integrator of democracy.' He wrote of the importance of religion and of how education should be a key part of the BBC mission. He rejected the potential vulgarity of the 'common man', while recognizing the equal potential for improvement: 'few know what they want and very few what they need. . . . In any case it is better to overestimate the mentality of the public than to underestimate it.' The making of money was not to be the purpose of broadcasting, the spreading of excellence was: 'As we conceive it, our responsibility is to carry into the greatest possible number of homes everything that is best in every department of human knowledge, endeavour or achievement.'[1]

Reith had set out the intellectual and moral boundaries of public service broadcasting. It was left to the Crawford Committee and the Post Office to create the architecture. The key design came in a memorandum from Sir Evelyn Murray, Secretary of the Post Office, to the Crawford Committee recommending that the BBC should be set up, either by charter or statute, as a public corporation with a representative governing body. Murray also emphasized the importance of the BBC being politically independent.

On 5 March 1926 the Crawford Committee reported that broadcasting in Britain should be organized on the basis of a monopolistic, non-profit system supervised by a commission of persons of 'judgment and independence' acting as 'trustees of the national interest'. The Crawford Committee also identified the trilogy of 'educate, entertain, inform' which has persisted throughout the history of broadcasting in Britain. On 14 July 1926 the government announced that from 31 December 1926 the British Broadcasting Corporation would come into existence, deriving its authority from a royal charter.

At the heart of the structure would be the universal licence fee, a device not just for raising revenues to pay the bills but one articulating the national status of the BBC and guaranteeing its creative and political independence. It

---

[1] John Reith, *Broadcast over Britain* (1924).

was not therefore simply a price mechanism for receiving a certain service. The licence fee as a dedicated source of revenue, whose yield was theoretically independent of annual governmental scrutiny, was in effect the guarantor of the constitutional independence of the Corporation. When Reith received the draft charter, with the 'no-advertising' clause, he commented: 'Should not the Corporation have liberty with regard to advertising as a supplementary source of revenue in case of need?' The central problem of all publicly instituted broadcasters is the relationship with the state. The licence fee would thus be seen as a brilliant device for establishing a distance between the organization and the apparatus of government. One does have to recognize, however, that a necessary precondition for such an arrangement was a remarkably self-confident and tolerant political élite, and that the tolerance remained in the gift of the state and as such could readily, though not necessarily easily, be withdrawn. The calculated imprecision of the BBC's relationship with the state—so British, so subtle, so devious—was one in which the BBC, in Tom Burns's memorable description, 'has been lulled, or gulled, into believing [the state] allows it all the liberty, independence, autonomy that can be hoped for, but which has proved, time and again, to be liberty on parole'.[2]

The Pilkington Committee noted that even if there were a number of different ways of raising revenue—licence, advertisements, sponsorship, subscriptions, government grants—'It is not a matter of indifference which is adopted: for the method of paying for broadcasting affects the character of the service of broadcasting. It is therefore a matter of constitutional significance.' Rejecting all the various other alternatives as compromising the integrity and independence of the BBC the Report observed, 'only the licence fee system implies no commitment to any objective other than the provision of the best possible service in broadcasting'.[3]

Intriguingly in the light of later events the Pilkington Committee also noted that one financial option was to allow viewers to pay only for those programmes which they would want to watch:

That is to say, it should engage in 'subscription television'. We note now that the fact of the BBC's being financed from licence revenue encourages the provision of a balanced service available to all. To finance the Corporation in whole or in part from the proceeds of the sale—to those who want and can afford them—of particular programme items would operate in a reverse direction. It would positively discourage and make more difficult the provision of a balanced service. We reject, therefore, as opposed to the purpose of public service broadcasting, the idea that the BBC should engage in subscription television.[4]

The Report went on to argue that any income from any source other than the licence would inevitably become a factor to be taken into account in

---

[2] Burns, *The BBC*, 21.   [3] Pilkington Report, 143–4, paras. 492–3.   [4] Ibid. 147, para. 504.

deciding the level of licence revenue, and however marginal initially would inevitably become significant:

We are convinced that financing the BBC out of licence revenue is more than an important feature of the Corporation's constitution. The BBC sees it as essential. We are sure it is essential for the BBC must remain free from any other commitment, express or implied, to pursue any objective whatsoever other than the full realisation of the purposes of broadcasting.[5]

Fifteen years later the Annan Committee added its thoughts and recommended 'that the best way of financing the BBC is by continuing the licence fee. The only possible alternative is a direct grant from the Exchequer from taxation and we reject this because we think it will undermine the BBC's independence'.[6] For sixty years the BBC had held to this position: if it in any substantial way were successful in the commercial field there would be inevitable and perhaps even immediate political pressure to deprive the Corporation of the licence revenue, gradually but in the end totally.

Of course, if viewed as historical texts these statements appear to the contemporary eye to depend on outmoded, unrealistic assumptions. If, however, they are viewed as statements of principle about the practices of an institution which in constitutional terms remains unchanged, one needs to ask what has altered to make such statements no longer applicable. The answer to that question lies in the net effect of ideological and technological changes.

The BBC therefore has an accurate view of how much revenue it can expect, because it knows the level of the licence fee as set by the government and it knows how many television receivers there are in Britain. The two problems which have historically bedevilled the Corporation are that some people fail to pay the licence fee, and that the revenue has a nasty habit of quickly falling behind costs.

The problem of licence fee evasion is a real one. In February 1983 it was estimated that there were 1.4 million licence evaders costing the BBC £55 million a year. By the time of the Peacock inquiry in 1985 the official figure was 1.6 million evaders and a loss of £80 million in revenue.[7]

The second problem of rising costs is by far the most important and intransigent. Historically the BBC has been able to keep up with costs through the growth in the total number of licences, first radio, then radio and black and white television, then black and white and colour licences. With the extra cost of the colour licence the BBC was guaranteed a steadily rising income. Once the total number of licences began to level off, with colour licences

---

[5] Pilkington Report, 147, para. 506.
[6] Home Office, *Report of the Committee on the Future of Broadcasting*, Cmnd. 6753 (London: HMSO, 1977) (Annan Report), para. 10.22, p. 132.
[7] Cf. Hansard, col. 1051, 27 Mar. 1985.

increasing by only 3 per cent a year, an even greater dependence was thrown onto licence fee increases. Between 1975 and 1981 there were five licence fee increases, compared with seven in the previous fifty years.

The pressure on a licence-supported public service system such as the BBC is, in such circumstances, to force it to go cap in hand to the government for an increase in the fee or to force it to turn to ever greater sources of commercial revenue, and increasingly to shift its ideological ground to accommodate these demands. Either way lies a Faustian bargain—on the one hand compromising the organization's political independence, on the other importing those commercial values which have been held to be anathema to public service principles. As Ian Trethowan wrote, 'The post-1973 inflation built up such pressure on the licence fee that the whole system was called into question. . . . Had inflation continued in double figures the BBC would have been forced to accept annual increases in the fee, and these would have looked indistinguishable from a yearly Government grant.'[8]

According to the late Charles Curran the 'undermining of the licence fee system actually began in 1962, after the Conservative Government's endorsement of the Pilkington recommendation that the BBC should undertake the construction and cooperation of a second television network'.[9] When the BBC launched the second channel it had been assured by the Conservative government that the necessary funds would be available. The BBC was therefore given the full proceeds of the existing licence of £4 which the public paid for the joint radio and TV licence. Since 1957 an excise duty of £1 had been charged on the licence.

The election of the Labour government in 1964 delayed further the consideration of any increase in the licence fee. An Inter-departmental Committee examined the BBC's finances and this was followed by an increase of only £1 on the combined television and radio licence. The BBC complained that this was not enough. In 1968 a supplementary colour television licence was introduced, an additional charge of £5 per licence. With the increasing sale of colour television sets this did much to stave off many of the BBC's immediate financial difficulties, though no one predicted the growth in colour sets at the levels which took place. In 1969 the Labour government agreed to increase the combined licence fee for radio and black and white to £6, a figure which the BBC regarded as 'once again, too little and too late'.[10] It was at this point that the BBC was forced to use its borrowing powers for the first time in its history. Curran says that when he and Lord Hill, then Chairman of the BBC, were negotiating directly with Prime Minister Harold Wilson about a new licence fee, the development of local radio, and the extent of the BBC's

[8] Ian Trethowan, *Split Screen* (London: Hamish Hamilton, 1984), 171.
[9] Charles Curran, *A Seamless Robe* (London: Macmillan, 1977), 75.   [10] Ibid. 86.

employment of musicians, Wilson insisted that the licence increase would only take effect in April 1971, well after the last legally permissible date for the next election.[11]

Wilson's loss of power in June 1970 left the decision to the Heath government, which duly obliged in July 1971 with an increase in the combined television and radio licence to £7 and the abolition of the radio-only licence. According to Curran: 'Once again we demonstrated that on the BBC's known commitments, and the existing state of its indebtedness, the new licence fee would be below the level demanded by the situation, even on the depressed figures for inflation which the BBC was being compelled to adopt in its forecasts in response to Treasury requirements.'[12]

The only thing which saved the BBC was the sudden rapid growth in the number of colour licences. Between 1971 and 1976 the total number of colour licences increased from 609,969 to 8,639,252, or by 1,316 per cent. The next increase in the licence fee did not come until April 1975, with a monochrome fee of £8 and a colour fee of £10, with a stipulation that this settlement was expected to last for at least two years. In those four years the general financial position of the BBC had worsened, and continued to worsen until the next increase in July 1977 when the monochrome and colour licences were increased to £9 and £12 respectively. Vitally, though, the government accepted that the increase was likely to be for only one year: the BBC was in effect receiving an annual grant-in-aid. In November 1978 the colour licence went up to £25, and the monochrome to £10.

In the light of contemporary debates about the future of the BBC, it is interesting to note that in November 1970 the Minister of Posts and Telecommunications was quoted in the press as having 'made it plain' that the BBC 'should not attempt to compete right across the board with commercial interests', and that the BBC should build on the things it does 'uniquely well' and 'what other companies cannot do'. This latter phrase was interpreted as suggesting that the BBC should perhaps concentrate on minority programming. Curran was quick to point out that this did not make sense since so-called minority programmes tended to be more expensive than more popular entertainment programmes. At the time a seventy-five-minute *Play for Today* series on BBC1 cost £25,000 an hour. A half-hour comedy such as the highly successful, and brilliant, *Dad's Army* or *Up Pompeii* cost about £7,500. A sports programme cost about £6,000 an hour, and a feature film £4,000 an hour. Curran went on: 'The same is true of radio. It is now argued (and often of course by interested parties) that we scrap Radio 1, the popular service the BBC undertook when the Government finally took action against the pirates. The saving would be no more than £750,000. It is in fact the cheapest of the

[11] Charles Curran, *A Seamless Robe* (London: Macmillan, 1977), 86.   [12] Ibid. 277.

radio services. The most expensive is Radio 4, which with Radio 3, represents the service to minorities which we are apparently being encouraged to expand.'[13]

Of more immediate concern to Charles Curran and his successor Ian Trethowan than the implications of the differential costs of programming was the looming gap which was beginning to open up between the salary levels inside the BBC and those offered by ITV companies. The problem for the BBC was the way in which the need to go cap in hand for an increase in the fee necessarily tied the Corporation close to the government's economic policies. The Labour government had introduced a pay policy in July 1975, but shortly before this the ITV companies had agreed pay increases of about 20 per cent. A similar BBC settlement was due to come into effect in October, only to be neutralized by the government's pay norms in August.

In 1977, when Ian Trethowan took over from Curran, he knew that in the following year the BBC faced the daunting problem of the renewal of its royal charter, the need for a licence fee increase, and the implications of government economic policies. A report in the *Financial Times* described him as being 'at the helm of a vessel apparently heading for stormy waters. Money is at the root of the BBC's current bout of evils'.[14] The starkest problem which the BBC faced was that the government refused any increase in salary levels for the BBC of more than 5 per cent, something which Trethowan in his memoirs says 'must rank as one of the more disreputable activities of any government in recent history'.[15]

The BBC was in fact suffering to a considerable extent from a bad bout of inflation. One commentator wrote: 'However much it juggles with its schedules and balances its books, the BBC is faced with rising costs in every field of its output, which its present income cannot begin to match.'[16]

Inevitably the relative cheapness of imported programmes became apparent when compared to the average drama cost of £81,000 an hour as against £39,000 in 1975; light entertainment at £45,000 compared to £23,000 three years previously; current affairs at £16,000 as against £10,000. *Starsky and Hutch* cost £7,000 an episode. Another development was the new thinking which began to emerge around this time about the virtues and possibilities of co-productions. The production of the drama *Tinker, Tailor, Soldier, Spy* for example was made possible only with American money.

By November 1978, still facing desperate problems with its staff, the BBC was asking to be allowed to grant its employees a 7.8 per cent pay increase, in keeping with the increase in the cost of living. The government said no, but in December agreed that the issue should be speedily dealt with by the

---

[13] Charles Curran, in *The Times*, 12 Nov. 1970.   [14] *Financial Times*, 8 Oct. 1977.
[15] Trethowan, *Split Screen*, 167.   [16] *Sunday Telegraph*, 15 Oct. 1978.

Central Arbitration Committee (CAC), which proceeded to grant the BBC a pay settlement of 16.5 per cent, way beyond anything which anyone had expected.

In November 1978 the government agreed to a new licence settlement of £25 for colour and £10 for monochrome, less than the BBC objectively needed, and again granted with the specification that it would last no more than a year. Seen from within the context of the large pay settlement this inevitably meant that the BBC's problem would be nothing other than sharpened. Shortly afterwards, in what Curran calls 'the crowning disgrace', the government increased the BBC's borrowing powers from £30 million to £100 million in order to meet the bills which would inevitably appear. This was in effect a rather cynical way of the government sidestepping the need for a proper increase until after the next election.

One almost inevitable consequence of the by now permanent and deep financial problems facing the BBC was the steady erosion of morale. One senior producer was quoted, anonymously, as saying early in 1980:

There's been a massive deterioration in the overall quality of the management . . . the place is falling apart morally, we won't make a stand on anything . . . those who run the BBC will do anything to trim editorially so as not to put the licence fee in danger . . . when Mrs. Thatcher said we need to put our house in order, she was bloody right. . . . Trethowan has no sense of vision or purpose . . . I don't know what we are going to do about radio . . . are we going to see the decline and fall of BBC Television after its Augustan Age?[17]

As the 1980s dawned the problems remained, not of creativity but of real financial difficulties. The journalist Graham Turner reflected an ever more widely held view when he wrote: 'what the new financial climate means in the short term is that the BBC now faces a considerable, and long overdue, trimming of sails . . . like all broadcasting organisations the BBC is both fat and self-indulgent.'[18]

In November 1979 the licence fee was raised for the fifth time in ten years. The new colour fee was to be £34, far short of the BBC's desired figure of about £42. The BBC was nevertheless still in the trap of having to beg on an annual basis for more money. To try and evade this difficulty a joint committee of officials from the Home Office and the BBC published a report on 23 November 1979 on how the BBC could best be financed. The Report recommended that the licence fee be continued but that its level should be based on an agreement between the Home Office and the BBC. The licence fee would therefore be determined by the government on the basis of meeting that agreed expenditure.

---

[17] *Sunday Telegraph*, 2 Mar. 1980.   [18] Ibid.

A *Times* leading article suggested that the only thing the BBC could do on its own was to remove union restrictive practices with which it was 'hampered', reduce its overweight bureaucracy, improve productivity, while all the while sustaining its quality production.[19] On 28 February 1980 the Board of Management announced that they were recommending to the Governors that they axe five orchestras, cut 1,500 jobs, limit regional broadcasting, and thereby save £130 million. These were desperate measures, aimed at seeing the BBC through the two-year period which the government had set for the present licence fee settlement, at a time when a likely annual inflation rate of 16 per cent was held to be optimistic.

The Home Secretary, William Whitelaw, replied in the House of Commons on 31 July 1980, when asked what extra help might be given the BBC, 'I believe that this House, through the licence fee, gave the BBC the necessary finances, and the Governors must seek to live within that limit.' Seventeen months later Whitelaw announced a new licence level of £46 for colour and £15 for monochrome. The BBC had asked for a £50 colour licence, which would have given it an extra £220 million a year, restoring in effect the cuts it had suffered since 1979. The BBC also wanted to develop and redevelop services: running BBC1 in the afternoons, something which it had not done since 1974; extending BBC2 until 1.00 a.m. Monday to Friday.

A new royal charter was granted in 1981 extending the life of the BBC until 1996 and guaranteeing its independence. The licence fee increase, which was to last three years, had provided a certain short-term security allowing for a modicum of medium-term planning. By September 1983 the opening shots could be heard of the new campaign for a licence increase. Alasdair Milne, the Director-General, in a speech to the Institute of Cost and Management Accountants spoke of how low the licence fee was compared with most other European countries, of how the BBC was making great efforts to raise monies through sales of programmes by BBC Enterprises, and crucially of how cost-effective the BBC was when compared to ITV: 'The crude annual cost per hour for ITV was £39,813 compared with a figure for BBC television of £29,614. So ITV cost 34% more.' He admitted that the licence fee, as a method of funding the BBC, produced inequities, one of which was that it fell heavily on old age pensioners. In mitigation, he argued, old people tended to watch more TV than young people and their pensions had increased over the period at a greater rate than the licence fee.

In February 1984 stories began to circulate in the press, quoting 'ministerial sources', attacking the declining standards of the BBC in general and in particular its showing of the mini-series from the USA *The Thorn Birds*. That source was the then junior Minister at the Home Office with responsibility

---

[19] *The Times*, 24 Nov. 1979.

for broadcasting, Douglas Hurd. It was a mixture of the amusing and frightening to the supporters of the BBC to learn that Hurd had not himself seen the programme but had been informed by his wife about its general shallowness, a conclusion she seems to have arrived at on the basis of viewing one episode. Whitelaw, stout defender of the BBC, was no longer at the Home Office and had been replaced by a stout defender of Thatcherite policies, Leon Brittan. Not many people could imagine him banging the table in Cabinet to defend the interests of the BBC or to express the eternal truths of public service. The BBC pointed out that *The Thorn Birds* had been very popular, reaching over 15 million people. There were few signs that such arguments were getting through to the government, most of whose members never watched television anyway.

The year 1984 was perhaps most notable as the year in which voices were raised saying that the time had come to rethink the way in which the BBC was financed and organized. The radical atmosphere spawned by the Conservative government of Mrs Thatcher had finally and seriously spilled over into a discussion about the future of the BBC, and therefore of public service broadcasting. There were three strands to this: that the BBC should take advertising; that it should be funded through subscriptions; and that it should be broken up into its constituent parts.

In April 1983 an article in *The Times* posed what seemed then to be the heretical question of 'do we really need the BBC?' A former Treasury official, Howard Davies, noted that the 'case for dismemberment or even abolition of the BBC is gaining ground among the Prime Minister's advisers'. He added: 'It seems that if Mrs. Thatcher has a second term there will be a radical reappraisal of public service broadcasting. The present structure—conceived in an era of optimistic collectivism—is creaking, expensive and out of touch with its taxpayer viewers.' Whatever the weaknesses of his analysis Davies was perfectly correct in his view that any electoral success for the Thatcher government would inevitably be followed by pressure on the BBC.

The Adam Smith Institute in a monograph published in 1984, *Communications Policy*, urged the government to privatize large, potentially profitable sections of the BBC, leaving behind a rump of worthy public service programme departments funded by a variety of different sources.

In January 1984 David Elstein, then a television current affairs producer, and subsequently a senior executive with a number of commercial TV companies, suggested that the solution to the increasing difficulties of the licence fee was to replace it by a subscription service, supplemented by advertising and sponsorship: 'Immediately the BBC would gain control of its own finances, by setting its own subscription level. Governments would no longer be held responsible for unpopular licence increases. Carrickmore syndrome would disappear. Non-viewers of BBC television would no longer have to pay for a service they do not use. The BBC would become truly answerable to its audience.'[20]

This idea that the BBC only receive payments from those who use it is analogous to electricity, gas, and the telephone; if you wish to have it you pay according to your usage. The immediate advantage would be that this would overcome the unfair system of the same tax—the licence—being charged to the Queen watching her television in Buckingham Palace and to Queenie Malone living alone in Buckingham Palace Villas on the limited income of a pension. The disadvantage is that while utilities like electricity, gas, and the telephone are deemed essential to all intents and purposes, BBC television is not. What was being proposed was to many a recipe for the total destruction of public service broadcasting, since funding from the licence fee and creativity of programme-making within the BBC were inextricably linked, the former a necessary precondition for the latter.

A call for the BBC to use advertising revenue is nothing new, and has been contemplated in some shape or form throughout its history. Indeed it is mostly forgotten that even John Reith allowed for some such possibility. In 1984 the issue was raised with particular vigour by, among others, Rodney Harris of the advertising agency D'Arcy MacManus Masius in an article in *Marketing Week*.[21] He suggested that by pegging the licence fee, and allowing the BBC to carry a small amount of advertising, say 15 seconds per hour in 1985, rising slowly each year, its revenue could be kept healthy without damaging its capacity to make quality television.

At the beginning of December 1984 the BBC officially submitted a claim for an increase in the licence fee to £65 for colour, and £18 for monochrome. Almost immediately Mrs Thatcher was letting it be known through selective press briefings that a figure of £55 was more likely to be approved, that she thought the licence was increasingly becoming an additional levy on the population, and that the Corporation might have to consider taking advertising. In reply to a question in the House of Commons she said that a 'number of people will . . . wonder why the BBC has to take on so many new programmes when their needs could be fulfilled by other programmes'. She had in mind the BBC's development of breakfast television and its continued expansion of the local radio network. Suddenly the papers were full of headlines such as 'Thatcher Enthusiastic about BBC Advertising'.

Much of the pressure for change was coming from Conservative backbenchers motivated by a powerful, if mainly ignorant, desire to see off the BBC, that most visible symbol of a public culture which was the antithesis of their beloved Thatcherism's commitment to private being. In *The Times* of 27 November 1984 the Conservative MP Tom Hooson wrote: 'If one cuts through

[20] *Television Today*, 26 Jan. 1984.   [21] *Marketing Week*, 28 Sept. 1984.

the BBC's idealised view of itself, what actually exists is a badly managed, over-staffed and over-extended empire.' Robert Jones, another Conservative MP, in a debate in the House of Commons on 19 December 1984 described the proposed increase to £65 as a 'whopping increase for anyone who is living on a restricted budget due to a fixed income'. He added that with a declining share of the audience due to competition there 'are bound to be questions about the legitimacy of the base for a compulsory tax, such as the BBC licence fee'. Another Tory, Michael Forsyth, argued that the 'time had come to think about radical action in terms of commercialising the BBC. . . . Auntie is in desperate need of surgery. BBC1, BBC2 and breakfast TV could be hived off as a separate company. The Board of Governors of the BBC should be turned into a sort of IBA. . . . That entity could then be funded entirely by advertising without any difficulty.'[22]

Thatcherism provided the intellectual framework, the campaign of Rodney Harris and company their rhetoric, and the BBC, through its application for a £65 licence, their excuse. Piers Merchant, Tory MP for Newcastle Central, summed up their views: 'By asking for a huge licence increase this year, the BBC is happily opening the door to a complete review of its financial base and its structure.'[23]

On 15 January 1985 the House of Commons was given a formal opportunity to say what it thought about the BBC taking advertising in a ten-minute rule bill proposed by Joe Ashton, a Labour MP. Ashton argued that the BBC's proposal to increase the licence fee to £65 a year would bear very heavily on the poorer section of the community who could not afford it. The bill was defeated on a free vote by 159 to 118.

The Ashton bill provided the peg for a sharp and sustained intellectual attack on the BBC. *The Times*, owned by Rupert Murdoch, whose own satellite television plans would to a considerable extent depend upon the demise of public service broadcasting, on 14 January 1985 launched the first of three consecutive editorials asking 'Whither the BBC?' The paper was asking such fundamental questions as: what is public service broadcasting and is the BBC version the only one? This searching inquiry did not seem to prevent the paper from concluding that the BBC 'should not survive this Parliament at its present size, in its present form and with its present terms of reference intact'.

In the following day's leading article the paper argued that the BBC was wrong to assert that public service values could and should be provided through the whole of its output and that arguments about the effects of advertising were no more than self-serving statements by broadcasters. It also began to hint that if there were financial pressures then it should reduce its commitment to those areas where commercial companies could provide, such

---

[22] Hansard, col. 485, 19 Dec. 1984.   [23] Ibid.

as entertainment, and emphasize those which would not be provided by such bodies, such as news and current affairs. The radical surgery was taken even further in the third leader in the series: 'The Government ... should consider quickly the establishment of a new broadcasting commission to auction franchises that are currently operated by the BBC. These franchises could form one or more than one of the services that the Corporation currently controls. Public service criteria would be constructed and strictly enjoined upon the franchise holders, all of whom would be allowed to take advertising under as little regulation as the commission thought appropriate to the smooth establishment of the new arrangements.' The BBC would be left to run a news and current affairs service.

The heart of the BBC's case remained that it provided unmatched value, a range of programmes that served a multiplicity of interests, that its whole history was one of providing both serious and popular programming, and that while the commercial system could occasionally produce truly excellent programmes it could not match the range and depth of excellence which the BBC constantly served up. In *The Times* the BBC's Director-General, Alasdair Milne, argued:

The basic premise of public service broadcasting, as I understand it, is this: if you address yourself to the nation as a whole, you must appeal to the nation as a whole— in all its diversity. All of us have amazing varieties of tastes, interests and curiosities. Each one of us belongs, at one and the same time, to majorities and minorities. What public service broadcasting must constantly seek to do is to provide enough satisfaction in the belief that allegiance to taste and interest is never certain, is constantly changing and that therefore you must offer the widest variety of programming.[24]

Milne's was a powerful, well argued, and basically simple case: no other conceivable arrangements for broadcasting could come anywhere near in range and quality to those services provided at a cost of 18p a day. This was however a time when the BBC, while putting its case for a £65 licence with some force, had an uncanny knack of shooting itself in the foot, exemplified by a small but revealing incident. In something of a show-biz commando raid, the commercial company Thames Television slipped in and bought the rights to the forthcoming series of *Dallas*. This was a bit like the BBC stealing ITV's long-running domestic soap opera *Coronation Street*. When the news of this broke the BBC was running the current series of *Dallas* but on the orders of the BBC's Director of Programmes, Michael Grade, the series was pulled from the schedule even though it had not completed its full run. The series, the BBC announced, would continue its run in the autumn. Uproar as distraught and furious fans besieged the BBC. Politicians asked questions about what

[24] *The Times*, 26 Feb. 1985.

looked to all like a petulant gesture by Grade with no concern for the feeling of the audience.

Such incidents fed the eagerness of Murdoch's various News International papers, *The Times*, the *Sunday Times*, and the tabloids the *Sun* and the *News of the World*, to maintain a crude but not ineffective offensive against the BBC. Fleet Holdings' *Express* papers and Associated's *Mail* also leapt on any story which might allow them to attack the BBC.

On 1 February 1985 the BBC sent to the Home Secretary the report of the inquiries into its efficiency by the firm of accountants Peat Marwick Mitchell (PMM), and simultaneously stepped up its campaign for a £65 licence. In a speech to the Parliamentary Press Gallery Alasdair Milne spoke of the licence as the 'best bargain in Britain'. He and the Chairman of the BBC, Stuart Young, took part in radio programmes, television interviews, press interviews, all the while explaining the importance of the licence increase they were seeking.

The problem remained that the BBC, almost inevitably, was out of step with the government and its supporters and that no matter what the objective merits of its value-for-money case, an increase in the licence fee remained unnerving to politicians, especially when those politicians had, as David Watt put it, 'a visceral objection to the BBC as the perfect embodiment of the old establishment, the paternalist expression of traditional middle-of-the-road consensus. Thatcherism and the Prime Minister herself being an iconoclastic reaction against just these things are naturally hostile to the BBC; they have also helped to create a polarized political and cultural climate in which Reithian aspirations find it hard to survive.'[25]

The first real indication of what the Government was intending to do with the BBC appeared in a piece in the *Observer* by Adam Raphael: 'An independent top-level inquiry into future financing of the BBC—investigating the merits of new sources of revenue, from advertising to sponsorship—is to be announced shortly by the Government.'[26] He also predicted an 8 per cent increase in the licence fee, taking it to £50. What was certainly clear was that it was Mrs Thatcher, and not just the Home Secretary, who was making the key decisions and that the inquiry was the price she was determined to extract from the BBC for any kind of increase.

On 27 March 1985 the Home Secretary announced a new colour licence fee of £58, and £18 for black and white, to last initially for three years. He announced also the setting up of a small committee under Professor Alan Peacock, an economist at Heriot Watt University, to look into the possibility and desirability of financing the BBC wholly or partly from other sources, particularly from advertising. The other members of the Committee announced shortly after were the economist Sam Brittan; former journalist, broadcaster,

---

[25] *The Times*, 22 Feb. 1985.   [26] *Observer*, 3 Mar. 1985.

and latter-day researcher Alastair Hetherington; philosopher Lord Quinton; businessman Sir Peter Reynolds; accountant Jeremy Hardie; and broadcaster Judith Chalmers.

The official statement from the Home Office said that it recognized the BBC's desire to improve and enhance its services in various ways but that 'there was a limit to what licence payers could reasonably be expected to afford'.[27] It also called on the BBC to 'achieve greater productivity than it had done in the past and had so far planned for the future; and that there was scope for the BBC to achieve greater efficiency through improved management procedures and strengthened management attitudes.'

The terms of reference of the Peacock inquiry were:

(i) to assess the effects of the introduction of advertising or sponsorship on the BBC's Home Services, either as an alternative or a supplement to the income now received through the licence fee, including

(ii) to identify a range of options for the introduction, in varying amounts and on different conditions, of advertising or sponsorship on some or all of the BBC's Home Services, with an assessment of the advantages and disadvantages of each option;

(iii) to consider any proposals for securing income from the consumer other than through the licence fee.

The immediate implication for the BBC was chilling in that for the first time the possibility of advertising was to be considered as a serious option. More practically the £58 fee meant a shortfall of £65 million over three years even if all plans for expansion and new development were jettisoned. Milne, however, was unbowed, arguing that there was insufficient advertising to go round, that the effects on ITV and other media would be disastrous, and that the BBC refused to become a rump broadcaster of worthy intellectual material and would sustain its commitment to popular broadcasting and an even split of the audience with ITV. He was also quick to point out that some of the opposition to the BBC was crudely self-interested. Fleet Holdings, owners of the *Express*, wanted the BBC out of breakfast television because of its massive investment in TV-AM. Murdoch wanted the BBC out of satellite broadcasting because of his ambitions there. Milne also saw a mood in certain circles to break up the BBC solely because it was big, powerful, and public.[28]

Robert Kilroy Silk for the Labour Party thought that Peacock was the wrong man to be leading the inquiry because his free-market views would lead him almost inevitably to favour advertising on the BBC. 'The introduction of advertising not only would lead to the lowering of standards in the BBC and independent television companies and to more demands for even greater

---

[27] Home Office press release, 27 Mar. 1985.   [28] *Financial Times*, 6 Apr. 1985.

advertising but would damage irreparably the ITV companies, commercial radio and local newspapers.'[29]

The *Report of the Committee on Financing the BBC*, the Peacock Committee, was published in July 1986. On the central issue which the Committee had been asked to address of whether the BBC should be made to take advertising the Committee was quite clear: 'BBC television should not be obliged to finance its operations by advertising while the present organisation and regulation of broadcasting remain in being.' They added that the fee 'should be indexed on an annual basis to the general rate of inflation'. The majority of the Committee favoured the privatization of BBC Radios 1 and 2 and local radio 'in whole or in part'. On the issue of television advertising it might have first appeared that the BBC had been reprieved, though a closer reading would show that underlying the intellectual basis of the Report was a commitment to 'consumer sovereignty'. At the end of the Report they said, 'If we had to summarise our conclusion by one slogan . . . it would be direct consumer choice rather than continuation of the licence fee.'[30] The Committee added: 'the true friend of "public service" programmes will realise that the present system for supporting them is unlikely to last far into the 1990s and that they will require for their future sustenance a combination of moves to a genuine consumer market and some direct support from the public purse.'[31] They added in the next paragraph:

Our own conclusion is that British broadcasting should move towards a sophisticated market system based on consumer sovereignty. That is a system which recognises that viewers and listeners are the best ultimate judges of their own interests, which they can best satisfy if they have the option of purchasing the broadcasting service they require from as many alternative sources of supply as possible. There will always be a need to supplement the direct consumer market by public finance for programmes of a public service kind supported by people in their capacity as citizens and voters but unlikely to be commercially self-supporting in the view of broadcasting entrepreneurs.

It seemed that the BBC had been saved. This was, however, less a case of parole, more a temporary stay of execution, determined by the fact that there was no way in which the selling of advertising on the BBC, that is of delivering blocks of viewing to advertisers, would be defined theoretically as the creation of individual consumer sovereignty. And neither did it seem possible to break the advertising monopoly without seriously damaging the financial viability of ITV. The logic of the argument was, however, quite clear: once the objective infrastructural conditions were present—primarily in the

---

[29] Hansard, col. 355, 17 Apr. 1985.

[30] Home Office, *Report of the Committee on Financing the BBC*, Cmnd. 9824 (London: HMSO, 1986) (Peacock Report), para. 711.

[31] Ibid., para. 591.

shape of some form of advanced cable network—the sentence could finally be carried out.

One immediate and obvious consequence of the Report was that on 4 January 1988 Douglas Hurd, the Home Secretary, announced the linkage of the licence to the retail price index. He also told the House of Commons that the government accepted the Peacock Committee's argument that the BBC should not be made to take advertising and should continue to be funded through the licence fee. The decision was an attempt to balance an increase in the Corporation's revenue periodically and securely with the need to ensure that the Corporation would face a strong incentive to practise efficiency and care in undertaking fresh commitments. The government also began to insist on a greater number of independent productions being purchased by the BBC.

Perhaps, however, the most powerful indications of the ways in which the financial wind was blowing were the appointment of Michael Checkland, an accountant, as Director-General and the rejection by the Governors of the man most people felt to be the living embodiment of public service values, Jeremy Isaacs.

The rise of Checkland to some, indeed many, eyes suggested not the internal imposition of financial change, but an external transformation of organizational character. Co-production, co-financing, implicit and explicit sponsorship, new services, foreign sales, the whole lexicon of commerce invaded the Corporation. Thus was implanted the idea of the importance of searching for more non-licence fee revenue. The sum totals remained relatively low, but what was clear was that commerce as an idea of how to fund the BBC had by the late 1980s become a legitimate and increasingly important part of its financial strategy. Depending on one's larger world view this development could be seen as either a useful source of extra finance with no greater implication for the public service character of the BBC or as the first pungent scent of winter on the wind.

The clues were everywhere. The BBC, for example, announced in February 1990 that it had agreed its first direct sponsorship tie-in via a $1.3 million deal with Lloyds Bank to support *Young Musician of the Year* and that it was also seeking sponsorship for its *Come Dancing* programme. In April 1992 the BBC announced that it was to join with Thames Television, which had lost its franchise for commercial broadcasting in the London area, in creating UK Gold, a satellite service drawing on the enormous archival resources of both organizations. The process of adding a little more commercially oriented money here and there seemed to be irreversible and inevitable as pressure increased on the licence fee. In July 1990 the then Home Secretary, David Waddington, warned the BBC that it must look for new ways to supplement the licence fee and to become more cost-efficient. He added that there was no guarantee that the licence fee would be fixed to the retail price index, implicitly suggesting that the value of the fee might in fact begin to decline. Waddington also pointed the finger at the fact that while commercial television staff had been cut by 15 per cent in the past three years, the BBC had only gone from 30,000 to 27,000. In this relatively slow decline was to lie the next vital stage in the BBC's history.

The Governors, led by the Chairman Marmaduke Hussey, set as they were on greatly paring costs, had run into an unanticipated obstacle: Michael Checkland, the Director-General. Checkland, an accountant, had been appointed in 1987 after Alasdair Milne's sacking. The assumption had been that he would see the BBC as a giant ledger and be amenable to greater fiscal rigidity, with all the consequences which would inevitably flow: a squeeze on spending, more internal financial accountability, and a reduction in staff. In the event Checkland refused to move too quickly or too far on the grounds that to do so would badly damage the creative fabric of the Corporation. The Governors, on whom history will not look kindly, saw in Checkland's deputy, John Birt, someone who was more 'realistic' and 'pragmatic' and thus more likely to wield the axe with the necessary zeal.

What we can see here is the slow process of utterly changing the nature of the BBC. The basic assumption which had taken hold in many minds, including those of the BBC's own Governors, was, as Sir Alan Peacock told the Edinburgh Television Festival in August 1990, that 'Whatever government is in power will be looking at other ways of funding the BBC.' The power of the assumption was in large part determined by a general shift in the minds of the political élite as to how a society should think about broadcasting. In a piece titled 'Reforming the BBC' The Economist argued that the BBC's central problem was economic not political, that costs were increasing faster than revenues. The only options were either to increase earnings or cut costs. It seemed unlikely that there were major new sources of funding available. For example, in the year ending March 1990 BBC Enterprises had sales of £184 million, with a pre-tax profit of £14.3 million. These were hardly impressive figures for an organization whose licence revenues were in the £1.5 billion range. The conclusions, at least to The Economist, were obvious: control costs vigorously and consider radically different sources of revenue, such as subscription.[32]

The problems of the BBC were further exacerbated by a serious decline in ratings. On 23 June 1991 the Sunday Times reported that Michael Checkland had addressed BBC employees on a video link the previous Thursday, offering a pep talk about the future of their jobs. The paper commented, 'If employees thought they detected an uncharacteristic nervousness they may have been right. Reports of plunging ratings and internal feuding could soon be getting more headlines than any of its programmes.'

---

[32] The Economist, 19 Mar. 1991.

Checkland's contract was up for renewal and there were increasing rumours that the Governors wanted to replace him with Birt. As the *Sunday Times* declared, Checkland and Birt, who it was being claimed had become bitter rivals, represent 'different visions of the BBC's future'.

By November the BBC1 rating was down to 32.9 per cent compared to ITV's 43 per cent. The cry was heard that the BBC was spending too little on entertainment and too much on John Birt's first love, news and current affairs. The figures on spending preferences were clear: in the first twenty-three weeks of 1991 ITV had 190 hours of popular drama, the BBC had 80 hours. In that time the BBC had spent £18.2 million on new drama, ITV £80 million. The perception was growing that under Birt's influence the BBC was abandoning popular television and moving up-market. Even here, however, the news was gloomy since by May 1992 two ITV current affairs programmes, *World in Action* and *This Week*, were getting a larger combined audience than the BBC's five weekly current affairs programmes combined.

The Governors' solution to these dilemmas was to announce that Michael Checkland's contract would be extended for eighteen months after which time John Birt would become Director-General. It was widely and correctly interpreted as a decision of fairly considerable idiocy. Again, however, it reflected the increasing desperation of the BBC. In November 1991 reports began to appear in the press that the Corporation, in the face of much tighter financial conditions, would shed 8,000 jobs, close various facilities, and privatize all kinds of activities. All these were to prove to be accurate predictions.

In the early winter of 1993 the government announced an extension of the licence fee until 1996, the date of the charter renewal. The BBC's fate was yet to be announced. It was impossible, however, to avoid the sense that times were perilous for the world's most famous broadcaster. The issue of money was substantively important but also clearly symbolic. As were other suggestions that floated threateningly through the ether. In his 1990 Edinburgh speech Peacock had suggested that the Governors be abolished; a thought which given their recent performance held some attraction. In November 1992 Peter Brooke, the Heritage Secretary, spoke of the need to establish a dialogue between broadcasters and the audience. The Government, he said, had 'sought to increase diversity and choice in broadcasting and to strengthen the role of audiences in determining which programmes and services are provided. We need to think more about the concept of broadcasting as a joint enterprise between broadcasters and audiences'.

It had thus become quite clear that the ever more prominent proposals about the BBC's future were no mere tinkering. Should the licence fee be diminished or abolished, should the Governors be abolished, then what would have been removed would be the two principal pillars on which the creative and constitutional independence of the BBC had rested. Into the vacuum so created would indeed flow that closer link between the broadcaster and the audience of which Brooke spoke. In such circumstances one would see the triumph of a consumerist, market ethos and the utter demise of the principles of public service broadcasting.

Much that was to happen under Birt was dictated by the brute reality of governmental edict. Thus was the BBC obliged to take a quarter of its programmes from independent companies, necessitating a reduction in its in-house resource and programme base. Thus was the licence fee indexed and, in effect, cut. Thus did the changes in ITV and Channel Four crank up the zealotry of competition. And thus, anyhow, was the *Zeitgeist* of Thatcherite and post-Thatcherite Britain all about reform, cost-cutting, and efficiency. Birt was to observe in 1993 that if the BBC had not changed itself 'the job would have been done for us'.[33]

Birt's best-known and most controversial initiative, Producer Choice, was in effect the establishment of an internal market. Rhetorically its intent was 'to ensure that as much money as possible is channelled towards the most creative ends, to the people who actually make the programmes'.[34] The fiscal rationale was that it allowed the BBC to cost all of its activities and thus root out its inefficiencies and thus save money. Opponents pointed to the appalling bureaucracy that was a consequence of costing everything from light bulbs to major drama.

Inevitably the intentions of the government were, as Birt took over, vague and threatening. In the summer of 1993 the Department of National Heritage received a Touche Ross report presenting options for the licence fee. One such was its reduction in relation to any saving that Producer Choice made. In the first months of his Director-Generalship Birt was assailed for his management style, cold aloofness, and personal ethics. It was however obvious to him and others that the only thing that really mattered was how the government would react to his changes in operating and financial procedures. And within that, the only thing that mattered was the fate of the licence fee. Birt's strategy was to persuade the government that because the BBC was putting its own house in order the licence fee should be protected. So, for example, the BBC agreed in November 1993 to budget costs of around 5 per cent a year to reduce its borrowing to zero by 1996. The net result within the Corporation was uproar and hostility at the implications and harshness of the new fiscal stringency.

Even among Birt supporters there was by 1995 a concern about the amount of bureaucracy which had been created and a fear that money was haemorrhaging out of the Corporation because of the increasing use of cheaper independent producers and production facilities. The real fear was that the BBC, a public *service*, was increasingly being treated as if it were simply another

---

[33] John Birt, 'The BBC', Fleming Memorial Lecture, 30 Mar. 1993.   [34] Ibid.

business. On 10 March 1995 even the then Foreign Secretary, Douglas Hurd, observed in a speech in Birmingham that 'Competition and market testing are important, but they are not ends in themselves. The BBC and the Civil Service are ultimately about public service . . . Service to other, service to the community, public service—different branches of the same tree'.[35]

When the government published its White Paper on the future of the BBC on 7 July 1994 the headlines told their own story: 'How Birt Persuaded the Conservatives to Call off the Dogs' was *The Times*'s headline; *Today* had 'The Man Who Saved the BBC's Licence'; 'Birt's BBC is Given its Reward' said the *Independent*; and the *Guardian* pointed to 'The Birting of the BBC'.

The White Paper had declared that the BBC would be granted a new royal charter and agreement to run for ten years from 1997; the licence fee (which stood at £84.50) would remain index linked and provide the BBC's main income, but would be reviewed before 2001; the BBC would be encouraged to develop its commercial activities, particularly in developing international TV services in co-operation with private sector partners, so that it emerged as a fully fledged global multi-media enterprise.

The modest hindsight which one can now have about the government's proposals makes it hard to see why the document was regarded as such a triumph for Birt. Of course it could be, and was, argued that, compared to threats which had been heard from the Conservative Party in the 1980s, this was indeed a remarkable turnaround.

The logic of this is that the sole or primary argument that proved persuasive was Birt's reforms. It seems likely that while those internal changes were a factor, of far greater significance were the changed political circumstances of the Conservative government. For it to have set about privatizing the BBC or breaking it up, given the likely public reaction, would have been an act almost sado-masochistic in character.

At best the White Paper was a holding operation, particularly in relation to the licence fee. The proposals to shape the BBC into a globally oriented multi-media corporation made some sense if one thought of the revenue possibilities for Britain. As an idea it is inevitably fatal to the maintenance of the public service character of the organization. Whether the BBC is seriously able to compete globally with the likes of Rupert Murdoch of News Corporation and John Malone of TCI is debatable. That it would be able to do so and retain a public service remit is ludicrous. The relationship between the government and the BBC increasingly has the feel of a marriage which is dead but in which the partners cannot quite steel themselves for the divorce court.

Nevertheless, by the 1990s, there was still much that was remarkable about the BBC, particularly in the sheer range of its services. There were notable

[35] Douglas Hurd, in B. Barnett, 'Choice Cuts', *Broadcast*, 17 Mar. 1995.

successes in drama, both popular and more challenging. So by 1996 Birt, who had demonstrated steely resolve, could claim he had not only won the battle for the BBC but had saved it from its own inclination to ignore political reality and thus lay the basis for its dissolution.

Such a view would however be grotesquely blinkered and short term. The creative traditions which continued to provide the excellence were the legacy of pre-Birtian times, the fruits of an ethos which fed off the work and philosophies of earlier generations of programme-makers and executives. What was beginning to go, however, was something of the edge, the grit, the radicalism which constituted the BBC at its best. Too much programming was now made for, and by, people who 'wear' cellular phones and nod approvingly at the niceties and conservatism of Blairism. It is interesting that in his Fleming Lecture, in a section called 'Pushing Back Boundaries', the example Birt cites is from that age which was allegedly mired in gross inefficiency and bureaucracy, Bleasdale's *Boys from the Blackstuff*.

The point, and this cannot be said too often, is that it matters not what the BBC was or was not doing in mid-decade. What mattered were the objective circumstances within which it was asked to operate, and those were powerful and, in the longer term, destructive. In the BBC's Annual Report in 1993 the Governors say, 'these are early days'. How right they were.

6 Conquerors, Culture, and Communication: The Foundation of Post-war Japanese Broadcasting

Admiral Tojo observed in 1943 that speech had to be used by Japan in its fight with the Allies 'as a bullet'. By 1945 Tojo and his colleagues had run out of both bullets and things to say. The United States, as the dominant member of the Allied powers, had decided to use 'information' in the broadest sense in its re-creation of Japanese society and culture, not as a bullet but more as a mixture of national group therapy, liberal democracy, and what they assumed would be a sublime new experience for the Japanese public. From his remarkable position of total power General Douglas MacArthur, as Supreme Commander Allied Powers (henceforward SCAP), could stand back from Japanese society, focus on the weaknesses and aberrations, dismantle and rebuild the soci[...] infrastructure, and recast the nation. It was within this context that th[...] war public service broadcasting system in Japan was to be establis[...]

The Instrument of Surrender stipulated the complete acce[...] filment of the terms of the Potsdam Proclamation of July [...]

surrender; the carrying out of all SCAP orders; the freeing of all POWs and interned civilians; and acknowledgement by the Emperor that he and his government were subject to the Allied command. Almost simultaneously the Emperor issued a proclamation and imperial rescript to the Japanese people which declared that he and the Japanese government had accepted the surrender terms, and ordered the armed forces to give up their weapons.

The development of occupation policy assumed Japan's incorporation into a post-1945 geopolitical reality which both reflected, and created, United States' strategic interests. It also exemplified the need to fashion this particular, conquered society in ways compatible with the political infrastructure of liberal democratic systems in order both to sustain those strategic interests and to offer evidence of the fundamentally benign nature of the new imperialism.

The work of the Allied powers in Japan, under the influence and forcefulness of MacArthur, was in many ways remarkably liberating. Women, minority groups, trade unionists, liberal democrats were all to benefit from SCAP's decisions. The supreme irony was that, as in Germany, the ability to re-engineer the society, so that its structure of militarism and ultranationalism was changed to one committed not just to the formal practices but also to the values of a liberal democratic parliamentary culture, depended totally on the fact that MacArthur was himself a dictator.

That remoulding of Japanese society necessarily entailed a process of intellectual reconstruction. Ideologies, values, traditions, sentiments, and prejudices had to be destroyed or at least re-engineered as an essential part of SCAP policy. Within that process were Allied ideas about freedom of information and culture, and within those rested the future of broadcasting.

As with any broadcasting culture one has to burrow through different layers of political and cultural experience and expectation. Broadcasting organizations do not exist as islands, any more than other organizations do. They constitute at least one element ⋯ ⋯ kind of social and cultural archipelago.

In general ⋯ ⋯ of Japan before its surrender had been a mixture of ac⋯ ⋯ es, of paradoxes and perplexity. The dominant ⋯ ⋯ on with an insatiable appetite for other people's ⋯ ⋯ sfying it. More informed and objective views ⋯ ⋯ character with her origin, history, environ- ⋯ ⋯ ions'.[1]

⋯ *The Chrysanthemum and the Sword* that both

⋯ e, to the highest degree, both aggressive and ⋯ c, both insolent and polite, rigid and adapt- ⋯ hed around, loyal and treacherous, brave

⋯ e First Year's Planning, Policy Formulation and

and timid, conservative and hospitable to new ways. They are terribly concerned over what other people think of their behavior and they are also overcome by guilt when other people know nothing of their misstep. Their soldiers are disciplined to the hilt but are also insubordinate.[2]

It is not a portrait of simplicity and straightforwardness. Indeed, one might be forgiven for saying that any society contains its complexities and contradictions, its poverty and its violence, and that that is no more than a socialized version of the human condition. It is not, however, every society which is subject to a process of total transformation, and it is therefore important to grasp just what it was that westerners thought they were transforming.

The extraordinary feature of the development of broadcasting policy in immediate post-war Japan is that one can so readily see the formation of the cultural geology. The American policy-making machinery had in fact been split between advocates of a soft peace and a hard peace, between those who believed in ripping apart the whole fabric of Japanese society and those who argued for taking the continuing strengths and merits of Japan and building on them, through such institutions as broadcasting.

Joseph Ballantine, Director of the Office of Far Eastern Affairs, was also a member of a key State Department committee known as the Coordinating Committee, one of a system of committees preparing policy papers for the period of occupation. He later observed that they had wanted:

to encourage those Japanese who in the past had shown progressive pro-Western tendencies, who had been suppressed during the military regime. We wanted to encourage them to come forth and assume leadership. We felt very strongly that the strong forces of example, tutelage, suggestions would be much more effectual in making the Japanese see the inconsistencies and the inadequacies of their traditional order of life, and they would themselves then be willing to make choices in favour of democracy and liberalism.[3]

Eugene Dorman, another influential figure who worked very closely with Ballantine, viewed the programme of the Occupation from the same perspective. Born in Osaka, Japan, in 1890, the son of a missionary of the Episcopal Church, he stayed in Japan until 1903 when he returned to the United States. He later returned and spent many years there as a Japanese specialist in the US diplomatic service. From 1944 until August 1945 he was Chairman of the Far East Subcommittee of SWNCC—the State, War, Navy Coordinating Committee.

He describes pre-war Japan as a graduated society in which the national purpose and objective was formulated at the very top of the social structure

---

[2] Ruth Benedict, *The Chrysanthemum and the Sword* (Boston: Houghton Mifflin Co., 1946), 27.

[3] Joseph Ballantine, Columbia University Oral History Collection, part 3, no. 199, Occupation of Japan Project.

and where the common people had been habituated to conform and support whatever had been enunciated at the top as the national purpose: 'National policies were not the formulation of the hopes and aspirations of the masses, but rather what a small group of people considered in the interests of the nation.'[4]

The fact of cultural and social stratification in Japan—a term used here in the broadest sense to include the sum total of social arrangements, ideas, beliefs, traditions, symbols—was embodied in the person of the Emperor. He embodied through his divinity the totality of Japanese life. The problem which faced the Americans was stark and simple: either to make him into a constitutional monarch stripped of his divinity or to hang him as an accessory to war crimes. Fortunately for him and history, the United States chose the former course. Not, however, without a good deal of debate.

Many within the State Department believed in the retention of the Emperor as head of state as an absolutely essential prerequisite for the successful occupation of Japan. One observed:

Anybody with any knowledge of the Japanese social structure as it had developed over a period of 1,500 years knew that there was nothing that kept the Japanese together as a unit other than the allegiance of every Japanese to the emperor as a living manifestation of the racial continuity of the Japanese people; that he embodied the racial continuity way back to the age of the gods. And that therefore if there were no emperor, the whole social structure would fall apart. And I could see that if the monarchy were disestablished, we would just have a collection of eighty million people; that the Communists were well organized and that it would be no problem at all for them to take over the country.[5]

A detailed view of 'current attitudes on the Emperor institution' was offered in a note in February 1946 from the Office of the United States Political Adviser in Tokyo. The note was intended to feed into the discussion about the future Japanese constitution and observed that

The central feature and foundation of the Japanese emperor system has been the sentimental attachment of the masses of the people for the person of the emperor, whom they regarded as deeply and personally concerned for their welfare and whose task they sought to ease by complying to the best of their ability with the orders issued in his name. Although his lofty and secluded position and association with the distant past surrounded him with an aura of pseudo-divinity involving reverence and awe, respect for his authority and obedience to his will resulted essentially from a very human affection which the people felt for him, and which they believed he felt for them, and relatively little from fear or superstition. This basic attachment remains as strong today as in the past, if not stronger.

---

[4] Joseph Ballantine, Columbia University Oral History Collection, part 3, no. 199, Occupation of Japan Project, 57.

[5] E. Dorman, ibid. 142–3.

It was only in the light of this kind of perspective that President Truman decided that the Emperor should not be executed, despite American public opinion which seemed to favour a more violent end to this deity.

In 1948 Ballantine was asked by George Kennan to advise the State Department 'on how to induce the Japanese to take greater responsibility towards their economic recovery . . . I said, well, you can't give me an easier chore than that. My advice is that you let the first team come back into action—the first team that you have purged. They were able to raise Japan from an insignificant congeries of feudal states into a first-class power in the course of 75 years. They can do it again if you give them a chance.'[6]

Purges were part and parcel of the effort to alter the structure of Japanese society. The purged therefore would inevitably tend to be people who had engaged not in some especially heinous crime but who because of their positions embodied the old structures and ideologies that had provided the lattice-work for militarism and ultranationalism and, thereby, war. From the perspective of a Ballantine or a Dorman occupation policies were now to emasculate, impoverish, and destroy those elements in Japanese society 'which might be counted upon to resist the Communists'.

The purges, then, from which broadcasting was not exempt, were an instrument of wider policy. To many eyes those policies were geared to the reformation of a whole nation through the introduction of such primary values as fairness, social justice, wealth distribution, equality, and so on.

The process was seen by the US military government as one of re-educating the Japanese mind, but doing so by involving the people themselves. A note in July 1945 concludes that

It is recognised that any basic changes in the ideology and thinking of the Japanese cannot be forced upon them from the outside, if such reforms are to have lasting value, but must be acceptable to the Japanese themselves. Consequently, military government will be faced with the extremely difficult task of not simply drawing up a reform programme and insisting on its acceptance but rather of convincing the Japanese that certain basic reforms are desirable and necessary and should be initiated by them.[7]

Inevitably a key to this process of re-education was felt to lie in the mass media. An instruction issued to SCAP on 1 November 1945 from Washington stated:

You will establish such minimum control and censorship of civilian communications including the mail, wireless, radio, telephone, telegraphs and cables, films and press as may be necessary in the interests of military security and the accomplishment of the purposes set forth in the directive. Freedom of thought will be fostered by the dissemination of democratic ideals and principles through all available media of public

---

[6] Ballantine, ibid. 62.   [7] Inter-divisional Area Committee for the Far East, Meeting No. 214.

information. . . . Freedom of religious worship shall be proclaimed promptly by the Japanese Government. To the extent that the security of your military occupation and the attainment of its objectives are not prejudiced you will ensure freedom of opinion, speech, press and assembly.[8]

On 22 September 1945 the United States had issued the key document defining its policy for the Occupation. It was entitled 'United States Initial Post-surrender Policy for Japan' and was the end result of a long, complicated, sometimes confused, often acrimonious debate about what to do with the country once it had been conquered. The 'ultimate objectives' of that Occupation included the proposal that: 'The Japanese people shall be encouraged to develop a desire for individual liberties and respect for fundamental assembly, speech and the press. They shall also be encouraged to form democratic and representative organisations.'

Even prior to the Occupation, at a meeting in the State Department on 17 November 1944 it was 'pointed out that a positive statement to the effect that military government should terminate the dissemination of ideas subversive of the purposes of the United Nations'—which had been accepted as policy—raised the question 'as to how it would be possible to maintain freedom of the press and at the same time suppress subversive ideas'. The implicit answer was that the freedom of the press would in effect apply only to those whose ideas were acceptable to the occupying forces. A certain realism, however, was added when one member of the meeting noted that they should be on their 'guard against thinking that we would be able to do too much in changing and developing the ideas of the Japanese and the Germans through the control of education or media of information'.[9]

There were in effect both negative and positive elements within the general policies of information control; on the one hand the extinguishing of the negativities of militant nationalism, and on the other the pursuit of positive ideals and attitudes which were not just a version of US ideals and attitudes but necessarily supportive of United States geopolitical interests. It was nevertheless recognized that the real buttressing of Allied interests would come through the filling of bellies rather than the filling of minds. At a meeting in Washington of the Far East Commission it was noted that the

average Japanese is certainly not greatly concerned with politics or the outside world at the moment. He is concerned with that basic thing, his stomach, and until he gets through worrying about his stomach and those of his children, he is not going to worry very much about whether his political affiliations are in the middle or on the right or the left.[10]

[8] Basic Initial Post-surrender Directive.
[9] Inter-divisional Area Committee, minutes, 17 Nov. 1944.
[10] Far Eastern Commission, minutes, 20 Mar. 1946.

From the point of view of the role and use of information, the most significant document was that which directed the establishment, in 1945, of the Civil Information and Education Section (CIE) 'to advise the Supreme Commander on policies relating to public information, education, religion and other sociological problems of Japan'.[11]

The particular activities of CIE were directed towards the elimination of ultranationalism and militarism from the education system, the revision of education curricula to include democratic ideals and principles, the establishment of freedom of worship, opinion, speech, press, and assembly, 'informing the Japanese public of the facts of their defeat, and ascertaining public opinion.'[12] It was also established to 'make recommendations on information programmes, through all media, reaching the Japanese public, to ensure their understanding of all policies and plans for political, economic and social rehabilitation of Japan and Korea'.[13]

These basic notions were ultimately translated into the new Japanese constitution, of which Article 21 declared, 'Freedom of assembly and association as well as speech, press and all other forms of expression are guaranteed. No censorship shall be maintained, nor shall the secrecy of any means of communication be violated.'

The role of CIE and the likely tone of its activities is illustrated by the background of the man appointed by MacArthur to run the Information and Consumer side of the Occupation. General Dyke in his civilian life had been Director of Advertising for the Colgate-Palmolive-Peet Company, and Director of Research of the National Broadcasting Company.

The issues and thinking behind the development of a communications policy for an occupied Japan are made clear in papers by a subcommittee of the State, War, Navy, Coordinating Committee (SWNCC) on 'Control of Media of Public Information and Expression in Japan'.[14] The immediate issue was that Japan had been a highly literate culture with an extensive media structure dominated by the state. Before 1937 there had been over 1,000 daily newspapers with a total circulation of almost 7 million. The principal news agency, Demei, founded in 1936, was a government-sponsored monopoly. Governmental control had taken the form of licensing, withholding of news, confiscation and suspension of publications, fines, and imprisonment. During the war centralized control had lain with the Board of Information. The total number of books and magazines published had, prior to 1941, been greater than in the United States. Publishing firms were licensed by the Home Ministry; books were subject to pre-censorship; and periodicals were reviewed by the police. Before 1941 there were more than 6 million medium wave radio sets, though

---

[11] SCAP General Orders No. 4, 2 Oct. 1945.   [12] Ibid.   [13] Ibid., para. 3 (b).
[14] 'Control of Media of Public Information and Expression in Japan', 20 Jan. 1945.

short wave sets were prohibited. A pre-war publication summarizes the official view of nature and purpose of broadcasting: 'There is no doubt that control of the radio industry in conformity with the national broadcasting policy can be most securely maintained by a monopolised management.' The Allied powers' view of the role of NHK during these years was sharper: 'From its inception in 1926 until VJ Day 1945, the B[roadcasting] C[orporation] of J[apan] served as a propaganda medium for the Japanese warlords.'

The SWNCC planning committee argued that

while it is desirable that military government use, to the greatest extent possible, the media of public information and expression in Japan to achieve its objectives and to prevent the revival of Japanese militarism, it is recognised that any program for the control of public information and expression must be designed so that it can actually be undertaken by military government. It is envisaged, therefore, that military government will utilize Japanese personnel and Japanese organisations as much as possible in achieving or carrying out the programme of control of public information.

The committee then outlined the general objectives of the control and employment by military government of 'media of public information and expression'. In the short term these were to ease the process of occupation. In the longer term, however, the objective was much grander, something which was in effect little short of reconstructing the psyche of the whole nation:

1. To eliminate among the Japanese the influences and doctrines of militarism and aggressive nationalism.
2. To develop a sense of individual political responsibility among the Japanese and the reorientation of their political thinking.
3. To inform the people of Japan of the ideals, concepts and principles of the United Nations as expressed in the Charter of the United Nations; and to encourage them in the development of an international as opposed to a national outlook.
4. To encourage the development of Japanese organisations and policies in the information field which will, in the post-occupation period, promote freedom of information and expression, develop a sense of responsibility for the proper use of these freedoms and increase popular participation in the discussion and decision of public issues.[15]

The objects to be pursued also included recognition of a range of key principles:

That men and nations owe obligations to each other. That the dignity and integrity of the individual must be respected by society and other individuals; and that the individual is not merely a tool of the state. . . . That citizens bear their share of responsibility for public policy. . . . That free communication between individuals, groups and nations is a necessary condition for the dissemination of truth and for national

---

[15] 'Control of Media of Public Information and Expression in Japan', 20 Jan. 1945.

and international understanding. . . . To create an understanding among the Japanese people that the failure to recognize these principles facilitated the development of aggressive nationalism and contributed to Japan's disaster.[16]

Within this general ideological background, the road to the constitutional formulation of broadcasting policy was dotted with a whole series of directives issued by MacArthur's headquarters. In September 1945 SCAP issued to the Japanese government a 'Memorandum Concerning Freedom of Speech'. The government was instructed 'to prevent dissemination of news, through newspapers, radio broadcasting or other means of publication, which fails to adhere to the truth or which disturbs public tranquillity. The Supreme Commander for the Allied Powers has decreed that there shall be an absolute minimum of restrictions upon freedom of speech.' The memorandum, however, declared certain subjects taboo, such as troop movements and 'false or destructive criticism of the Allied Powers and rumours'. Radio broadcasts 'for the time being' would be 'primarily of a news, musical and entertainment nature. News, commentation [*sic*] and informational broadcasts will be limited to those originating at Radio Tokyo studios. The Supreme Commander will suspend any publication or radio station which publishes information that fails to adhere to the truth or disturbs public tranquillity.'[17]

On 24 September 1945 SCAP issued a

Memorandum Concerning Disassociation of Press from Government: further to encourage liberal tendencies in Japan and establish free access to the news sources of the world, steps will be taken by the Japanese Government forthwith to eliminate government-created barriers to dissemination of news and to remove itself from direct or indirect control of newspapers and news agencies.

On 27 September 1945 came a memo 'Concerning Further Steps toward Freedom of Press and Speech'. It noted:

The Japanese government forthwith will render inoperative the procedures for enforcement of peace-time and war-time restrictions on freedom of the press and freedom of communications. . . . A report will be submitted to the Supreme Commander on the first and the 16th day of each month describing in detail the progressive steps taken by the Japanese Government to comply with this order and the orders of 10 September and 24 September.

On 4 October SCAP issued a memorandum 'Concerning Removal of Restrictions on Political, Civil and Religious Liberties'. This called upon the Japanese government to remove anything which sustained 'restrictions on freedom of thought, of religion, of assembly and of speech, including the unrestricted discussion of the Emperor, the Imperial Institution and the Imperial Japanese Government'.

[16] Ibid.   [17] SCAP, 'Memorandum Concerning Freedom of Speech', 22 Sept. 1945.

The Occupation was in effect to be a colossal civics lesson, achieved through what the Committee designated as the 'Control Programme'. Extremely tight controls of information of any kind were to be imposed during the immediate post-surrender 'emergency period', during which time Japanese would be sought out 'to whom may be intrusted [*sic*] the re-establishment of Japanese information services under military government supervision'.

A whole series of conditions were thus laid down by the SWNCC for each of the media concerned, within the general parameters of what one might call controlled licence or national parole. Running through each was the clear desire to develop the liberal democratic notion of free expression. For example, for the publication of magazines, books, and pamphlets it was argued: 'In order to permit the development of self expression and a free public opinion, Japanese publications should not be required to serve as channels for military government information.' What would be closed off, of course, were any publications promoting militaristic or nationalist philosophy. For radio broadcasting the SWNCC paper stipulated immediate military control, gradually being replaced by more extensive Japanese involvement. The paper added:

It is impossible at this time to state whether such eventual licensing might permit monopoly broadcasting. This question should be examined in the light of the then existing conditions taking into account our general policies with respect to information monopolies, the practice in other countries, the desires of the Japanese and, in particular, whether monopoly broadcasting could be developed in Japan along non-political lines as in England.

It was from within this context that NHK was to be created.

7 The Making of an Institution: The Rebirth of NHK

Broadcasting in the mind of the conquerors was to be both a consequence, and sustainer, of the new liberal democratic culture. The creation of the conditions under which radio broadcasting could assume its role in the programme of re-education and democratization required the removal of government controls, the improvement of efficiency, and the development of administrative machinery that would be independent, stable, confident, and responsible, and strong enough to prevent any attempt to re-establish government domination. To achieve these ends, the Occupation established three specific objectives: (1) to require establishment of a sound regulatory, management, and financial structure, (2) to stimulate production for reconditioning of stations, wire lines, and home receivers, and (3) when and if it became practicable, to permit competition.[1]

In a memorandum of 11 December 1945 SCAP outlined the plans for the reorganization of the NHK. MacArthur established 'an institution of public service', an advisory committee of fifteen to twenty Japanese citizens of both sexes from all parts of Japan 'to advise the President of the Broadcasting Corporation of Japan. This committee will represent the professional, business, educational, cultural, religious, labour and farming elements of national life.'

[1] Internal report, Civil Information and Education Section (CIE), 'Radio Japan' (1947), 16.

The immediate task of the Committee was to make three nominations for the office of the President of the NHK, the final decision lying with SCAP. The Committee would then advise the President and Board of Directors of NHK

on general policy matters. The committee will consider among other things, a code of ethics for broadcasting to be submitted through the Corporation and the Board of Communications to this headquarters, and reorganisation of the Broadcasting Corporation of Japan to allow full participation by the Japanese public in ownership of the Corporation.[2]

The character of Japanese broadcasting was put somewhat more prosaically by General Dyke, the head of Information and Education for SCAP. He told a meeting of the Far Eastern Commission held in Washington in 1946 of the setting up of the Advisory Committee and its relationship to the President of JBC. He added:

the whole thing has got to be reorganised. It is shot full, as everything in Japan, of bureaucracy and Nellie's sister and cousin are running the music department only for the reason they are Nellie's sister or cousin. There are some smart people there. We plan to bring over a mission sometime in the middle of the summer representing radio experts, in the same manner as we have done on education. The future of Radio in Japan is wide open, and thus is a good question for this Board. What is best for Japan in radio? Shall it have, let us say, the American system which is completely commercial? Shall it have its present system, which is, let us say, similar to the type of thing you have in Great Britain, BBC, which is supported by a tax on subs[cribers]? Shall we have the Australian system where you have a combination of both, ABC and also commercial radio, or what? At the moment the answer is obviously this: we will keep it the way it is as long as it best suits the needs of the occupation, and we will continue to explore.[3]

At a meeting of the Allied Council for Japan (ACJ) held in Tokyo on 11 December 1946, the issue of the kind of broadcasting organizations which Japan should have was raised. W. MacMahon Ball, representing the UK, Australia, New Zealand, and India, observed:

I think the particular way in which the radio stations in Japan are owned and operated is something that should ultimately be determined by the Japanese people themselves . . . there is considerable variation among the Western Democracies in the way these things are done. In the United Kingdom there is a single monopoly, a public corporation, the BBC, which operates and owns broadcasting. I understand that in the United States radio stations are owned and operated by private companies. In Australia, we have tried to make the best of both worlds. We have an Australian Broadcasting Commission, which is modelled largely on the British Broadcasting Commission [sic], but alongside of that, we have a number of commercial broadcasting stations. I feel

---

[2] SCAP, memo, 11 Dec. 1945.   [3] Far Eastern Commission, minutes, 20 Mar. 1946.

therefore that it would be very difficult indeed for us to say that one particular type of ownership of operation was more democratic than any other type. Nevertheless, at the present time, it does seem very important that there should be Allied control of the material broadcast in Japan; and since it is more economical and more efficient to exercise control at one point rather than at a number of points, over one organisation instead of over several organisations, I think it would be inopportune at the present time to encourage or approve the establishment of independent commercial broadcasting companies in Japan.

The Soviet representative, Lieutenant-General Derevyanko, responded by raising the question of the forms of ownership, organization, and management of NHK. The Chairman, George Atcheson, who was deputizing for MacArthur, suggested that the answer was contained in a study which had stated: 'Radio broadcasting in Japan is a monopoly of the JBC, a non-profit juridical body under the supervision of the Communications Ministry.'[4] Derevyanko wanted to know to what extent and in what manner governmental control of broadcasting in Japan was being realized and what 'specifically has been done in the course of this year to democratise Japanese broadcasting?' Having received no answers which satisfied him, two meetings later Derevyanko returned to the subject, only to say, not surprisingly, 'I have come to the conclusion that at present it is not expedient to recommend the creation of private broadcasting in Japan; that under present conditions it is more expedient to have State exploitation of radio stations in Japan, under the supervision of the Communications ministry.' He did so in order to ensure that the Occupation retained control of broadcasting and because

the introduction of private broadcasting would lead to the concentration of broadcasting in the hands of the most powerful financial, industrial companies, and would deprive new democratic organisations of Japan which do not have sufficient means for using broadcasting in the interest of furthering democratisation of Japan.[5]

The membership of the Radio Advisory Committee (RAC) is an interesting illustration of the kinds of figures and personalities on whom SCAP was relying to build the new Japan. In January 1946 Shigeyoshi Matsumae, Minister of Communications, announced the appointments to the Advisory Committee from the SCAP-approved list of candidates, including businessmen, an agriculturalist, a scientist, academics, publishers, lawyers, a housewife, and two young people.

At its first meeting General Dyke and other members of SCAP explained to the members the purposes of the Committee. It was being asked to make recommendations about the future of radio in Japan; draft a code of broadcasting ethics, nominate to SCAP the names and brief histories of three

[4] Minutes of meeting, ACJ, 11 Dec. 1945.   [5] ACJ, minutes, 8 Jan. 1947.

candidates for the office of President of NHK; similarly nominate an executive committee of from three to five members; make recommendations about the reorganization of NHK, including screening out 'all personnel not qualified by reason of personal habits, training, experience, or prior association with militaristic or non-democratic groups and provide for the hiring of capable personnel', and 'insure well-balanced programmes, which will promote the democratisation of Japan'. The existing Board of Directors of NHK was to play no part in the nominations since, as one note put it, 'it [the board] was not considered fit to play any important part in a democratic reorganisation of radio because of its war record as a pawn of the militarists'.[6]

The RAC came up with the necessary three names for president in February 1946: Iwasaburo Takano, a 76-year-old lawyer; Kinnosuko Ogura, a 63-year-old scientist; and Michihara Tajima, a 62-year-old banker. They chose Dr Kinnosuko Ogura because of his 'iron will, creative power, cultural refinement and cool scientific mind'. It was also believed that he would 'meet the least opposition from reactionary elements'.[7] Ogura's tenure was extremely short and he was replaced in April by Iwasaburo Takano, President of the Ohara Institute of Social Problems. There was opposition to Takano but SCAP made it clear that they were perfectly happy with his appointment and that if the Board of Directors disapproved they would be sacked 'on the premiss that members are not qualified by investment in the corporation or high qualities of democratic leadership to represent the Japanese people'.[8]

Not everyone was happy with the character of the members of the RAC— also known as the 'Broadcasting Advisory Board'. A senior figure inside military public affairs said of the members:

especially evident is the fact that this body was appointed by the Japanese Ministry of Communications and approved by GHQ. Could it be possible that these omnipotent 'control agencies,' CIE and CCS, approved this collection of ideological mugwumps for the establishment of an 'advisory body' to a free and democratic broadcast channel of public information? I would be willing to bet even money that G2 or its Civil Intelligence arm was not consulted . . . Note especially that Hijikata Yoshi, our old Moscow-trained buddy in things theatrical in Japan, holds a membership card. . . . Strongly recommend that this information be brought to the attention of G2 for action; the original memo was rightfully designed to terminate control by instrumentalities of the Japanese government, but it is apparent that an advisory body has been established which could conceivably effect special-interest group ideological control.[9]

On 16 October 1947 the Civil Communications Section of SCAP convened a meeting to outline its views about the development of legislation on the

---

[6] 'Memo: Radio, Research and Information', 26 Jan. 1946.   [7] CIE Radio, memo, 12 Mar. 1946.
[8] CIE Radio, memo, 13 Apr. 1946.
[9] Memo, Public Affairs Division, SCAP: Ch./PPB, 14 Apr. 1947.

future of Japanese broadcasting. In attendance were representatives of the Japanese Ministry of Communications, the NHK, the CIE Section, and CCS. The SCAP view was that the law 'should provide a sound basis for the development of all techniques of broadcasting, meaning standard broadcasting, international broadcasting, frequency modulation, television and broadcasting facsimile'.[10] SCAP also felt that this basic legislation should reflect a number of very general principles: (1) freedom of broadcasting, (2) impartiality, (3) fulfilment of public service responsibility, (4) observance of technical standards. They were also informed that the basic legislation must establish an organization to regulate all forms of broadcasting.

The organization was to be an 'autonomous organisation', completely separate from other executive branches of the Japanese government:

Whether it is created as an organ reporting to the Diet or not, is not of importance at this particular point, but it must be an autonomous organisation. It must be completely separated from the Ministry of Communications, Ministry of Education, Finance and any other ministry and will not report to any ministry. It is the type of organisation that is not to be dominated by any political party, by any governmental 'clique' or any governmental group, nor is it to be dominated by any private corporation or group or association of individuals.[11]

The organization was to be compared to the Tennessee Valley Authority or the New York Port Authority in America:

an organisation to serve the public, to be controlled, idealistically speaking, by the people of Japan who make known their desires and wishes through their constitutionally and democratically elected government. . . . SCAP suggests that the law provide for the development of privately-owned broadcasting companies in Japan so that when economic conditions permit, there can be developed in Japan competition in broadcasting, that is between private companies themselves and between private companies and this public authority. In other words, the law will permit the development in the future of a system of broadcasting which is comparable to the present Japanese railroad system, namely, both a public authority operation and private operation.[12]

Hence, with the development in the future of two systems of broadcasting, one broadcasting by a public authority and the other private broadcasting, this public authority would necessarily have to consist of two main elements:

The first main element is a supervisory or regulatory group. This supervisory or regulatory group will determine policy in accordance with the terms of the statute and will regulate by licence or otherwise all broadcasting, including the operating group of the public authority and all private broadcasting companies. The second main element in this public authority will be the operating group. This element will actually operate

---

[10] SCAP, note, 22 Oct. 1947.   [11] Ibid.   [12] Ibid.

the broadcast facilities which will be transferred to it, mainly those which are now being operated by the Broadcasting Corporation of Japan.[13]

The basic law, SCAP added, must in very clear and definite language establish the guarantees of independence and, in addition, give special emphasis on the guarantee of programmes prerogatives with no interference from any group, 'clique', or any other small or large body: 'It must be a public service organisation devoted to the welfare of the entire people and no segment of the people, large or small, organised or unorganised, should dictate to it.'[14]

With respect to the matter of finance, SCAP had no objection to capital financing through the governmental sources and operational financing by means of a listeners' fee. Certainly with the competition between the public authority and private enterprise, the authority would have to have the right given to it by statute to enforce listeners' fees from the owners of all radio sets.

It was pointed out that while the various suggestions were very general, in drafting the details care should be taken that each detail supported the basic principles:

For example, it is fundamental that the public broadcasting authority not be dominated by any particular group, either governmental or private. If there are appointed or elected commissioners to the broadcasting authority, such a detail as the length of service of the commissioners would be very important. Their terms would not all expire at the same time so as to permit the appointment of a majority of the commissioners by the party then in power. Also, the length of the terms should be sufficiently long so as to permit continuity and prevent the authority from reflecting the rise and fall of political parties or the influence of various groups.[15]

The Japanese themselves had not been slow in offering their ideas as to how a future broadcasting system should be structured. In fact, by January 1948 the RAC, the Ministry of Communications, the management of NHK, and the labour union at NHK had all offered their own scheme.

It is not surprising, given the highly purposive character of the Occupation, the restoration not just of the fabric of democracy but of the myriad threads of the democratic mind, that much effort was given to thinking through the standards of practice and codes of ethics which were to prevail within broadcasting. Both general and specific standards were identified in the extensive SCAP document.

General Code Policies:

Religion—Freedom of worship should be respected, with no attacks made on race or creed; should be presented by recognised organisations, with emphasis on broad truths and avoiding controversy. Appeals for funds or sale of publications opposed.

---

[13] SCAP, note, 22 Oct. 1947.   [14] Ibid.   [15] Ibid.

Race, Creed, National Origin, Color—Unfair attacks or disrespectful references not acceptable.

Profanity, Blasphemy, etc.—not acceptable.

Sex—Good taste should be criterion, with double entendre avoided in dramatic continuity and dialogue. Abnormalities and sex crimes not acceptable. Divorce should be handled with due respect to sanctity of marriage.

Alcoholism and Narcotics—Not to be portrayed as desirable or prevalent.

Crime, Horror—Criminals should not be depicted favourably; e.g. detailed accounts of crimes, brutal killings opposed; kidnapping not acceptable; seduction and rape to be avoided unless necessary to programme.

Physical and Mental Afflictions—Should be handled in good taste.

Simulation of News—Non-news and fiction not to be depicted as authentic news.

Legal and Medical Advice—Not acceptable.

Sports—Data on prevailing odds not acceptable if gambling would be encouraged.

Specific Program Standards:

News should be treated fairly, accurately and without sensationalism. Commentaries and analyses should be clearly identified. Broadcaster should have complete control of news from source to microphone, with newscasters and analysts responsible only to station. Alarm and panic should be avoided. Good taste should govern.

Politics—Time should be allocated in conformance [sic] with FCC rules and Communications Act. This includes public proposals subject to ballot. Dramatization opposed. Though not a censor, broadcaster should check for compliance and libel laws.

Public Problems—Allotment of time should respect programme balance and public interest, with fair presentation of issues. Specific periods advised for controversial issues, with clear identification. Equal time advised for opposing viewpoints, with dramatic treatment, announcement copy and solicitation of funds or membership opposed.

Religion—Attacks on race or religion opposed, with programming by responsible groups; major emphasis on broad truths; controversy avoided, as well as solicitation of funds or sale of publications.

Crime and Mystery—Commission of crime should not be made attractive, with violence and horror avoided; law enforcement officers should be treated with respect; criminals should not be depicted sympathetically; details of crimes not desirable; murder, brutality and torture opposed; no kidnapping, suicide should not be treated as solution to individual's problems.

Child Programmes—Careful control of content advised, with adherence to high social standards and respect for parents, law and high ideals. Programmes should entertain; contribute to development of personality; avoid torture and supernatural if likely to arouse fear; avoid profanity and vulgarity; no kidnapping; programmes should not end with such suspense that listener may have bad reaction; no appeal on behalf of character or continuance of programmes through boxtop offers; avoid contests which might send children to strange places.

To this particular note an American officer had appended his own handwritten version of the ethical standards which should apply:

1. Primary function of broadcasting in Japan is advancement of Japan as democratic nation. Mission of NHK is to provide education and information in such manner as will assist in advancing and in safeguarding democracy and peace.
2. In order to achieve this, broadcasting must attain high standards. This requires freedom of medium and assumption of full responsibilities.

    a. be effective (quality and popularity);
    b. a freedom;
    c. responsible to the people.

In September 1946 the Broadcasting Committee of NHK (which had been established in 1937 as a means of evaluating the merits of programmes and making recommendations to NHK) presented to Takano, President of NHK, a new draft radio code expressing the aim of democratization. The principle articles of the code as approved by the Committee were:

Article 1: Radio in Japan has an important duty as a public organ to assist actively in the regeneration of Japan as a modern democratic country and to raise her to the level of an accredited member in the family of nations.

Article 2: Radio in Japan will not be subordinate to commercialism and must be impartial. . . .

Article 4: Radio must do its best to exterminate feudalistic customs and militaristic ideas in Japan.

Article 5: Radio must contribute to the completeness of democracy, respect of fundamental human rights, and improvement of the national morality.

Article 6: The persons concerned must pay close attention to the improvement of the cultural life of the salaried masses who command an absolute majority of listeners.

Article 7: The persons concerned should make impartiality their guiding principle. . . .

Article 9: Japanese radio must work for the widespread dissemination of proper language habits and must weed out the language's ambiguity.

Takano died in May 1947 and of more immediate concern to his successor, Tetsuro Furugaki, was the nature of the legislation which was being prepared for the future of Japanese broadcasting. In the previous two years, when legislation was being prepared by the Ministry of Communications, Furugaki had been a key figure in the preparation and articulation of NHK's views on its future and the general future of broadcasting in Japan. It had become clear to Furugaki and his colleagues at NHK that the Ministry was seeking to strengthen government control over broadcasting. Furugaki outlined the Corporation's views on the draft legislation:

1. As the basis of the drafting, we should adopt democratic attitude of legislation necessitated by our acceptance of the Potsdam Declaration.
2. [NHK] is recovering its natural character as an institution of public service from its past weakened position caused by extreme control of its operation by

government authorities. As the result of such control the people of Japan have
had no voice in the management and operations.

3. The policy of [NHK] should be established by the President who is independent
of the Ministry of Communications with the exception that he would be guided
by and be responsible to the Minister of Communications in the matters enu-
merated in the memorandum for record from SCAP [11 Dec. 1945].

4. In all dealings with radio enterprise of [NHK] the listeners, as a whole, should
be the cardinal factor.

5. As to the editorial policy in the making of radio programmes, the Management
of [NHK] should be given complete responsibility and all rights, free from any
interference from the outside.[16]

The immediate proposal of the Ministry of Communications was to vest
complete control of nation-wide medium wave radio broadcasting in the
Broadcasting Committee which would then function democratically. The
object of the Committee was to promote the public welfare through the broadcasting of current topics, culture, entertainment, and so on. The legal character
of the Committee would take the form of a corporation. The Committee itself
would be elected from every class of people and would provide the central
management body of the broadcasting enterprise. The body doing the electing
would be 'composed of intelligent citizens, representatives of the Diet and specialists appointed by the government'.[17] In addition seven committee members
would be appointed by the Prime Minister with the approval of the House of
Representatives. A prevalent view among some Japanese newspapers was that
this law would imply a reappearance of bureaucratic control through state
ownership and public management of the broadcasting enterprise. Not so, cried
the ministerial legislators, who argued that the Committee would not be placed
under governmental supervision, that it would be able to own property, and
that it would constitute a special juridical person with a right to decide its
own policy: 'It is neither state ownership nor public party.'[18]

Soichi Kawana, head of the rather blatantly named NHK Propaganda
Section Fighting Committee, commented: 'Real democratic broadcasting will
be born from democratization of NHK, and self-satisfied democracy is no use
at all. We agree to the government plan to appoint seven committee members, but we think it is better to organise a committee composed of ten representatives each for the Diet, listeners and workers.'[19] Another important
structural objection was raised by Shinichiro Watanabe:

I am absolutely against the national control of the broadcasting enterprise, because
this enterprise will be operated at the discretion of the government officials in the
system of national control. Monopolistic enterprise is apt to become stagnant. I hope,

---

[16] Tetsuro Furugaki, memo, 3 June 1947.   [17] *Shimbun Kyokai Ho*, 25 Aug. 1947.   [18] Ibid.
[19] Quoted Radion Denka Shimbun, 6 Sept. 1947.

therefore, as many private broadcasting stations as possible will be established because improvements can only be brought about by competition.[20]

Nyozekan Hasegawa noted: 'There will be various forms of national control and like in England national control is successful. I am therefore of the opinion that there is room for investigation.'[21]

On 9 June 1948 the Japanese government submitted the new broadcasting bill to the Diet. The two key provisions were that NHK would become a special juridical person based on law and that in future private broadcasting companies could be established. The legislation rearticulated all the social and moral intentions which had been so extensively discussed in the previous three years. The organizational key lay in the 'broadcast committee' established as

a board of the Premier's Office under the jurisdiction of the Prime Minister. This committee will be the supreme competent administrative organ. The form and power of this committee will resemble the merged powers of Great Britain's Postmaster General and the American Federal Communications Commission system. The committee will comprise five members appointed by the Prime Minister subject to approval of both Houses of the Diet. Detailed regulations concerning qualifications of the members are established in order to prevent interference by political parties and the Diet. . . . The broadcast committee appoints seven directors of NHK through the Prime Minister subject to approval of both Houses of the Diet. . . . Those who wish to establish private broadcasting stations must receive permission to do so from the Broadcast Commission.

One commentary observed that the 'most important feature of this act is the fact that the broadcasting Committee is modelled after the British pattern'.[22] In effect the control of broadcasting moved from the Ministry of Communication to an emanation of the Prime Minister's office, with the control of frequencies residing with the Dempa-cho (Electric Wave Bureau). A critic writing in *Choryu* felt that this new structure 'may be regarded as a new system of "bureaucratic regulation" by the old political parties and the Government officials'. He added, drawing the comparison in the legislation between Britain and Japan,

people should not forget that Japan is different from England in its history of democracy. It should not be taken for granted that Japan has been thoroughly democratized because it has the appearance of a democratic state. In Japan the three great political parties, influential Cabinet members, and even the Prime Minister, who are elected by the Diet, seem to retain vestiges of undemocratic ideas and systems. It will be easy to surmise the character of a 'broadcasting committee' whose members are to be appointed by the Prime Minister with such a political character. Moreover we all know that Japanese people tend to become bureaucratic in positions of powerful organisations.

[20] Quoted Radion Denka Shimbun, 6 Sept. 1947.   [21] Ibid.   [22] *Choryu* (July 1948).

It is too early for Japan to imitate the British. Still, the plan of the Communication Ministry spells progress, because it aims to reorganise NHK, which is being severely criticized by the public. The fact that NHK leaders strongly oppose the plan is evidence of its progressive character.[23]

The new tripartite broadcasting legislation was reintroduced in the Diet in November 1949. The three bills had as their stated objectives (1) establishing necessary technical regulations to conform with international radio conventions; (2) transferring control to a government agency representing the people in conformity with the spirit of the constitution; and (3) breaking NHK's monopoly and clarifying its legal status. Those three bills were the Radio Law, the Broadcast Law, and the Radio Regulatory Commission Establishment Law.

During consideration by the Telecommunications Committee of the two Houses, the bill to establish a regulatory commission was amended to place it under Ministry of Telecommunications control. Sponsors of the bills, supported by SCAP, insisted on an independent agency. To ensure enactment of a satisfactory measure, MacArthur wrote to Prime Minister Shigeru Yoshida, expressing approval of the Radio and Broadcasting Bills but asking further consideration of the Regulatory Commission Bill.[24] He pointed out that, as amended, the bill would not safeguard the commission against partisan influence. He explained that the provision that made a state Minister the chairman and gave the Cabinet authority to reverse decisions of the commission violated the principle of independence and would make the agency a mere advisory committee of the Cabinet. Removal of these provisions would provide the essentials of statutory independence.

The central question had been whether the structural link between NHK should be with the Ministry of Telecommunications or with the Prime Minister's office. In the first instance the problem turned on the question of the financial support for NHK. The draft of the Broadcasting Law prepared by the Radio Regulatory Agency of the Ministry of Telecommunications suggested the possibility of a financial subsidy. The view of SCAP officials was that this would in effect make NHK a government agency. This would also be the case if the Government Board of Auditors were responsible for any audit of NHK books.[25]

On 18 June 1949, a discussion conference was held at SCAP in the office of Brigadier-General Back to consider the draft outline of the Broadcast Bill which had been submitted by the Ministry of Telecommunications on 17 June 1949. The draft proposed that a Broadcast Council be established in the Ministry of Telecommunications, reporting directly to the Minister. It provided for the operation of the NHK under a Broadcast Advisory Committee, the membership of

---

[23] Ibid.   [24] General MacArthur to Prime Minister Yoshida, 5 Dec. 1949.
[25] SCAP, note, 16 June 1949.

which would be appointed by the Corporation with the approval of the Minister of Telecommunications. The draft bill also placed final authority with the Minister for the approval of officers of the NHK, for the establishment of the level of listeners' fees, and so on. The bill continued, as in previous drafts, to allow for the start of commercial broadcasting.

With the exception of the final provision none of the points was acceptable to SCAP officials. A meeting was therefore convened on 20 June 1949, again in Back's office, between CCS, CIE, Mr Masuda, Chief Cabinet Secretary, and Mr Ozawa, to discuss the points on which CIE and CCS would like the Minister's consideration. First that a Radio Regulatory Commission consisting of from five to seven Commissioners be appointed by the Prime Minister with the approval of the Diet. This Commission would be responsible only to the Prime Minister and the Diet and not to the Ministry of Telecommunications since its functions as a regulatory agency would overlap the operations of several ministries.

Brigadier Back also outlined suggestions regarding the legal operation of NHK. These were that a Board of Directors should be chosen by the Prime Minister, with approval by the Diet, consisting of eight people fulfilling various requirements such as regional representation, political affiliation, non-purgees, no local or national government officials, representatives of no other informational media. The Board would elect a Managing Director from existing qualified NHK personnel who would become the ninth member of the Board of Directors. A Chairman of the Board would then be elected. Following the initial appointment of the Board by the Prime Minister, subsequent vacancies would be chosen by majority vote of the Board of Directors and presented to the Diet for approval.

The initial response from the Ministry was unfavourable because of the proposal that the Radio Regulatory Commission should report straight to the Prime Minister and not the Ministry of Telecommunications. Compromises were suggested, but SCAP was insistent that the line of responsibility should be directly to the Cabinet and not the Ministry. The time had come for a heavy hand:

Following the departure of the Japanese from this meeting, CCS and CIE representatives discussed the advisability of issuing a SCAPIN directing the Japanese Government to incorporate our suggestions in a Broadcasting Bill to be presented the next session of the Diet, should the Cabinet reject these recommendations. In accordance with Memorandum 28, such a SCAPIN can be issued if it is considered that the Japanese Government is failing to perform its functions effectively or satisfactorily. It was agreed that such a SCAPIN should be issued if necessary to guarantee that a Broadcasting Bill which will insure the freedom of radio be enacted at the next Diet session.[26]

[26] D. Herrick, CCS, note, 28 July 1949.

In essence, then, while a compromise had initially been sought, the members of SCAP were quite prepared to get very tough to ensure that its view of the future structure of broadcasting in Japan would prevail. Further demands for change were made at a meeting on 22 August 1949, with Mr Amijima and Mr Tori who had drafted the Radio and Broadcast Laws for the Ministry of Telecommunications. They were asked to recommend to the Ministry that the provision in the draft Radio Law for a right of the state Minister, acting as chairman of the Radio Regulatory Board, to disagree with a decision of the Board and seek Cabinet reversal of that decision be removed. CCS and CIE recommended that the President of NHK be elected by the Board of Governors of the Corporation and not by the Prime Minister. In addition it was to be made clear that whoever was elected to the presidency had to be so on the basis of broadcasting experience rather than on any other qualifications. It was expected, said a note of the 22 August meeting, 'that a new draft of the Bill incorporating all suggestions of CCS and CIE will be submitted within a few days.'

An immediate problem for SCAP was that NHK objected strongly to the contents of the new legislation. The Corporation sent its objections to the Broadcast Law to SCAP. These were:

(a) giving the National Diet authority to determine the radio listening fee. Their objections to this seem to be vaguely based on the present social and economic conditions of Japan;

(b) BCJ is opposed to any audit of its books by the Government Board of Audit;

(c) BCJ considers it unwise to have its Board of Governors exercise too much control over the business functions of the Chairman (or President) of the Corporation.[27]

The response from SCAP to the objections from NHK was firm and extensive:

NHK is permitted to collect a listening fee (in fact, the Government will actually collect the fee through its post office system) by reason of law passed by the Diet. In other words, the National Government is assessing every radio listener for the right of receiving broadcasts. Those radio listeners have the right through their representatives in the Diet to determine what that fee should be. That is democratic government. The people need a postal service, and the people through their representatives in the Diet determine their postal rates. Rice and private railways are in the nature of private enterprise. Gas and water charges are either municipal or prefectural operations.

A radio receiving fee must be established on a national basis, and the only appropriate agency is the National Diet. NHK's document gives the impression that NHK does not trust the National Diet. If the Government cannot be trusted, then SCAP's mission has completely failed and nothing in Japan can be trusted. NHK views with

---

[27] Ibid.

respect to the fee can be presented to the Diet through the State Minister who will be Chairman of the Radio Regulatory Commission; or the President or Board of Governors may have direct communication with the Diet committee which is considering the matter. It is recommended that management and staff members of NHK be brought to realise that they are trustees, and only *temporary* trustees, of a corporation in which not any of them invested any money, that the Corporation is owned by the people of Japan. The President has not inherited any life position with NHK. He holds his position because of his ability and experience, and because of the trust and confidence the people have in him. Also, since NHK is one medium of disseminating democratic ideals, its management should be encouraged to put faith in and be willing to abide by democratic government.[28]

The drafts of the Radio Regulatory Commission Establishment Law, the Broadcast Law, and the Radio Law received the approval of the Japanese Cabinet for presentation to the Diet in its extraordinary session and were presented to the SCAP Government Section on 24 October 1949. An immediate bone of contention regarding the Radio Regulatory Commission Establishment Law was that its clauses made possible a large degree of government control of radio, especially a reference to the Prime Minister's prerogative to change the decisions of the Radio Regulatory Commission should they fail to suit him or the Cabinet (Article 19). It was the consensus that these articles of the Law were aimed to give the government control over informational media in Japan in general since, if these articles became law, a precedent would be set for future regulation of other matters of great concern to the Japanese.

A basic problem for SCAP, however, lay in the fact that one section, CIE, which had been involved in the discussions during which the legislation was drafted, had in effect accepted the terms of the draft. The compromise was necessary, it was argued, on the grounds that while not completely satisfied with the Law as it stood, CIE staff felt that it was a step in the right direction. It was CCS's opinion that even though it seemed to make possible some control by the party in power over communications, this Law was preferable to no new legislation which would continue to place radio completely under the domination of the Ministry of Telecommunications. CCS was of the opinion that Cabinet supervision over the Commission would, in effect, act as a safeguard. The rest of SCAP was a bit more sceptical of this 'since, unlike the American people, the Japanese public, press and radio is, at the moment at least, less apt to organise a concerted campaign against government mismanagement'.[29]

CCS further believed that the passage of these radio laws would at least ensure continuance of certain basic points in them beyond the end of Allied occupation. The drafters of these bills had been in the United States for some

---

[28] A. Feissner, CCS, 12 Sept. 1949.   [29] SCAP, note, 26 Oct. 1949.

months studying the operations of the Federal Communications Commission and in general the regulations were patterned quite closely after those which established the FCC in the United States.

These men seem to be sincere in their objective of creating legislation which will allow for a free radio in Japan, though it is quite obvious that the officials of the Ministry of Telecommunications itself have no such altruistic motives. CCS feels that an independent body will not last beyond the end of the Occupation but that such Laws as are here drafted concerning radio and communications stand a chance of continuing in their basic form.[30]

Japanese hopes as well as anxieties for the future of broadcasting were summed up in an editorial in the *Nippon Times*:

Since the radio was introduced into this country 24 years ago, [NHK] has been the sole broadcasting organ under the strict supervision of the Government through its Ministry of Communication . . .

The evils that may emerge from a monopoly in any field and particularly in that of public information and education are too obvious to be recited. Yet it must be pointed out that a single national radio system is not necessarily injurious to a democratic nation. Great Britain, that staunch champion of human rights and individual freedom, has only the BBC. But the balance there between free speech and national interests, between private enterprise and public welfare, is effectively maintained.

The licencing of private radio stations under the proposed broadcasting bill will mean the advent of competition which in turn will infer the development of improved programmes from a technical and artistic standpoint and wider choice of programmes for listeners. But the introduction of commercial Broadcasting will also mean the 'merchandising' of programmes. The radio programme with the greatest public appeal will gain the best paying sponsor who will thus be assured of the widest advertisement. Herein lies the possible appearance here of the worst evils of commercial broadcasting.[31]

The official response by SCAP to the proposed legislation came in a letter from MacArthur to the Prime Minister:

I am in full accord with the principles incorporated in these proposed laws and find no objection to the first two named [the Radio Law and the Broadcasting Law]. With respect to the third bill, namely the proposed Regulatory Commission Establishment Law, careful study discloses certain features which merit further consideration.

Specifically, the proposal to entrust the regulation of broadcasting to a regulatory commission recognizes the desirability of a form of governmental agency which, while new in Japan, has been successfully developed over a period of 60 years in the United States. There it has found its greatest usefulness in those fields of modern economic activity where, because of the technical and complex nature and constantly changing conditions of the activity to be regulated, the Legislature, while able to formulate

---

[30] Ibid.   [31] Editorial, *Nippon Times*, 14 Feb. 1949.

national policy and define broad standards, must delegate to a regulatory body wide latitude within the framework of the statutory objective to prescribe the necessary detailed regulations, make rulings, decide specific cases and enforce compliance. The commission in the exercise of its complex regulatory functions is thus called upon to exert a combination of legislative, judicial and executive authority. The privileges which such a regulatory commission may grant or withhold are invariably of great value and the field in which it regulates is directly affected with the rights and interests of the people at large. These considerations make it mandatory that any such regulatory commission possess the following fundamental characteristics:

1. Its membership should consist of citizens equipped by broad knowledge, background, experience and sound judgment to make wise decisions on the issues and problems involved, assisted by a professional staff of qualified specialists in the area of regulation.
2. Decisions of the commission should be reached by concurrence of a majority of members of equal standing after full discussion and deliberation; and
3. The commission should be insulated from direct control or influence by any partisan group or other agency.

The independence of such a regulatory commission is not, of course, absolute. The power of initial appointment of members and their removal for cause, the safeguards of required public hearings by the commission and review of its acts by the courts, control over the commission's annual budget and, finally, the power of legislative investigation, all constitute powerful restraints and checks available to the executive, judicial and legislative branches of the Government to guarantee that the commission operate within the framework of national policy as established by law.

The plan of your Government incorporates fully the first two of these basic characteristics and also contains the necessary checks on the commission's powers. . . . In one respect, however, the proposal is deficient in that the commission is not adequately safeguarded against direct control or influence by an outside partisan group or agency. Indeed, the requirements that a State Minister be chairman of the commission and that the Cabinet have authority to reverse decisions of the commission completely negate the principle of independence and render the commission a mere advisory committee of the Cabinet. If these two provisions are removed the Government's plan will meet the essential tests of statutory independence and will further insure its free and impartial operation in the best interest of the public.[32]

In February 1950 the Telecommunications Committees of both Houses considered the three radio bills. Susumi Ejiri, managing editor of *Shimbun Kyokai*, for example, thought that 'supervision, leadership and control by the government as provided in the bills are too strict and NHK will lose its independence'.[33]

Of particular note was Furugaki's speech to the House of Representatives Telecommunications Committee on 7 February 1950:

[32] General MacArthur to Prime Minister Yoshida, 5 Dec. 1949.
[33] Quoted in *Shimbun Kyokai Ho*, 6 Feb. 1950.

I am in favour of this Bill and so wish its passage of the Diet . . . Truly the radio broadcasting enterprise has peculiar as well as intricate characteristics and functions which cannot be seen in any other type of enterprise. Therefore, it is not right to judge radio with other similar enterprises such as newspaper, motion picture, or such things as lecture meetings, schools, or railroad or power distribution. . . . The Radio broadcast setup of this country to date is quite similar to that of British BBC, and we have had a great deal of things to learn from that pioneer and leader of senior radio business. But the present new Bill seeks for a combination of public radio form with that of American free competitive enterprise. It seems to me that the idea is taken from the type now in operation chiefly in Canada and Australia . . .

About three years ago, problems as to what is the most peaceful and democratic form of radio management in Japan were brought before the sessions of the Allied Council for Japan several times. At the time, some delegates favoured a single national operation, while some stressed a dual system of government and private enterprise. Then a British delegate gave his view and said that the form of radio broadcasting enterprise in its greatest peaceful and democratic function should not be the same considering the peculiar circumstances of a country. This is really a reasonable statement, and up to this day there is yet no ideal form existing in the whole world, each form has its own merits and demerits. Therefore, however good a system and form foreign radio laws and regulations [are], I think we cannot apply them in this country just as they are unless we consider Japan's special topographical nature, economic circumstances, cultural standard, progress of radio broadcast enterprise, wavelengths allocation and the extent of radio receiving sets distributed among the nation.

Therefore, such a move as denouncing a monopoly form as undemocratic or trying simply and hastily to assimilate the single public radio broadcast to the case of newspaper with a statement that 'If we have only a single newspaper available in Japan, the situation must be the same as the monopoly radio enterprise,' are both notions which totally ignore the nature of the wave-science called radio. At the same time these arguments do not see the reality existing in Britain where both paper and public opinion have fully matured or do not see the reality existing in other nations. As everyone knows, in Britain communications and newspaper enterprise have attained a wonderful development, but as far as radio is concerned, it has been taking the system of a single monopoly public enterprise in conformity with the circumstances of Britain. . . . Especially, the BBC's third network is doing the things that could never be done by other forms but a monopoly enterprise. This kind of work is so good that the radio of any other nations *can never* follow . . .

It seems to me that the public radio broadcast be placed at the center of Japan's radio activities to be heard at every nook and corner of the nation with free enterprise commercial broadcaster attached to it in order to rectify each other their shortcoming and to develop their good points. In this sense, the Bill is surely a progressive and ambitious law. Some quarters, however, have been heard accusing the new measure which, according to their words, grants too much protection to NHK, and I feel it very strange. What is the protection given to NHK? That is the protection of public broadcasting, the only aim of which is to give benefits to the entire population, that is in other words—the protection of the public itself. It is senseless to talk about too much protection for the people . . .

Secondly, I wish to talk about the freedom of broadcasting. . . . The freedom of broadcasting cannot be obtained only with production of programmes. The independent radio broadcasting cannot be established unless the whole body of the public enterprise, including independence of finance, personnel and organisation, are attained. For this point, the regulation of the new bill should be reconsidered for its part.

In short, he wanted the Board of Governors of NHK to be totally independent and not responsible through statute to any external agencies. To maintain the public service nature of NHK, he suggested, 'it is better to trust the Board of Governors, and direct criticism of people or Diet should be invited and that is the more realistic approach.' And then in words which might well have been uttered by his Reithian colleagues on the other side of the globe, he ended:

In short, the object and main target of the public radio is people and not a group of advertisers, capitalists, investors, or a certain particular organisation or individual who represent a definite ideology . . .

I hope the public organ nature of public radio can be guaranteed at the same time as the public cultural property can fulfil its duty, I hope, its autonomy to be established and guaranteed.[34]

Press critics immediately challenged the analogy which Furugaki had made between the position of the BBC and that of NHK:

Whenever anyone begins criticising NHK's radio monopoly, NHK leaders point out in self-defence that BBC is also a monopolistic broadcasting enterprise. NHK president Furugaki has stated at public hearings in the Houses that BBC is carrying on broadcasting on a monopolistic basis. . . . I doubt whether NHK can be compared with BBC, on the basis of outward appearance.

If for our purpose we temporarily consider Europe as one country, England, being a small country, is merely one of several European broadcasting areas. But Londoners may listen to broadcasts from Paris, Berlin, Antwerp, or anywhere else in Europe . . .

NHK broadcasting in Japan is a monopoly without competitor either in Japan or in neighbouring countries, because Japanese cannot listen to overseas broadcasts with their inefficient radio receivers. I therefore think that arguments stressing the similarity between NHK and BBC are fallacious. I believe Furugaki is aware of this, because he was formerly London correspondent for *Asahi Shimbun*.[35]

There was enormous interest in the press about the future of NHK, largely because the owners of newspapers were themselves looking to become involved in applications for private stations which would therefore be in direct competition with NHK. Between November 1949 and April 1950 three major newspapers, *Asahi*, *Mainichi*, and *Yomiuri*, published between them about thirty editorials concerned with broadcasting. The overwhelming emphasis

---

[34] Tetsuro Furugaki, speech to House of Representatives Communication Committee, 7 Feb. 1950.
[35] *Shimbun Kyokai Ho*, 20 May 1950.

within these editorials was the attacking of NHK and the pointing up of the need to develop private, commercially based television.[36]

In the early summer of 1950 the three key pieces of legislation were introduced into the Diet. The Radio Law (Law No. 131, May 1950) repealed the old Wireless Telegraph Law and was designed to ensure fair and efficient utilization of radio waves. It authorized the establishment and government licensing of new private radio stations, and fixed standards for equipment, rules for operation, and qualifications for radio operators.

The Broadcast Law (Law No. 132, May 1950) established national radio broadcasting policy, outlined the reorganization of NHK, and provided licensing procedures for commercial stations authorized to broadcast paid advertising. National policy was stated to be (1) to regulate broadcasting to serve the public welfare and to assure its sound development, (2) to assure the maximum availability and benefits of broadcasting to listeners, (3) to secure freedom of expression with guarantees of impartiality, integrity, and autonomy of broadcasting, and (4) to contribute to the healthy development of democracy by clarifying the responsibility of broadcasters.

The Law forbade interference with, or any regulation of, programmes except under powers specifically provided by the Law; required correction of false statements; and banned broadcasting likely to harm international relations. The Act incorporated from the original radio code the principles that broadcasts were not to distort facts and were to treat issues from all angles. They were made to apply to private as well as NHK broadcasts. While NHK was still prevented from carrying advertisements they were permitted on private stations on condition that they were identified as such and that political advertising was made available to rivals on equal terms.

NHK was assumed to belong to the people because the radio spectrum was public property and because NHK was supported entirely by listening fees. The objectives of the section of the Act relating to NHK were (1) to make management responsible to the public, (2) to prevent political domination and to safeguard its freedom, (3) to give it clear legal status, and (4) to make it financially accountable to the people. To achieve these ends, NHK was completely reorganized as a quasi-governmental corporation. Policy-making responsibility was assigned to a Board of eight unpaid Governors, appointed by the Prime Minister with the consent of the Diet, and executive management to a Board of five Directors.

The Board of Governors replaced the thirty Directors elected by the old membership representation. Each Governor was to represent a geographical district and all were to be chosen from such various fields as education, culture, science, and industry. Not more than four could belong to any one

---

[36] Editorial, *Asahi*, 1 May 1950.

political party. Government employees, political party staff members, and people with business interests in radio, radio equipment, or newspapers were declared ineligible.

The Board of Directors was to consist of the President, appointed by the Board of Governors, and a Vice-President and three Directors appointed by the President with the approval of the Governors.

The old corporation was dissolved by refunding the original membership subscriptions, although the old stockholders retained their free perpetual listening licences. The new corporation was made financially accountable to the government. Budget and plans were to be presented annually through the Radio Regulatory Commission and the Cabinet to the Diet for advance approval. Full business reports were to be audited by the Board of Audit and submitted to the Diet at the end of each year. The Law provided that listeners with standard receiving sets should pay fees established by the corporation with Diet approval and sign contracts with the corporation. Radio research, to be financed by government subsidies, was made an NHK responsibility.

The Radio Regulatory Commission Establishment Law (Law No. 133, May 1950) created an agency comparable to the United States Federal Communications Commission to regulate the entire field of radio. It provided that the Commission should consist of a Chairman and six Commissioners appointed by the Prime Minister with Diet approval from among persons of wide experience and knowledge, who could be expected to make fair judgements concerning the public welfare. Members of the Diet, political party staff members, and radio entrepreneurs, manufacturers, or dealers were declared ineligible for membership. Not more than four members could belong to one political party.

Conforming to the suggestions of MacArthur, the Commission was made directly responsible to the Diet, assuring its freedom from domination by a ministry or the Cabinet. SCAP advisers regarded the creation of the Commission as the most important occupation accomplishment in the field of communications. The Commission was activated on 1 June, the date when the Radio Law came into force, and a former Vice-Minister of the Ministry of Communications became Chairman. The bills received the assent of both Houses in April 1950, were promulgated in May 1950, and came into effect on 1 June 1950. Public service broadcasting in Japan had been created.

8 Conquerors, Culture, and Communication: The Intellectual Roots of Post-war German Broadcasting

This chapter is about the establishment of public service broadcasting in post-war Germany. Or, perhaps more accurately, it is about the intellectual history within which that history is embedded. If I had to try and summarize the ideals of 1945, avoiding all that fine detail of passionate collisions of parties, political rows, and social divisions, the argument would go something like this. The Allied powers were haunted by their inheritance, the shattered remnants of a gangster state, the ultimate abuse of centralized power. Their thinking, however, was also much influenced by a sense of the pressures which political parties had placed on broadcasting before Hitler came to power in 1933. Despite its great artistic achievements German broadcasting had not then been in a healthy condition. It was over-centralized, state controlled, neutered, devoid of the independence and freedom of speech which might have made it an effective weapon in the defence of the Weimar Republic. The regional broadcasting organizations were grouped together under the Reichsrundfunkgesellschaft in which the Post Office held the majority of shares. All the activities of the broadcasting companies were closely controlled by political committees on which representatives of the government and of the political parties sat side by side, a relationship which slowly descended into regular pre-censorship by the political parties of programmes dealing even remotely with political subjects. The Reith of German broadcasting, Dr Bredow, spoke of how the dead hand of party political control led to colourless reporting, a lack of actuality, and an unnatural neutrality towards the events of the day.

The question after 1945 thus became one of how to create, among other things, an information system which would not be squashed beneath the weight of the state and which therefore could watch over the political system and thereby guard against future abuse. Scan the world and there was only one possible model to adopt, one which had at its heart the idea of its independence, the public service broadcasting model. The difficulty was that this model was not something which magically flowed from a set of institutional arrangements. Nor was it something which would be created by simply putting onto paper a lot of good intentions. The model was the evocation of a political culture which recognized, nurtured, and supported the presence within it of a force, a powerful instrument of dialogue, which engaged with the state but which was separate from it, not just institutionally or politically, but morally. And since institutions consist of people, the model presupposed that sufficient men and women, at all levels, could be found who were able to divorce themselves from partisanship. What was being laid down then was the idea that broadcasting in Germany should be devoid of pressures which might narrow its vision and social role and therefore undermine its ability to be of social good.

Much of the planning for the occupation of Germany was done by the European Advisory Commission on which sat British, Russian, and American representatives, and which emerged from the Moscow Conference of Foreign Ministers in October 1943.[1] The basic decisions are by now familiar, that Germany would be divided up into occupied zones, each with its own military governor. The four military governors—Eisenhower, Montgomery, Zhukov, and de Lattre de Tanigny—constituted the Allied Control Council. A central secretariat, the Control Commission, would be established. Much of the planning for the British element was done from August 1944 onwards, by Ivone Kirkpatrick and Major-General Kirby.[2]

---

[1] A detailed discussion of the EAC can be found in Philip E. Mosely, 'The Occupation of Germany: New Light on How the Zones Were Drawn', *Foreign Affairs*, 7 (1950), 28.

[2] Cf. I. Kirkpatrick, *The Inner Circle* (London: Macmillan, 1959), 57.

The Allied attitude towards Germany had a certain ambivalence in that it was never precisely clear, for example in Roosevelt's thinking, whether or not the war was being fought against the whole German people, or just against the Nazi Party and the military machine. The precise details of how the military government would function were incorporated in a *Handbook for Military Government in Germany prior to Defeat or Surrender*. In particular, this outlined that the 'administration shall be firm. It will at the same time be just and humane . . . you will strongly discourage fraternisation . . . military occupation is intended (i) to aid military operations; (ii) to destroy Nazism . . . ; (iii) to maintain and preserve law and order; (iv) to restore normal conditions among the civil population as soon as possible.' The United States War Department Field Manual 27–5 stated: 'To the extent that military interests are not prejudiced, freedom of speech and press should be maintained or instituted.'

At the end of 1944, the *Handbook* was replaced by a directive known as JSC1067 which declared that Germany was 'not to be occupied for the purpose of liberation but as a defeated enemy nation'. The British accepted JSC1067 so long as SHAEF was in existence, but once zonal military government had been established they went their own way. There was, however, an obvious punitive element which went beyond the banning of contact between Allied soldiers and German women, the most important aspects being reparations, dismantling of capital equipment (viewed by some commentators as a foolish act), the trial of war criminals, and denazification (which were clearly necessary if the efforts to create the new society were to prevail). JSC1067 also set forth propaganda directives—to inculcate a sense of war guilt and to assure the extirpation of Nazi, pan-German, racialist, and military ideology. In a sense, however, this Directive posed a real dilemma for the control of information. On the one hand it required the purging of the existing information services, the inculcation of new ideas, and the expunging of old ideologies; on the other military government was expected to permit the maximum freedom of speech compatible with military security.

The same conflicts and dilemmas were to exist in Japan, though the effective unity of control in Japan as opposed to the zonal system for Germany and the very real divisions of power between the Allies—America, Britain, Russia, and France—meant rather different situations in practice.

Technically all the authority in occupied Germany was vested in the Allied Control Council which derived its authority from the third of the proclamations signed in Berlin on 5 June 1945. The first two proclamations had declared the unconditional surrender of Germany and laid down the terms to be imposed, and divided Germany into zones, with Berlin having a quadripartite government. The Council—on which sat the four commanders-in-chief and military governors in the four occupied zones—first met on 30 July 1945 and announced its formation to the German public in Proclamation No. 1. Any decisions and any text relating to those decisions had to be agreed unanimously. The detailed work of organizing and running the conquered nation was actually done by the Coordinating Committee on which sat the four deputy military governors, and it was this Committee which effectively constituted the administration of occupied Germany. Meeting twice a week to prepare the agenda for the Council it was described as a body 'whose importance can hardly be overestimated'.[3]

Two functions were perceived by the US military in their information services: control of information in the occupied territories; and propaganda to those territories. The actual structure of information control inside Germany had three goals: the destruction of the Nazi propaganda machine; reconstructing the German information services; fostering of desired ideas and attitudes among Germans. The methods of control involved licensing, registration, instruction, and training. Military government law number 191 prohibited the operation of all German and Austrian information services without Allied permission. After that, anyone wishing to engage in any form of information activity—newspapers, theatres, films, publishing—had to be licensed. Such activities as singing, printing, book-selling could only be undertaken by registered performers.

There were sharp internal disagreements about how to interpret evidence about political complicity. On balance, however, 'it was considered that some loss in available talent, and injustice in some cases, was justified by gains from applying rigorous standards of political delousing in a field so critically important to political beliefs as that of information'.[4]

The principal developments in the policy framework for information control after 1945 were embodied in four documents: two directives of the Control Council for Germany (No. 40 on 12 Oct. 1946; No. 55 on 25 June 1947); a decision of the Council of Foreign Ministers at Moscow in April 1947; and a new directive to the American military governor in Germany on 11 July 1947. Directive No. 40 laid down general policy to be followed by German press and politicians. In effect, the Directive allowed complete formal freedom of speech, subject to certain general and explicit restrictions:

1. With due consideration to the necessity for maintaining military security, the German democratic parties and the German press shall be allowed to discuss freely German political problems. Comments on the policy of the Occupying Powers in Germany are allowed. The publication in the German press of factual information on world events, including informative articles taken from the foreign press, is also allowed.

2. Members of German political parties and the German press must refrain from all statements and from the publication of reproduction of articles which:

   [3] Michael Balfour, 'Germany', in A. J. Toynbee (ed.), Four Power Control in Germany and Austria 1945–1946, Survey of International Affairs 1939–1946 (Oxford: Oxford University Press, 1956), 327.
   [4] Directive, Control Council for Germany, 11 July 1947.

(a) contribute towards the spreading of nationalistic, pan-Germanic, militarist, fascist or anti-democratic ideas;

(b) spread rumors aimed at disrupting unity amongst the Allies or which cause distrust and a hostile attitude on the part of the German people towards any of the Occupying Powers;

(c) embody criticism directed against the decisions of the Conferences of the Allied Powers on Germany or against the decisions of the Control Council;

(d) appeal to Germans to take action against democratic measures undertaken by the Commanders-in-Chief in their zones.

3. Offenders will be prosecuted for any breach of this Directive.

The April 1947 Foreign Ministers' conference agreed to facilitate further development of the democratic German press and to establish in the whole of Germany a free exchange of information and democratic ideas. These intentions were translated into Directive No. 55, which authorized:

1. ... the free exchange of newspapers, magazines, periodicals, films and books published in different zones of occupation and in Berlin.

2. This exchange shall not be limited by Zone Commanders except by the requirements of military security, the needs of the occupation, the necessity of ensuring that Germany carries out her obligations to the Allies and the necessity of preventing a resurgence of national socialism and militarism. Each Zone Commander will retain the right to take such measures as he may deem necessary against any publications or any persons who violate these provisions, subsequently informing the Allied Control Authority of his action; he shall in addition have the right, if he so chooses, to raise the question of the application of such measures before the appropriate body of the Allied Control Authority—the Information Committee of the Political Directorate.

3. This exchange of information and democratic ideas shall not be subject to any pressure of any sort, administrative or economic on the part of the Central Government or Land Governments.[5]

The Directive of 11 July 1947 to the commanders-in-chief superseded the fragmentary JCS1067. It called for 'the creation of those political, economic and moral conditions in Germany which will contribute most effectively to a stable and prosperous Europe'. The provisions for public information were:

a. You will, in the United States Area of Occupation, supervise, encourage and assist in the development by the Germans of media of public information designed to advance the political and cultural objectives stated in this directive.

b. You will arrange through the Allied Control Council for the implementation of the decision of 23 April 1947 of the Council of Foreign Ministers on the free exchange of information and democratic ideas by all media in all of Germany.

---

[5] *Gazette of the Control Council for Germany*, 16 (31 July 1946).

c. You will develop and maintain organizations and facilities for the operation of media of information, including those sponsored by Military Government, designed to further the objectives of your Government.

The section on cultural objectives is important as a directive for information work:

Your Government holds that the reeducation of the German people is an integral part of policies intended to help develop a democratic form of government and to restore a stable and peaceful economy; it believes that there should be no forcible break in the cultural unity of Germany, but recognizes the spiritual value of the regional traditions of Germany and wishes to foster them; it is convinced that the manner and purposes of the reconstruction of the national German culture have a vital significance for the future of Germany. It is, therefore, of the highest importance that you make every effort to secure maximum coordination between the occupying powers of cultural objectives designed to serve the cause of peace. You will encourage German initiative and responsible participation in this work of cultural reconstruction and you will expedite the establishment of these international cultural relations which will overcome the spiritual isolation imposed by National Socialism on Germany and further the assimilation of the German people into the world community of nations.[6]

In June 1946 the American military governor, General Joseph McNaney, informed the German authorities responsible for framing new *Länder* institutions that they must meet certain standards if they were to be regarded as democratic including, in the information field: 'The basic rights of the individual, including freedom of speech . . . must be recognised and guaranteed. Control over the instrumentalities of public opinion such as the radio and press, must be diffused and kept free from governmental domination.' It was not necessarily easy and, as Thompson points out, 'The initial contacts revealed the extent to which earlier German traditions covering control of speech, press and radio had penetrated the German representatives chosen to formulate standards for the new regime.'[7]

As far as the model for radio was concerned the United States recognized that while it wanted to avoid following the traditional European model of a state-controlled service, an American advertising-supported system was equally inappropriate: 'The device of a public corporation, financed chiefly by fees for licensing individual receiving sets, but free from government control, along the general pattern of the BBC, appeared to be the most likely solution.'[8]

In the first two years of ICD control the US authorities had licensed 45 newspapers; established a German news agency; created 5 radio stations; licensed 312 publishers, 10 film producers, 439 theatre producers, 129 music publishers; registered 9,071 book publishers, printers, and lending libraries; registered 58,000 individuals; established 20 US Information Centres; and opened 975 film theatres.

[6] Directive, 11 July 1947, p. 258.   [7] Ibid.   [8] Ibid.

It is important to understand that, after the initial conquest of Germany and Japan, the mood switched in the Allied mind to becoming less of a conqueror and more of a creative force within the new German and Japanese societies which were to be created out of the ashes of the old. The basic impulse was to construct a liberal democratic community. Before such a community could be created, however, there was a fundamental necessity to establish an understanding and empathy among the population for those principles which provided the political morality without which that state could not exist. The occupation of both countries, therefore, was not just about the establishment of the institutional artefacts which go to make such states. It was also about the creation of a new consciousness, a new set of intellectual commitments and imperatives. The central problem facing the Control Commission in Germany and SCAP in Japan was not physical destruction—awesome though that was—but an intellectual desert and a spiritual wasteland in Germany and a deeply reactionary and hierarchical order in Japan. Civilization met the remnants of barbarity and reactionary tradition and in the collision communication in general and broadcasting in particular were always bound to be important tools in the rebuilding.

Byford-Jones was a young army officer in the occupied zone from 1945 to 1946, and the year after leaving he wrote his impressions about life in the zone, but particularly in Berlin, in an interesting book called *Berlin Twilight*. He refers to the fact that in early 1946 there were 'events' in Hamburg which were variously described as 'disturbances' and 'food riots'. He went from Berlin to Hamburg to have a look at the situation himself:

That Hamburg was suffering could be seen on the faces and in the bodies of the men more than the women; in the women more than in the children. But many children were ill, though parents made sacrifices to give them food. There was increasing absenteeism in schools as there was in factories. The streets of the city were the streets of a hungry frightened place, haunted by the long-since remembered spectre of starvation. Old women were to be seen scavenging around messes. Young girls waited in main streets to meet the provider of chocolate and cigarettes, the magic currency on the Black Market, where unrationed bread and even tinned meat were to be found. . . . The people looked pale, tired, apathetic, almost spiritless.[9]

Of anything that could be described as riots he found no evidence, though there had been some raiding of shops and bakeries, quite simply because most of the population had eaten their monthly ration of bread with half of the month still to go. At about the same time, Stephen Spender, who was touring the zone and keeping a diary, wrote: 'Perhaps I exaggerate, but the homelessness of thousands of people, the ruins, the refugees, the distress, the hunger, haunt me, and since I have no statistical picture in my mind I do not even

[9] W. Byford-Jones, *Berlin Twilight* (London: Hutchinson, n.d. [1948]), 65.

know whether I do exaggerate.'[10] The pain and suffering of the German people in Hamburg and elsewhere distressed even more the English socialist and publisher Victor Gollancz, who wrote a whole series of pamphlets urging that their treatment be better, their conditions be improved, and that there be a much less marked difference between the apparent opulent life-style of the military government and that of the German people. 'The Atlantic Hotel', Spender noted when he arrived there in 1945, 'is . . . the most grandiose Mess for officers I have ever been to. It also contains very grandiose-looking officers.'[11]

Stephen Spender's diary of 1945 contains the details of many conversations and thoughts. He refers for instance to a conversation with a Dr Kroll, who had been put in charge of cultural affairs in Cologne by Konrad Adenauer. The discussion turned to young people and Kroll claimed there was a spiritual and intellectual vacuum, that the young people of Germany were like 'dry sponges'. They had returned from the war often to find themselves without family, without home, and had to ask themselves, not 'what shall I do?', but rather 'what shall I think?' He continued, 'Then they find that they have no values, no guidance, no general culture which they can bring to bear on their situation.'[12]

Whatever the explanation, and there seem to be as many as there are people to offer them, it was taken for granted in 1945 that something had gone drastically wrong with German culture and society and the men of the CCG spent endless hours in conversation with their German subjects trying to work out just what it was.

In October 1945 the Control Commission began publication of a magazine to be distributed to British personnel in the zone. Known as the *British Zone Review* it was described as a 'fortnightly review of the activities of the CCG (British Element) and Military Government'. It is an intriguing document because it is now possible to see it as a kind of voice of British thought—in all its perplexity—during these years, both at the decision-making level and among the rank and file. In only its third edition a page 1 editorial asked 'Quo Vadis?' and declared, 'we shall succeed in our task [in Germany] only if we know what we want to do and set about the doing of it in an orderly manner undistracted by any hysterical advice which may pour in upon us from irresponsible quarters.'[13] The sixth edition asked 'Can we reeducate Germany?' It argued that everyone 'serving in the Control Commission military Government must, at one time or another, have considered whether it is possible to effect a radical and lasting change of heart in the hard working, efficient, inflammable, ruthless and warloving German people with whom we have been at war twice in our generation'. The CCG was, it concluded, fighting

---

[10] Stephen Spender, *European Witness* (London: Hamish Hamilton, 1946), 219.   [11] Ibid. 217.
[12] Ibid. 58.   [13] *British Zone Review*, 27 Oct. 1945.

1,200 years of German history, but despite this burden 'much can be done to accelerate this mental process by plain, objective reporting of the scope and progress of the disarmament measures in the German press and broadcasts'. The information media, run by Information Services Control, were to be used 'to bring home to the German people the progress and reality of disarmament, and also to help in their reeducation and in the reorientation of their minds, and to stimulate in them a mental attitude which it is hoped will be helpful to themselves, to us and to the world'.[14]

Interestingly enough, the man who was running the Public Relations/ Information Services Control (PR/ISC) section of the CCG in the British zone, Major-General Alex Bishop, in his (unpublished) memoirs seems much less concerned with any 'problem of the German mind' and far more concerned with the sheer difficulty of making the zone work. Bishop was a professional soldier. During the Second World War he had been working in the Cabinet Office, the War Office, and then the Political Warfare Executive. In June 1945 he was told that he would be running PR/ISC in the occupied zone. In May 1946 while retaining those duties he also became deputy chief of staff to General Sir Brian Robertson, the deputy military governor in the British zone. In spring 1948 he became Regional Commissioner of *Land* Nordrhein Westfalen.

Given his tasks it is perhaps not surprising that his concerns revolved more around logistics than matters of the head. He was not unaware of the battle of ideas, but thought that all would be resolved, particularly the prevention of a communist take-over in Germany, so long as Germany was restored economically. He was particularly perturbed, certainly in the initial stages, with the dilemma of seeing through a denazification programme which removed from the market many who were skilled and able: 'It was . . . clear that unless the German people were helped to transform the conditions then existing into a situation which would provide a bearable if modest standard of living it would be impossible to prevent the spread of communism throughout the whole country.'[15]

PR/ISC was in effect a Janus-headed creature, trying both to influence opinion in Britain and to get on with the job of influencing Germany. In August 1945 it was 'charged with the responsibility on the one hand of seeing that the world was properly informed about conditions in Germany and on the other with reconstructing German information services on sound lines'.[16] The Public Relations Branch had therefore put a good deal of effort into servicing foreign correspondents, with its Information and Liaison Group letting correspondents know what was happening in the British zone. To the British military government journalists were the link to a public back home which

---

[14] Ibid. 8 Dec. 1945.   [15] A. Bishop, 'Memoirs' (unpublished), 23.
[16] *British Zone Review*, 5 Jan. 1946.

was far less enamoured with the country's role in Germany than were CCG personnel. Bishop wrote of this time:

We were . . . all aware that the civilian population in our own and other Allied countries, who had suffered so grievously throughout the six years of war, should have reservations over the employment of British and allied resources in manpower and material on the reconstruction of the German economy, when so much was needed to repair the home economies, disrupted and shattered by the war. . . . We had to find ways of making known to the people at home the dangers that existed, and what had to be done to overcome them. We went out of our way to help our Press correspondents to see the problem that crowded in on us, and to understand what we were trying to do.[17]

Alfred Dickens, an Englishman who was running a newspaper in Lübeck, states in his account of the Occupation that one of the problems of the British attitude back home was that the Germans were seen as 'all the same' when, he argues, they were not. He even constructs a ten-point typology of the German character. At the same time though he himself implicitly defines, as the central concern of his book, the understanding of 'the German problem'. Similarly, Michael Balfour, one of the foremost historians of the period, later offered a list of 'German traits', 'arrogance and aggressiveness in victory, submissiveness in defeat', an emphasis on masculinity, an exclusion of tenderness; sexism; a 'disposition to violent and sadistic behaviour'; an emphasis on status; the exaltation of the collective whether it be the state, the army, the party, over the individual. He further points to a tendency to introspection and refers to Thomas Mann who 'once remarked on the divorce [in Germany] of the speculative from the socio-political element of human energy and the complete predominance of the former over the latter. The weakness of German thought has been a preoccupation with high sounding theories and words which, when closely examined, prove either meaningless or commonplace; an inability to accept criticism and therefore a tendency to blame others, for example the Jews.'[18]

The immediate problem for the Commission was that there were insufficient 'unblemished' Germans to man all the posts which were needed to make the new state function. The problem, however, was not one of having to leave Nazis in position, but of just how clear understanding of the principles of political morality expressed by the Commission was among those other Germans who were to be the building blocks of the new state. In effect, looking at the situation from the perspective of broadcasting one can see that the German problem on the ground in the years after 1945 was not the Nazi problem. If one takes as a litmus test the declared intentions of the Allies in, for example, employing a BBC model for the future of German broadcasting, one could

---

[17] Bishop, 'Memoirs', 82.   [18] Balfour, 'Germany', 328.

never rest in hope that denazification would of itself provide the pointer to a successful future. There was something else which points to a fundamental difference between Allied consciousness and that of the German élite which emerged in the post-war period.

Ideas and values are the very stuff of communication whether in the direct sense of news services or in the more submerged layers of drama and entertainment. It is probably for this reason that the process of recreating the German mind (and no matter how patronizing that now seems, that *was* what the whole process of occupation was about) figures prominently in the diaries and recollections of British personnel in the British zone. It was almost as if western society were engaged in a debate with its own darker side.

This inner tension within the information services worked itself out in two ways: in the style of journalism to be practised in the revived media; and in the debate surrounding the principles and values and culture which were to infuse that style. In effect, the creation of the style of journalism was itself to be part of the exercise in political democracy. When he opened a German press exhibition in Düsseldorf, Bishop said that the first and greatest duty for the press was:

for the purpose of honestly and factually informing the reader how his fellow country-men and the rest of the world act or think . . . to provide the reader with that information on which he can base a well-informed healthy judgement of events. Its second duty is to provide the reader daily with a sound unbiased commentary on these events and thoughts. The importance of correctly carrying out these two duties in countries which are governed by parliamentary democracies cannot be overemphasized, for parliamentary democracy cannot exist successfully except where there is common sense and goodwill . . . we desire an independent press but we do not wish to recreate the *Anzeiger*, which through its colourless political mentality contributed to the fatal lack of public interest in government during the Weimar Republic. Nor do we wish to create a press whose sole function is to blare forth the political propaganda of one or other party.[19]

Dickens commented in his diary on a 'pleasant and useful' piece written by the first German journalist he employed, about the revival of the postal service in June 1945. His entry for the time reads:

the length these German journalists accord to their literary flourish and background material must be seen to be believed. This article for example though written by an otherwise slick journalist with a quite first class sense of humour and with Berlin experience, contained references to Louis XIV, Thomas Mann, and an alleged quotation from an unnamed British poet. The Germans tend to read and write in roundabout minds—their own word 'umstandlich' is the only one exactly expressing this idea. They love

[19] *British Zone Review*, 29 Nov. 1947.

the literary and historical trimmings which the bulk of the British press, since the coming of Northcliffe, has abandoned.[20]

For Dickens the real problem lay in what the seriousness and earnestness of the style represented: 'their tendency to adopt an abstract and pseudophilosophical approach to the most matter of fact things easily becomes an insidious vice.'[21] The task of the CCG therefore was to change the whole style of the German press, if only because that style was felt to embody styles of *thought* which were alien to the new society. There was a dilemma, though, in that it was still necessary to employ people to produce the papers who, if circumstances had been more favourable, might not have been employed at all. Journalists for example could be either 'safe men' of mediocre ability and mediocre political convictions, or 'brilliant, determined, self confident, affected, nevertheless by semi-Nazi geopolitical and racialist ideas'.[22]

Some Germans protested that the proposed changes in style were wrong-headed and could only be counter-productive: 'Dr Vogel complained that in addition to the whims of local military gods, he was also at the mercy of the idea held by certain authoritative British journalists in Hamburg, that the entire German press should be altered in character. He disagreed with this policy. He said that he thought the Germans could best be reeducated by papers to which they were accustomed and he said that they would never get to care for "tabloid journalism".'[23] Spender's views on this matter are best summed up by his description of German newspapers as looking 'like a Lutheran tract printed in Gothic type'.[24]

It is clear then that from the point of view of the members of the Control Commission there *was* a German problem, a problem of thought and culture, which could be eradicated to an extent through the process of denazification, but which could not be totally eradicated overnight, and which tended to persist in the prosaic but important area of journalistic style.

Dickens had a very specific and clear view of what he understood to be the kind of society they were creating in Germany, a creation moreover which aimed to help buttress 'western democracy' and 'European civilisation'. It was to be a society of

free elections, freedom of political opposition, freedom from arbitrary arrest and political police forces, freedom from party-controlled judicial systems and a host of other freedoms which the Anglo-Saxon nations have done so much to propagate. And by the survival of European civilisation I mean the unbroken development of spiritual and cultural life as known in Europe during the last thousand years, a life based in its turn upon the twin foundations of the Graeco-Roman and Hebraic-Christian worlds. This seems to me to be the kernel of our human inheritance. . . . All these things

---

[20] Alfred Dickens, *Lübeck Diary* (London: Gollancz, 1947), 111.   [21] Ibid.   [22] Ibid. 203.
[23] Spender, *European Witness*, 195.   [24] Ibid. 196.

matter little to communists and crypto-communists here and in Germany; still less do they matter to the self-appointed scientific regimenters who, setting no value on spiritual freedom, naïvely suppose all the ills of the human race to be curable by material means alone.[25]

Germany then was to be both an experiment and a buttress: an experiment, like no other in history, apart from the one which was taking place simultaneously on the other side of the earth, in the self-conscious creation of liberal democratic culture; a buttress against the 'Beast in the East'.

Dickens's perception of individual Germans, usually journalists, is very interesting. He refers to a discussion he had with a young, university-educated woman journalist: 'She struck me as the very type of young woman who, while not a Nazi in the sense of being a supporter of the late regime, remains nevertheless enveloped in those narrow, national values which formed the basis of such creeds as Nazism.'[26] This conversation led him to consider the problem of morality faced in the post-war period and those values which the victors could bring to it. The young woman's arguments, he says, illustrated

The triumph within so many German minds, not so much of Nazism over democracy, as of the State-worshipping philosophies over higher forms of moral philosophy. In short the study of Kant has met with appalling neglect in the country of his origin. I am convinced that a vast number of young German intellectuals will need above all reintroduction to the elementary concept of a moral law, lying outside the all too often opportunist demands of the State. They need first to become convinced of the existence of a rule of law . . . Our educative responsibility does not end with educational reform in the narrow sense. We need to elaborate and work our whole new European system in correspondence with such an idea. This is the only real significance I can attach to the cant phrase 'winning the peace.' But here a snag appears: so many of the interested parties amongst us have no use for religion or philosophy: most have either rejected, or forgotten, both Greece and the Bible. They replace them by some cheap ersatz in the Machiavelli–Materialist tradition, some system which seems to correspond with facts better, but which is, in reality, yet another system pitched just a little below, just a little to the animal side of the actual standards current in our historic Europe. Yet far worse are the new Barbarians. Of these the ones from the Steppes are the most excusable; the ones from Birmingham and Detroit the least so. They are people, often those in responsible positions, who read nothing beyond detective stories and the penny papers, men whose ideas on human relations [apart] from a few nursery reflexes are based on the law of the jungle. . . . Poor Europe with your beliefs in Mercy, Humanity, Truth and Personality; Europe of Plato and Paul, of Augustine, Dante, Milton, Voltaire, Schiller, are you now completing your life-cycle? Miserable City of Man, have you at last been betrayed by the barbarians within your gates? Have you been purged of the German barbarians, only to fall into the hands of his non-German imitators, less cruel, but almost as narrow-minded, ignorant and deluded?[27]

[25] Dickens, *Lübeck Diary*, 340–1.   [26] Ibid. 107.   [27] Ibid. 109–10.

There is a certain English eccentricity to Dickens's role in the occupied zone; his is the culture of the Oxford high table, all classics and claret. In a conversation with a German economist he described the European tradition which he valued as not

about the interplay of predestined national roles and materially determined politico-economic forces; it centred rather about the moral and intellectual achievements of that strangely fruitful tension between Christianity and Humanism one associates with the old idea of Christendom. 'Ah excellent' cried Dr. Hess with an air of an adult allowing to a child his little day dream. 'A typical example of the English or rather the Oxford, point of view.'[28]

He then offers his thesis of how the German problem relates to a rupture in German history and culture: the context is another conversation with Dr Hess:

He talks so much about the tradition of Western Europe and yet he knows so little about its foundations, about Hellenism and Hebraism, about the essentially Latin and rational character given to the Christian tradition by centuries of scholastic and humanist influence . . . I begin to see more clearly the technical deficiencies which mark many highly educated Germans. My judgement may at first seem odd and academic, but I think it is of real importance that these people are essentially lacking in a sense of continuity with the Middle Ages, with the earlier centuries of our western achievement. . . . The German mind is still weakened by that comparative gap in its own cultural tradition during that period between Luther and Lessing. . . . Will Germany ever become a really integral part of the West or merely use its intellectual techniques to create a new barbarism? We have just displaced by force those latest and crudest barbarians, the Nazis, and it now remains for the German intellectuals who have truly understood the western tradition to wage the fight for it within the German mind.[29]

Dickens was echoing a familiar theme in any discussion of Germany's culture, the conflict between the achievements of its literary culture, the Germany of Goethe and Kant, and the barbarity of its political culture, a collision of Mind and Might. In Goethe's words, 'two souls, alas, reside within my breast'.

There was then current among members of the CCG in those early, painful, and difficult months after the end of the war a version of 'the German problem' which might have varied in terms of the details but which nevertheless amounted to a consensual view both about the absence of liberal democratic culture in German society, culture, and history, and about the very real difficulties faced in trying to create such a culture in terms of both its intellectual and institutional manifestations. The re-creation of broadcasting was to be both metaphor and mechanics in this project.

[28] Dickens, *Lübeck Diary*, 120.   [29] Ibid. 210–11.

9 Conquerors, Culture, and Communication: The Creation of Nordwestdeutscher Rundfunk

In December 1945 Major-General Alex Bishop, in charge of the development of information services within occupied Germany, wrote to the BBC. Bishop, responsible among much else for the development of radio and film in the British occupied zone, had re-established broadcasting in the British zone in the shape of Nordwestdeutscher Rundfunk, based in Hamburg with offices and studios in Cologne. He described its function in his letter to the BBC as being

to provide for the British Zone of Germany a Home Service on the lines of the BBC Home Service. . . . To retain its audience and to build effectively a new tradition in German broadcasting, NWDR must not be too obviously edifying, and information not too obviously instructional. Excessive attention by NWDR to the political and historical re-education of the Germans will destroy its credibility and it follows that the overt presentation of 'world' and 'British' views of current and past events should be conveyed to the German public mainly by other means.[1]

[1] A. Bishop to BBC, PID, FO, 15 Dec. 1945, in CCG Files, FO Library, File No. 63824/1, 1944–6.

Bishop also referred to the kind of programmes the station should have: news, 'actuality', talks, and discussion giving the views of commentators within the British zone; schools broadcasts; serious and light entertainment. It was to be a low-key, straightforward broadcasting station. The more aggressive 'missionary' work was to be the task of the BBC's German Service which was to offer, apart from a broad-based news service, what Bishop described as:

Cultural programmes using every means provided by radio technique to reflect to the German audience the literature, art, scholarship, music, theatre, film and science of the outside. . . . Talks and discussions intended to reintroduce Germans to the values and traditions of Western Christian civilization, and to correct past German distortions of the facts of history.[2]

NWDR was not to be a British mouthpiece but an 'instrument which, though serving our purposes and conforming to our general ideas, could be regarded by the Germans as essentially their own'. Bishop candidly pointed out that in keeping with this policy they had rapidly transferred a considerable measure of responsibility to the German staff 'while retaining a small English staff at all the key controlling points'.[3] It gave the illusion of democratic control with not much of the substance until such time as the occupying powers allowed an independent Germany to emerge.

The initial implementation of the policy fell on the shoulders of another former BBC man, W. A. (Rex) Palmer. In the early months of 1946, two main problems concerned Bishop, Palmer's superior:

Firstly, there is that of inducing the German staff to enter into the spirit of our ideas, instead of just conforming to them mechanically. This cannot be done by regulations but only by personal influence. The second problem concerns the basis on which NWDR should be constituted when the time comes to hand over even more completely to the Germans. While we do not contemplate any such steps immediately, it may not be delayed for more than two years.[4]

These were the major problems for him and he turned to the BBC as the only possible source of moral and personal support. He observed to Haley: 'I am clear that we do not want commercial broadcasting. The alternative is a public corporation for which the BBC is the obvious model. Similarly in connection with exercising influence at present, it is clear that the BBC is the chief source of our inspiration.'[5]

Bishop's problem was in finding the correct mix of personal authority for the people running NWDR and the precise articulation of the structure and organization of this BBC of the north German plain. The vision and authority

[2] A. Bishop to BBC, PID, FO, 15 Dec. 1945, in CCG Files, FO Library, File No. 63824/1, 1944–6.
[3] A. Bishop to W. Haley, 10 May 1946.   [4] Ibid.   [5] Ibid.

did not, however, reside in Rex Palmer: 'I am forced to the conclusion that it is my duty to remove him now, providing a successor of heavier calibre can be found. It is here that I turn to you.'[6]

Haley felt that this was an obligation the BBC should try to meet, and on 9 August 1946 suggested the name of Hugh Carleton Greene to take over the job of running the NWDR. In September the Commission formally announced that 'we are today making a formal offer of appointment to Mr. Hugh Greene as Head of the North West German Broadcasting Organisation'.[7]

In 1945 the Foreign Office had issued a very general paper on the 'Policy of British Information Services for Germany'.[8] This referred to the need to consider very carefully the techniques to be employed in offering information to the German public, techniques, moreover, which, it said, 'will play a primary part in re-educating the taste of the German public to new standards so that they may unconsciously become more accessible to the ideas and standards for which Great Britain stands'. It declared one of the aims of the services to be 'to create a German mentality which will last beyond the period of Allied control and which will by inclination come to identify German interests with the policy of Britain and her allies'. To achieve these aims the information services would have the objectives of 'the eradication of the militarist and National Socialist ideologies and traditions of which the basis is that might is right and that the necessity of the state knows no law'. The creation of a sense of the rule of law was to be of paramount importance along with 'a respect and taste for impartial reporting in the spheres of both historical writing and day-to-day news'.[9]

On 1 October 1946 Hugh Greene arrived in Hamburg to continue the reconstruction of Nordwestdeutscher Rundfunk. His brief, at least in his own mind, was to continue and enhance the relatively liberal atmosphere in the station; to obtain legal status for it as an institution in public law, independent, centralized, and financed by licence fee to ensure constitutional continuity once the post-war world settled into normality.

Shortly after he arrived, he collected together the employees of NWDR to tell them of his intentions and hopes for the future. The station, he said, would not be the voice of the conqueror, but the voice of the conquered, of the new Germany. On one point he was clear, 'that one of the tasks of the coming months and years will be to secure the independence of the broadcasting service . . . from the individual political parties and from any essential future government agency.' The model for the station would be the BBC, his prime purpose 'to make available the experience I have been able to gain for

---

[6] Bishop to Haley, 11 July 1946.
[7] J. McDougal, Control Office for Germany and Austria, to W. Haley, 11 Sept. 1946.
[8] BBC German Service File, 29 May 1945.   [9] Ibid.

the further setting up and securing of a new German broadcasting system which accords with German needs'.[10]

The problem was how to secure those needs. Who was to define them? Greene's belief was that it was for the broadcasters themselves within the public system to define them since the presiding assumption within the basic model, the BBC, was that it had, in an almost metaphysical sense, a *relationship* with 'the public' not as a group of partial interests but as a collective entity which was composed of different interests and different needs.

From the British standpoint the key to the future success of German broadcasting would lie in the discovery of those vital mechanisms and conventions which distanced NWDR from the political establishment but which would not, in so doing, isolate it. The immediate requirement was to buy the time necessary for the development of those traditions of independence, open-mindedness, and tolerance which were held to be the real bedrocks of the BBC's reputation. The BBC's work had in practice depended on its being suspended in a life-giving atmosphere of acquiescence to its role, status, and position within British culture. Without that atmosphere all the institutional devices in the world could not but fail to create an independent organization. It was never really likely that the re-creation of that supportive environment would be achieved.

The key year in the task of establishing the constitutional framework for public service broadcasting in Germany was 1947. The day of the conqueror's departure was rapidly drawing close and it was only common sense to try and persuade the future controllers of Germany that here was a model for broadcasting at its best.

Greene was later to describe the statute which established NWDR as a compromise between the desirable and the attainable, leaving room for interpretation, with no intention of it being a strait-jacket hindering the development of a living organism. Strait-jacket or not, the ideas which were to shape the station had already been well established at the very beginning of the constitution-making process. This is made clear from a memorandum in the BBC's files which, though it is undated, was, on the basis of internal evidence, written some time in late 1946 or early 1947. Entitled 'The Future of Broadcasting in the British Zone', it begins:

It is presumed in this paper that for political reasons and owing to the inexperience of the German staff, control of broadcasting in the Zone must be kept in British hands at any rate until the late summer of 1948. In planning subsequent devolution to the Germans it is technically impossible to use the *Land* units as a basis for the broadcasting organisation since, even if the frequencies were available the *Land* unit is too small a basis. On the other hand there is an obvious danger in putting broadcasting

---

[10] Hugh Greene, note for lecture to NWDR employees, Hamburg, 27 Oct. 1946.

in the hands of a national government. The middle course of organising broadcasting on a zonal basis is proposed in the following paper. The resulting organization would have the advantage of being technically sound and providing a forum for the expression of local or regional views. It is true that the organisation proposed for the British Zone is unlikely to be matched by parallel organisations in the other Zones. Any future national government will thus be presented with a continual temptation to intervene with the idea of setting up a more uniform national organisation and it is difficult to provide the *Land* governments with sufficient incentive to defend an organisation based on the Zone and not on the *Länder*. Nevertheless it is submitted that the advantages of the proposed organisation outweigh its disadvantages and that no better solution can be found.

The paper then considered the 'Proposed Status of NWDR after the Withdrawal of British Control':

(a) It is proposed during 1947 to give NWDR legal status and a character as a public corporation along the lines of the BBC.

(b) The Director General of NWDR will then be responsible to a board of seven or eight Governors, whose duty it would be to safeguard the political independence of NWDR and to take an active interest in the programme, financial and staff policy of NWDR. They will be appointed in the first instance for differing periods to prevent the retirement of the whole body of Governors at the same time, and will be paid a salary. These Governors will be chosen not as specialists or as representatives of particular interests of localities but as persons of judgment and independence who will represent the interests of the whole body of listeners. It is most undesirable that any concession should be made to the idea of political parties being allowed to nominate Governors. The first governing body should be appointed by the Control Commission. It is suggested that, in agreement with the Zonal Advisory Council, in order to keep the choice of Governors free from political influences a body of ex-officio trustees should be appointed which should be responsible for the appointment of the Governors. The suggested trustees are the Minister Presidents of the three *Länder*, the Mayor of Hamburg, the Rector of Goettingen University, the President of the Zonal Trades Union Council and the presidents of the most important Women's, Youth and Cultural Organisations in the Zone.

Throughout 1947 the trickiest question was how to guarantee the independence of NWDR. Much time in particular was taken with the legal status of NWDR as a corporate entity and with the thorny question of who controlled the transmitters. In autumn 1947 the Control Commission noted 'the difficulty of establishing NWDR as a public corporation free from governmental control within the framework of present German legislation'. The proposal therefore was to establish NWDR and then to change German law to ensure its independence of government and party politics and also to put it 'beyond the reach of the normal administrative powers of the government such as would enable a would-be totalitarian regime to get hold of this essential means of publicity by controlling perhaps just departments of government'.[11] Their conclusion was that the broadcasting institutions should control the transmitters.

By November 1947 the Control Commission was recommending the establishment of NWDR 'as an institution of Public Law' independent of the state. This was formally agreed by the Control Commission in December 1947, on 30 December 1947 the NWDR charter was officially handed over, and on 1 January 1948 what had previously only been an institutional extension of the political will of the military government gained legal status. It was one of the signs that the Occupation was drawing to an end, though for the time being the military government retained the power of censorship and the power to approve any appointments made to NWDR.

The structure of NWDR consisted of two main bodies: the Hauptausschuss and the Verwaltungsrat. The Hauptausschuss (or Principal Committee) consisted of sixteen members and was intended to be the equivalent of the monarch, who in Britain appoints the Board of Governors of the BBC. The members consisted of the presidents of the *Länder* of Nordrhein Westfalen, Lower Saxony, and Schleswig-Holstein; the Mayor of Hamburg; the President of the central judiciary; four representatives from education; one representative each of the Catholic and Evangelical Churches; the leader of the German Trades Union Congress; the leader of the north-west German journalists' union; a theatre manager; the President of the state music academy in Cologne; the President of the joint industrial and trade board. The Hauptausschuss elected the seven members of the Verwaltungsrat (Administrative Board), NWDR's executive committee analogous to the BBC's Board of Governors. This body in turn could appoint the Director-General. At the time Greene wrote: 'It is laid down in the Charter that the members of the Administrative Board may not represent any special interest of any kind and may not accept instructions from any outside quarter in connection with the conduct of the office.'[12]

In an interesting memorandum commenting on the charter a member of the Control Commission, Alan Huet-Owen, pointed to a number of its less obvious features. He noted: 'for obvious reasons the Charter stipulates that the operation of NWDR shall be completely independent of State and Party influence. This means, for example, that the Minister-President of Lower Saxony is a member of the Principal Committee of NWDR only by virtue of his high office, even though he had been elected to this high office as the candidate of a specific political party. It could therefore happen (at least in theory) that all members of the Principal Committee (and indeed of the Administrative Committee) belonged to one political party without formal

---

[11] Internal memo, Control Commission for Germany, 11 Dec. 1947.
[12] *British Zone Review*, 31 Jan. 1948.

violation of the Charter.' He further observed: 'In Great Britain the Board of Governors of the BBC is ultimately appointed by His Majesty. In Germany, there is as yet neither Crown nor any other supreme institution above party politics. For the purpose of the NWDR Charter a substitute was created in the form of a Principal Committee of 16 members. With unimportant exceptions, memberships exist by virtue of office, not by election.'[13]

Thus, even though ostensibly the membership was not there to represent particular party political interests, one could not separate that element out. That was the kernel of the problem facing NWDR, and the rest of the new broadcasting system in Germany, from which many problems would come in future.

Greene wrote at the time:

My period of complete personal dictatorship here came peacefully to an end last Saturday when the Board of Governors of NWDR came together for the first time. It's a very good lot of people on the whole and, as I had hoped, Grimme, the Minister of Culture in Niedersachsen—a man I like enormously—was elected Chairman. Now I've got to find a DG and then I shall have turned myself out of a job.[14]

Grimme explained his view of the role and purpose of broadcasting in a piece he wrote in the *NWDR Yearbook 1949–50* entitled 'The Ethos of Broadcasting'. Grimme saw broadcasting as a cultural instrument, though he also recognized it as inevitably politically sensitive. His 'vision', if one can call it that, was of a service not simply chasing popularity, but also seeking to bring out the cultural best in the listeners. He assumed a relationship between the making available of cultural goods and the cultural and social enrichment of the community. Broadcasting, Grimme concluded, was more than just news, more than just entertainment, more even than edification—it was the centre of family life, instructive, an instrument for making people conscious of the new Europe and Germany's role within it. German broadcasting was to be 'an ambassador of the German spirit and also the spirit of the good European'.

Almost immediately, however, things began to go wrong.

Early in 1949, Alan Huet-Owen, the British Liaison Officer with NWDR, wrote to ISD about the emergence of a certain amount of 'internal friction' in NWDR created by the fact that 'Dr Grimme apparently has been imposing his personality on the organisation in an autocratic way'.[15] Senior members of NWDR had been saying to Huet-Owen that Grimme was making decisions without consulting them, even where their own departments were concerned. There was in particular much ill-feeling about Grimme's proposal to bring with him as his personal adviser a Dr Pleister, described as 'a man with an unsavoury

---

[13] Alan Huet-Owen, memo, 3 Feb. 1948.   [14] Hugh Greene to his mother, 14 May 1948.
[15] Alan Huet-Owen to Deputy Chief, ISD, 5 Feb. 1949.

political background'.[16] A delegation from among the senior staff visited Grimme and informed him that, should Pleister be appointed, they would resign. Greene, aware of the problems, along with the members of the Hauptausschuss also advised Grimme against the appointment. Grimme acceded to the pressure but had clearly made a considerable error of judgement in ever thinking of making Pleister his adviser. It was one example among other incidents.

The issue was whether such difficulties were born of Grimme's innocence and inexperience or resulted from a deliberate effort to ease out people, like Schnabel, wedded to the notion of independence for broadcasting. Grimme apparently made 'little effort to accept and continue the ease and informality with which the affairs of NWDR had been conducted over the past years'.[17] He was, however, an experienced politician and not one of whom the description innocent and naïve readily springs to mind.

In his efforts to ameliorate what he saw as a potentially deteriorating situation in NWDR Huet-Owen was beavering away trying to persuade the key personnel of the organization to stay on and persevere.

The problem, as they were discovering very quickly and very painfully under Grimme, was that NWDR was about an ideal, about an emotional and intellectual commitment to a notion of broadcasting which was peculiarly British, but which inevitably depended very much on the personality of its chief exponent. Autocracy was tolerable so long as it remained creative and visionary, as had been the case with Reith, or benevolent and kind, imaginative and tolerant, as it had been with Greene. Grimme's problem and therefore NWDR's problem at this stage seemed to be that he had neither the personal authority to control events, nor the necessary imagination to inspire people.

At the end of February 1949, Greene visited NWDR in his new capacity as special adviser, keen to come to grips with the problems which were now besetting his creation. He was less worried about the situation than Huet-Owen had been, describing it as 'a very German crisis, magnified out of all proportion by typical German hysteria and by typical German inability to cooperate in a normal way with their own fellow countrymen'.[18]

Greene did however pin-point 'one aspect of recent events' which he was correct to find 'rather disturbing':

an attempt made by some of Grimme's advisers to get members of the SPD into key posts in the organisation. The villain of the piece seems to be . . . Wenzlau, who has been so indiscreet in his support of SPD interests that there is almost a case for demanding his dismissal on the ground that he has infringed the NWDR Charter. He is intensely unpopular in NWDR, is universally regarded as a bad influence on Grimme, and I suggest that gradual and discreet efforts should be made to get him removed.[19]

[16] Alan Huet-Owen to Deputy Chief, ISD, 5 Feb. 1949.   [17] Ibid.
[18] Hugh Greene to Chief, ISD, 1 Mar. 1949.   [19] Ibid.

In April 1949, three members of the ISD, Thomas, Grinyer, and Brigadier Crowe, had a meeting with Grimme to discuss the 'internal difficulties' in NWDR. This followed an article in *Neue Zeitung* on 9 April which had the title 'Dispute about Hamburg's Station Director—Herbert Blank and his Strasser Past'. It accused Blank of having been a member of the 'left wing' of the Nazi Party and a collaborator of the Strasser brothers and Roehm. It also said he had written a pro-Nazi novel, *SS*. Grimme had decided to give way on this sensitive issue and argued that he had never intended this to be a permanent appointment.

Grimme lashed out at the attitudes of some of his staff and complained to Grinyer that even before he had taken up his post at NWDR 'intrigues against him were started'. The article in *Neue Zeitung* attacking him 'was further proof of the disloyalty existing among staff. . . . He was thoroughly tired of being blackmailed by threats to resign every time things did not run the way his staff wanted them to run and he had come to the conclusion that he would have to accept a few resignations if he wanted to establish a happy administration. . . . He rejected any idea that he was trying to get rid of the pro-British element in the organisation as ridiculous.'[20] There was however a rumour going round the station that Raskop, Grimme, and Blank had made a list of those who would have to go, amounting to almost a third of the staff.

In other conversations Grimme was allegedly arguing that his problems lay in the attitude adopted by the Administrative Council. He said that

his position as General Director, as defined in the Charter, left him few actual powers, especially in relation to the Verwaltungsrat which was interpreting the relevant passages of the Charter in so literal a manner they were not content with giving him general directives as to the conduct of affairs in NWDR, but often insisted on intervening in matters of administrative detail in a manner which tended to qualify still more whatever independent authority he had.[21]

It could be argued that these were mainly internal tensions. There was another, potentially more serious, problem for the long-term development of German broadcasting. A memorandum in April was intriguingly titled 'Scrutiny of Applicants for Employment with NWDR'. This pointed out that the existing instruction for scrutiny only covered 'the political screening with regard to a National Socialist past. The question of widening the scope of political scrutiny is under consideration.'[22] ISD reported to the military governor:

A request has been received from NWDR for the establishment of some kind of machinery for vetting employees and free-lancers working for NWDR. The request is a result of a recent experience with the employment of a free-lance journalist on NWDR,

[20] D. Thomas to Dept. Chief (Plans), ISD, 'Internal Difficulties in NWDR', 14 Apr. 1949.
[21] T. Grinyer to Brigadier Crowe, Zonal Executive Officer, 16 Apr. 1949.
[22] ISD memo, 12 Apr. 1949.

who proved to be implicated in communist activities. This matter has been discussed with Political Division, who consider that it would not be advisable to set up a special machinery for this purpose. They advocate that, generally speaking, the Germans should make their own decisions. With regard to political commentators and senior employees, however, it would appear necessary to undertake some kind of vetting.[23]

The basis for this judgement was that their 'political unreliability' might implicate the military government as well.[24] The whole question of political commentary was raised in an abrupt manner when in April 1949 Dr Worliczek, the chief political commentator, resigned his position 'under circumstances which indicated that Grimme and Blank desired this change and were thinking of reducing political commentaries in the NWDR programme'. Worliczek was regarded by the British as 'perhaps the only commentator who was not susceptible to the growing trend of national self-consciousness, and was distinguished by a balance of approach to matters of foreign affairs and German politics which, from our point of view, made him highly acceptable. It appears to me unlikely that NWDR will ever again find a commentator of his knowledge, experience and European outlook.'[25]

What was not made clear was whether the alleged political activities of the free-lance, which provided the pretext for the request for more vetting, had actually affected his work. If they had, then that of itself would represent an indication of a profound problem, the inability or refusal of the staff to recognize the immediate need to keep manifest politics out of their work. The more accurate way of seeing this request for greater scrutiny would be that it followed from a Board of Governors which was itself more and more political, saw broadcasting as part of a party political game, and was concerned almost solely with carving up NWDR between the SPD and the CDU. Such a view of things was definitely not what the British had in mind.

Much of 1949 was taken up with the laborious but necessary task of preparing the charter of NWDR for the ending of military government. All along the British had been conscious of the difficulties which might follow their departure and had sought informal as well as formal means of maintaining their lasting influence. There is, for example, among the CCG papers an undated list prepared from intelligence sources of NWDR employees with a DM figure next to their names. Against some names, for example Axel Eggebrecht's, someone had pencilled in 'Yes', a footnote explaining that this person is 'known to Applegate as being regarded with confidence by Broadcasting Branch as being pro-British'. On 12 May 1949 Grimme had informed Grinyer of his intention to 'displace' Eberhard Schutz, to suggest to Eggebrecht and Hans

---

[23] ISD to MI Governor, 'Testing of NWDR Employees or Free-lancers for Communist Sympathies', 1949.
[24] Memo of record, Grinyer, 26 May 1949.   [25] Ibid.

von Loyewsky that they enter into new contracts as free-lance contributors, and to suggest to Karl Wirtz that he resign his position in return for a year's salary. Rumours abounded that efforts were being made to rid NWDR 'of any remaining personnel who dated from the days of British control, and that it was openly boasted among NWDR staff that the "British spirits" were to be eliminated' though they did not know whether 'to blame Dr. Grimme, with his increasingly despotic ideas' or Raskop. The consensus was that the whole thing was an SPD-inspired affair to gain control.[26]

Almost on cue, on 16 May 1949, fifty-one dismissals were announced, though to be fair when one looks closely at the evidence the context seems to have been at least in part the need for economic cut-back as well as party political reasons. The NWDR budget for 1949–50 had been severely cut. ISD later argued that

The financial management of NWDR had been somewhat lavish in the past and the organisation was certainly overstaffed. A reduction of expenditure seems therefore justified, particularly in view of the shortage of money which followed the currency reform. The administration was however also clearly intent on getting rid of what they considered undesirable personalities in the process. As a result a list of 51 dismissals was issued containing the names of prominent staff members. The notices of dismissal had been clumsily worded.[27]

The dismissal notices were in fact then withdrawn and new redundancies arranged. Schutz had also been suspended, and not dismissed, for a 'serious indiscretion' in suggesting that the NWDR authorities 'were installing apparatus for tapping all office telephones'.[28] A number of the dismissals were allowed to stand and some senior officers resigned or were dismissed.

The most important departures were described by ISD to the British Foreign Office, and included Dr Worliczek, chief political commentator; Axel Eggebrecht, 'one of the two or three most popular broadcasters, a temperamental man who is believed to stand far to the left'; Eberhard Schutz, 'a disgruntled man'; and Haberfeld, the Berlin Intendant, 'whose financial administration had been somewhat careless'.[29]

On balance the Control Commission tended to agree with Grimme's interpretation of the structural weaknesses of his position, and that the underlying causes of the crisis, lay, at least in part, in the abrupt transfer of the organization into entirely German hands. It had, they felt, been very much easier for a British Director-General to allow his staff considerable freedom since he had ultimately complete power, whereas the German Director particularly under the new charter had to establish his authority in a very different way.

Edwards of ISD gave a fuller account of the situation and its implications:

---

[26] Memo of record, ISD, 11 Aug. 1949.   [27] Ibid. 20 Aug. 1949.
[28] Ibid. 11 Aug. 1949.   [29] Ibid. 25 May 1949.

Party-political considerations have not so far played an important part within the organisation. It is perhaps a pity that the personalities chosen by the Principal Committee
(Hauptausschuss) as members of the Verwaltungsrat, outstanding as they are, all have
their party affiliations. The Verwaltungsrat consists of four SPD and three CDU members one of whom (Raskop) is the Chairman. With the Director-General also a member of the SPD, the influence of the SPD should be stronger than that of the CDU.
However, neither Raskop and Grimme nor the members of the Verwaltungsrat seem
to consider themselves as agents of their respective parties. They are, of course, loyal
to the political conceptions of their parties but they are not working on factional lines.
It is encouraging to see that the organisation has so far maintained its independence
of party interests both in its attitude and in its personnel policy for which reason
Schumacher apparently is as dissatisfied with Grimme's as Adenauer is with Raskop's
performances from the party point of view.[30]

Whatever the personal flaws of Grimme and Raskop, the most telling and
damning fact to the historical eye is that only six months or so into German
control of the NWDR, any assessment could take, as part of its case, a political
calculus in which SPD was measured against CDU. In terms of its original
intentions the NWDR experiment was, by the spring of 1949, in an appalling
mess. Greene himself was so disgusted with some things that he decided to
sever his links as Special Adviser.[31]

In June 1949 a new Intendant was appointed. Troester was a former deputy
head of the Berlin station who, 'though not brilliant, has a cool head and a
faculty for managing people, and appears to be able to get on with his superiors, colleagues and subordinates'.[32] Generally however it was held that, at least
for some time to come, Troester's equanimity and affability, along with his
practical sense, would 'outweigh what he lacked in intellectual and artistic
stature. He will be received by a house whose relative calm is partly due to
expectancy and partly to exhaustion'.

Grinyer discovered that much of the trouble and disturbance had come from
free-thinking individuals—almost maverick-like characters—who were wedded
to the memory of public service broadcasting as the British had conceived of
it. Of course they could be pacified or removed, and thereby controlled, but
not without quenching much of the spirit of that commitment—which was
both intellectual and emotional. It was a difficult position for the British controllers to be in.

By July 1949 things were calmer, partly because of the influence of Troester.
However, Sir William Haley, the BBC's Director-General, and Ian Jacob, the
BBC's Director of Overseas Services, who had just visited NWDR were dis-
turbed by the obvious friction between Grimme and Raskop: 'the cause of their
disquiet appeared to be that NWDR were rapidly losing the BBC traditions of

---

[30] Memo of record, ISD, 25 May 1949.   [31] Ibid. 11 June 1949.
[32] ISD to Foreign Office, 11 Aug. 1949.

objectivity and freedom from party politics which it was thought Mr. Carleton Greene had successfully implanted and Herr Grimme would carry on.'[33]

What one sees is an internal development in which a combination of internal political manœuvrings and idiosyncratic behaviour caused NWDR to lurch away from some of the ideals which had been present at its birth. If its equation for broadcasting included a role for the political parties then it would in no sense be described as fitting the public service model. The interesting point is that political manœuvres and wrangles did not just emerge as the Germans took control but were *institutionalized* in the process of setting up the transition from British to German control.

By February 1950 it was clear that Raskop would not be reselected as Chairman of the Verwaltungsrat. The question of his successor therefore assumed importance: 'It appears likely that Professor Dovifat, his Deputy, may be chosen, since Dr Grimme and members of the Verwaltungsrat appear to feel themselves bound by a tacit agreement, dating back to the transfer of control, whereby a Director General of SPD, Protestant, North German background should be balanced by a CDU, Catholic, Chairman of the Verwaltungsrat. Dovifat would meet these conditions.'[34]

They did indeed feel 'bound by a tacit agreement', and when at the end of March 1950 Raskop was not re-elected as Chairman, he was replaced by his former deputy, Professor Dovifat, with von der Gablentz as deputy Chairman. Both Dovifat and von der Gablentz lived in Berlin and both were members of the left wing of the CDU, with Dovifat a Catholic and von der Gablentz a Protestant. This latter act of delicate political balancing was a result of the 'tacit agreement' to which the members of the Verwaltungsrat had earlier expressed their sense of commitment. In a note to Jacob, the BBC's Director of Overseas Services, Greene explained the origins of this agreement:

Before the appointment of Grimme as Director-General, I made an agreement with Herr Arnold, PM of Nordrhein Westfalen, that if he would agree to Grimme's appointment it should be regarded as reasonable that the chairman of the Administrative Board should be a member of the SPD and a Protestant. This agreement has since been regarded as binding.[35]

A certain calm descended, but beneath the surface there was a much more significant remnant of the early days, one that was to have serious long-term consequences: the institutionalized involvement of the parties. That could not be removed now, only more or less controlled, with the gradual withdrawal of the British Control Commission accelerating the level of party political activity. This built-in partnership was possibly inevitable and certainly not unique to Germany. What one saw in those years from 1945 to 1950 was a microcosm

[33] Hugh Greene, 'Notes on the Situation in NWDR', 2 Feb. 1950.
[34] Hugh Greene to Ian Jacob, 'NWDR Situation', 8 May 1950.   [35] Ibid.

of the central problem of the whole notion of the public service organization, its relationship to its surrounding political culture which is always threatening, always scratching away at the door.

From its birth then the child was deformed. The fall-out, not from the war alone, but from the very core of the German spirit, had penetrated into and mutated the conception. The doubt, so powerfully expressed by characters as diverse as von Zahn, Eggebrecht, Schutz, and Dickens, as well as the whole of the CCG, about the ability of that spirit to encompass the values and assumptions which were the very stuff from which the British conception of broadcasting was woven, was by 1950 all too accurate an understanding of the German situation. In effect, at the inception of post-war German broadcasting, the political parties in German society were institutionalized within the structure.

It is vital to understand this, given that the formation of the political parties preceded the formation of the modern German state. It was not, therefore, as has sometimes been suggested, that party political influence came in through the back door of having representatives on the Hauptausschuss. The British had taken a gamble that the representatives on the Verwaltungsrat would leave their party political clothes at the door of the Funkhaus. There was no guarantee that they would. Certainly in the period covered here the differences seem to have been over the broad intellectual directions of NWDR rather than over any party political squabbles. This was bound to be so since the station, like all other institutions in the rebuilt society, hung in a state of suspended animation betwixt and between the old masters of the Central Commission and the new masters of the *Länder* governments. The party political involvement which lies at the heart of the German broadcasting system was the bastard child of an ill-conceived relationship.

Fundamentally, any public service broadcasting organization exists because it is allowed to exist, is allowed to have a coequal existence with the political estate. The other side of the coin is that any public broadcasting organization exists under a perpetual threat of annihilation. The model for the German development, British political culture, had successfully been able to develop a context in which had emerged a tradition of the fourth estate, the bedrock of which was a certain toleration of free comment and criticism. That tradition had been a long time growing and even then rested uneasily on its base at any time of crisis. In Germany the fourth estate was fashioned in a society in which the other estates did not even, at that time, exist. The battle was, to borrow Hugh Greene's metaphor, not only for the soul of NWDR, but for the soul of the new Germany. NWDR was no more than one front in that campaign.

Maybe it was the nature of its birth, a powerful initiation, a medium for influence and power which the new political class—appearing out of camps and exile and pain and frustration—were eager to control and guide. There was no basic meanness of spirit about this, it was and is the instinct of the politician to seize the means of creating the future. It is a universal phenomenon and only the most self-confident of societies, the most assured political establishments, are willing to grant a certain freedom for the separate articulation of its nature. In only a handful of instances have these conditions prevailed. Amid the physical, emotional, and intellectual rubble of defeat it was almost inevitable that the architects of the new state would not have that self-confidence. The bickering between Raskop and Grimme thus was more than just pettiness. Rather it represented the birth pangs of the emerging struggle between the SPD and the CDU. The various other hostilities, the accusations of right-wing bias and left-wing bias, of conspiracy and corruption, were battles which linked with the emergent struggle to define the ways in which the new state would fashion itself.

PART III

New Communications

10 Video Kombat and Highway-Building

There are certain moments in history when the pace of change quickens and the force of its impact becomes apparent, and 1993 was one such moment. It was a time when waves of corporate decisions broke on the shores of the old order, when the imperative of commerce and the immanent characteristics of technology seemed to be approaching critical mass. It was also a time when the collisions between old and new became contained within very particular events and individual biographies. Two men in particular figured prominently in what was to prove to be an extraordinary year in communications. John Malone of Tele-Communications Inc. (TCI) and John Birt of the British Broadcasting Corporation (BBC) both sought to capture, and shape to their own ends, the shifting ecology of the media. Malone seemed to be the master of ceremonies, organizing the theatre of the new, setting the scene for the twenty-first century. Birt desperately tried to change the BBC as an organization without appearing to betray its traditions. His was very much the high-wire act, without net.

In an age in which the possession of money and fame are more often than not the same thing it is remarkable that a man who is known by his peers to be the single most dominant figure in the cable industry, who is more powerful and more ruthless than any network president has hardly any public persona. The only thing most people know about him is that he is someone to fear. 'He has by the nuts some of the most prominent people in the entertainment business,' says one studio executive, adding that 'no-one in his right mind would talk about him on the record.' Another, well-known television executive was quoted off the record in the trade press, as saying of Malone: '. . . nothing happens in this industry without his blessing. Everyone has to kiss his ring.'[1]

Malone in fact has come to embody and, to a considerable extent, drive the change which engulfs all forms of electronic communication. Here, if anywhere, is the Prince of Darkness or the Prince of Light, depending on one's own disposition, of the post-industrial order. Malone is a mathematician by training. In 1972 he moved to Colorado to work for Bob Magness, an Oklahoma rancher. Magness had begun developing cable in the 1950s, starting a small cable company in Memphis, Texas. He moved to Montana and then Colorado where he settled in Denver and established his new company under the title of Tele-Communications Inc. He was in considerable debt until Malone came on board and began to expand the company. Magness remains the Chairman and chief shareholder, but is today very much in the background. TCI and Malone's other company, Liberty Media, apart from the huge stake in US cable, also have interests in cable systems in Europe, in TBS, the Discovery Channel, and QVC. In the USA it is in 10 million cable homes, controls 25 per cent of the American cable market, and has revenues of $4 billion. A recent commentary noted: 'It's conceivable that TCI could one day control the country's key communication systems . . . Malone realized early on that in a quasi-monopolistic industry like television he needed to amass a power base to acquire leverage: the bigger he was the better deals he could cut.' He therefore started to buy small cable companies when they came on the market, at what seemed like inflated prices. By the end of the 1980s Malone had done 482 deals, an average of one every two weeks.

In the very early years of his cable career John Malone began to demonstrate qualities that were very quickly to place him at the forefront of the cable revolution. He combined his not inconsiderable intellectual ability, a total commitment to endless hours in the office, and a real gift and zeal for doing deals. By the 1980s he and his company TCI were emerging as the most dominant force in the development of a medium which was to change the landscape of American television. The patter was clear, the persistent and determined acquisition of small cable franchises across the country slowly growing into an enormous and some thought all powerful presence. The scale of Malone's achievement was measured by the fact that he very much had a pivotal position in the strategic development of American television. There wasn't much that could happen, within the market or in Congress, without his concurrence. This was to prove crucial in later debates about the digital revolution and cable. Inevitably there were many enemies made along the way, most notably the then senior senator from Tennessee, Al Gore, who was known to be

---

[1] Quoted in *Multichannel News*, 23 Jan. 1995, p. 5.

furious with the way in which the cable industry as a whole treated its customers.

In 1987, when Ted Turner ran into trouble after the purchase of the MGM/UA film library, it was Malone who put together a consortium to bail out TBS for $568 million in order to prevent it falling into the hands of the networks. Malone emerged with 25 per cent of the stock of TBS, three board seats, and effective control of Ted Turner.

In the spring of 1993 Barry Diller joined Malone to run his QVC network. Diller was the former head of Paramount Pictures and was widely seen as Malone's stalking horse for bigger things. Diller was also seen as essentially motivated by the pursuit of wealth. 'David Geffen had a Gulf Stream and Barry Diller wanted one,' jokes one top entertainment executive. 'That kind of competition might be what's driving the whole future of telecommunications forward.'[2]

What has to be realized is that the QVC deal—which involves at the pro-gramme level the selling of the likes of hair-care kits and porcelain statuettes—was clearly only a stepping stone. The year 1993 was to reveal just how large those steps would prove to be.

At some point in the very early days of the 1990s the boundaries between computers, telephone, television, movies, and radio communications began to blur in a serious way. Other countries had stolen a march on the United States. In Japan there were extensive trials to define the architecture of what had become known as the information society. In Britain cable companies were offering telephone services as well as programmes to their customers. In Germany and France there was a keen desire dating from the 1970s to move in the direction of a post-industrial world. There was much rhetoric, a library of books, numerous conferences all declaiming the new age. It was not however until certain events, particularly in the USA, happened that one began to sense a real and fundamental quickening of the pulse of change.

A number of moments stand out. In 1985, Rupert Murdoch's News Cor-poration bought 20th Century Fox from an oil tycoon, Marvin Davis, for $600 million and laid the basis for establishing the fourth US network, Fox. Also in 1985 Turner Broadcasting Systems paid $1.5 billion for MGM to guarantee a supply of programming for the TBS superstation. In 1988 Sony paid $2 billion for CBS Records and in 1989 $3.4 billion for Columbia Pictures; it already owned Tri-Star and thus controls about 20 per cent of the US movie box-office and sits on a huge film library, which was really the point of the purchases. In 1990, the giant Japanese corporation Matsushita bought MCA/Universal for $6.1 billion, thus gaining control of Hollywood's largest television and film library. In January 1990, Time Inc. bought Warner Communications for $14.1 billion to create Time-Warner Inc., a multi-media company with major

---

[2] Ibid.

interests in film and television production, publishing, and premium cable channels. In August 1992 TCI announced that as of 1994 they were going to introduce digital compression, which in lay terms meant that where there had been 40 channels or so in the average cable home there would now be four or five hundred. The actual implementation of the plan was put on hold, but few doubt its eventual operation.

All of these developments suggested that this was no longer playing with change, this was ramming it through at an extraordinary pace in a development which seemed to be on a par with the creation of the printing press in the fifteenth century and that of television itself in the late nineteenth century.

In late August 1993 the CBS network announced that it would not be asking cable companies for cash payments if they carried its programmes on their systems, as it had a right to do under the terms of the Cable Act of 1992. The networks' capitulation—and that was a word used extensively in the press commentary on the situation—seemed to be one more toll of the bell for traditional television, because the cable industry had made it quite clear that if the network persisted in its demands they would simply yank it from their schedules. In May 1993 US West, one of the regional telephone companies which emerged from the breakup of AT&T, decided to invest $2.5 billion in a Time-Warner venture to develop advanced technology for consumer video services, one of the first major signs that what was slowly evolving was not so much a rivalry between telephone and cable but a natural alliance driven by the technical convergence of telephone, computers, and television.

In July 1993 Rupert Murdoch announced that News Corporation was acquiring a majority stake in the Hong Kong-based pan-Asian Star TV which theoretically had a potential audience of 2.8 billion people from Israel to Japan. On 23 September 1993 the FCC announced the terms under which the auctions of the radio spectrum for 'PCs', personal communications systems, would take place, a sale which would raise billions of dollars for the federal government. It became very clear, very quickly, that the cable industry was eyeing this new opportunity, which once would have been regarded as the sole preserve of the traditional voice communication industry, such as the telephone companies and the cellular phone industry.

In September 1993 a take-over struggle developed over the purchase of Paramount Communications. As the battle developed no one, other than two or three individuals, knew that it was merely a related sideshow in another development of truly titanic proportions. At the centre of the fight for Paramount was Martin Davis, Paramount's chairman and chief executive, who agreed to a $7.5 billion merger with Viacom, owner of MTV and much else, and controlled by the forceful and determined Sumner Redstone. The appeal was quite simple to understand. Redstone's Viacom, which had been built on movie theatres, had expanded into cable television and thus, like everyone else in the industry, wanted to ensure that they had the 'software' to go with the hardware. Paramount was an obvious choice since it was one of the last remaining studios that could be purchased. When Redstone, on 13 September, announced his plans to buy Paramount he caused an enormous flurry of interest among those who were themselves thinking of expanding their media interests. Two figures in particular very quickly announced their own interests: Barry Diller and Ted Turner.

On 20 September Diller, Chairman of the highly successful shopping network QVC, offered $10.1 billion for Paramount in what was described uniformly in the business pages as an 'unfriendly bid'. Diller's bid was not only larger than Viacom's, with a much larger cash element, it was also backed by Malone, whose Liberty Media company shared control of QVC with Diller. The reasons for the scramble for control of Paramount were put clearly by Ted Turner, who already owned the MGM film library, and in whose company, TBS, John Malone's TCI is a major investor: 'I have more than 3,000 old movies and no new movies except for television movies. If you are going to be a big player you have got to have the product.'[3] Paramount has a library of 15,000 television programmes and 2,000 feature films. The company also owned Simon & Schuster, one of the world's largest publishers, two sports teams, and the Madison Square Garden sports complex.

Viacom responded to the QVC bid with a number of lawsuits, one of which sought to have it blocked on the grounds that John Malone was the real power behind the bid and that he was trying to monopolize the cable industry, a claim which had a manifest and significant level of plausibility. They also put together the financing of an increased offer for Paramount, including $1.2 billion in support from Nynex Corporation, a regional telephone company, and $600 million from Blockbuster Entertainment Corporation, whose fortune had been made through its chain of video stores. Nynex's involvement reflected a growing interest among the USA's telephone companies in the entertainment industry. In May for example US West and Time-Warner had entered into just such an arrangement. On 17 October two other media conglomerates, Advance Publications, with interests in publishing, newspapers, magazines, cable television, and Cox Enterprises, with cable, broadcast, and newspaper interests, offered $500 million each to add to the QVC bid for Paramount.

At the very same moment as the struggle for Paramount between Sumner Redstone and Barry Diller was receiving extensive coverage in the business pages, another, less contentious, but perhaps none the less important story emerged, with the announcement of a new MTV service, MTV Latino, covering Spanish-speaking Central and South America, with an intended audience of 3 million to 5 million homes in twenty countries. MTV Networks was also

---

[3] *Sunday Times*, 26 Sept. 1993.

planning to put other services into the region, such as VH1 and Nickelodeon. An MTV official is quoted as saying, 'There's one last area for us, which would be South and Central Africa.'[4]

Behind the fight for Paramount was a notion that had become highly prevalent in the 1980s, the notion of synergy, natural alliances of companies in which the whole is bigger and better than the sum of the parts. The evidence of benefits was by 1993 somewhat limited. The debt incurred to finance the mergers, clashing corporate cultures, and the drag effect of large new bureaucracies undermined the original synergistic ambitions. However, what was happening in the cable industry was somewhat different in that logics of merger, while clearly touched by the usual avarice and ambition, even megalomania, seemed to be demanded by the very nature of the increasingly dominant technologies. For example, the alliances fashioned out of the pursuit of 'software' houses seemed inevitable given the simple emerging fact of life, that the massive increase in the technological capacity to communicate was not paralleled by anywhere near the same level of productions to put on the technology.

As if to complicate things even further Paramount announced in October that it would join forces with Chris-Craft Industries to start a fifth television network. The service would begin in 1995 and offer four hours of television each week over two nights. The key to this lay in the fact that Paramount was already producing thirty hours of programming a week, including such highly successful syndicated programmes as *Star Trek: The Next Generation*, *Entertainment Tonight*, *The Arsenio Hall Show*, and *Hard Copy*. The announcement also contained the fact that the network would première a new series, *Star Trek Voyager*. The notion behind the proposal was the putting together of a network of ten already owned stations, the acquisition of existing independent stations, and the creation of a superstation to be carried by cable systems. On opening night the new network would reach 27 per cent of the television households in the country, building eventually to about 70 per cent. The assumption was that Paramount was taking the initiative in a situation in which other companies, such as Time-Warner and Diller of QVC, were known to be exploring the possibilities of a fifth network.

This was an extraordinary development since there had been much comment in previous years, as cable had grown, that the era of networks was over. What was becoming clear was that what was really in decline was the idea of what we might call the full service network. All Paramount-Craft had in mind was a mainstream entertainment service dominated by battle-proven programmes such as *Star Trek*. The emergence of the new network would further shrink the number of independent stations, thus reducing the number of outlets for off-network syndication.

---

[4] *New York Times*, 27 Sept. 1993.

The events of 1993 made clear that one of the key issues to be resolved by governments, in the USA and elsewhere, would be how to construct a new policy environment which could handle the fact of convergence. The regulatory systems and policy regimes in place were constructed at a time when different forms of communication—telephony, print, broadcasting, movies, computing—were technologically, and therefore institutionally, separate. Come the superhighway, that is no longer the case: digitalization of messages and optic fibre cable bring *everything* together.

Britain had led the way in creating a policy which favoured cable companies, including American ones such as TCI, by allowing them to offer their British subscribers telephone services, in competition with BT, but not allowing BT to offer audio-visual services. Britain had in fact become a test bed for the telephone company–cable alliance that the Bell Atlantic–TCI merger came to symbolize. TCI for example was in a joint venture with US West called Telewest and operated the largest cable franchise area in the UK with 180,000 television subscribers and 120,000 telephone subscribers. US West and TCI were investing $1.8 billion in their British operations. Nynex was investing $3 billion in its UK cable interests. Other cable–telco ventures, Southwest Bell–Cox, Bell Canada–Jones, were investing hundreds of millions more.

If the barriers were coming down between previously discrete systems and processes then inevitably the way was being opened for someone or some corporate entity to own whatever configurations were now possible. What we can see then is a movement in two directions. One reflects the natural propensity of capital to seek monopoly, with conglomeration creating fewer and fewer players controlling the market. The other reflects the need to find new markets to sell products, either through niche programming, to a particular society, or by finding new markets in other countries.

It is inevitable that the huge American conglomerates will do even more to dominate international markets in the way in which they dominate the US domestic market. So we see the inevitable spread of the availability of CNN, TNT, the Cartoon Network, VH1, MTV, Nickelodeon around the world. Equally the ambitions of Murdoch to take his Sky services, particularly Sky News, around the world are very clear. NBC bought a 75 per cent share of Superchannel, giving it a possible 60 million European cable homes to enter. Time-Warner is taking its HBO service to many different countries. Cox, an Atlanta-based media conglomerate, has taken stakes in UK Gold, which dips into the archives of the BBC, Thames, and UK Living, a life-styles channel oriented to women. Pat Robertson's International Family Entertainment bought the British commercial television company TVS after they lost their franchise, and brought the Family Channel to the UK.

In September 1993 MTV Europe, which has its headquarters in London, arrived in Cyprus and Turkey through arrangements with local broadcasters and cable operators. In January 1994 MTV used compression technology on one of its four satellites to increase the capacity from one to four channels. Its revenues were about $70 million a year and it is believed to be the first pan-European service which is making money.

On 1 October 1993 the QVC channel, a joint venture between the USA's QVC and Sky, went on the air, the UK's first 24-hour, 365-days-a-year shopping channel. There was some potent symbolism: the importation into Britain, home to what many regarded as the most highly developed public service system in the world, of the emergent high-tech. banality of American television culture. The foundation to these developments was the emergence of a number of major companies which seemed likely to dominate the future of communication: AT&T, Bell Atlantic, British Telecom, Matsushita, Microsoft, News Corporation, Nintendo, Philips, Sega, Sony, Time-Warner, US West, QVC, and Viacom.

On 13 October 1993 there was an announcement at a press conference at the Hotel Macklowe in New York which bested even the frenzied activities of the rest of the year. John Malone of TCI and Ray Smith of Bell Atlantic announced a deal which dwarfed any other in history, the purchase by the telephone company Bell Atlantic of 100 per cent of the stock of TCI and Liberty Media, both dominated by John Malone. Announcing the $33 billion deal, Malone pointed to the underlying technology which would allow the integration into a single stream of communication of telephony and television information, all with the interactive capability traditionally associated with the computer. The new company would, through TCI's existing interests, have the biggest number of cable subscribers in the USA; stakes in several cable programming services such as 49 per cent of Discovery Channel; a 23 per cent share of TBS, and thus of WTBS, TNT, CNN, sports franchises, MGM, video and film production; 100 per cent of Liberty Media, and thus 18 per cent of Black Entertainment Network, 15 per cent of the Family Channel; 22 per cent of QVC, and, possibly, Paramount Communication. It would also have the whole infrastructure of Bell Atlantic's telephone system.

The real implication, or at least ambition, was summed up by a comment by Vice-President Al Gore: 'The Administration supports any development in the communications marketplace that is pro-competitive and fosters the development of an open, interactive information infrastructure.'[5] Gore himself during the course of the 1992 presidential campaign had popularized the notion of building an 'information superhighway' or, as he labelled it, a national information infrastructure (NII). The allusion was to the highway-building programme of the 1950s which was seen as having been such an important part of the general prosperity of those years, and in which Gore's father had been a prime mover. The problem was that both philosophically

---

[5] *New York Times*, 14 Oct. 1993.

and fiscally the US federal government was in no position to provide the huge amounts of money necessary. The proposed merger of Bell Atlantic and TCI both symbolized the character of the emerging information society, but also, if allowed to proceed, created a corporation sufficiently large and so inclined to commence building the superhighway in earnest. Ray Smith told the press conference announcing the merger: 'This is a perfect information age marriage. Together we will make the information highway a reality.' Together the two companies had a market capitalization of about $60 billion. The sense that here was the reinventing of America was palpable in the flurry of media coverage and comment which followed the announcement.

A fibre optic network would be created which would allow anybody on it to send and receive any amount of information in any form—words, video images, sound, or graphics. The technology envisaged the traditional television set being transformed into a powerful computer, only one of whose applications would be the old-fashioned possibility of 'watching' television. The response from Viacom, which was still trying to buy Paramount, summarized the concerns of some people about the place of John Malone in these developments: 'TCI's ability to dominate our nation's cable network and information infrastructure is virtually unlimited. It is time for our nation's lawmakers and the communication industry's leaders to take a hard look at the record and the power of John Malone.'[6] The question which was obviously raised by the merger was whether or not the new vertically integrated corporation, which would control a significant proportion of the hardware and software of US communications, had monopoly implications which would prove unacceptable.

The merger was overwhelmingly greeted by gasps of amazement and a widespread sense that here at last was the real reinventing of America. The most significant reaction was a flurry of other acquisitions and mergers. It has been calculated that during 1993 there were something like 160 multi-media deals with a value of $75 billion.

A good sense of how discourse about the information highway had evolved is captured by a full-page advertisement in the *New York Times* on 5 January 1994.

This time, the monopoly is the map and the clock. And MCI has an astonishing plan of liberation from them.

Today, we inaugurate the nation's first transcontinental Information Superhighway —part of an overriding vision for the next century that bears the name networkMCI.

The roadbed for this highway is SONET fiber optic technology, with the power to move information 15 times faster than any SONET

25 YEARS AGO, WE TOOK ON THE LARGEST COMPANY ON EARTH.

network available today. Coupled with SONET will be ATM switching technology, giving the network self-healing capabilities within a subsecond.

[6] Ibid.

Together, they will shrink the distances between humanity with everything from broadcast quality videophones, to long distance medical imaging, to universal access to information, to worldwide Personal Communication Services.

The first traveler on the New York-to-L.A. portion of this superhighway will be the Internet. MCI, in one of telecommunications' best-kept secrets, has been providing Internet connections for the last half decade.

It now empowers 20 million people to conduct a worldwide conversation with each other via computers.

What networkMCI will do is unite the human voice and data and video image and interactive multimedia for the entire nation and beyond.

MCI, together with its partners, will invest more than $20 billion over the next six years to create a veritable brain trust for the Information Age.

TODAY, WE TAKE ON SPACE AND TIME.

The space-time continuum is being challenged. The notion of communication is changed forever. All the information in the universe will soon be accessible to everyone at every moment.

And all because of a dream known as the Information Superhighway and a vision known as networkMCI.

This advertisement is an interesting example of the language which surrounds the so-called superhighway. Implicit is the assumption that we live on the cusp of change. Not just any kind of change, but major change which will strike this society with the same force as the industrial revolution. In short, the assumption is that America, and behind it other societies, is being reinvented. Internet has become the metaphor for the new age and its proponents. It is an argument born in part out of a sense of wonder at the possibilities of the technology allied to a firm conviction, clearly held with some force by the Clinton administration, that unless the United States does reinvent itself then it will slowly decline as the economics of global life demand a post-industrial condition. On 11 January 1994 Vice-President Gore addressed a 'Superhighway Summit' at UCLA. In his speech Gore prodded the industry players—who will build superhighway—to think about the broader public interest, and 'challenged' them to link all classrooms, libraries, and health clinics to an interactive video and data network by 11 January 2000. At the same meeting however John Malone repeated his view that home shopping, gaming, and entertainment video on demand would create the revenues to spend the billions of dollars to build the National Information Infrastructure. In this he was echoing the comments of Ray Smith, who will chair the new TCI–Bell Atlantic conglomerate. In December 1993 Smith told the Western Cable Show that five 'killer applications' will help finance their plans to bring two-way video services to 1.25 million homes by the end of 1995 and to 8.75 million homes by 2000. The killer applications he outlined were: video-on-demand, home shopping, video games, programming, and direct-response advertising. Mixing his metaphors he described these killer applications as 'plums ripe to be picked'.

If metaphors are required to delineate the future it is, from Smith's rather than Gore's standpoint, one of 'Blockbuster Video meets the shopping mall in your living room'. Such evolution may indeed be significant, but it hardly constitutes a shift in the axial principles which define this or any other society. Here is the old order in new high-tech. garb, but deeply challenging to other parts of the old order. The *New York Times* in a piece titled 'Newspapers Race for Outlets in Electronic Marketplace' stated:

The rapid development of electronic information technologies have placed the American newspaper industry at a crossroads. New methods of delivering information to desktops and living rooms are threatening the economic foundation of the $45 billion newspaper industry, historically one of the most lucrative and influential of American businesses. Newspaper companies are racing toward electronic media of all kinds in an attempt to pre-empt the competition.[7]

The assumption is that NII will provide 'paths for new vendors to compete cheaply in the sale of news and other information'. Walter Wriston, the former head of Citicorps and a leading proponent of market forces in the areas of communications activity, observed:

Information technology has created an entirely new economy, an information economy, as different from the industrial economy as the industrial was from the agricultural. And when the sources of the wealth of nations change, the politics of nations change as well. . . . Information technology has forever changed the way the world works. It has changed the way wealth is created. It has changed the concept of sovereignty as borders become totally porous. Advanced technology does not produce wisdom. It does not change human nature nor make our problems go away. But with much trauma and dislocation, it does speed the world on its journey to more freedom for more people.[8]

What we can see emerging are two models for the future, which have become subsumed within the generic concept of the National Information Infrastructure: Internet—centrally concerned with 'information'—and super-highway—critically concerned with 'pleasure'. The question is which of these models will prevail, what will be the impact of the one on the other, or will they live side by side, satisfying different social needs? These are important but difficult questions to answer.

Underlying the ambitions of superhighway—and those numerous other formulations of the information society in many different countries—is, as was seen in Wriston's words, an assumption: that the larger consequence of these developments is a change in the character of society, a shift in its material being, in its sense of self, mores, values, conventional assumptions. This formulation leaves out something which it is absolutely vital to grasp: that societies cannot

[7] Ibid. 17 Jan. 1994.
[8] Walter Wriston, *The Twilight of Sovereignty* (New York: Charles Scribner's Sons, 1992), 186.

evolve materially without a concomitant shift in their mental or intellectual being. It is clear that if there is a condition of 'the new' then that has to be definable according to a set of structures—material and intellectual—such that we can readily see that we have become something different from what we were, that not just the forms of economic activity have changed, but the axial principles that define the society have also changed. The relevance of such change and possible impact of NII was put well by Krishan Kumar: 'If the passage from the industrial to the post-industrial society ever occurs it must live up to the promise of its name. The post-industrial society must contain a principle and a direction very different from that of the industrial, just as the latter distinguished itself from its pre-industrial forms.'[9]

The likely development of NII thus needs to be considered on the basis on which it affects social institutions (business, education, the family, the mass media, politics, trade, government) *and* the habits of life and thought of the population. However, as evidenced by the contrasting language of Gore/MCI and Malone/Smith, the advanced character of NII is being incubated within the old culture. One finds the conceptual and preferential 'genetic' fingerprints of the old all over the new. For example, home shopping or video-on-demand are old activities in new garb, with very different dynamics and consequences from those of, say, the financial analyst or the university professor using Internet.

Consider the relationship of NII with such social institutions as the family, education, government, and citizenry, establishments of public culture and the entertainment industry. The NII has the capacity to bring into the *family home* a wide range of services, to allow people to work from home, to send and receive messages in text, audio, and video, to commune with like-minded individuals through 'cyberspace', to construct communities that do not exist in any meaningful physical sense but which 'act' as if they did, to structure each individual's own informational and entertainment environment. But what of the price of such home-centred provision—price in both the literal and metaphorical sense. Will those with disposable incomes be able to opt in to the new services while those on lesser incomes are excluded? Will we have a society of information haves and have-nots? And what of the idea of isolation, the idea that the more inward we become in terms of the patterns of our lives the less cohesive our sense and sharing of community becomes? Is there not a clear and dangerous relationship between the sociological construction of the tendency of more people to live alone and the technologies' capacity to nurture that condition? And what is to be done to address these issues?

In *education* the NII can clearly begin to provide access to bodies of information and teaching aids of which previous ages could only dream. There is clearly the potential for major educational empowerment, and for the

---

[9] Krishan Kumar, *Prophecy and Progress* (London: Allen Lane, 1978), 327.

enhancement of the educators' goal of producing a literate, skilled, and capable population. But the very same structure delivers to the child enormous numbers of new sources of simple entertainment. In particular it provides young boys with a hugely enhanced capacity to play video games with all their implicit capacity to construct new and very different forms of 'literacy' which fundamentally challenge traditional educational practice.

Citizenship and *governance* quite possibly receive a major boost as the provision of information for political discourse, analysis, and understanding becomes unparalleled. But then the technology provides for a new Age of Distraction in which the desire and ability to pay attention to the governance of human affairs is kicked aside as ex-citizens do other things, like watching movies, or living in cyberspace, or editing their own football game.

The technology of communications allows unprecedented access to a *digitalized culture*, from art to books to music to the theatre, to the whole storehouse of the artefacts of the human adventure. But at a price and at the expense, maybe, of the public library, the art gallery, the subsidized theatre, the repertory company, the local music store, the movie theatre.

The *entertainment* industry can offer more, with the widespread assumption that by the millennium most cable homes will have upwards of 500 channels available. So more 'choice' in a quantitative sense will be available but is it more of less, an explosion of the banal and mediocre rather than the special and the creative? And as the audience fragments, relocating itself in niches of taste, so go the networks and with them the ability of any medium to service the whole society-as-community. Perhaps one of the most significant entertainment uses of the new communications infrastructure will be video games. In the US video games rake in $5.3 billion annually, which is about $400 million more than movie box-office receipts, and global sales equal $10 billion. What this means is that video games strategically became one of the cutting edges of the efforts by huge corporations such as AT&T, Time-Warner, and TCI to develop interactive television. Video games lie at the intersection of Hollywood, Silicon Valley, and the information highway. The video-game capacity of the interactive age would be one way to get children to persuade their parents to sign up for new services.

The video game Mortal Kombat, for example, released in September 1993 with a $10 million media campaign, was expected to bring in $150 million by Christmas 1993, equivalent to the revenue for a major hit movie. One of the most aggressively ambitious video-game companies is 3DO, using initially CDs to service its 32-bit Multiplayer but eventually looking to use interactive cable. 3DO is backed by Time-Warner and Universal Studios, working with the successful video-game company Electronic Arts. Sega has also entered into an agreement with Time-Warner and TCI, who will create a special Sega channel that would give subscribers access to fifty games each month. Sega has also entered into an agreement with AT&T which will allow video games to be played anywhere in the world over ordinary telephone lines. More and more video games are being based on successful movies and television programmes, to the extent that the two productions tend to happen at the same time. And all the while lurking in the realms of distinct technological and commercial possibility waits virtual reality.

Two models, two worlds; reinventing America, or merely using technologies to extend the boundaries of that which already exists; a new sophisticated citizenry or a new ignorance drowning in trivialized pleasures and an obsessive teleconsumerism; accessing the post-industrial Alexandrian library or Mortal Kombat 50; or a mix of all of the above?

The debate that is gathering force in the United States is about the future of the society, how it would be ordered, what its central dynamics would be, where the benefits would flow. It is a debate where the extraordinary nudges against the banal: for example, the ordering of cheap trinkets from a home shopping channel or young boys playing endless hours with video games whose defining characteristics are the vividness and extent of their violence.

The early 1990s, and in particular 1993, saw a quickening pace, providing a clear glimpse of the key motifs that would characterize the future direction of communication. There were equally important developments elsewhere, no more so than in Britain, which flowed from a profound sense of a changing world in which an old communications order would need to accommodate to the new. The nature of the debate under way is, however, very different from that in the USA.

London, the National Film Theatre, 9 March 1993

It was a curious sight. On the stage of the National Film Theatre sat Jeremy Isaacs, the former chief executive of Channel four, the current general director of the Royal Opera House, and the man many cognoscenti felt should have been the Director-General of the BBC, interviewing John Birt, former commercial broadcaster and the man who was the actual DG of the BBC. The curiosity, however, lay not in the format but in the initial focus of the questioning.

'Would you like, John, to explain to our audience who the secretary was who got the £15,000?' 'No I won't, Jeremy, it is not right that I have to reveal every detail of my personal matters. I don't intend to.'

Curious indeed. The world of television was in a state of turmoil and change, and here was the head of the Corporation being asked about 'filthy lucre'.

The details were simple enough. It had emerged in the spring of 1993 that John Birt was not employed by the BBC even though he was its head. His company John Birt Productions (JBP) was paid a consultancy fee by the BBC and John Birt, who with his wife was one of only two directors, paid himself from the fee. It was an unusual arrangement for someone in his position, but not unique. Indeed as he readily pointed out it was commonplace in the world from which he had come, commercial television. It was a simple and perfectly legal way of avoiding tax. Behind the simplicity of the facts, however, lurked other, more troubled forces.

In the first case, someone spotted that JBP paid £15,000 to a secretary. Who was this person and why on earth did the Director-General of the BBC need to pay for a secretary, from moneys provided by the BBC, when he had at his disposal several private secretaries and a whole secretariat? Could it be, the cynical mutterers were heard to yell, not whisper, that the 'secretary' was none other than Mrs Birt? No one would say, and it did not matter because the rumour was more useful than any truth. Here was a chink in the armour, an Achilles' heel of the man who had come to represent change of a profound kind in the organization and, possibly, mission of the BBC. This was not a controversy about tax arrangements. This was a battle for an institution which was adored by many, who regarded it, not without some justification, as easily the greatest broadcasting organization that has ever been.

It emerged however that his terms of employment, and thus his tax arrangements, had had the seal of approval of the Chairman of the BBC, Marmaduke Hussey. This did not help since it was widely known that Birt had become DG because Hussey wanted him to 'sort out' the BBC. He was thus the man to prepare the BBC for the 'inevitably' more competitive environment of the 1990s. But could he change it in such a way that it was fiscally fitter and still this remarkably creative national public broadcasting service?

The Annual Conference of the Radio Academy, Birmingham, England, 13 July 1993

The speaker was 58 years old, famous for a rather crumpled appearance, dishevelled clothing, a calm urbanity of manner. In 1985 he was voted the twenty-seventh most influential person in India, from where he had been broadcasting for the BBC for the best part of thirty years. He was, observed the London *Times*, 'regarded by many as one of the world's finest broadcasters'. Here on this day in the Midlands of England, Mark Tully was addressing several hundred workers in, and lovers of, radio. His speech was a savage assault on what was happening inside the BBC, and in particular on the actions and policies of the man who was technically his boss, the Director-General, John Birt. Tully's concern was with change in the BBC which he took to be revolutionary. He also seemed troubled, as were others, that the new regime proceeded by mocking and denigrating the old, which was painted as having been overly bureaucratic, inefficient, and wasteful.

Tully responded that under the old regime management was centrally concerned to protect the position of the producer—the point of creativity. After the Birtian revolution the whole institution had become top heavy and rigid, smothering the creative potential of the production staff.

The response to Tully's speech was remarkable. In the first instance he received a standing ovation from the attendees at the Conference, many of whom worked at the BBC. Other commentators, such as Brenda Maddox, penned supportive pieces. Maddox, in a column in the *Daily Telegraph* the following day with the headline 'Big Brother's Reign of Terror at the BBC', observed:

Mark Tully is right. Conversations with a range of senior staff—from the regions as well as London, programme-makers as well as administrators—all yield the same message that the BBC's respected New Delhi correspondent delivered yesterday in Birmingham. The BBC is ruled by fear, secrecy and sycophancy.

Especially fear. It is simply not possible for a journalist to talk to anybody within the BBC about the BBC without hearing—usually repeatedly—the desperate plea, 'This is off the record? You promise not to quote me? I've got a family to keep.'

Thus reassured (although he did not dare to send a fax for fear that it would be traceable), one executive declared, 'Tully is an extremely brave man. The licence-payers are paying millions for a dream-world from which a lack of instinctive flair is being disguised by being methodical.'

. . . Tully kindly said that 'Stalinist' may be too strong a word for the regime now in power. If so, others suggest 'Maoist'. There are the reindoctrination courses in which BBC staff are shipped into a specially refurbished headquarters in London and given 'structural walk-throughs' of the new organisation.[10]

The day after Tully's barrage, Birt spoke to the Radio Academy in his own defence:

So let me confront some of the black propaganda that has been obscuring what's actually happening in the BBC.

First, let me address those critics outside the BBC. They come in many forms: traditionalists, opportunists, society's hecklers, ever ready with a quote, and there's even the odd old BBC soldier sniping at us with their illusions, still telling nostalgic tales of the golden days when no one bothered much about management, when all was creativity and romance.

But either they are ignorant of, or they conveniently ignore the changed universe in which the BBC now operates—changes not of our making . . .

I'd like to say a word or two about yesterday's missive from Our Own Correspondent, Mark Tully. I am grateful for the dignified and carefully argued case he made yesterday. It was obviously heartfelt; and I want to preserve much of the ethos that Mark holds in such affection.

[10] *Daily Telegraph*, 14 July 1993.

But I have to say to Mark, first, that the BBC is a living part of the society it serves. It must change and develop and learn from what happens around it.

Second, the BBC must draw in the best talent from outside as well as promote the best from inside the BBC. He makes management in the BBC sound like they all wear a uniform. He should come and meet them . . .

Mark also said yesterday that 'there is a very real sense of fear among staff which prevents them speaking their minds'. I can tell you that's not my experience. The BBC is blessed with one of the most intelligent, articulate, questioning and sceptical work-forces in the nation . . .

Radical reform was the only option for the BBC for a hugely important reason . . . the BBC's financial circumstances have been completely transformed in the past few years—and not for the better. For decades the BBC had been cushioned by real rises in its income, drawn from a number of sources. That golden era is over . . .

So I say to those who look back with nostalgia to a bygone age, please face those realities.

If you really care for the BBC, bury the hatchet and stop fighting old wars. Recognise we are building on the BBC's most cherished values and on its best traditions . . .

Join us in the fight to win a new charter based on the promise of a creative, alert BBC, clear about its programme purposes. It will be a modern well-managed institution, not afraid to adapt and change, looking forward with confidence and backwards with affection for Auntie and respect for a great programme tradition. It will be an institution ready and fit to take its place in a new and beckoning century.

Birt was to a considerable extent correct. The world had changed. But the issue which he was really raising was whether his harsh medicine could lay the basis for a reinvigorated Corporation that would carry into the twenty-first century the traditions and programme excellence which had made the BBC the dominant broadcasting organization of the twentieth century.

There was, however, another perception that danced across the mind's eye, that Birt was no more than a symbol, that rather than the midwife to a new golden age of public service broadcasting he was mortician to an age now past. The world was changing; the 1980s were the Passchendaele of public broadcasters. In the events of 1993 in the United States, in the betrothal of the technology of abundance to the ideology of the market-place, there lay the future, and for those who treasured the memory of the past, the words of Max Weber, the nineteenth-century sociologist, hauntingly returned: 'Not summer's bloom lies ahead of us, but rather a polar night of icy darkness.'

Yet a larger context would inevitably come into play in shaping the destiny of commercial television in Britain. In winning their franchises in 1992, and in commencing broadcasting in January 1993, the ITV companies were in effect being asked to shed the tradition of public service which had been such a vital characteristic of the old commercial system, generate sufficient income to be able to pay their fees and advertising levy to the Treasury, and maintain their commitments to producing quality programmes. All of this to happen in an environment increasingly defined by large multi-national corporations with large global ambitions. It is important to remember that while the ITV companies remained a highly visible part of the life of Britain, in economic terms they remained relatively small when compared to say the Bertelsmann group in Germany or Silvio Berlusconi's Fininvest Corporation, or Murdoch's News Corporation. The total capitalization of all the ITV companies is equivalent to about $6 billion (at 1993 rates). The capitalization of the company formed through the proposed merger of TCI and Bell Atlantic is in the region of $60 billion. The terms of the legislation which had established the new ITV system made some, limited provision for internal mergers, but extensive provision for European companies to invest in any given ITV company. The system to many observers seemed highly vulnerable, weak even in the face of huge international forces. It came as no surprise then that in late November the government let it be known that it would 'relax' the take-over rules for ITV. Immediately at the end of November Carlton, which already had the London weekday franchise, announced that it would make a bid for one of the other major companies, Central Television, a move which would give Carlton about a third of all television advertising revenue in Britain. The move was interpreted not only as a way of developing the company within Britain, but as a step towards developing the company globally. Here was one more piece of evidence that the likely future of television was not national, but a transnational process dominated by a small number of large corporations.

The shift in the public service character of ITV seemed even more precipitous, more final, and more fundamental than anything that was taking place at the BBC. Both were, however, obviously linked to the shifting organization of global communication. The managerial revolution of the BBC, the destruction of public service commitments within ITV and the creation of new conglomerates among the companies continue apace. It seems not just unlikely, but impossible, that the future will be different.

11 The New Television in Britain

The early development of new media systems in Britain had all the characteristics of a meteor shower on a dark night. The dark night was a Britain depressed by unemployment and economic decline; the shower was cable and satellite, the television vanguard of the information society, briefly illuminating the surrounding gloom. Like a meteor shower it vanished rapidly, leaving all as it was before. Yet the furious debate about cable and satellite after 1979 did leave one lasting intellectual legacy. It brought to the fore arguments about the development of the whole of British culture which have challenged and continue to challenge dominant ideas of the relationship between public culture and the state.

At the beginning of the 1980s, one could detect a stirring of an interest and anticipation about the future of cable television. Travellers had returned from across the ocean with tales of wonder at the exploits and new-found wealth of a curious creation called Home Box Office. A British thesis was developed —by the captains of industry and by lowly, but ambitious, entrepreneurs in the provinces: if only one could develop cable television in Britain, then similar wealth would be at hand with limitless prospects for the future. The thesis gained a patron. Mrs Thatcher was convinced that a resolution of Britain's economic crisis lay to a considerable extent in transforming Britain from a country whose wealth lay in manufacturing, to one whose wealth lay in processing information. This conjunction of dreams born of private greed and political opportunism provided the necessary political and economic conditions in which the information revolution could be planned.

The 'new cable age', 'the third age of broadcasting', 'beyond broadcasting', 'the new communications technologies', 'the post-industrial society' were slogans which spawned a thousand conferences, seminars, television programmes in the early 1980s.

The subterranean themes within the debate about cable and satellite—the need for deregulated services, the virtues of the market in cultural choice and by extension the problematic nature of public support for culture, the irresistibly seductive force of the economic salvation which was deemed to reside within a vastly expanded technological capacity to communicate—had taken hold and begun to reshape the whole mental ecology of communications in Britain. Whatever happened it seemed likely that the world of broadcasting would never be the same again (any writer on this subject is necessarily indebted to the marvellous work of Tim Hollins, whose *Beyond Broadcasting: Into the Cable Age* is the definitive study of the history and growth of cable TV in Britain).[1]

The Slow Birth of Cable

The relaying of broadcast signals through wire to overcome problems of reception, and at the same time serve as a source of commercial revenue for small companies, developed slowly but surely in Britain from the 1920s onwards. Rediffusion claims to have installed the world's first cable network, for the relay of a single radio channel, in March 1928. By 1950, nearly 1 million homes received their radio programmes by wire, representing about 8 per cent of radio licences. Equally slowly but surely, the industry became dominated by a number of large companies, a trend which was further emphasized by the use of cable to relay television services.

The first British cable television system was installed by Link Sound and Vision Ltd. in Gloucester in 1951. Growth before the coming of independent television in 1956 was limited, but ITV appears to have given cable a considerable boost. While the number of television sets in Britain doubled between 1956 and 1961, subscription to cable television increased tenfold to 554,700. By 1966, over 1 million people received their television signals by cable, and by 1973 the number of homes peaked at roughly 2.5 million (13.8 per cent of those with television).

In 1972 the Conservative government granted a licence to Greenwich Cablevision to develop local programming. The government also announced the availability of other licences for similar projects. The companies welcomed the opportunity and there was clearly an expectation that more lucrative uses

[1] Tim Hollins, *Beyond Broadcasting: Into the Cable Age* (London: BRU/BFI, 1984).

of cable would follow. The demise of the Heath government in 1974, the emergence of a far less sympathetic Labour government, and the appointment of the Annan Committee to look into the future of broadcasting made such prospects dim indeed. Annan, indeed, was to call cable 'a parasite'.

The return of a Conservative government in 1979 reversed the persistent anti-cable trend of previous years. In a speech to the annual luncheon of the Cable Television Association (CTVA) on 13 November 1979, the Home Secretary, William Whitelaw, breathed new life into old ideas:

Subscription television can offer an additional service to the public and if it proves to be a service that the public wants to have, and is prepared to pay for, then it is reasonable to try it. But we need to ensure that subscription television—and the rate at which it might be introduced—does good not harm. There must, therefore, be adequate safeguards. . . . Subscription television should not be allowed to weaken and impoverish the existing off-air broadcasting services. . . . There is need to consider the effect of subscription television on the cinema industry, and also to consider what other rules should be applied regarding programme content. . . . Technological advances cannot be ignored. As a country with its living to earn in the world we cannot afford to be left behind, but I hope what I have said this afternoon has reassured you that the government believes that cable television has an important role to play in a broadcasting system which we want to preserve and develop.[2]

In November 1980 Whitelaw approved thirteen licences for pay-cable schemes to be run on the existing systems of seven companies. Licences were initially for two years and allowed extra charges to be made to those people who wished to receive an additional channel of feature films, entertainment, sport, and, it was hoped, an element of local programming. The industry, however, was not overflowing with gratitude and felt that what was being allowed was too little, too late. One senior figure from Rediffusion said at the time: 'We say enough of this mucking about with pilot schemes, now is the time we should be allowed to get on with it!'[3]

In September 1980, the Cabinet Office's Advisory Council for Applied Research and Development (ACARD), established by the Labour government in 1976, had presented a report to the Cabinet on the importance of information technology (IT). In particular it recommended the creation of a department to co-ordinate policy on computing, telecommunications, and information handling, and suggested, in view of the IT implications of teletext and mobile radio, that broadcasting should also be brought within this brief. Moreover, it expressed its opinion that 'a first class, modern economic communications system is . . . essential for effective application of IT'.[4]

---

[2] William Whitelaw, speech to Cable Television Association, 13 Nov. 1979.

[3] Quoted in Hollins, *Beyond Broadcasting*, 62.

[4] Advisory Council for Applied Research and Development, *Information Technology* (London: HMSO, 1980), 41.

Although it scarcely mentioned cable television, the ACARD Report never-theless raised speculation that a transfer of broadcasting responsibilities from the Home Office to the Department of Industry (D.o.I.) would lead to a more rapid and progressive approach. The D.o.I.'s function, after all, was to pro-mote industrial initiatives, whereas the Home Office saw its role more in terms of protecting society. The Report's main impact, however, was to raise govern-ment awareness of the industrial and employment potential of IT, the world market for which it valued at some £50 billion a year and growing at 10 per cent annually in real terms. Within weeks a Minister for Information Tech-nology was appointed and a special section created within the D.o.I., although the Home Office retained its broadcasting responsibilities.

Consultation between the two departments, however, became increasingly necessary, particularly in relation to decisions on satellite broadcasting. Indeed by the time of the Commons debate on direct broadcasting by satellite (DBS), in March 1982, even the Home Secretary was describing the 'opportunities for an industry and jobs' as 'the central factor' in a decision which would radic-ally alter the character of Britain's broadcasting services.

The Prime Minister was herself taking an increasingly personal interest in the opportunities offered by information technology. In early 1981 Mrs Thatcher promoted Kenneth Baker, long one of the most vociferous exponents of IT in the House of Commons, to the post of IT Minister, and in May gave her personal approval to the designation of 1982 as Information Technology Year. There followed a series of discussions on the best way to pursue the issue, and the Prime Minister's close involvement was reflected in the out-come. In July 1981 she announced the formation of an Information Technology Unit in the Cabinet Office itself to help 'promote the use of IT within gov-ernment and . . . seek to ensure the overall coherence of Government policies towards IT, particularly insofar as they span the responsibilities of more than one department'.[5]

In addition, an Information Technology Advisory Panel (ITAP) was estab-lished, consisting of leading members of IT industries, particularly computing and electronics, though no one with any media experience.

On 22 March 1982, the ITAP published its report on 'Cable Systems'. Its first paragraph signalled what was to come:

Modern cable systems, based on co-axial cables or optical fibres, can provide many new telecommunications-based services to homes and businesses. The initial attrac-tion for home subscribers could be the extra television entertainment channels. However, the main role of cable systems eventually will be the delivery of many infor-mation, financial and other services to the home and the joining of businesses and homes by high capacity data links.[6]

---

[5] Hansard, HC Deb., 2 July 1981.

[6] Information Technology Advisory Panel, *Cable Systems: A Report by the ITAP* (London: HMSO, 1982), 7.

Thus was established the whole logic of development for cable television which has since been followed by the Conservative government. Like all important shifts of emphasis the key lay not in the technology or even the economies. Rather it lay in the underlying systems of values which the Report articulated:

We believe cable to be an essential component of future communications systems, offering great opportunities for new forms of entrepreneurial activity and substantial direct and indirect industrial benefits. However, the initial financing of cable systems will depend upon none of these things, but upon estimates of the revenue from additional popular programming channels. We consider the long-term potential of cable systems will go through an initial phase when their attraction will be based on 'entertainment' considerations. It is, though, essential that the technical specifications set for new cable systems should not preclude the transition from this initial phase to a subsequent phase when cable really does provide a full range of interactive services.[7]

The image they offered was of the entertainment 'engine' pulling the information society 'train', which struck some observers as akin to someone having argued in the eighteenth century that the immediate purpose of building the canals and railways was for the amusement of canoeists and trainspotters.

High-capacity cable systems, the Report argued, could provide a wider selection of services more efficiently than traditional broadcast and telephone systems. New types of television programmes could be produced for specialist and minority audiences—for ethnic, religious, educational, and cultural subgroups as well as for truly local community interests. A wider choice of conventional television programmes could also be provided as well as very recent films to those who wished to pay extra for them. Advertising could benefit as producers of specialized products found it easier to target their particular specialist audience than the undifferentiated mass which commercial broadcasting currently supplied. New information services, on the videotext principle, would also become available, as would new ways of buying and selling, through electronic viewing and ordering of goods—everything from groceries to houses. This would save both time and precious natural resources, as it would reduce the amount of time spent travelling. In a similar fashion, 'in serving homes and businesses alike, a cable system makes possible new work relationships'. Cable could offer everything from the transfer of digitalized business data to the continuous monitoring of a home security alarm system, and all much more efficiently than existing 'narrowband' telephone lines. The ITAP pointed admiringly to developments in other countries, such as France, West Germany, the USA, and Japan. The intended effect was to tap that deep-seated anxiety, now part of the British popular consciousness, of being left behind by developments in other countries.

[7] Ibid., para. 8. S, p. 48.

The Report suggested that to cable half the country would necessitate capital investment of at least £2,500 million, with another £1,000 million going into information, security, and other cable-related services. A large domestic market would be provided for cable equipment manufacturers, computer hardware and software companies, programme and enhanced service providers, and producers of office equipment and other information technology systems. Cable, the ITAP members believed, was as inevitable as information technology itself, and both needed to be promoted. To do so would be to minimize imports and open up international markets. Whilst conceding that some countries would protect their indigenous cable and IT industries, the Report concluded that there would be 'sizeable export opportunities'. The industrial benefit of cable could, therefore, be tremendous and the effect on employment possibly 'substantial', a message which was certainly very welcome to a government then facing over two and a half million unemployed and an economic slump which was getting progressively worse.

The money to fund cable development would, they proposed, be raised by attracting private investors: 'Cable systems offer large business opportunities with good chances of profit. We can see no need for any public funds to be used to establish them.'[8] They were equally optimistic that with the development of cable television no harm would be done to the existing broadcasting service, that local newspapers would not be harmed, and that the film industry would benefit.

ITAP was, above all else, eager to get things moving and called for speedy action in its by now famous aphorism 'a delayed decision will be the same as a negative decision'. The nub of the Panel's argument was that speed was essential lest the existing industry disappear and Britain be subsequently forced to depend on foreign hardware. Rapid cabling would be more probable using private investment than public money; this did, however, depend on the service provided being made sufficiently attractive to draw in cable subscribers. For although the long-term interactive and information technology potential of cable systems was the principal objective, it was their character as an entertainment service which would be the initial chief attraction.

For its part, the government embraced ITAP's philosophy. As William Whitelaw declared in the subsequent Commons debate, 'The Prime Minister has made clear the Government's determination to secure the advantages that cable technology can bring to this country.'[9] Those advantages were economic; this, from the standpoint of public service broadcasting, was the crucial intellectual development.

---

[8] Information Technology Advisory Panel, *Cable Systems: A Report by the ITAP* (London: HMSO, 1982), paras. 5.15–16.

[9] Hansard, HC Deb., 22 Mar. 1982.

The Report brought into focus the questions of how one got from the present worthy, regulated system of broadcasting to a system of abundance which might need no regulation, and would serve industrial policy and economic needs. In this sense the ITAP, whatever the limitations of its Report on cable, has had a seminal influence on all subsequent discussions about audio-visual communications and telecommunications policies.

On 22 March 1982, the same day as the ITAP Report was published, Mr Whitelaw announced 'an independent inquiry into the important broadcasting policing aspects' of cable development, under the chairmanship of former Cabinet Secretary Lord Hunt of Tanworth. The inquiry was to

take as its frame of reference the Government's wish to secure the benefits for the United Kingdom which cable technology can offer and its willingness to consider an expansion of cable systems which would permit cable to carry a wider range of entertainment and other services when consistent with the wider public interest, in particular the safeguarding of public service broadcasting; to consider the questions affecting broadcasting policy which would arise from such an expansion, including in particular the supervisory framework; and to make recommendations by 30 September 1982.[10]

In short the questions about the future of cable were no longer ones of 'if' but 'how' and 'how much'. Within the space of a few short months the government and commercial and industrial interests had hijacked the debate about the future of British television culture.

There was, however, a rising concern over the character of the ITAP Report and the government's apparent tendency to envisage the development of a deregulated cable television system. Colin Shaw, then Director of Television at the IBA, in a memo in May 1982 captured something of this feeling when he argued that too hasty a charge into new technologies could seriously damage overall programme quality and weaken the viability of the existing public service authorities. He confessed that 'history was littered with men and women who failed to see progress when it was staring them in the face', but added that some men and women, by saying 'Yes, but', must have spared mankind 'at least a few of its greater follies'.[11]

He defended the existing broadcasting ecology by describing it as a 'kind of public library offering not only best sellers but the book which is perhaps in demand only once every six months. Both are available for the same price —either the licence fee or the sum attributable to advertising in the price of goods at the grocer's'. But cable operations, said Shaw, would be paid for by subscribers, and the operators would have to supply a constant stream of

---

[10] Hunt Committee, *Report of the Inquiry into Cable Expansion and Broadcasting Policy*, Cmnd. 8679 (London: HMSO, 1982) (Hunt Report), 1.

[11] Note, Broadcasting Research Unit, May 1982, Colin Shaw, Director of Television, IBA.

exclusive events and entertainment if they were to entice viewers away from the existing services.

There seems likely to be a considerable scramble for the more desirable properties. What happens to the public library in those circumstances? You ask for a popular novel but it isn't being stocked. If you want it, you have to pay for it, but if you live in the wrong place you might still not be able to get it because it hasn't been worth any-one's while to open a bookshop. If cable services are to reflect economic factors, as the government seems to be saying, then the first places to be cabled will be those main centres of population where investment will be rewarded most rapidly. What happens to the people who live in less profitable areas?[12]

A report in *The Times* on 19 March 1982, on the eve of the publication of *Cable Systems*, announced that Mr Whitelaw was concerned about the con-sequences of a large increase in the number of television channels: 'The fear is that standards will slump, with pornography and other substandard material being broadcast by unscrupulous operators.' And when speaking to the Par-liamentary Information Technology Committee on 10 June 1982, Mr Whitelaw suggested that both cable and satellite had the potential to change the face of British broadcasting. He added:

In welcoming the new we must see to it that we do not lose what is worth preserv-ing in what we have. The challenge to government is, I believe, to catch the tide of technical development while at the same time securing an orderly revolution. I think we have to recognise that the pace of change in today's world does make it neces-sary to devise new policies and re-examine old ones much more quickly than we have been used to. Our industry must clearly be in the best position to compete in the ever-changing world of telecommunications. That is why we could not afford to defer decisions on DBS and cable while large committees of inquiry spent two or three years listening to evidence.[13]

The Hunt inquiry into Cable Expansion and Broadcasting Policy presented its report to the Home Secretary on 28 September 1982. It asked: should cable be subject to regulation? if so, of what kind? and how could public service broadcasting best be preserved? The answers were almost totally those which had been put forward by the cable television lobby. Lord Hunt made it clear that while there should be some regulation it should be neither too detailed nor too inflexible. He further stated that a formal franchising procedure would be desirable and that a national cable authority (not the IBA) should be estab-lished, but that once the franchise had been awarded, oversight should be react-ive rather than constant.

The fears of the BBC and IBA were not rated very highly. Although the Committee admitted that forecasts of how much advertising revenue cable

---

[12] Note, Broadcasting Research Unit, May 1982, Colin Shaw, Director of Television, IBA.
[13] William Whitelaw, speech to Parliamentary Information Technology Committee, 10 June 1982.

might attract were 'hedged around with uncertainties', it did not feel that independent broadcasting revenue would be seriously affected. Nor did it believe that BBC and ITV would lose any significant proportion of their audiences to cable channels. In any case, if cable was going to succeed it would need both to be popular and to attract advertising revenue.

There were many negative reactions to the Hunt Report and great scepticism, even cynicism, as to whether or not the Committee had had sufficient time to come to grips with issues. Something of the weakness of the Report was well captured in the remarkable optimism of the following statement: 'In the longer term, we have faith in the British film and television industry's ability to expand and satisfy the market, provided the cable operators encourage this and do not continue to rely unduly on low-cost material available.'[14]

Something of the superficiality of the whole debate about the future of television was captured in the short, sharp, shallow character of the Hunt Report. It did not come to grips with the wider social questions raised by cable development, nor the very real financial questions which it was clear would inevitably emerge.

In its evidence to the Hunt Report, the BBC said

its attitude to the expansion of cable was neither fatalistic nor Luddite, but it did not believe something should be done just because it was technically possible, without counting the social cost. It had taken a 60-year investment in skill and dedication to create the present system of public service broadcasting, which was universally acknowledged to be a national asset. It would take a much shorter time to erode the value of that national asset if the new cable services were permitted an operating philosophy made up of quick-kill methods of financial control, a cynical view of public taste and no concern for social side effects.[15]

The immediate effect, it was suggested, would be that parts of the nation would be deprived of soccer's Cup Final—offered as a kind of exemplar of the inherent exclusivity of cable as opposed to the inherent universality of broadcasting. Bill Cotton, then the BBC's Director of Development, pointed out that 'nearly 20 million people watched the FA Cup Final this year. But by the end of the decade, with the free-for-all unregulated system, it was possible that only half that number would still have the privilege of choice and then only if they could afford the cable subscription charge'.[16]

Hunt and his two colleagues rejected the argument that the IBA should be the central franchising and oversight body, and recommended therefore the creation of a new cable authority.

Lord Thompson of the IBA, writing in the BBC's house journal *Ariel*, was quick to respond:

[14] Quoted in Hollins, *Beyond Broadcasting*, 75.   [15] Ibid. 69–70.   [16] *Ariel* (Oct. 1982).

The Hunt Report claims that it wishes to avoid real losses in the range and quality of public service broadcasting and that it recognises the need for 'limited safeguards'. The IBA believes that if its recommendations were to be accepted they would be bound to undermine the standard of public service broadcasting both in ITV and in the BBC.

The report claims too that cable will supplement and not rival the existing services. But the lack of adequate oversight exercised in the public interest means that rivalry will be inevitable with consequences of considerable concern to the public broadcasting or on the interests of the viewer.[17]

The government, however, had not been persuaded that the standards of broadcasting with which Britain was associated were no accident, rather the consequence of careful planning. The most important characteristic of the traditional version of public service broadcasting was not the imposition of some élitist view of the public good, but ensuring that money was spent on programmes which, using simple criteria of likely commercial popularity, would not otherwise be made. That linkage of principle and structure which lay at the heart of most British TV success was what cable TV seemed to be challenging.

In April 1983 the government published its White Paper *The Development of Cable Systems and Services*. It set out four elements which lay at the heart of the Conservative government's strategy: cable investment should be privately financed and market led; regulation should be as light as possible so that investors were free to develop a wide range of services and facilities; flexibility was necessary in the regulatory framework so that it could be continually adapted to meet changing conditions: despite this light and flexible approach, a small number of key safeguards should be applied to guide cable development to ensure that existing broadcasting and telecommunications services were maintained.

The White Paper came down heavily in favour of a national cable authority, with a small staff, without direct day-to-day supervisory powers over cable operators; its central task, initially at least, was to award franchises. The White Paper was also notable for its lack of enthusiasm for the interactive services that had previously been the central plank in the government's arguments for cable. It specifically barred cable operators from offering data communications, one more extraordinary decision in the light of the original intentions of the policy. Equally curious was that while the obvious technology of the new systems was optic fibre, the choice was to be left to the operator to use either switched or tree and branch configurations, using coaxial or optic fibre cable. The operators whom the Authority was to franchise had to carry all four terrestrial services (BBC1, BBC2, ITV, Channel Four) and the UK's five potential direct satellite

---

[17] *Ariel* (Oct. 1982).

services, along with any other terrestrial and satellite services from wherever they might originate, thus implicitly accepting an open skies policy.

The Cable and Broadcasting Act received the royal assent on 26 July 1984. The first Chairman of the new Cable Television Authority was Richard H. Burton, the retired Chairman of Gillette Industries, with no track record in either broadcasting or technology.

By the autumn of 1984, Britain had the basic legal structure for cable television, though not very much money to get it established. Almost immediately things began to go wrong. An ill wind had blown from the Chancellor's budget in the spring, in which he removed tax concessions on capital expenditure. Unfortunately, the budgets of the various companies that had entered the field presupposed that those concessions remained. Market research results also began to show what many had known for some time, that there was no massive public demand for new entertainment services. In October Visionhire, the second largest operator, announced that it was withdrawing from cable television, having failed to find a buyer for its business and blaming the government's delay in awarding new franchises and the changes in capital allowances in the budget. A week later Rediffusion, the largest cable television business in Britain, announced that it was selling its interests in cable to Robert Maxwell's Pergamon Press.

In 1985 the government was still trying to talk cable television into existence without actually doing anything in particular to provide the wherewithal. On 1 March 1985 Geoffrey Pattie, the new Minister for Information Technology, in a speech in Swindon, which had been the first town in Britain to receive multi-channel TV, declared that '1985 will be the year of opportunity for cable'. Pointing to the contribution which the cable industry could make to the prosperity of Britain, he observed: 'Cable means investment in new technology and jobs, and this is why the government attaches a high priority to the success of the industry.'[18] In the same week the Cable Television Authority announced the areas which would be advertised for franchise applications, the first to be announced by the Authority. The Authority's declared aim was to announce five new areas for cable every four months, with the notion that by 1990 about 4 million homes—20 per cent of the country—would have access to multi-channel cable.

What followed was far from a happy period for cable operators. A largely pessimistic realism was the order of the day. Those who were prepared to start were hampered by the delay in setting up the Cable Authority and delays by the Department of Trade and Industry in distributing licences. In addition, the subscriber take-up rate has been much lower than the 35 per cent originally

[18] Geoffrey Pattie, speech to local business leaders, 1 Mar. 1985.

envisaged by many operators. By 1993 there were just 5 per cent of homes subscribing to cable.

However bleak the picture by the late 1980s, money started to flow into the development of franchises. The investment, however, was coming not from within Britain, but from across the Atlantic. Companies such as United Cable Television, Pacific Television, TCI Jones, Intercable, US West, Time-Warner began to spend hundreds of millions of dollars in Britain, rapidly becoming the dominant force. The rationales for this were several. There was an increasing sense in the United States of the need to develop new global markets. The most powerful argument was captured in an interview with Gary Bryson, head of US West's cable interests abroad, when he observed: 'our strategic interest is in the voice and data area . . . The UK is the only place in the world where you can legally do voice, data and video today . . . Our role in the UK is not to manage the cable business, it is to manage the telecommunication services within cable systems.'[19]

The concern thus was not with the provision of programme services; that was relatively incidental. The concern was with developing integrated communication systems, offering telecommunication and audio-visual services. It was the vision which had captivated Thatcher and her colleagues at the beginning of the 1980s. In a rather shrewd move the Conservative government had introduced legislation which allowed cable companies to offer telephone services in competition with British Telecom, but prevented BT from offering video services in competition with cable. It was a policy to favour the need of the large American companies, to structure the so-called market in such a way as to persuade the US companies to invest in Britain. It worked.

But here was not a British success story, rather an American entrepreneurial adventure. Bryson added, in a revealing comment, 'the experience we're getting in the UK is highly relevant'. The nature of the relevance was put in almost brutal terms in 1993 when John Malone told a trade conference in the USA that Britain was rather like Spain in 1938, a place where they were able to test their heavy weapons for the real and coming struggle. And that real struggle would come in the USA when the cable companies were allowed to offer telecommunication services and the telephone companies to offer video services. Britain had become a laboratory for other people's experiments.

Satellite Rising

The other development of major significance to the future of public service broadcasting is the development of direct-broadcasting satellite television. In March 1980 the Home Secretary, William Whitelaw, initiated a study of the

---

[19] *Broadcasting*, 14 Aug. 1989.

'implications of establishing a United Kingdom direct broadcasting satellite service by about 1985'. The study, which appeared in May 1981, emphasized that the government would not wish to finance such a project and that programme services would be either provided or supervised by the existing broadcasting authorities. In his foreword to the study, the Home Secretary stated that the government was prepared to give serious consideration to an early start to a British DBS service with one or two television channels and possibly other information services. 'This approach', wrote the Home Secretary, 'would need to be consistent with, and indeed built on, our existing broadcasting arrangements and institutions, as the existing services are for the majority of the population.'[20] The government's general welcome for the Report meant that the United Kingdom had arrived at a watershed in terms of national communications policy.

The government allocated two of the five British DBS channels to the BBC, and gave it permission to commence transmissions in 1986. The BBC had in fact put in its bid for two channels in 1980, its attitude towards satellite from the mid-1970s onwards being more positive than that of the IBA, which was preoccupied with the start of the fourth channel and breakfast television.

In keeping with its consistent policy of spearheading developments in broadcasting, or at least pre-empting competition, the BBC made it clear from the outset that it was interested in providing a two-channel DBS service to the British public: DBS1, a subscription service with a scrambled signal of new films, and DBS2, a 'window on the world', not scrambled and showing British and foreign programmes. The radio channels available would be used for stereo sound on DBS1 and 2, and other high-quality stereo music channels.

The BBC, when planning the DBS policy in the late 1970s, had not thought either that it would be alone in developing a DBS service or that if it were it would be asked to bear the full brunt of the development cost, particularly for the 'hardware', if this were to be essentially of British manufacture. Nor had it envisaged the forced development of cable, at least not for many years, or that communications satellites would play any significant role in British audio-visual distribution before the advent of DBS in 1986.

If the BBC had embarked on DBS partly to help protect its financial position in the last decade of the century, opinions by the autumn of 1983 had become sharply divided about the viability of the whole development. The borrowing of the substantial sums necessary constituted an expensive mortgage not only on the BBC's DBS budget but also on future BBC programme production, the essential life-blood of the organization. There were serious questions whether this was a proper use of the licence-payers' money, on which ultimately any borrowing would depend.

---

[20] 'Direct Broadcasting by Satellite: Report of a Home Office Study' (London: HMSO, 1981).

Equally serious was the whole principle of whether or not the idea of a subscription service was compatible with the principles of public service broadcasting. For example, how did it square with the basic principles of universality of payment and universality of provision?

In the late 1970s the Independent Broadcasting Authority had wanted to delay the advent of satellite broadcasting in the United Kingdom. The IBA argued that satellite channels might upset the delicate broadcast ecology of the country and thus should not be encouraged before the late 1990s.

The IBA's reluctance was linked to its concern to preserve the principle of public service television in the United Kingdom: no two television companies should be forced to compete for the same source of revenue. This principle had been observed at every extension of the broadcasting system, and its very observance was one of the reasons why the accommodation for the second commercially financed television channel posed such a problem. All those firms wanting to advertise in the United Kingdom still had to deal with what is basically one entity—the ITV-IBA system. A powerful view within the IBA was that it could hardly accommodate a national satellite channel supported by advertising revenue which would inevitably represent competition to ITV companies. Such competition, it was alleged, would not be beneficial to programming.

The IBA gradually concluded that international developments would inevitably affect its operation and that of the ITV companies. On the one hand the unspent advertising revenue in some Continental countries, together with the willingness of many Europeans to view English-language programmes, presented a considerable business opportunity for the expansion of commercially financed English-language television. On the other hand the same potential market could be tapped by other organizations, which in due course could interfere with the British monopoly of ITV companies by attracting the attention of British viewers. Such developments would clearly represent for the IBA system a competition for British advertising revenue.

In the latter half of 1981, when government thinking became clearer, the IBA began to move towards a more positive attitude. In one of its submissions to the Hunt Committee, the IBA declared itself eager to supervise cable broadcasting by being made responsible for licensing cable companies and presented its claim for the second two DBS channels that might be available in the United Kingdom. In March 1982, when the BBC was allocated its two channels, the IBA was ready with its own plan, and showed some indignation at not having received a firm promise.

The IBA's proposal, published in May 1983, claimed that unlike cable, with a multiplicity of channels, DBS was a limited resource and thus should be looked after by publicly accountable bodies. The Authority declared its wish to contribute to the extension of choice offered to the public via DBS by being able to offer not only advertising-supported services but also pay television, thus sustaining the present duopoly in broadcasting and preserving the parity between the two public service bodies, the BBC and the IBA.

It was not long, however, before the real financial and structural difficulties of the BBC and IBA schemes began to become clear. In a devastating attack in *The Times*, in a piece titled 'Satellite TV: Will the BBC be Lost in Space', Brenda Maddox dissected, with clinical efficiency, the economics and the pretensions of the BBC's satellite plans. She concluded: 'The best move for the BBC would be to back out of DBS.'[21] Six months later the BBC announced that it was shelving its plans for unilaterally developing a DBS service.

It immediately began to look for partners to share the costs and risks, and found an eager one in the IBA. In 1984 a consortium emerged of the BBC, the IBA, the independent television companies, and a number of organizations concerned with the hardware and software potential of the new media. This consortium became known as the Club of 21, the number of different organizations concerned. At the beginning of 1985, however, the whole thing collapsed because of fears of the high cost and doubts about potential revenue.

Later in the same year the IBA was asked by the government to take another look at the possible development of the DBS system under the umbrella of the IBA. By November a dozen organizations, broadcasters, and industrial companies had indicated their interest in taking part. In the same month the news that Robert Maxwell was to start an English-language entertainment service using a French satellite further fuelled the belief that satellite television was at last beginning to take off.

Things then began to develop apace as the contract to develop Britain's first DBS service was awarded to the BSB consortium on 11 December 1986 in a contract to run for fifteen years. The consortium consisted of such companies as Anglia and Granada Television, Virgin, the Bond Corporation, and Pearson. BSB planned to offer a dedicated film service funded by subscription, and three other services funded by advertising: a children–family channel; a news–live–current affairs–magazine–sports channel; and a general entertainment channel. Its business plan, which included total start-up costs of £600 million, with a £100 million programme budget in the first year, depended almost totally in its opening years on the subscription channel.

On the same day that BSB gave evidence to the Home Affairs Select Committee, a very different idea was being floated with the Committee for the future provision of a subscription-based film service. This idea put forward by the Rank Organization was to develop a new terrestrial system. This would have the advantage, being considerably cheaper, to create as a transmission system and in the charges for the reception.

[21] *The Times*, 22 June 1983.

The official submission from Rank to the government in December 1987 had stated that they proposed

to launch a service to be broadcast on UHF or possibly VHF which would offer programming, i.e. feature films, sports events and popular drama series. The service would be broadcast in scrambled form and a decoder would be required by subscribers in order to unscramble the signal. Rank is satisfied that from a technological point of view such a service is now feasible and indeed a similar service (Canal Plus) has been in operation in France for three years and has proved to be an outstanding success.[22]

The idea from Rank which predicted a 3 million household penetration had been implicitly raised in the Peacock Report which had suggested subscription payments for existing terrestrial systems. In October 1986 the government commissioned the consultancy firm CSP to report on whether pay television could be introduced, whether people wanted it, and how it would affect the BBC. CSP reported in July 1987. They had concluded that there was considerable demand for subscription services, and that BBC2 should be switched to such a form of financing. The Report also concluded that there was plenty of space available on the airwaves for extra subscription channels. It also suggested use of the 'downtime' or unused hours of BBC2 and Channel 4 for the downloading of premium items such as films on a subscription basis.

The preferred solution put forward by the CSP Report was that at least one more TV channel should be provided for a subscription service. The report estimated that one pay-TV channel costing about £10 a month could attract 30 per cent of households.

There was very much an air of desperation about all these measures, a sense of trying any and every new idea in an effort to establish the new media, create new television markets, and break the public service monopoly of the BBC and the then ITV. The new age was, however, even at the end of a decade of Tory nurturing, proving a very slow birth.

The approach of the government remained clear. One report noted that behind the government's policy 'lies the DTI's determination to apply standard cost-benefit analysis to an area of British life previously tempered by cultural considerations'.[23] The commentator's tone was a mite ironic and the piece was headed: 'High Price of a Satellite Success.' In January, in a more optimistic—or, as it was to prove, naïve—mood, Anthony Simmonds-Gooding told the American publication *Broadcasting* that their 'research suggests' that out of 20 million British households, 6 million are 'very, very prone to buy', with 2 million 'early adapters', 3 million within two years, 5 million by three

---

[22] Rank Organization, proposal for the development of subscription television, Dec. 1987.
[23] *Independent*, 15 June 1988.

years. He added: 'We begin to break even and make real profits somewhere between year two and three.'[24]

One of the immediate problems for BSB was that in February 1989 Murdoch had started broadcasting his Sky service into Britain, though sales of its receiver dishes were to say the least laggardly, and by the early summer of 1989 the new service was losing £2 million to £3 million a week. In an aside the *Sunday Times* added that 'Murdoch, it seems, has enough capacity to carry Sky's debts and wait for the tide to turn'.[25]

Far more important for BSB, however, was that its start-up costs were £750 million, the second most expensive venture start-up in British commercial history. It was thus beginning life carrying a huge debt-burden which would need to be serviced. There were also doubts about the financial security of Alan Bond, one of its major financial backers, delays in the launch of the satellite it would use, and serious questions about whether the dish it would sell—the famous 'squarial'—even worked.

On 15 October 1989, in an interview on Channel Four, Murdoch had said that he would subsidize Sky for five years and called on BSB to abandon its own statellite and join Sky on board the Astra. Even as Murdoch was speaking rumours began to circulate about his increasing financial problems. His company News Corporation had been built on borrowed money, carrying a burden of $5.5 billion. Between July and September 1989, News Corporation's pre-tax profits fell 47 per cent.[26]

By November 1990 it was clear that there was insufficient market capacity for two satellite services. BSB collapsed and agreed to a merger, which was in effect a take-over by Sky, the new company to be called BSkyB.

In December came the news that Alan Bond—who was also deeply in debt in Australia—was selling his shares in BSB to Robert Maxwell—who in turn owed creditors $1.4 billion.

Murdoch's financial troubles worsened and the business press were full of stories about News International's immediate demise. In one day, 20 December, the stock of News Corporation dropped 20 per cent on the Australian stock exchange. On the same day a documentary on Channel Four examined Murdoch's financial problems.

Simmonds-Gooding was unemployed, Bond bankrupt, Maxwell dead and disgraced, but Murdoch survived. BSkyB by 1993 was received in about 10 per cent of British homes and clearly had to be taken seriously. It was the rise of BSkyB perhaps more than any other event which led to the Director-General of the BBC, John Birt, telling his employees that they should prepare for the inevitable decline in their share of viewing to at least 30 per cent.

[24] *Broadcasting*, 23 Jan. 1989, pp. 152–4.   [25] *Sunday Times*, 21 May 1989.
[26] *Observer*, 19 Nov. 1989.

The Assault on ITV

The Thatcher government decided on a number of other changes which it articulated in the White Paper, and in the legislation introduced into Parliament in 1989. In some senses these were even more significant than anything that was happening to cable or satellite. The government's plans heralded the most significant transformation of the character of the British broadcasting system since its creation in the 1920s.

In June 1989 the government announced that the franchises for the ITV system would be auctioned off when the current ones expired at the end of 1992. Thus, rather than a company having to convince the then IBA of the merits of its programme intentions, it would now also have to bid for the particular piece of the radio spectrum on offer.

There occurred one of those interesting moments when an old order met and fought the proposed new one, with no immediately obvious sense of which would prove triumphant. It must be understood here that the British commercial television system, ITV, as constituted between 1955 and 1992 was every bit as important to the traditions of public service broadcasting as the BBC. Granada Television, for example, had been voted at the Banff Festival the best broadcasting organization in the world. It was legendary for such programmes as *Brideshead Revisited* and *Jewel in the Crown* and so much more. ITV was, in short, a remarkably creative *and* profitable system. The initial government plans seemed set to put the torch to the thatched-hut for purely ideological and monetary reasons.

When the Broadcasting Bill was introduced to Parliament at the end of 1989, it was Tory backbenchers who immediately led the call that the franchise bids should be judged on the basis of the likely range and quality of the programmes that would be produced as well as the size of the cash-bid.[27] George Walden, a former Education Minister, told his constituents that the bill would lead to a collapse in TV standards: 'We in the Tory party bemoan the yob elements in our society, yet we are likely to get "yob tv".'[28] The call for maintaining quality in programming was suddenly heard from many different places: 'A year ago market zeal would have ruled out such views as belonging to the extinct philosophy of the nanny state. But the wind has changed rapidly. Tory MPs do not wish to be held accountable for the end of British television.'[29] Television producers formed the Campaign for Quality Television. And the whole auctioning process was described variously as 'a fiasco' and an 'infantile crudity' in its conception. *The Times* intoned: 'auctioning terrestrial commercial television was always intended to benefit the Treasury not the television viewer. The result must be fewer resources

[27] *Observer*, 19 Nov. 1989.　　[28] Ibid. 10 Oct. 1989.　　[29] Ibid. 10 Dec. 1989.

available for programme-making and thus for competing with the cheap products on offer from the American television industry.'[30]

The government had relented at one level and placed in the legislation a
'quality threshold' which any applicant had to pass whatever the amount they
were bidding. There were, however, very few observers who did not believe
that the future of ITV was quite likely to be rampantly commercial. The effect
on the BBC was hardly likely to be benign.

[30] *The Times*, editorial, 17 Oct. 1991.

12 Broadcasting and New Technologies: The Case of Japan

In July 1983 Nintendo marketed its 'family computer' or Famikon. By March 1986 6.3 million sets had been sold, one out of five TV-owning households. By comparison there are only about 1 million personal computers in homes and offices in Japan. The most popular game for playing on the Famikon was Super Mario Brothers, which sold 3 million copies, along with almost 1 million copies of a book explaining how to play the game. The aim of the game was to reach the imprisoned Princess by passing through areas in eight worlds. Even skilled players took three hours to achieve this act of chivalry, and research showed that 1 in 5 boys aged between 10 and 15 years spent on average 1 hour 10 minutes every day playing these games. Indeed, such became the intensity of involvement that television viewing among primary and junior high school students went down to 50 minutes a day, and various companies approached Nintendo to use the minicomputer as the terminal of a 'Famikon' network, linking up households throughout Japan.

The extraordinary scale of the 'Famikon' phenomenon led one commentator to observe that the ' "famikon" had become the leader in the new media race of cable, teletext and videotex, not to speak of DBS or HDTV. It is, in fact, threatening conventional television business.'[1]

---

[1] Shinichi Shimizu, *Developments in Japanese Broadcasting* (Tokyo: NHK, 1986), 3.

The video-game phenomenon was to spread across the globe and become a multi-billion-dollar industry. It was perhaps the first and possibly most potent metaphor for the new age of communications. Nothing captured better the extraordinary, even bizarre, evolution of modern audio-visual culture in Japan and elsewhere than the idea that young boys, and not so young boys, spending hours rescuing a video princess challenged the stability of one of the most highly developed TV cultures in the world. Even if we allow for a certain hyperbole what was perfectly clear was that NHK was yet one more public service broadcaster entering on troubled and uncertain times.

The sixty-first anniversary of broadcasting in Japan fell on 21 March 1986. Masato Kawahara, the then President of NHK, outlined four goals for the coming years: (1) to develop the DBS service, (2) to develop the use of HDTV, (3) to expand the domestic use of teletext broadcasts, (4) to rationalize operational management structures, and to develop subsidiary enterprises. A week later, when the National Diet approved NHK's draft budget for fiscal 1986, it affirmed these goals as well as calling on it to maintain neutrality and editorial independence; to secure extra sources of revenue to forestall any increase in receiving fees; and to continue to provide its audience with the 'last and most comprehensive possible programming service, diversified and balanced for all sectors of the population'.[2]

What could be seen evolving was a by now familiar mix of increasing financial pressure, the temptations and threats of the new media alongside a continued commitment to public service values and purpose. NHK was itself coming ever closer to one of the more profound combinations of modern culture: the lingering desire of governments to maintain the national broadcasting organization at the very same time as they encouraged developments in communication which by their very nature could only succeed by diminishing and preferably destroying the national broadcasting organization.

The difficult spiral within which NHK is trapped is a familiar one. The number of households concluding new contracts diminished, with the net result that NHK's income had been increasing by only about 2 per cent a year. At the same time increasing numbers of families failed to pay the fee. Costs, however, were rising by more than 10 per cent a year. The end result was the cyclical need of NHK to go cap in hand to the government and the Diet, a position which is never good for the operational independence of any broadcasting organization.

One obvious solution was for NHK to shed staff and to seek other sources of revenue. NHK's interest in DBS was stimulated, in part, by the ability of satellite communication to reach areas which remained inaccessible to terrestrial transmissions. The more powerful argument was that a premium on the licence fee was quite possibly a major new source of revenue. In addition a

---

[2] Ibid. 7.

revision of the 1950 Broadcast Law had allowed NHK to establish 27 subsidiary companies, including 20 joint-stock companies, 7 non-profit corporations, and 2 public welfare organizations. By 1989 these were contributing ¥4.5 billion—about $32 million. There was also a larger strategic aim in the establishment of these subsidiaries. As one leading Japanese commentator put it: 'The main aim of NHK's policy on its subsidiaries is understood not to be "extra income" but the formation of a media business cooperative between the non-commercial NHK and its commercial subsidiaries and continue to dominate the broadcasting media world in Japan.'[3] The response of commercial broadcasters was hostile, accusing NHK of an 'expansionist policy' and seeking to create an 'NHK conglomerate', which 'will go further on the way to commercialization . . . contrary to the idea of a non-commercial broadcasting institution [which] cannot be permitted'.[4]

In January 1985 NHK Enterprises Inc. had been established to distribute NHK programmes at home and abroad, develop co-productions, stimulate independent production, and produce programmes for the commercial and cable television markets.

Perhaps more than any public broadcaster on earth, NHK was being buffeted by the technological and ideological reinvention of the western industrial democracies. The former President of NHK, Tomokazu Sakamoto, has called the 1980s the 'new period of fruit-bearing for technological innovation'. On the occasion of NHK's fifty-fifth anniversary he announced with touching, if perhaps naïve, optimism:

The deeper we find ourselves plunging into what is variously called an 'era of change' or an 'era of uncertainty', the higher shall we raise the torch of public broadcasting with the unflinching determination to overcome all difficulties that may await us in our future path. We will do everything in our power to contribute to the promotion of people's happiness and to their brighter future through our continuous efforts to safeguard the freedom of speech, as we keep on advancing with our eternal trust in mankind.[5]

Japanese Broadcasting in the New Age

To the outside observer there is a stark, almost cold and awesome, rationality to Japanese culture and society. The crispness of organization, the sense of order, the need—emotional perhaps but rational in its manifestations—for clearly defined goals and purposes on which everyone agrees have underpinned the quite extraordinary development of this society since the defeat of 1945.

[3] Shinichi Shimizu, The Changing Face of Japanese Broadcasting: Toward a Multichannel, Multimedia Era (Tokyo: NHK, 1991), 15.
[4] Ibid.   [5] Tomokazu Sakamoto, quoted ibid. 16.

Nowhere have these elements of the Japanese social order been more manifest than in the development of new communications policies. That singularity of vision and purpose, contained within long-term strategic plans, is the yeast in the technocratic dough of Japanese developments in broadband communications, computers, and all the attendant apparatus needed to taste the new age. Beyond that, however, the intellectual and cultural cohesiveness creates an inevitable sense of both the totality of the vision and its meaning in human terms.

The immediate post-war development of broadcasting in Japan had to be viewed against the vast project in social engineering which was otherwise known as the Occupation. So today one has to look at what is happening to broadcasting in Japan against a different but equally vast drawing board on which is being plotted a whole new social engineering project. There is one element to this which appears highly problematic, the belief that in the very act of perfecting the ability to communicate one can achieve harmony in human affairs. The occupation of Japan, however one might view it in geopolitical terms, had many virtues, not the least of which was an understanding that harmony flows from the successful exercise of benign and enlightened social values and the successful implanting of a moral and democratic culture.

Any discussion of the relationship between public service broadcasting and new communications policies therefore necessarily enters the heart of a debate not just about the future of public service broadcasting but also about the self-conscious, long-term plan to transform the character of the second greatest economy on earth.

The concepts of 'post-industrial society' and 'information society' are by now familiar if somewhat vague concepts. The themes and issues have been picked up elsewhere in most industrial societies. Nowhere, however, is the effort quite so self-conscious, quite so determined, and so aggressively pursued, as in Japan. Kazuhiko Goto, a leading Japanese observer of communications developments, refers to the distinction and ill-consequences of allowing the new age to evolve on the basis of what he calls 'spontaneous development'— known elsewhere as 'market forces'.

The post-war communications system in Japan revolved around the principle of governmental monopoly of public telecommunications; and of NHK as a special public corporation in competition with commercial enterprises.

As elsewhere this structure has been severely undermined by both technological and socio-economic developments. On the one hand the vast capacity of cable, especially optic fibre, and satellite to communicate both enhanced the business possibilities of telecommunications and simultaneously destroyed the idea of audio-visual communication having to use a scarce resource. The distinctions between different communications media became blurred as multiple use of a single form of transmission became technically and economically feasible. At the same time, the drive to control public spending for greater efficiency and consumer-oriented services established the logic of privatization and deregulation which had as its most obvious manifestation the privatization of NTT. Broadcasting in general, and NHK in particular, is no more than a bit player in a game of global proportions and yet it finds itself faced with theoretical decommissioning precisely because of these wider events.

In Britain the official view was that the information society could be created on the back of a demand for more and more entertainment, offered by new cable services which would happily coexist with public service broadcasting. In Japan, however, there is a real expectation that peaceful coexistence is viable. There remains a considerable level of satisfaction with the status quo in TV, as yet no great demand for more entertainment services on the part of the audience, and a primary interest in the telecommunications possibilities of broadband cable systems and satellite systems rather than new entertainment TV channels: a basic interest in the economy rather than the cabaret.

This is not to say that there is no interest in expanding TV services as a new source of entertainment. Some Japanese businessmen did become enthralled by the message which seemed to be emerging from the United States of the considerable amounts of money to be had through subscription television. This has, however, not captured the official imagination to anything like the extent to which it did in Britain. The emphasis in Japan has been on the development and deregulation of telecommunications services and using the power and influence of the state to ensure that in the future telecommunications and information infrastructures in Japan are adequately developed to meet with the needs of the post-industrial society.

There has been a remarkable self-consciousness about this, resting in part on the deep-seated need of Japanese society and culture to arrive at consensual decisions about problematic areas and issues. As one observer noted:

In the past several years . . . as new technologies and new media are accepted as applicable to communications, the need for an integrated policy for the nation's communications system has come to be strongly acknowledged among the interested parties. In other words, they have come to realise that leaving the new communication technologies and media to their spontaneous development may eventually rebound against the national interest. Thus they have come to consider that it is necessary to establish a nationwide consensus as to the social functions and desirable utilization of the new communications media, and the social values to be realised by such media.[6]

The point was reaffirmed by Meguma Sato, Minister of Post and Telecommunications, speaking in Tokyo in September 1985. He said:

[6] Judith F. Geller, *Japanese Public Broadcasting: A Promise Fulfilled* (New York: Aspen Institute for Humanistic Studies, 1979), 57.

When we talk about an 'advanced information society' what is envisaged is a society in which all its members—including the individuals, families and corporations—are linked into a nationwide and multi-layered telecommunications network, which enables the smooth flow of information and easy access to the information needed and thereby brings into reality the activation of industry and society and an affluent and comfortable life of the people.[7]

He added that telecommunications was essentially an important way of writing 'the whole world into a single network' and of 'guaranteeing the solidarity of mankind as a whole'. Masato Kawahara, then President of NHK, spoke of the contributions of new technologies to 'the furthering of mankind's happiness and development of culture'.

That process of definition included the establishment by the Ministry of Post and Telecommunications in July 1980 of the 'Study Committee on the Diversification of Broadcasting' which reported in March 1982. The Committee established a number of basic objectives for (1) the further spread and improvement of broadcasting services; (2) the diversification of programmes; (3) the diversification of the means or methods of offering broadcasting services, involving the active introduction of new technologies.

The method proposed by the Committee for paying for these new services was pay TV, a development which it was recognized might challenge the public and political acceptability of the receiver fee: 'Therefore, if pay-television is introduced into Japanese society, it will be necessary for concerned parties to clarify the theory behind the present NHK viewers' fee system so that the TV user/payee audience can fully understand the relationship between the pay-TV system and NHK's fee system.'[8]

There are television receivers in about 99 per cent of Japan's 30 million households with access to between four and eight TV channels. Average viewing is 3 hours 6 minutes on Saturdays and 3 hours 46 minutes on Sundays (a pattern which shows a slight decline over the past five years). In short, Japan is a society in which TV is ubiquitous, where there is an almost total saturation of homes by television programmes.

In March 1982, the Research and Study Council on the Diversification of Broadcasting, an advisory body to the Ministry of Post and Telecommunications, published the results of a survey conducted in Tokyo and in Kofu in Yamanashi prefecture to the west of Tokyo. Respondents complained about the lack of variety in programmes and wanted more music, films, and news, in that order, along with more information on health, medical treatment, hobbies, and learning. In October 1982 NHK also conducted a survey which

---

[7] Meguma Sato, speech to annual conference of the International Institute of Communications, 9 Sept. 1985.
[8] Shimizu, *Developments in Japanese Broadcasting*, 15.

examined the wishes of the Japanese public in terms of future services. On the question of whether they wanted more channels, 26.8 per cent did, 63.2 per cent wanted no more, 6.3 per cent thought there were too many already, and 3.7 per cent did not know.

Japan as a Multi-channel Society

As in most other industrial societies cable television developed in Japan simply as a means of distributing clear pictures to areas which would otherwise not receive them. Television had started in Japan in 1953 and by the end of the 1950s most urban areas were covered by signals from NHK and commercial broadcasting stations. At the same time many MATV and CATV stations were established in areas where the mountainous terrain made reception extremely difficult. Most of these stations consisted of a joint reception facility established and operated by a local voluntary organization of residents. All that one had to do was to inform the Ministry of Post and Telecommunications that one intended to establish the facility. There were a few cable systems which offered both retransmission and local original services, but 80 per cent of these systems were small and provided less than 100 subscribers with clear retransmission pictures.

NHK was obliged by law to provide a service to the whole of Japan and actively assisted in advising on the construction of local cable systems, and from 1961 started covering some of the costs of such developments. The net result was that during the 1960s more than 5,000 new cable systems were built. Cable, however, was then viewed as being no more than one further means of receiving NHK's signals and those of commercial television stations not otherwise available.

Slowly there were efforts to begin production of programmes for cable systems. In July 1968 Nippon Cable Vision network (NCV) started services in Tokyo just before the beginning of the Mexico Olympics. The company planned not only to provide retransmission facilities in Shinjuku by linking together shops and houses whose reception had been affected by the creation of tall buildings but also to extend its services to the rest of Tokyo and to produce its own programmes. Both NHK and the commercial TV companies were becoming increasingly nervous at the implications of the NCV plans. They therefore refused to give their retransmission consent to NCV. In a manœuvre probably unique to Japan, the Ministry of Post and Telecommunications resolved the conflict by bringing together the broadcasters and NCV on the Joint Operating Committee for the CATV System in Shinjuku Districts which in turn was given retransmission rights. Kobayashi describes this as 'one of the most typical approaches adopted by the administrative body in Japan to settle a certain conflict through, as it were, the centralization of competing interests on a single organization'.[9] Nevertheless, here was the kernel of the debate about the development of cable: whether to allow the whole thing to expand and reap the alleged rewards of the services through broadband cable, or to impose controls in the interests of an orderly supervision of the existing ecology of communications.

The immediate reaction of the Ministry of Post and Telecommunications was to impose stricter controls and in 1969 a bill was introduced into Parliament which would have required the licensing of cable systems. A hail of criticism at what was seen as a reactionary and unnecessary measure persuaded the members of Parliament to reject the proposal. Having thus failed to get new legislation through the front door, the government tried a back-door method. It proposed the establishment in each prefecture of non-profit Cable Vision Foundations and indeed four were established in Tokyo, Kyoto-Osaka-Kobe, Nagoya, and Fukuoka. The Foundations were to be made up of various participants including NHK, commercial local TV stations, newspaper publishers, the Nippon Telegraph and Telephone Public Corporation, power companies, electronics firms, and banks. In Tokyo NCV joined the Foundation. The point was that in placing the control of cable systems within the shell of the Foundation through an administrative measure the Ministry of Post and Telecommunications had succeeded in gaining control because under Japanese law a non-profit foundation is obliged to obtain permission for each of its activities.

What emerged, however, was that very few viewers complained of the problem of reception because of tall buildings—the ostensible reason for establishing the Foundations being that they would ensure good reception—and even fewer were prepared to pay extra money to obtain their better pictures. In short the new cable organizations were not exactly inundated with would-be subscribers. Other prefectures simply did not bother to establish the Foundation. For the Ministry it was back to the drawing board and back to attempting to introduce a new law.

A Cable Television Broadcast Bill was introduced into Parliament in 1971. Criticism of the proposed legislation was once more widespread. It was said that the bill was wrong to specify cable as supplementary to TV; that it did not come to grips with the future potential of cable, for interactivity for example; that it was wrong to try and control the content of communications over cable; that bodies other than just the Ministry should be involved in licensing—the assumption being that those other bodies would be more liberal minded. Perhaps the most powerful opposition to the regime of control over

[9] Kazuhiko Goto, *Japanese Project for Direct Broadcasting Satellite Service*, Studies of Broadcasting 19 (Tokyo: NHK, 1983), 9–48.

cable proposed by the Ministry of Post and Telecommunications came from the increasingly powerful Trade and Industry Ministry. It wanted a 'liberal'—or deregulated—structure for cable to enhance its telecommunications and therefore economic prospects.

In 1972 the Cable Television Broadcast Law was passed by Parliament. It stipulated among other things that any cable station with more than 500 terminals required a licence from the Ministry of Post and Telecommunications. While the principle of the Law was that it was the facility which was licensed rather than the enterprise, the Cable Law made it clear that the actual content of original programmes for cable must comply with the provisions of the Broadcast Law which governs off-air broadcasting. The assumption here is that while the means of transmission may be different there is little or no distinction to be made between cable TV and broadcasting in that both are viewed in the home where, for example, children might be present. There was no provision in the cable legislation for the use of cable for interactive services. The law governing cable television quite specifically excluded its particular use for information purposes which presuppose the existence of interactivity. Hence the inclusion of 'Broadcast' in its title.

From January 1976 to December 1977 the Ministry of Post and Telecommunications undertook an experimental cable service at Tama New Town, west of Tokyo. Known as the Coaxial Cable Information System (CCIS), a variety of services were offered to a small number of participants. These included a retransmission service, original broadcasts, a pay-TV service, a flash information service, a facsimile newspaper, a still picture request service, and so on. At Scuba City a similar government-sponsored interactive coaxial cable experiment was established.

At the end of March 1990, there were 6.172 million homes served by cable (about 18.6 per cent of the 33.4 million TV households). Most of these received rebroadcast signals from the main broadcasting organizations. However, about 100,000 households subscribed to 120 multi-channel CATV facilities engaged in new programming services. The Ministry of Post and Telecommunications estimates the figure will rise to 13 million (41 per cent) by 2000.[10]

By the late 1980s there was, nevertheless, a sense that the development of cable television had been considerably inhibited by excessive regulation and infrastructural development costs. NTT, which had been privatized in 1985, exacerbated matters by charging high rates for the use of its facilities, for example where cable was to be strung from its telephone poles. While the planning for the information society was, as we have seen, long-standing and grand, what had been missing was the desire, or imperative, to force the growth of cable within Japan. The information society may have fundamentally been

---

[10] Shimizu, *The Changing Face of Japanese Broadcasting.*

about the economic development of Japan, but the export-led growth of the 1960s, 1970s, and 1980s, combined with a deep-seated fear of the implications of changes in communication for the coherence and stability of Japanese culture, served to dispel any zealousness in making new policy to usher in the new age.

However, in December the Japanese government, faced with serious difficulties with the economy, woke up to the economic potential of the cable industry. In 1994 a study group established by the Ministry of Post and Telecommunications (MPT) concluded that full-service cable TV networks and multiple service operators (MSOs) should be promoted. The study argued that the cable TV industry could grow from ¥100 billion to ¥2.7 trillion by 2010, with 30 million subscriber households. By that date the study predicted that multi-media businesses would generate 2.43 million new jobs and a market worth between ¥23 trillion and ¥56 trillion.

The reduction of restrictions on ownership and encouragement for the formation of MSOs rapidly attracted investment from such American conglomerates as Time-Warner and TCI. By 1994 there were 9.5 million homes subscribing to cable TV, 22.9 per cent of all TV households.

Further support for cable emerged in 1995 when the Japanese government formally adopted a plan to build a nation-wide fibre optic network at a cost of $980 billion. The Ministry of Post and Telecommunications announced in 1994 'that it will continue to encourage favourable conditions for technological development through the establishment of a special loan programme, tax incentives and general subsidisation'.[11]

Paralleling such fiscal inducements are attempts to deregulate the cable and telephone industries in ways which closely resemble policies in the United States and Britain. Most significant is the proposal to allow cable companies to offer telephony, and NTT to offer video services.[12]

There are now under way in Japan numerous multi-media experiments, sponsored for example by MPT and NTT. The 1994 MPT Report *Reforms toward the Intellectually Creative Society of the 21st Century* highlighted 'technology as the key to solving the country's social and economic problems. These include an ageing population, over-concentration of people in the Tokyo metropolitan area, and Japan's economic recession.'[13] The actual language of the Report was remarkably similar to that heard many times in the previous three decades: 'We find it difficult to solve these various problems using the

[11] Delbert D. Smith and Brigitte L. Adams, 'Converging Technologies, Converging Regulation: Telecommunications Policy in the US and Japan', *Intermedia*, 23/6 (Dec. 1995–Jan. 1996), 24–6.
[12] Mark Schilling, 'Why and Where Multimedia is Gathering Momentum', *Intermedia*, 23/6 (Dec. 1995–Jan. 1996), 15.
[13] Annelise Berendt, 'Vision and Viewers: The Social Focus of Multimedia', *Intermedia*, 23/6 (Dec. 1995–Jan. 1996), 22.

conventional methods of industrialised society, based on the movement of people and goods and the consumption of vast amounts of energy. Rather, we should approach our problems from the perspective of info-communications to seek solutions making full use of information and knowledge.'[14]

In NHK's 'Mid to Long Term Plan', published in January 1995, the provision of multi-media services is articulated as a public service commitment. This is the essence of NHK's Integrated Services Digital Broadcasting (ISDB) which offers digital pictures, sound, and data with video-on-demand, 3D, HDTV, smart TV, interactive participation of the audience, and electronic newspapers.

Satellites and High-Definition Television

One other area of major development has been the extensive planning for direct broadcasting by satellite in which Japan has taken major steps.

DBS has developed in Japan in the context of other satellite developments, dating back to the N-1 project of technical experimental satellites in 1975. There followed a whole series of meteorological, experimental, and communications satellites over the following ten years. The first broadcasting satellite, BS-1, was launched on 8 April 1978 and ceased to function in June 1980. This was used for various tests by the Ministry of Post and Telecommunications with the help of NHK and NSDA. In order to control the use of such satellites the Telecommunications Satellite Corporation was established to operate communications and broadcasting satellites that were in practical use. TSC began work in August 1979, 50 per cent owned by the government, 50 per cent by NTT, KDD, NHK, and with a capitalization of ¥7 billion. A satellite control centre was opened in Kimitsu City on 2 August 1982.

In January 1984 the BS-2a satellite was launched. The intended primary use for this was to solve the problem of poor reception in mountainous areas, isolated areas, and those parts of cities affected by high-rise buildings. Despite NHK's 7,000 relay stations and 10,000 facilities for community viewing, there were still an estimated 420,000 households where terrestrial reception was difficult. The cost of the two BS-2 satellites has been estimated at ¥61 billion (about $US265 million), with NHK paying 60 per cent and the government 40 per cent. The development of the satellite, however, greatly worried commercial broadcasters, and a report from the National Association of Commercial Broadcasters in March 1981 stated: 'The BS-2 may be called an NHK satellite, since it has only two channels, and thus, to us, the commercial broadcasting companies, how the so-called second generation satellites expected to be launched from now on are to be utilized will become a matter of the

[14] Quoted in Annelise Berendt, 'Vision and Viewers: The Social Focus of Multimedia', *Intermedia*, 23/6 (Dec. 1995–Jan. 1996), 22.

greatest concern.'[15] DBS has a national coverage which potentially undermines the local nature of commercial television stations—a localness already considerably undermined by their domination by programming from the major stations in Tokyo.

When NHK tried to start broadcasting with the BS-2a in May 1984 they discovered that two of the satellite's three channels, including the back-up channel, had ceased to operate. NHK was therefore only able to operate one channel using programmes from the General Television Service. It had been estimated that dissemination of DBS receiving-dish-and-converter sets would reach 100,000 a year, reaching half a million households within five years. Given the problems which developed, it is not surprising that by the end of 1985 there were only 61,400 DBS households. In February 1986 the BS-2b back-up satellite was launched, providing for two new NHK channels. NHK paid ¥36.6 billion, 60 per cent of the total production and launch costs of BS-2a and BS-2b. The government covered the rest of the costs.

In July 1987, using the BS-2 satellite, NHK started a new 24-hour TV channel with news, sport, and music programmes. By April 1988, according to reports from NHK, the number of households receiving the satellite broadcasts was 580,000, including both individual and communal reception. The other channel available is used to broadcast NHK programmes to remote regions of the country. Initially, the cost of receiving dishes was in the region of ¥300,000. At the time, the Daichi Kangyo Bank announced that it would make special loans available to allow people to purchase the dishes. NEC then announced that they would be marketing a satellite TV broadcast-receiving system for ¥100,000, and Fujitsu General Ltd. announced that they would be producing TV sets with built-in DBS tuners. The projections for growth were that sales of satellite TV receiving systems would reach 1 million units in three years, and 3 million in five years.

A further four channels were made available with the launch of BS-3a in 1990; two used by NHK, one by the University of the Air, and one by the Japan Satellite Broadcasting Co., a consortium of 190 leading enterprises, including commercial broadcasters, trading firms, and advertising agencies, to start Japan's first commercial DBS broadcasts in 1991. The costs of BS-3a, ¥79 billion, are being covered by NHK (43 per cent), the government (35 per cent), and the JSB (21 per cent). In December 1994 NHK had 6.37 million subscribers to its satellite-delivered services.

The commercial DBS company JSB started business with an initial capital of ¥26 billion ($186 million). Much of this was spent on buying programme rights to films, musical shows, and sports. It spent another ¥42 billion ($300 million) on programming.

---

[15] Shimizu, *Developments in Japanese Broadcasting*, 30.

In April 1991 JSB started a 24-hour service of scrambled programmes, principally new movies from Hollywood and entertainment. The initial signing-on fee was ¥27,000 ($193) and ¥2,000 ($14) per month viewing fee. By 1993 there were 1.26 million homes (about 4 per cent of all television homes) receiving the scrambled signal. A new generation of DBS satellite, BS-3b, was launched on 25 August 1991 carrying NHK's two-channel 24-hour service, and JSB's pay service. By 1993 there were more than 7 million households (about 20 per cent of all television homes) receiving NHK's unscrambled signals.

In August 1995 Direct Multi-Channel (DMC) launched JCSAT3, with sixteen transponders offering a possible 96 channels. In August 1997, digital SuperBird C with sixteen transponders was launched, and Hughes Corporation launched a 100-channel satellite. The MPT is also examining the digital future of Japan's BS system.

As the number of channels has increased the immediate problem, as elsewhere, is to find programming. It is widely assumed that given the nature of the society such programming will need to be heavily Japanese. Such a situation is assumed to favour NHK and certainly has led to a noticeable level of confidence within the organization that they will more than weather the storm of the digital age. It is, however, portentous that the one body of viewers which NHK is currently losing is the young.

The development of HDTV was given a considerable boost with the new generation of BS-3 satellites. The Ministry of Post and Telecommunications reserved one of the four BS-3b transponders for HDTV. In the spring of 1989 two multi-partner companies, Japan Hi-Vision Inc. and Hi-Vision Communications Inc., were established to meet the expected demand for high-definition programming. JHV was formed by NHK, commercial TV, and leading electronics companies.

Besides broadcasting, NHK pioneered a wide range of commercial applications of HDTV technology, including video production, video theatres, education, film editing, printing, electronic publishing, and so on. The MITI and the Ministry of Post and Telecommunications have played key roles in the promotion of Hi-Vision and in building the supporting infrastructure. For example, MPT planned a 'Hi-Vision City' programme to equip twenty-four model cities with HDTV systems, with equipment in art and science museums. Not to be outdone, MITI promoted the 'Hi-Vision Community' project, designating thirteen cities and towns as model communities. MITI's own estimate was that the HDTV market of Japan would be worth ¥1 trillion ($7.7 billion) by 1995, and ¥5.329 trillion ($44 billion) by the year 2000. More than 5,000 hours of HDTV programming—sports, music, documentary, and drama—have been broadcast. Thirty-nine per cent of this was sport, 22 per cent music, 24 per cent documentary, 15 per cent drama and movies. In 1993, there were 400 public locations for viewing HDTV and 12,500 sets for private use. The industry estimate is that by 1997 there will be 5 million sets and 10 to 15 million by 2000. The likely growth of HDTV depends on the costs of the monitors. When NHK started the one-day experimental Hi-Vision in 1959, the price of the receiver was ¥20 million (about $200,000). When in 1991 experimental broadcasts were extended to eight hours a day, the price was ¥4 million ($40,000). In 1993 a 32-inch HDTV monitor cost between ¥900,000 and ¥700,000 ($9,000 to $7,000). By 1997, when normal HDTV services commenced prices were in the region of $3,000.

Along with the development of HDTV, NHK's technical laboratories began in 1971 to develop flat-screen television technology. They quickly decided to employ plasma technology and in June 1992 exhibited a prototype 40-inch PDP (plasma display panel) flat screen for HDTV. The screen is carpeted with about 1 million pixels, like tiny red, green, and blue fluorescent lights. The set is 8 cm. thick. The plan was to have such screens commercially available in time for the opening of the Winter Olympics in Nagano, Japan, in 1998. And beyond HDTV, according to the Japanese, lies UDTV, ultra-definition television, with 2,000- to 4,000-line systems. These sets would offer images equivalent to perfect, 20/20 vision of reality. And beyond UDTV lie 3D, holographic, and virtual reality systems.

Such has been the growth of both DBS and CS communication that it has been estimated by the NABJ Research Institute that by the year 2000, the audience share of terrestrial television will only be 50 per cent. NHK itself estimates that by 2000 there will be more than 20 million satellite households.

The Vision of the Information Society

The Japanese vision of the future begins with a sense of how the economy is changing. It is tied to the aspirations of Japan to move from a society based on the export of manufactured goods to one based on the utilization of information through its production and distribution. Masahiro Kawahata notes the widespread belief that Japanese economic growth was slowing down, particularly in those areas which had led its growth: steel, manufacturing, and assembly industries such as electrical appliances and cars. He added:

Japan should not cling to such past glory but start seeking a new way as a trading country. There is no model for her to follow. Under such circumstances one suggestion would be a combination of the information processing and communication technology . . . the society is undergoing a transition from industry orientation to information orientedness; the centre of industry is shifting from physical production to intellectual production.[16]

[16] Masahiro Kawahata, quoted in 'Report on Present State of Communications in Japan, Fiscal 1984' (Tokyo: Ministry of Post and Telecommunications, 1985), 7.

This is necessarily a massive subject since it entails, in fact, the efforts of a country which now provides one-tenth of the total global national product to transform the roots of its wealth. It is, however, precisely that kind of thinking which has lain behind the development of communications policy in Japan in recent years, and it has to be said it goes a long way further than the rather narrow, poverty-stricken imagination which has so far guided related policies in countries such as Britain.

In July 1980 a new regulatory agency was established in Japan's Ministry of Post and Telecommunications, called the Telecommunications Policy Bureau. The Bureau took over responsibility for all national and international telecommunications. Its main task was enormous: to assess and articulate the convergence of telecommunications and data-processing, reveal the implications of this for social needs, and propose new policies.

A ministerial council was set up, consisting of twenty-four people drawn from industry, academia, the press, NTT, and KDD. A secretariat for the Council was provided by the Research Institute of Telecommunications and Economics (RITE). What emerged was a key publication, *A Vision of Telecommunications Policy in the 80's*, a report which did much to influence the whole development of Japanese communications policy. It was eventually a vision of the next ten years, of the relationship between society and technological development in telecommunications.

It pointed to the fact that in the 1980s Japan would have to contend with circumstances which were increasingly constrained. Slower overall economic growth would be met with increased demands for public welfare programmes. Hope would lie in the development of knowledge-intensive industries. It noted also that there had in recent years been remarkable progress in the basic telecommunications technologies. This had led to the greater use of computers, the digitalization of the telecommunications network, the development of mobile communications, and the widespread utilization of optical and satellite communications. Of particular interest, the Report felt, was the convergence of telecommunications and data-processing made possible by the computerization of information-processing technology. This opened up the possibility of a vast array of new data services, data communications, facsimile, and videotext. It pointed to the increased use of computerized information and communication systems both within and between systems. In addition there was increasing appeal for the home user: 'It will help to enlarge people's living space by means of tele services.'

In that concept of 'living space' was contained a key notion in the thinking behind the information society. The authors of the Report speak of the social goals for the early 1990s: 'they must include not only increased vitality but also more human contact. . . . While it appears that the development of informatisation will bring about more "man–machine communication" or "machine-to-machine communication" the real purpose is to increase human contact and make people more responsive'.

In the first instance, however, the purpose of these developments lay in their strategic importance for the future economic well-being of Japan: 'the swift progress in communications technology is leading to more sophisticated and diversified needs in industry, the home, and local administration. In such times the industrial sector must emphasise higher productivity and increased management efficiency and activity. Telecommunications must assume a leadership role in modernising the industrial structure of the 1980's. . . . telecommunications policy in the 1980's demands a comprehensive approach incorporating a long-term vision and giving proper attention to international relationships including Japanese participation and the protection of national sovereignty.'

The Report speaks of the emergence of new media and the convergence of existing media. All areas of communication—wireless and wired, fixed, mobile, broadcasting, public telephony, non-public telecommunications—which had previously been administered separately would need to be administered collectively, systematically, and as part of an integrated communications policy: 'a planned administration with a long-term vision will be required in the formulation and implementation of comprehensive programmes.'

It paints a picture of the future: 'telecommunications has now attained the status of a main infrastructure, functioning not only as a nervous system through which information is transmitted but also as a "brain," as a sophisticated processor of information that is now indispensable to daily life in home and industry. Pursuing this way of thinking, we can see that the universal use of telecommunications gives it the attributes of a jointly owned natural social resource.'

The 'Information Network System' was seen as a logical formalization of the relationship which can exist between telecommunications and computers as the infrastructure of the information society. One of the principal architects and exponents of INS, Yasusada Kitahara, stated:

It is necessary to digitalise the telecommunications network, and efficiently and economically to provide all kinds of communications services, including such non-telephone services as facsimile, data communications, and visual communications. It is also essential to establish a comprehensive system based on the integration of computers and digitalised telecommunications networks. This comprehensive system will integrally link digitalised telecommunications technology and computer to provide for the transmission, storage and processing of information.[17]

It stands in total distinction from all previous notions of communication—telegraph, telephony, telex, etc.—precisely because they evolved as separate

[17] Yasusada Kitahara, *Information Network System* (London: Hutchinson, 1983), 5.

but parallel developments. The essence of INS is that it fuses different forms of communication into a single structure. From that structure flow a range of services from video conferencing to digital telephone sets. Kitahara in his book on INS refers to three structural bases for the operation of the system, what he calls Business Telecommunications Centres, Home Telecommunications Centres, Information Processing Centres. Note, however, the optimistic character of the vision:

More than simply transmitting information, each Home Telecommunications Center will help satisfy basic needs for learning, self enlightenment and amusement, thus serving as an interface between one's social and private life. Users will be able to select from the various services available, the optimum configuration for them and use it efficiently and reasonably....

INS will come to be considered one of the key elements in the social and economic infrastructure of post-industrial society. It will contribute towards increasing productivity, intensifying knowledge and saving energy. It has great potential to help resolve conflicts between industry and society, and it will play a role in improving education, dealing with the problems of elderly citizens and promoting better international cooperation.... Telecommunications will provide a way for individuals to use their time more effectively . . . leisure will be increased, and the ability of people to use their free time for cultural purposes will be enhanced.... INS will be a humanitarian force because it will free people from numerous mundane daily tasks.[18]

In September 1984 field testing of the INS model began in Mitaka-Musashino, a suburb of Tokyo, and Kasumigaseki and continued until the end of March 1987. The point of the testing was (1) to check the performance of the new technology, examining system reliability and system debugging; (2) to study possible INS services and their utility value; (3) to research the impact on individuals, industry, and local government.

The particular uses currently being examined include home shopping and banking; assistance with studying; home medical information and consultation; communications within and between businesses; video teleconferences; the creation of satellite offices; local government information service; video display of key events. In short the model service is specifically structured so as to examine the domestic, community, and business implications and uses of INS.

What one can see then in Japan is the development of a clear sense of the new information society; the development of a number of highly advanced, well-funded projects to test the social, infrastructural, economic configurations of this new socio-cultural order; and a recognition that the sea-change of the information society need not just be a drifting-in with the tide of entertainment fed by superficial consumer needs.

---

[18] Yasusada Kitahara, *Information Network System* (London: Hutchinson, 1983), 9.

The Japanese conception of the information society is an industrial imperative transmuted into a philosophical vision. A more cynical response might be to say that it is easier to justify the enormous expenditure implied by such things as INS if they contribute to the greatest good of the greatest number than if only the interests of large corporations are served. Clearly, however, the notion is that the two are inseparable, but what is particularly important from the point of view of the concerns of this book is that all thinking about the future of communications in Japan presupposes a high measure of deregulation and privatization.

The Impact on Broadcasting in Japan

In the initial planning for, and thinking about, the Japanese information society there was a long period in which it was clearly felt that television and radio would remain largely unaffected by the process. It was certainly difficult to detect the same kind of fear which began to prevail in European broadcasting systems. More recently, however, the mood seems to have changed as planning for new cable and satellite TV systems gathered pace, and as both NHK and the commercial broadcasters began to assess their less than certain future and to plan strategies to ensure their continued survival.

One commentator writing from within NHK observed: 'NHK must secure an ever more stable financial base as a public broadcasting service, to meet the ever multiplying public needs for information in the era of new media. This is an important problem for the future operation of NHK, in order to secure a secondary source of income besides the receivers' fees, while striving for broader roles for public broadcasting.'[19] NHK's revenue is only equivalent to 25 per cent of the total revenue of commercial broadcasters, but its public role, its need to respond to the possibilities opened up by technological developments, and its need to serve the whole of the country without obvious preference and despite geographical difficulties inevitably puts a strain on its finances.

In an age of massive multiplication of outlets for communication NHK holds to a sense of its own social responsibilities and a basic optimism. It recognizes the virtues of the new media such as CATV, videotext, VCR, DBS:

These peripheral media have features of their own lacking in broadcasting, such as increased individuality, selectivity, 2-way communication, and no restrictions on time or recording capacity. However, the proven merits of the broadcasting system today —such as its efficiency as a means of transmission, its overwhelming popularity, the

---

[19] Yoshinaga Ishii, 'The New Media and Public Broadcasting Service', *Studies of Broadcasting*, 21 (Mar. 1985), 77–94.

superior quality of programme software and the economical cost of reception—will continue to attract the public. . . . In fact, the role of broadcasting in our communities, creating a common environment of communications for the public, may only gain in importance. . . .

We at NHK feel it our responsibility, especially in the days of the new media, to maintain a wide variety of programme services, adequately reflecting minority views, while endeavouring to provide the public with reliable programmes of high quality. We believe this is very important for the healthy development of democracy in our country.[20]

This view of the continuing importance of the social responsibility of a public broadcasting system able to insulate itself from a crude pursuit of audience ratings was strongly affirmed in *The Report of the Council on Long-Range Prospects for NHK* prepared by opinion leaders outside NHK and submitted to the Corporation's President in 1982. More recently there were notable calls, for example from Moriyoshi Saito, President of Mainichi Broadcasting, for NHK in effect to narrow its remit, offering 'high quality public service and universal programming of news and information and culture and education'.[21]

What is beginning to worry Japanese broadcasters is that the rules which affect their activities may not apply to audio-visual services which use telecommunications systems. The Broadcast Law lays down a whole series of prescriptions governing the output of both NHK and the commercial companies. Article 44 states that they must 'not disturb public security or good morals and manners' and shall be impartial and provide cultural and educational programmes.

The implication of much of the thinking inside Japan about the relationship between the broadcasting institutions and future communications environments envisages a number of possible scenarios. All the scenarios begin with the basic assumption that by the turn of the century there will be more satellite communication; more cable penetration; and a vastly enhanced telecommunication network characterized by the transmission not only of data but also of audio-visual images.

A final thesis which has evolved in Japan is that there will be an inverse relationship between the number of channels available for transmitting programmes and the amount of control which will be exercised: 'it may be safely said that channel multiplication will proceed in the future, and it will accelerate as time goes by, so that it will lead toward removing the rigid framework of the control of broadcasting.'[22]

[20] Yoshinaga Ishii, 'The New Media and Public Broadcasting Service', *Studies of Broadcasting*, 21 (Mar. 1985), 12.

[21] Shimizu, *The Changing Face of Japanese Broadcasting*, 52.

[22] Yasuhiro Iyoda, 'Changes in the Broadcasting System and their Impact on Commercial Broadcasters', *Studies of Broadcasting*, 21 (Mar. 1985), 49–76.

The implication is that the 'need' to control diminishes with the increased capacity to communicate. It is assumed, for example, that Japan will at some point bow to the inevitable and adopt an open-sky policy that will permit the commercial reception of programmes from any of the satellites in the Asia–Pacific region. One commentator observed: 'deregulation in each country is essential if we are to make the most of satellite technology. For many countries in this region deregulation is a long way off, yet it is clear that technological advancement cannot be stopped and the only productive solution is for us to take advantage of it.'

As a result, the special laws such as the Broadcast Law, the Wireless Telegraphy Law, and the Cable TV Broadcast Law slowly wither to be replaced only by more general legal prescriptions drawn from criminal, civil, commercial, and anti-monopoly laws. In this eventuality, public service broadcasting will have been destroyed not by some rapid act of social violence but by the slow dawning before the eyes of a future generation of its irrelevance.

13 A Stricken Place: The Condition of American Public Television

Introduction

In the closing weeks of 1994 there appeared in the pages of the *New Yorker* a special advertising section. There was something apposite about the location, for here was the magazine of cultivated America, a magazine which applauded itself with the unctuous ditty of 'possibly the best magazine that ever was'. Here was brahmin culture, clever culture, ironic culture, sophisticated culture, correct culture, big vocabulary culture, anointed culture. This was definitely not a rag to be found next to the check-out in Safeway rubbing shoulders with the *Inquirer*. And here in an act of what was, indeed, extreme unction was the special advertising section. The subject was public broadcasting. Glossy, carefully crafted, the declaration was of the merits and quality of the output of public television, past and future. Here were the motifs and icons of a self-belief of institutional worth: *McNeil-Lehrer*, *The American Experience*, *Frontline*, *Tony Brown's Journal*, the great and good, the senior clerics of the established church of American public broadcasting. Standing in front of that most ubiquitous of public television's symbols, *Sesame Street*'s Muppets, was Ervin Duggan, as cerebral, urbane, and decent a figure as had ever occupied the presidency of PBS. The glossy pages of the advertisement were an iconography of an institution that had become a sanctuary for a certain type of American public television. On offer was the worthy, the intense, the serious, the upright, the correct, the self-consciously caring, curious, and learned. It was an iconography that screamed its loathing for the shallowness and trivialities of the rest of American television, and thus for all those 'ordinary' Americans who seem more readily to watch commercial than public television. The pages were not just a statement of difference, they were a sanctification of the serious soul of the institution and of those who defined it and used it. The earnestness of the showcase was almost pompous, speaking of a profoundly developed sense of worth, but apparently little inkling of mirth, of a concept of 'the civilized' but little grasp of pleasure, of the need to inform and educate the society, but somehow forgetful of the importance of entertaining it as well. In other words public television in the United States had become, perhaps always was, priggish. Where it projected a certain intelligent populism it was more often than not borrowed, often from Britain, and thus not really populist at all, rather a borrowing from the 'art' of British television. It was achingly obvious, for example, that nowhere in the imagination of the diasporic community that is American public television was there the creative ability, focus, or traditional craft to produce say *Prime Suspect*, let alone a *Fawlty Towers* or an *Are You Being Served?* All these years, it suddenly became clear, *Masterpiece Theater* had been not some statement of the brilliance of the system but a metaphor for a fundamental weakness that would at some point become apparent and destructive.

None of this would have mattered very much in terms of the wider debate internationally about the future of public broadcasting had not there come murmurings that the future lay in the American public television model. Some, such as Rupert Murdoch, declared it loudly, arguing that populist television should be left to the commercial station and that public television should plug the gaps, do those things that the market system did not deliver, in short, emulate the American way of doing things. More worrying was that quite serious and powerful public broadcasters were having similar thoughts: this may have been a love that could not speak its name too loudly, but it was definitely an increasingly significant closet desire. Understanding the character of American public television thus begins to take on an increased significance.

American public television approached 1995 in the knowledge that the Republican Party now controlled Congress and, in the shape of Representative Gingrich, would be asking some difficult questions about federal support for the Corporation for Public Broadcasting (CPB) and thus in part for the whole system. It approached the coming storm in a particularly ill-prepared way. Much of its difficulties were obviously not of its own making. The decline of the public sector was by this date a universal phenomenon, but elsewhere the defences were stronger, more articulated, undergirded by the continuing place of the public broadcaster at the centre of the journalistic and imaginative life of the society as a whole. In the United States, almost uniquely, there was no profound guiding theology, no figures around whom had gathered an ethos, a demonstration of the importance of the institution to the society, no language melding abstract purpose with operative reality. The chant in the USA was muted, distantly heard from remote corners of the commonwealth. But the really curious thing, certainly to this observer, was that in so far as there was a body of belief within the system it spewed forth a remarkable false consciousness that saw not its marginalized condition, not its continuing lack of substantive relevance to the larger society, not exile, but power, influence, and captivation of the public-as-audience.

The concept of false consciousness is always contestable and I do not think I have ever used the category before in relation to a social group. To make this point, a scrap of early history is needed here. Localism was built into the structure of public broadcasting from its inception. It was a structural condition that was encouraged, even mandated, as the federal government in the 1960s and 1970s was determined to ensure that a government-sponsored system would not adversely affect the networks. Public television was never meant to have the significance and centrality of public broadcasting in other countries. The debate which was never undertaken was whether or not such a structure could possibly serve the larger public interest, or even that of the local community. It has to be remembered, and will certainly be argued here, that much of the weakness and inefficiency of the system stems from its structure, its diasporic nature that fuels gross fiscal inefficiency and inhibits the construction of a core philosophy of broadcasting without which one cannot incubate these talents and successful programme strategies that speak to the largeness not the narrowness of the society. This condition was a deliberate act of political vandalism. But it is a vandalism that has over the years been translated, particularly by the managers of the numerous stations, into something joyous and benign. In short, much of the public broadcasting community is in denial, shackled to its own ways of seeing.

It is possible that something of the ferocity and fervour with which disciples assert the validity and importance of the local structure lies in the fact that whatever its objective inadequacies it does rest on one important piece of the mythos of American culture and society, the closeness and smallness of community, the American version of *Gemeinschaft*. In a 1927 essay John Dewey commented:

American democratic polity was developed out of genuine community life, that is, association in local and small centers where industry was mainly agricultural and where production was carried on mainly with hand tools. It took form when English political habits and legal institutions worked under pioneer conditions. The forms of association were stable, even though their units were mobile and migratory. Pioneer conditions put a high premium upon personal work, skill, ingenuity, initiative and adaptability, and upon neighborly sociability. The township or some not much larger area was the political unit, the town meeting the political medium, and roads, schools, the peace of the community, were the political objectives. . . . The imagination of the Founders did not travel far beyond what could be accomplished and understood in self-governing communities. . . . We have inherited, in short, local town-meeting practices and ideas. But we live and act and have our being in a continental national state.[1]

It is debatable whether this dewy-eyed view of the life of the Republic ever existed. There is no argument, however, that what was being created in the nation-state was a continental, integrated, industrial and agrarian society with a collective sense of self, seething with a sense of ideological purpose.

It is not then especially fanciful to see a certain symmetry between this larger sensibility and an intellectual and organizational architecture for public broadcasting—a hankering after the local in an irresistibly continental age. Here was a profound difference from other systems which sought to speak to, represent, and bind together collectively the nation, the society rather than its particularities and constituent pieces alone. As a result, however, the institution could never seem to recognize that the only public broadcasting institutions which could survive, let alone thrive, were those that welcomed—not shirked—intelligent populism, and which sought to build a truly national mandate. One of the lines of the advertisement campaign in the *New Yorker* reads: 'There's always something special on PBS. From historical pilgrimages and the war against poverty to a celebration of the senses and reducing youth violence, upcoming public television programmes are sure to enthrall and enlighten the most demanding viewer.'[2] That latter is a fascinating phrase loaded with patricianism, even paternalism, that would have satisfied John Reith. Every single example mentioned of upcoming programmes is a documentary or educational, which might be said to be an important part of television, but which in themselves can never build the audience base without which the 'public' in public broadcasting becomes an empty concept.

I have already suggested a level of denial and falsity of consciousness in the positions adopted at all levels of the public television system. Paradoxically, the consequence of critique of and challenges to that system serves only to feed the denial and the falsity. Certainly there is an atmosphere of siege once more surrounding public television. Dole and Gingrich and their congressional colleagues, the Heritage Foundation, Laurence Jarvik, and the Center for the Study of Popular Culture, the columnist and television personality George Will, numerous editorials in conservative newspapers and magazines are all

---

[1] John Dewey, *The Public and its Problems*.   [2] *New Yorker*, 28 Nov. 1994.

saying that public television is biased or unnecessary or in need of being laid to rest.

The consensual view from those who broadly define themselves as the supporters and friends of public broadcasting appears to be that these conservative attacks demonstrate the tough times which public television faces. They also seem to be held as a kind of badge of merit, the significance of the institution defined by the significance of those who assault it. In fact the attacks deflect from the discussion which should be taking place about the service offered this society by public broadcasting. Springing from such overtly partisan and, often, crudely simplistic viewpoints the criticisms have served the institutional status quo by providing the establishment of public broadcasting with the comforts provided by the quality of its enemies. If one is being attacked by the Republican leadership or right-wing intellectuals paid for by conservative businessmen then one must be doing something right. It is a sentiment which has bred an unfortunate complacency, typifying what Galbraith described as a 'culture of contentment'. The net effect has been to inhibit the discussion which should be taking place about the fundamental problems of the organization, funding, and purpose of public television in the United States, a debate which is taking place within every public broadcasting system around the world save the US one.

The certainty of rectitude is fed by what appears to be a deep ambivalence towards the public-as-audience. One gets a very real sense that from within public television American culture and society are viewed as something to be kept at arm's length, a dark and dangerous continent smothered in corrupted values and ethics, peopled by the Fallen of mass culture, beyond redemption. Public television is to be a protected zone, safe and serious and pure, a kind of televisual green-lung amidst the devastation. Translated into programming terms the logic is that any programme which is too popular should more properly appear on commercial television. Here, in fact, is one of the basic conceits of the American public television community: that if you are attracting too many viewers, if you are too popular, then you must be doing something wrong. Not so hidden within this notion is a clear disdain for the American popular mind. This suggests also a rejection of one of the richest traditions of public broadcasting elsewhere, a belief in the ability of the creative programme-maker to marry quality with popular appeal, a real faith in the potential of the 'ordinary' citizen-as-audience member to grow. Indeed one might argue that it was here within this core thesis that public broadcasting most profoundly connected with democratic culture and practice, which must assume not just the sovereignty of the individual but also his or her potentiality. If this interpretation of the disdain by those within American public broadcasting is in any way accurate—they will of course squeal that it is not—it must thus rank as the single most worrying fact about the system.

Public television is available in more American homes than any other single network—more than NBC, CBS, or ABC, more (by far) than any cable service —yet it only gets about 2 per cent of all viewing. The reason is not primarily to do with competition since, even when the viewing menu was restricted in the years before cable, public television's viewing was still marginal. The answer can only lie in what I have been suggesting: dysfunctionality in organization, fiscal recklessness, conceptual confusion all amplified by the hubris of a cultural élite which, it seems, has a deep fear of the 'mob'. At 2 per cent one has to question public television's claim to be a national broadcaster.

The rise of the multi-channel society in the United States, ahead of anywhere else on earth, has brought into sharp focus aspects of public television and its place within American society which are inherent, but which had, until the new television, remained largely invisible. The problems confronted by public TV, fashioned by the Public Broadcasting Act of 1967, are conceptual and structural. At the conceptual level the Act maintained public television's educational role but added a more general role, such that it now matched the definitional trinity of most public broadcasting organizations—informing, educating, entertaining. Structurally the two axes which constituted 'the system' were local and national. This duality in both concept and structure, like two tectonic plates rubbing against each other, was, and remains, an inevitable source of tension.

What one can see in American public television are, then, conceptual and structural confusion; a myth around the concept of the local; a nervous ambivalence about the audience; and the withering impact of competition.

Conceptual Confusion

The Carnegie Commission Report of 1967 preferred 'public television' to 'educational television' as a way of suggesting ' "education" in the broad sense of informational and cultural programming as well as instructional'. It seemed to want to enliven and soften the dry, forbidding instructional image and to have the system become a more general, entertainment service. However, in all the years since, 'public' broadcasting has never clarified the distinction or the exact relationship between the two models. Indeed, it appears to shuffle uneasily between them according to whatever funding sources it is addressing at the moment.

For many state governments and certain entrenched federal bureaucracies the public broadcasting community presents the view that the nation is a classroom and it, public broadcasting, is the teacher. To corporate sponsors it presents itself as a popular, generally up-market, 'good' entertainment vehicle, particularly capable of drawing élite, higher-income, and politically powerful audiences. To confused congressional leaders it slips back and forth between these images, and few on the Hill or in most prior administrations have succeeded in pinning it down.

The debates about the implications of change, of where public TV and radio should go, are far from new. They simply, today, have a fresh urgency. One has only to consider, for example, the argument about an enhanced (or is it rediscovered?) 'educational' role for public television. Henry Becton, President and General Manager of the WGBH Educational Foundation, wrote, 'At the start of the 1980s, WGBH could aptly be described as a television and radio broadcaster. Today, as we head into a new decade providing a far wider range of services, WGBH can more accurately be called an "educational telecommunications center".'[3] He went on to describe the potentialities of developing 'interactive software, home video cassettes, educational print materials and videotex columns; we address the needs of the business sector through such services as satellite teleconferencing'.[4] The late Michael Rice wrote, responding to earlier versions of this argument, and with his usual robust brilliance, 'This is a treacherous ambition.'[5] In May 1988 *Broadcasting* quoted Bruce Christensen as saying the PBS would 'focus increasingly' on education, training, and international services. Perhaps the most futuristic description of a reconceived public broadcasting service has come from George Hall, then head of public television's Office of New Technology Initiatives, and James Fellows, President of the Central Educational Network. Hall offered '[t]he brave new word TelePlex . . . to label what was once strung out as a "public telecommunications center complex" '.[6] Fellows elaborated: 'The invention of TelePlex makes it possible to describe public television's new institutional framework— not just a station or channel, not just a television network or a one-way video service—but a genuinely new concept with a new name.'[7]

Whatever is meant by the 'educational' remit of public broadcasting, its case is not served by the fact that the nation overwhelmingly plays hooky. There simply is not much of an audience for American public broadcasting, whether as compared to its foreign counterparts or more pertinently to its free, open, and rapidly changing commercial competition in the USA. On the instructional side, public broadcasting has a minimal presence in the schools. There is no educational radio to speak of anymore, and educational television is available in only about one-fifth of the nation's classrooms, where it is little used. The private Whittle Channel One, the CNN Newsroom, and several other

---

[3] Henry Becton, paper presented at the inaugural meeting of the Hartford Gunn Institute, Chicago, Ill., 30–1 Aug. 1993.
[4] Ibid.   [5] Rice, 'Public Television', 22.
[6] George Hall, paper presented at the inaugural meeting of the Hartford Gunn Institute, Chicago, Ill., 30–1 Aug. 1993.
[7] James Fellows, ibid.

services are much more widely available, and heavily used, and increasingly ubiquitous. Whatever is wrong with American education, public broadcasting has not offered any remedies. The situation is quite similar at the college level where, after years of having almost exclusive rights to the use of television in higher education, the universities have provided little off-campus, in-home instructional service. It is notable that, during the past five years, the Mind Extension University developed by Jones Intercable almost completely outside the conventional public system has joined forces with a number of universities to provide over two dozen formal, telecourse degree programmes nation-wide, clearly modelling itself on the BBC's own, much praised, Open University.

Structural Confusion

Les Brown, a well-respected observer of television, former editor of *Channels*, and former senior fellow at the Freedom Forum Media Studies Center, has noted: 'There is very little produced domestically [by public television] that is distinguished. The really big stuff that everyone writes or talks about is imported from England.'[8] The reason, Brown suggests, is that the system is a distribution mechanism, not a network, 'for a set of local and jealously independent public television stations. WGBH wants to be the main producing station, KCET wants to be the main producing station, none of them can produce worth a damn anyway. Nothing they've done has been world class.' These are challenging words since of all the givens of the ideology of public television the most universally accepted one is that it offers a 'quality' service. There is in fact real confusion about the very idea of quality—expressed in rather frustrated tones by someone familiar with the 20th Century Fund Task Force inquiry into the future of public broadcasting: 'There is a muddle (there is no other word for it) in the minds of most Americans over the concepts of "quality" and "popularity." That is precisely the problem with the Task Force. Not a single member of the Task Force appears to think the two ideas can be—or should be—compatible. Again and again they have proposed prescriptions for public TV that confine it to a ghetto—an educational ghetto, or a public service ghetto, or a cultural ghetto—but always a ghetto.'[9]

It may well be that one could argue that the idea of 'quality'—what it means, how you get it—has proved elusive in even the most successful public broadcasting communities. One would, for example, search long and hard within the historical discourse and documentation surrounding the BBC to find a meaningful definition. The philosophy, there as elsewhere, has essentially been

---

[8] Les Brown, quoted in Robert Knafo, 'Making PBS Worth Watching', *Connoisseur* (Sept. 1989), 160–2.

[9] Private communication to author from a member of the Task Force.

one of 'we all generally know quality when we see it'. One could also perhaps argue, in sympathy with the American system, that, even if there is a cultural ghettoish tone to its output, in serving such tastes public television is contributing to the general diversity of American television culture. The difficulty with this latter argument is that at one and the same time it seeks to universalize narrow, somewhat class-based taste to a population which not unreasonably is less than welcoming, and at the same time leaves the provision of popular culture to providers who could not care less about concepts of 'quality'. Trailing as a consequence of the implicit Reithian patricianism of American public television is the brute reality that for most Americans most of the time there is no felt 'need' for public television and many other distractions.

The issue of production—quality or otherwise—is anyhow largely academic for the greater part of the public broadcasting system. The Boston Consultancy Group, in a study commissioned by the CPB, reports that according to PBS statistics for the fiscal year 1991, of the 345 public television stations—345! —with their 11,215 full-time employees, the vast bulk of programming was made available by just eleven stations. Three hundred stations contributed not a single programme.

The organizational structure of American public broadcasting is a bizarre combination, at one and the same time, of the monolithically bureaucratic and the anarchically fragmented. There is within public broadcasting an unwieldy combination of university, state, and local education authority stations serviced by a confusing array of state and regional organizations, all overlain by an indescribably complex national bureaucracy represented by the welter of organizations known as the Corporation for Public Broadcasting (CPB), the Public Broadcasting Service (PBS), the American Program Service (APS), National Public Radio (NPR), American Public Radio (APR), the National Association of Public Television Stations (NAPTS), the Children's Television Workshop (CTW), and myriad other federal, foundation, and corporate funding and programming agencies. It has been widely reported that this chaotic structure severely restricts the creation of significant services by permitting a complex pattern of competing interests who spend more time arguing over their respective turf than designing and producing programmes. As one public broadcaster himself put it long ago, 'Public television is one long meeting occasionally interrupted by a program.'[10]

From time to time they have even proposed major adjustments that would reduce the confusion, creating a much more rationalized, efficient system of multiple, distinct national programme services and complementary local stations that might even compete successfully with all the new commercial services. Yet the elements of the system are so regularly at loggerheads with

---

[10] Private communication to author from a member of the Task Force.

one another that any intelligent plans along these lines are watered down and reduced to only minor rearrangements of the chairs around the table. One member of the 20th Century Fund Task Force on the Future of Public Broadcasting observed: 'I do not think our report will have much of an impact, and there is so much inertia built into American public broadcasting that my guess is there will be little change until people sense a real crisis. While I have not entirely given up, I am not optimistic.'[11]

The seriousness of the situation is revealed in the outcome of two major changes initiated in 1989–90. Because many producers could not break through the complex programme decision-making and funding process involving the local, regional, and national agencies, legislation in 1989 diverted some funds from traditional mechanisms and forced a certain rearrangement of responsibilities in Washington. It appears that from one perspective all that has been accomplished is the evolution of yet another new national organization, the Independent Television Service (ITVS), whose constituents have a decidedly leftist hue and whose capacity to receive funds seems to run ahead of their ability to make programmes that people wish to watch. Another effort at national reform can be seen in the appointment of a 'programming czar' (or czarina) at PBS who, the *Wall Street Journal* suggested in 1990, has been steering public television toward production of soap operas and game shows. The spin was typical of those forces inside American society who see worthiness in parched erudition and absent imagination. The task of this new 'czarina' (Jennifer Lawson was appointed to the post) was to help develop a national programme schedule that would spread the appeal of public television—rather in the way in which *Morning Edition*, *All Things Considered*, and Garrison Keillor have transformed NPR into a key part of the national radio system. Lawson found life less than easy and was eventually eased out of her position.

The Myth of the Local Community

It could be argued that the justification for public broadcasting stands or falls on the extent to which it represents and serves its local communities. There is, as has already been suggested, little evidence that it does either.

While it is true that the number of public stations continues to proliferate—due in large part to the continued stimulus of a federal funding programme for new facilities—it is unclear what they add to each community. Public broadcasters justify the need for all these stations on the grounds of increasing coverage and the ability to give voice to the different licensee organizations. But for some time now public broadcasting coverage has been nearly universal, and the amount of local programming, especially in public television, is almost

---

[11] Ibid.

negligible. The overall prime-time programming of a college station, a community station, and a state authority station will be almost identical even if they are available in the same city. One need only scan the schedules of the three stations available in the Washington, DC, area to understand this reality. Where is the differentiated local voice and diverse set of interests in all this? As an editorial in *Broadcasting* forcefully stated in 1988: ' "the principle of localism" remains the enemy within.'[12] The same editorial noted that the core problem of public TV was not the centralized decision-making function of CPB, but 'rather the political squabbling and factionalism that impede that decision-making. Considering the competition, particularly from cable, for public broadcasting's target audience, a home divided could ultimately become a house of cards.' In effect, monies made over to public broadcasting are feeding a body at war with itself.

This problem is compounded by the manner in which the United States has evolved sociologically. It is a simple fact of life—well recognized by, for example, advertisers—that the idea of the local community is *passé* and that the USA is defined by a vast array of different taste cultures. Since those taste cultures dot the whole nation, clearly only pan-national services are likely to be relevant. With its relentless local ideology which does not match objective realities, however, public broadcasting has set its face against such a manifestly nationally organized service. It thus ends up expressing a commitment to ways of life which were always more mythologized than real—someone observed that if Norman Rockwell were alive today he would have to introduce himself by saying 'I'm Norman, I paint lies.' The funding of public broadcasting, particularly television, is, too often, spending to nurture nostalgia.

A specific illustration of the localism problem came several years ago from a supporter of public broadcasting, who also happened previously to have been one of its major station officials. The late Michael Rice wrote that 'mostly the problem is with the delusion caused by the officially promulgated, long perpetuated ideal that local stations exist to do local programming . . . [with the odd exception] local programming on public TV has not persuaded viewers of its indispensable value. However heretical, it is time to admit that apart from local news, genuinely local programs have been given their fair test. Except in rare instances, they are of marginal value and disproportionate expense.'[13] Figures produced almost a decade after Rice made this observation seem devastatingly to support his contention. Again according to BCG the cost of producing programmes at the local level in the fiscal year 1989 was $570 million—a figure that includes overheads, studio costs, salaries, etc. of the local stations. This was 43 per cent of all public television expenditures, but produced only 7 per cent of total broadcast hours. Figures for the fiscal year

---

[12] *Broadcasting*, editorial, 22 Aug. 1988.   [13] Rice, 'Public Television', 17–18.

1990 amplify the observation that the structure of localism is fiscally inefficient to the point of irresponsibility. Perhaps, however, the most telling figures are comparative ones, for example the monies available to say CBC in Canada and the BBC. In the fiscal year 1990 CBC had revenues of approximately $988.3 million, and the BBC $1.57 billion. In the same period about $1.5 to $1.6 billion (no one really knows) flowed through the US public broadcasting system. Clearly the CBC and BBC—two highly developed national broadcasting organizations—are vastly more effective, in programme terms, in spending their monies. Or consider that just one station, WNET in New York, had an operating budget of $120 million in 1990. CNN—operating three national and international networks, 24 hours a day, running nineteen foreign bureaux— had a budget of only $312 million. There is also an increasing disparity between the amount of money which the cable industry spends on programmes and that which public television spends on its national schedules. In 1990, for example, Disney, Discovery, A&E, and CNN spent $358 million on programming; PBS spent $201 million on its national schedule. And all the signs are that cable services will continue to increase their spending, PBS will not.

In light of this analysis it is only fair to conclude that the structure of localism has failed and that it is culturally irrelevant and a major financial drain on the system. This situation is the single most important reason why in an institution with total revenues for the fiscal year 1994 of $1.89 billion, only 10 per cent was spent directly on programming.

The Public Broadcasting Audience

Public broadcasters like to claim that they reach 120 million Americans or nearly half of the population each week, though recently one PR campaign boosted this figure to 200 million. Furthermore, they claim that this audience is a cross-section that 'mirrors' the demographics of the total US population. Unfortunately, this interpretation of the statistics is a rather selective reading of the data. For one thing, the so-called weekly 'cume'—the total number of homes reached by public TV—includes anyone who is reported to have viewed once for only fifteen or twenty minutes. The actual audience for any given public television programme is, in fact, quite minuscule.

The average prime-time rating for public television in all TV households remained steady for many years at only 2.6–2.8 per cent. In the mid-1980s the growth of basic and pay cable began to undermine even this small base. David LeRoy, the premier public broadcasting audience analyst, reports that by the autumn of 1989 the average prime-time rating had fallen to 2.1 per cent (less than 2 million households).[14]

---

[14] David LeRoy, unpublished research report (1990).

Something else became apparent by the late 1980s. Nielsen reported that PTV members who pledged money demonstrated a 'disturbing predilection' for the likes of Arts & Entertainment and Discovery. One observer was quoted as saying, 'the very people who had fed us were now feeding the lions who would devour us.'[15]

Finally the claim of representativeness in the cumulative audience is spurious. Among the prime-time audience, where the vast majority of the regular viewing occurs, the demographics are skewed markedly toward higher socio-economic characteristics—the élites public broadcasting likes to deny, except when seeking 'underwriting' (sponsorship) from corporate funders. The cumulative weekly audience, which in fact represents quite light viewing attention and loyalty, is said to be more balanced only because the much smaller audiences of children's programming are folded in with the more regular prime-time viewers. In a report to public television stations in February 1992 LeRoy pointed out that the figure was now 2 per cent and that the 'cume' was the lowest since 1984.[16]

Perhaps the most telling evidence of the lack of real impact and audience loyalty is in the figures associated with those who actually donate to public broadcasting. By its own admission public broadcasting can count only 10 per cent of its already small regular audience as paying members. Of course the viewing desires of this particular audience are as legitimate as any other. The problems lie in the way in which the force of their fiscal presence is a significant factor in crippling the ability of American public television to reach out and touch other audiences.

The Impacts of Competition

In spite of all these problems, the most profound reality that public broadcasting must face is presented not by its interior structural, definitional, and demographic problems, but by the rise of the 'third age' of TV and radio. The broadcast situation has changed dramatically in recent years. Over 60 per cent of American homes now subscribe to cable, even more have VCRs, and the large majority have more than one television set. The launch of the direct broadcast satellite services offering more than 100 channels will almost certainly have a heavy impact, especially in those homes which cable cannot economically reach. Those developments will be enhanced in the short term by the introduction of digital compression technology which before the end of

[15] Quoted in Knafo, 'Making PBS Worth Watching', 160.
[16] David LeRoy, unpublished research report (1992).

the decade may well make 500-channel cable homes the norm. In the medium term new fibre optic cables, high-definition television, and increasingly interactive cable-data systems will only further decimate the already small public broadcasting audience, offering the educational, cultural, and informational programming which public broadcasting used to claim for its own.

The inevitable recognition by any government of any political hue of the strategic industrial and economic significance and necessity of the wiring of the nation—the 'information superhighway'—will make inevitable a role for the Baby Bells (the regional telephone companies), alongside cable, in the provision of all kinds of information and video services. Such involvement will only serve to enhance massively the trends described.

In response cable interests will, indeed already do, work hard to provide the public service elements that were admittedly so lacking in the old network-dominated broadcasting system. It was that shortcoming within commercial broadcasting that led to the policy of federal support for public broadcasting after the mid-1960s. Now, however, with the technological advances of the 'third age' and its proliferation of special audience cable programming of all kinds, the old rationale for public support of non-commercial alternatives is at the very least undermined. Thus the claim to fame of public broadcasting, for example that it offers programming that the commercial system does not, is losing plausibility and rhetorical force. The range of genres available from the new media equals, indeed probably surpasses, those of public television.

Conclusion

With a deliberate argumentativeness, one might conclude that there is within American public television an extraordinarily inefficient use of available resources. There is also a complete failure to address the needs of this society, broadly defined, as public television in the USA turned its back on the mainstream of those cultures which now define this society. Public television is thus nowhere near as good as it could be, in terms of the character and range of the programming it offers and the lives it could touch. Public television is not 'local', merely balkanized. Public television can thus not provide a counterpoint to the social, political, moral, economic, and ethnic centripetal forces that threaten this society. Public television has little or no imaginative programming vision and thus no developed sense of excellence. There is little or no capacity or, with rare exception, courage to look at itself with a cold, unblinking eye.

As a result others have begun to do that for it. There is of course a high rhetorical element to these concluding observations, though they are closely tied to the kinds of questions which are being asked elsewhere. The layers of structure, institutions within institutions; the bureaucracies piled on bureaucracy; the tribalism of the local structure; the extraordinary siphoning off of funds into things other than programmes; the apparent absence of energy and excitement and innovation; those tones of a culture in exile; all these problems and more lead one to conclude that there is a powerful need for a searching public inquiry into the state and future of American public television.

The key to all successful public television is coherent thinking, coherent structure, and coherent, consistent, and untainted funding. Any public inquiry into the condition and future of public television will need to address these issues first. The answers to everything else flow from their resolution. And any such inquiry would therefore need to consider basic changes in the organization and funding of public television. Put simply: are these now appropriate to a multi-media age? Or is there a need for a total restructuring of the organization of public television so that a proper, and efficient, national programming service can become a reality? Any such inquiry would need to look very closely at the forms of funding. And in such a searching examination nothing should be sacred, including what I take to be the central mythology of public broadcasting, that the stations serve the local community and the nation.

Inevitably, though I realize this is highly contentious, consideration would need to be given to extending the logic of commercial sources of revenue: yes, advertising. Advertising *per se* is not the source of the problem of the commercialization of television, rather the linking of the raising of advertising to ownership and control of the system. People get greedy. But if the link is prevented then advertising simply becomes cash in the bank to pay for programmes. If this were not the case, how would one explain the undoubted success of Independent Television in Britain, or of Channel Four, both of which have been responsible for remarkable television over many years and yet both of which are funded by advertising?

The examination of these structural questions would be a necessary and central part of any inquiry into the future of public television. However, that would need to be paralleled by a consideration of the purpose of broadcasting. There is no point in having an institution if it has no proper or clear purpose. And the character of the programmes offered is ultimately the only testimony to such purpose. Everything else is housekeeping.

The preservation of the status quo within American public television may broadly serve the needs and interests of those inside, and that tiny portion of the American public which attends to its offerings. It does not, because it cannot, serve this society in any broader sense. And yet this society desperately needs a competent television service, and only the idea of public television, well organized and funded, has within it the inherent potential to so serve.

A Postscript

The titles of books, like those of articles, should make a virtue of their brevity. The title of this piece is almost certainly not readily apparent. It is, I have to confess, an ironic play on what I take to be the basic problem of public television, its marginality to American society. The phrase 'a stricken place' is borrowed from a comment by Norman Mailer about the media coverage of JFK's funeral.

One of the most compelling arguments for national public broadcasting is its ability, particularly in difficult times, to embody the broad sentiments and sensibilities of the whole, national community. There are numerous examples from around the world of this phenomenon. In writing about JFK's funeral, Mailer noted how American television, which for a brief space of time became in effect a public service system as commercials disappeared from the airwaves for several days, brought the nation together for a moment in the 'same stricken place'. That is not something that American public television has ever done, or could ever do.

PART IV

The Ceremony of Innocence

14 The Ceremony of Innocence: A Conclusion about the Condition of Public Service Broadcasting

Those involved in public broadcasting, either by doing it or thinking about it, have become fascinated, often frustrated, about such notions as how to sustain creativity, diversity, excellence, fairness, that whole canonical structure which has defined the narrative history of public broadcasting. How can, for example, the BBC or NHK or any of the national broadcasters survive? And what can they survive as? Buried deep in our concerns lies the spirit of the Enlightenment, the idea that the world can be a humane and rational place serving the needs and wishes of the people, liberating their potential and corralling their darker impulses. Implicit within this position is the further view that such service will not be rendered by the political or commercial spheres. Only a detached realm of public provision will be up to the task. The public broadcasting community consists in effect of optimistic humanists who believe that a broadcasting service can and must be sustained whatever the historical conditions.

The question is whether it is any longer viable or relevant in the modern world. I choose that last phrase carefully since I set my face against notions of the post-modern where there are no fixed meanings, no certainty, and where reason has been placed in its coffin. I take the world to be a highly rational place, defined by the needs and interests of private corporate culture, which unfortunately depends for its continuity on the sustaining of an irrational sub-stratum fed by a trivialized mediated culture. It is one thing to point to the need to provide for, and to sustain, cultural values and diversity, quite another to be blind to the real nature and strength of the forces which have been beating away at the intellectual plausibility structures of public broadcasting.

The discussion of any social institution is inscribed with a discourse fash-ioned from the values of the particular ideologies which are historically preval-ent. The fate of any institution is always—though rarely overtly—determined by the character of that discourse. There has to be a conceptual proximity between *the idea* which informs the institution and the philosophical, socio-logical, and cultural terms which provide the context within which it rests and by which it is formed. Nowhere more so than in the realm of broadcasting. If however we conclude that there is disjunction between 'the idea' and the context then all the declarations about preserving, in this case, public broad-casting will be for naught. The thought which has come to inform this book more than any other is that the fundamental problem which public broad-casters face lies in the shakiness of the very idea of a public good and public interest.

There is nevertheless a language which *can* be developed which begins to make clear the continued importance of national public broadcasting organ-izations. The terms of that language are paradoxically fashioned by precisely those forces which caused the crisis of public broadcasting in the first place. Such language is, however, drowned out by much noise, that Babel of confu-sion which characterizes the attempted reinvention of public broadcasting.

I was fascinated to read accounts of the BBC's press conference in 1993 for the release of the Corporation's thirty-five-page blueprint for the future. There is much talk of streamlining, structural change, programme strategy review, market testing of support services, new working methods, productivity targets, annual performance review making the BBC more efficient and accountable— as opposed presumably to the various possible negative permutations of that couplet. The Director-General, John Birt, is quoted as saying, 'Bureaucracy is what you have when you have very unclear lines of responsibility,' and noting that the organizational review 'should be creatively stimulating and highly enjoyable. Exactly what we all joined the BBC to do.'[1] If these quotes are accur-ate then the first is plain wrong and someone should loan Birt the collected

---

[1] *Financial Times*, 12 Jan. 1993.

essays of Max Weber, and the second worrying in that one would have hoped that people joined the BBC to communicate well, produce programmes, offer information, and so on.

None of this is surprising. It reflects a confusion of purpose, and a belief in the techno-fix of management theory, usually from the United States—which is not exactly a paragon of effective efficiency. It is all a bit like painting over rust—it looks shiny but it continues to decay from beneath. What we are witnessing here is a version of something which characterizes—in my view defiles—much of modern life, the triumph of technique over principled, humane purpose. In this instance we are dealing with management technique, the idea that in the application of management theory lies the answer to the 'problem'. It is unclear how far this is true of the making of widgets. It seems unlikely to be so for public broadcasting. Efficiency and accountability to what end and with what presumed consequence? I am reminded of a comment by Neil Postman. He was writing of the social sciences, but the parallels with public broadcasting are interesting: 'One becomes fastidious about method when one has no story to tell. The best people in our field have, with few exceptions, been almost indifferent to the question of method.'[2] The real function of such exercises is to be seen to be doing something, and to worry less about *why* you are doing that something in the first instance.

This is not to say that there is no response which the public broadcaster can make. But such response must lie in an examination of a set of questions which have long animated the sense of purpose of the public broadcasters: the relationship between the institution and the society, and in particular the things that can be done *for* the society. For today and tomorrow that purpose flows from the larger issue of governance in the modern world.

This book, then, has been about what public broadcasting was, and what has happened to it and why, and what, if any, solutions there might be. The potentiality to serve cultural values, diversity, excellence can only be understood from within those larger questions. I do not approach this task with any massive optimism, only a certain hope. Max Weber, a child of the Enlightenment, was haunted by its consequences, the incarnation of reason in bureaucracy and the fundamental denial of what it is to be human. Sitting amidst what may well be the planet's future, contemporary American society, one does get a sense of what he meant. A certain hopelessness sets in as the triumph of the banal and the morally and creatively impoverished appears complete. Yeats expressed this feeling well:

> Turning and turning in the widening gyre
> The falcon cannot hear the falconer;
> Things fall apart; the centre cannot hold;

---

[2] Neil Postman, *Conscientious Objections* (New York: Knopf, 1988), 18.

Mere anarchy is loosed upon the world,
The blood-dimmed tide is loosed, and everywhere
The ceremony of innocence is drowned;
The best lack all conviction, while the worst
Are full of passionate intensity.

The Condition of Public Broadcasting

The most obvious evidence of troubled times is the stark fact that governments, in country after country, have introduced new policies which at a minimum make life difficult for the public broadcaster. At worst governments have
obliterated such organizations. Equally worrying is the case when public broadcasters act as gravediggers to their own funeral by acknowledging in almost
welcoming terms that their share of total viewing will inevitably dwindle. The
curious thing, for example, in the BBC's position that they will move to a '30
per cent share' is that no argument was offered as to how they would be able
to prevent the slide carrying on below that level, nor even of what the implications would be to sustain a political rhetoric in favour of the licence fee.

This is not to suggest that there have been no bad times. The past decade,
for the reasons already explained, has been truly awful for the public broadcasting community. In almost every case they have had their organizations,
funding, and purpose challenged. Such a triple assault is of course no accident
since those three elements are inextricably linked. Something of the success
of those who would challenge public broadcasting has been in their ability
to nudge the concerns in the direction of thinking about 'housekeeping', as
the bureaucratization and corporatization of broadcasting continue apace.
Considerations of wider purpose—more abstract, difficult, and contentious—
wither through inattention.

The process of change within public broadcasting has connected with other
significant economic, political, and structural developments, which at the very
least will be seen to undermine the integrity of public service broadcasting.
In particular, one might characterize these as: the shift to the global, the decline
of the public sphere, and the fragmentation of social order. If we look at daily
life around the globe there are all kinds of currents, contradictions, disillusions,
reactions, disintegrations. Despite the often heard notion of the homogeniz-
ing impacts of globalism, it remains perfectly clear that there is no singularity
in the social and intellectual practices of the planet. Indeed, there are massive
collisions and differences, though it remains unclear as to whether these represent a pattern of social order which is likely to persist or the birth pangs of a
new, pluralistic order, more able in the long run to satisfy human aspirations.
Whichever of these scenarios defines the next century the consequences for

public service broadcasting are potentially profound, a profundity amplified by the character of communication technologies which will certainly be part of that future. For the public service broadcaster there is a fearful symmetry between the character of those technologies and the character of the emerging age.

Difference and diversity may be socially formed, but they are helped along the way by new systems of communication, developed in the past two decades, which are profoundly individualistic and definitely not collective, public, shared, or coherent.

The importance of this can easily be seen if one considers that in almost every country where public service broadcasting has been developed a central and common part of the lexicon of justification for the public sphere is the power of the shared moment, when the broadcasting organization becomes the national theatre, schoolroom, debating chamber, chapel, spectacle. It is in those moments, the canon holds, that broadcasting transforms us as a social species into a community infused with, and animated by, shared values and morality.

If we live in an age in which coherent and stable social relationships are in doubt, we also live in one in which the idea of coherent, stable, objectively valid belief systems are equally questioned and uncertain. Public service broadcasting really requires the persistence of both, since in its innermost beliefs it assumed that there were coherent populations to which it could speak, and recognizable hierarchies of value within which that speech could be formed. Incoherence and a relativity of values thus become fundamentally destabilizing for the public broadcaster, and yet both are immanent within the crudely, but forcefully, defined democratic cultural practice known as the market.

Much of this is known to the point of cliché. What seems to be less clear among the public broadcasting community is the way in which a real dilemma, even profound contradiction, is now embedded in the public policy regimes of the industrial democracies that we studied. On the one hand, there is residual support for a public sector in broadcasting. On the other, there is eager support for nurturing new systems of communication whose very nature calls into question the stability of the public system. There is nowhere, no society large or small, that is not harbouring, to greater or lesser extent, the ambitions of post-industrialism, and thus of digital communications technologies, and thus of more television accessed in different ways.

There is, however, something else about this new television which is profoundly significant. Several phases of the history and future of television can be defined and projected: (1) 1930–75: limited terrestrial TV; (2) 1975–2000: multi-channel TV; (3) 2000–20: digital, HDTV, interactive TV; (4) 2020–50: full interactivity; (5) 2050+: video holography and virtual reality. As one tracks across these phases, two tendencies can be seen: the de-institutionalization of the media; the shift to communications as essentially about easy pleasure and sensory experience. There are clear implications here for the premisses which undergird the use of traditional notions of television, particularly in its public forms. The reference here is not just to the massive amplification of the amount of simple, even trivial, pleasure which characterizes commercialized television, nor even the manifestly non-linear expressive forms of MTV culture, but also to the curious, perhaps even irrational process of grazing across multiple channels, viewing several channels at once, the amplified visuality of HDTV (reason does not really need 1,125 lines), and the emergence of interactive systems, most notably virtual reality systems. One does not need to be a technological determinist to suggest that technologies clearly have a powerful capacity to bring to the surface tendencies, dispositions, desires that have lain dormant and unrealized. It is equally true that there are all kinds of social forces which shift and cajole forms of thought and behaviour. A retribalization, for example, of the modern world is clearly something with more than mere rhetorical or metaphorical force. People, not all but many, find comfort in associations founded in gender, ethnicity, generation, music, life-style, sexual practice, memory, significations of difference, the multifaceted drawing of lines between self and the other. Whether this constitutes a retribalization is a moot point, but whatever it is, whatever the social tectonics that have fashioned it, the result seems to constitute not something which is benign and munificent, rather something which is troubled, unstable, alienated, and definitely not communal or caring.

A conclusion then can be drawn about the new communications. Its very nature constitutes a fundamental taking apart of that sense of the collective which is a precondition for the continuity of public service broadcasting. However, we delude ourselves if we do not acknowledge that such a process could not happen if the individuals who constitute 'the public' were not complicit. One further tendency, then, which needs to be considered and which inevitably affects the performance of public service broadcasting is captured by a phrase which, appropriately, gained currency in the United States in the early 1990s: 'dumbing down'. It is a concept which is perhaps better 'felt' than articulated, a sense of the corrosive influence of the main currents of popular culture: linguistic poverty and therefore a mental and moral poverty, daytime soaps, tabloid television, and the trivialization of public discourse, an evangelism of the ephemeral, the celebration of the insignificant, and the marginalization of the important, cults of empty celebrity.

A broadband culture can and will do nothing but encourage these tendencies. The rhetoric of broadband culture is that it is liberatory, that it constitutes the architecture for a new Jeffersonian plebiscitary democracy; that it offers, through the ability to communicate in 'cyberspace', new harmonies, new but nevertheless authentic virtual communities and relationships formed along paths of new ways of speaking to each other; access to unbounded sources of information; new forms of political praxis; unlimited sources of entertainment. The relationship between the rhetoric and reality, however, remains problematic, and certainly begs a set of questions about concepts of public interest, public good, and public culture which have not yet been properly addressed. In fact it is not clear, given the character of the various developments, whether one can even have a public policy on communications in which society through its nominated institutions has some capacity to guide its own evolution, and in which the new 'television', born out of economic strategy, is nevertheless cocooned within a civic ethic, touched with a sense of the whole as well as the parts, possessing a sense of responsibility to a public as well as a private interest. *That* is the fundamental crisis of public communication and public culture.

If there is any plausibility at all to these arguments—and there clearly is —then it suggests that within the next two decades the landscape of communications, and thus society, will be drastically altered, and new technologies, new services, new markets, new audiences will predominate. It is the fall-out from these developments which can be detected in public service broadcasting organizations the world over, and which has been translated into a number of changes inside public broadcasting. It is this larger context, and the challenges which have been thrown up in most national public broadcasting organizations, that have translated into the search for new definitions of mission; organizational and structural change; a new policy environment; new proposals for the funding of public broadcasting; important shifts in programme philosophy; and in particular into an examination of the crucial question of social 'location', much talk of streamlining new working methods, productivity targets, greater efficiency and accountability. Should the public broadcaster be upstream, mainstream, or downstream, popular or élite, lowbrow or highbrow, universalistic or particularistic?

The most obvious aspect of organizational response in public broadcasting has been to shrink the size of the institution, to make the organization more efficient, thus easing the pain caused by the reluctance of governments the world over to do anything other than squeeze the amount of the public treasury put into public broadcasting. The argument for 'downsizing' is overwhelmingly taken for granted by most public broadcasters, as is watching overheads, being very selective about capital expenditure, investing as wisely as one can in new systems that employ fewer people, and trying to channel as much as you possibly can of financial resources directly onto the screen. Such has been the extent of this process that it is now plausible to suggest that 'efficiency' is the single most dominating concept in the field of public service broadcasting.

The difficulty with downsizing is that not all organizations are quite so obviously overstaffed. Nor is it always clear where to stop the downsizing, especially if the process of reorganization begins to impact on those vital but intangible commitments from which many public broadcasters, and therefore their audiences, have greatly benefited. For example, one of the strengths of public broadcasting historically has been its ability to nurture talent, and to reflect on its own worth and purpose. More often than not that has not only been the function of particular departments but has also been a consequence of having the overall capacity to bring someone along—say a new writer or director or journalist—at a pace which allows their natural talent to mature. It is clear that the ability of most public broadcasting organizations to develop talent is ever more diminished: no 'space', no institutional memory; more dependence on an independent sector whose only concern is survival; less time to think.

One possible shift in the model of broadcasting as a result of fiscal pressures leading to downsizing is from broadcaster-producers, which has traditionally been the dominant model, to broadcaster-publishers, of which Channel Four is one version and the American networks another. The principal theoretical arguments for this model lie in the possibility of offering a greater diversity of 'voices' from an independent sector. The pragmatic arguments have much more to do with the economics of television, that this way of doing things is cheaper. The key question here is whether or not in slimming down the large public broadcasting organization, for example, by introducing internal markets and producer choice and allowing funds to flow outside the organization, one triggers a kind of cultural anorexia. There is an important, but highly abstract and intangible, argument that successful public broadcasters tend to be 'largish', with sufficient creative mass to find, nurture, and give space to talent across a range of genres. Shrink that size too far and the institution becomes impoverished.

What is clear is that in many instances the attention of senior public broadcasters has moved away from thinking about programmes to thinking about efficiencies and saving money. One consequence of these financial pressures is that something of the language of public service broadcasting has disappeared. In country after country, one sees a shift from having key decision-makers with a commitment to using broadcasting for some decent social purpose to those who think and act more like accountants.

Recent statistics about public broadcasting in Europe can help give us a slightly more quantified sense of what has been happening. They suggest considerable development in basic productivity. Between 1988 and 1994 the average total of programme hours transmitted each year increased by 55 per cent. During the same time there was a reduction in staff of 12 per cent. What these figures suggest is a much higher level of efficiency, through the reduction of overhead costs, the streamlining of organizational structures, reductions in support services, new production methods, and so on. The figures also show, however, as the European Broadcasting Union (EBU) Report puts it, 'public service broadcasters having to sacrifice in recent years some of their more prestigious programmes and to devote resources to programmes of a more simple nature'.[3] Many organizations increased output by introducing morning and afternoon transmissions and extending night hours between 1988 and 1992. In some places—Finland (YE), Israel (IBA), the Netherlands (NOS), Portugal (RTP), and Switzerland (SSR)—new channels and channel extensions have been established to meet competition.

Public broadcasters have retained a constancy in the proportion of owned/co-produced/commissioned (OCC) programming. That is, they have not come to rely overly on imported or repeat programming. Total volume of output between 1988 and 1992 increased by 20 per cent, while OCC productions increased by 23 per cent. There were increases in the output of all genres between 1988 and 1992. The biggest growth was in fiction (57 per cent), news (45 per cent), information (20 per cent), arts/humanities/sciences (29 per cent); light entertainment went up by 10 per cent, music by 11 per cent, sports by only 3 per cent, and religion by 15 per cent. The percentage share of viewing shows a marked decline. One might add that these are consolidated figures including situations where there is as yet little or no competition, such as Austria, Hungary, Ireland, Poland, and Sweden. The decline in audience share is especially marked in Belgium, Germany, the Netherlands, and Spain, i.e. in countries where the national public broadcasters have faced aggressive national competition.

Personnel numbers have been constantly reduced since 1988, with the largest decreases in the smaller organizations. Between 1988 and 1994 the decline was 12.9 per cent (alongside the 55 per cent increase in programme output). Hence, if nothing else, European public broadcasters can at least claim major increases in productivity. Expenditures increased by 52 per cent between 1988 and 1994, with a further 7.7 per cent between 1994 and 1995. If we allow for general inflation, the maximized internal inflation, and the increased number of hours, real expenditure declined, i.e. costs per programme hour diminished considerably.

Between 1988 and 1994 income increased by 54 per cent, with an expected increase between 1994 and 1996 of 6.6 per cent. Reliance on the licence fee has increased, though in most instances numbers of licence payers have effectively plateaued. The major loss has been advertising revenue. In this situation mixed funding becomes an essential for the majority of public broadcasters if they are to remain effective in the face of competition. The average amount of advertising revenue for all organizations is 28 per cent. The EBU Report draws a very interesting conclusion about these figures: 'fears sometimes

[3] EBU, *Report on Public Broadcasting in Europe* (Geneva: EBU, 1993), 10.

expressed that having too high a dependency on [advertising revenue] might adversely affect their public service mission are ill-founded.'[4] Sponsorship remains financially insignificant. Other sources of income (sales, publications, etc.) have remained constant at between 8 and 9 per cent.

Downsizing, however, does seem to be here to stay and with the shrinkage goes a whole galaxy of new accountancy procedures, zero budgeting, producer-centred budgeting, internal markets, privatization of services, and so on. Wherever one goes the same basic process can be seen: ever greater pressure on the monies made available for public broadcasting, whether that be from the public treasury, the licence fee, forms of sponsorship, advertising, or variations on all of the above. What is quite clear is that the introduction of more efficient and effective budgeting and accountancy procedures, which in themselves may be perfectly laudable, nevertheless in a broader historical sense constitutes a serious shift in the priorities and characterization of broadcasting within society.

Another tendency that needs to be considered is that of the pressures to shift from traditional to new forms of funding, for example, subscription and pay. Governments seem to be increasingly attracted by funding mechanisms that are painless to the public treasury and can also be sold as enfranchising the viewer and listener. However, if one begins with the proposition that the proper function of the funding of public service broadcasting is not only to provide the resources for the organization to operate, but also to put some distance between the programme-maker and the audience, then this fiscal mechanism becomes much more problematic. The classical theory of public service broadcasting holds that funding should guarantee the integrity and uncompromised nature of programme-making of whatever kind, not reduce it. Pay broadcasting intimately involves the broadcaster and the audience with inevitable, obvious, and powerful compromises. Almost without exception executives with whom we spoke, while recognizing the pressure on sources of funding, argued strongly for a core of coherent, index-linked revenue with integrity—whatever the mix of licence, advertising, and state funds. At the margins there was a willingness to be more entrepreneurial, looking for new ventures and sources of money—so long, however, as it remained at the margins. The question which will inevitably emerge as alternative sources of additional funding are sought is, at what point will the general integrity of the organization's programme-making activity be called into question?

All the abstract thinking and wishful thinking in the world will be for naught if there is no money to pay for public broadcasting. Perhaps therefore the first and most fundamental question which has to be raised is how a public service in communications can be paid for. In a sense, everything depends on the

---

[4] EBU, *Report on Public Broadcasting in Europe* (Geneva: EBU, 1993), 12.

answer to that question. Traditionally funding has come from the public purse, whether that be a licence fee paid by the householder or a direct subvention from government, sometimes supplemented by other incomes from sponsorship, advertising, residual sales, and so on. The most contentious issue thus becomes one of whether in the foreseeable future the public purse will continue to deliver, and if not what will be the replacement funding, if any? Here we can begin to see the real difficulties of foresight, prophecy, future analysis, because the answers to these questions depend upon the actions which will be taken by governments, who in turn will be determined by the multiple decisions of the electorate, and heaven alone knows what those will be. Then there is the issue of the larger economic climate. Funding public broadcasting was always, though this was rarely if ever stated, a kind of largess, a feeding off the fat of the economic growth of the twentieth century. It is barely contentious to argue that the body politic is somewhat slimmer, or at least is presented as such ideologically. The major industrial societies are now, as much as ever, vastly wealthy but with major inequities in distribution and a prevailing orthodoxy that nurtures a deep resentment at the idea of sharing the wealth. Pervading the whole political, and therefore financial, climate is the larger issue of the general condition of western industrial society. If that is the case then quite clearly the issue of the resolution of the crisis of public broadcasting depends to a considerable extent on the evolution of that socio-economic order.

There is a widespread understanding among public broadcasters that the absolute prerequisite for maintaining appropriate funding is the maintenance of a meaningful audience, and the prerequisite for that is producing programming which is popular. Two issues immediately rise to the surface: how many is enough? and what does the word 'popular' mean?

There is an inherent tension in the relationship between the programme-maker and the audience. The impulse of the public broadcaster is to offer a service to the audience without pandering, to put a certain distance between themselves and those who will watch the programming. The impulse of the commercial broadcaster is to remove the distance, to get close to the declared wants of the audience.

Here one runs into a veritable minefield of sensitivity, a bruising encounter with the modern difficulty of making prescriptive judgements of others' behaviours. Left to its own designs does popular culture gravitate towards the laudable or the dire? This is a question loaded down with dangerous words and even more dangerous assumptions and implications. Popular culture is clearly not a singular construction, and what exactly is that which is laudable, that which is dire, and who are we to draw such distinctions? The fact of the matter is that it is impossible not to see the distinctions between the two concepts: Geraldo Rivera set against Ed Murrow; *A Current Affair* nose to nose with *See It Now*, 911 versus *Hill St Blues*, *Neighbours* compared to a Dennis Potter play. If one seeks to suck the marrow out of the bone of life it is not difficult to see the differences, the enhanced pleasures and insights set against the unimaginative, the voyeuristic, the shallow.

More than one public broadcasting executive has agonized over the relationship between maintaining public service principles and producing popular programming, with a suspicion that the more popular one was, the less integrity one would have. It is, however, very clear that there is a wide assumption that the ability and desire to pursue excellence in production and nurture creative staff will be seriously challenged, and that the genres of public broadcasting programmes will be increasingly homogenized as such important forms of production as the single play, the innovative documentary, original children's programming, the analytical and searching current affairs programme, original comedy are allotted fewer and fewer resources, and the impulse to co-production and co-financing and international sales becomes relentless. Alongside such developments by regimes which have decided to go head to head with commercial and populist competition go decisions which are indicative and revelatory of the issue of the proper 'location' for public service broadcasting. For example, there are surprisingly interesting and revealing debates that take place around when is the most appropriate time for the main evening news programme. The *News* takes on considerable significance partly because, more than any other programme, that is the moment when the public broadcaster speaks to and for the nation. It is also almost invariably a successful audience-puller for the national broadcaster. Thus quite intricate debates can build up around when it should be scheduled, and those debates become more irritable when there are pressures of competition which, for example, lead the director of programmes to want new blocks of time available for even more audience-grabbing programming.

A related and dangerous argument is that public broadcasting should not be popular, that the place for public broadcasting, especially television, is somewhere 'up-market' where it can provide those programmes which the market fails to deliver. One sees this argument in the writings of Heritage Foundation member Laurence Jarvik, and the speeches of US Congressman Phil Crane, who called for the abolition of federal support for the Corporation for Public Broadcasting on grounds that CPB-supported programmes can 'flourish in the private sector without the hand or wallet of Uncle Sam'.[5] Andrew Neil, former editor of the London *Sunday Times* and adviser to Rupert Murdoch, has argued: 'Much of what was the preserve of the public service monopoly will now be—is now being—provided by the market, and it will be a waste of the funds we devote to public service broadcasting to spend them on

---

[5] *Congressional Review*, 23 Oct. 1991.

programming that the market can do just as well and, sometimes even better.'[6] From these standpoints, the public broadcaster should withdraw from game shows, sitcoms, sports, popular drama, films, and bought-in TV series. The gaps which the public sector should fill are performing arts, 'serious' drama, serious journalism, and analysis.

The proposition, especially for a Murdochian employee was disingenuous. However, it does touch on a problem which is not difficult to define but extraordinarily difficult to resolve. The claim to fame of public broadcasting, that it offers programming which the commercial system does not offer, is losing plausibility and rhetorical force. The difficulty of dealing with this for the public broadcaster stems from the fact that his or her rhetoric tended to hang its legitimacy on the peg of offering a diversity and range of programming.

Sometimes such possibilities are welcomed by those public broadcasters who have either wearily given up in the face of constant assault and battery, or never did like the populist tint of modern public broadcasting, or, increasingly, are more concerned with the creation and keeping of personal empire than with meaningful purpose. There is, however, a larger school of thought which remains determined to hold to the centre ground of their respective societies. In doing so, they articulate—sometimes overtly, sometimes subtly and intuitively—an argument *for* public broadcasting which is profound.

The fact of the matter is that range and diversity are not now, and never were, the final issue. The principle which lay behind the commitment to range and diversity was that only in this way could one bring something else to the many facets of life-as-lived. That something else was the commitment to 'quality' and 'standards', and the belief that the worth of a genre lies not in its arithmetic role in creating diversity but in the character of the programmes offered from *within* the genre. From this perspective the nature of public broadcasting would be that any programme offered, whatever the genre, should be the best of its kind, the best it can be. The argument against game shows on public broadcasting would thus have to be that they inherently cannot be worthwhile, which is *not* an especially easy case to make. And, in fact, we have seen examples of game and quiz shows which defy the commercial, down-market stereotype, rich with literary allusion, social consciousness, and humour.

If this perspective is adopted it provides the basis for a confrontation with the argument that, for example, public broadcasting should not be in the business of news, only analysis, because there is such a thing as a 'quality' news programme and a 'poor' news programme. The argument should also ask questions of the phrases 'drama with a mass appeal' as opposed to 'serious

[6] *Sunday Times*, 1 Sept. 1991.

drama'. What is the difference between 'mass' appeal and 'broad' appeal; what does 'serious' mean; why not seek to produce drama of the highest standards—defined how you will—which also seeks to be watched by as many people as possible? and was not Shakespeare—to borrow an almost clichéd example—popular in his day? Or would one exclude a Paddy Chayefsky or a Dennis Potter because they are popular as well as serious? And at what point for example does 'mass' appeal actually begin?

The problem—and this has to be confronted—is that the concept of 'quality' is impossible to define in the abstract, and is inevitably judgemental and hierarchical. Nevertheless it remains true that the subjectivities which ooze from any examination of 'quality' or some such phrase as 'the best of its kind' make this a far from easy position to defend. One might even suggest that the idea of quality programme-making only had meaning so long as no one ever seriously asked what that meaning was. This is, perhaps, why some, maybe many, public broadcasters find it easier to think of taking the 'things the market doesn't do' approach saying 'we are better because we're different', rather than that of 'we are better because we are better'. It has been axiomatic to public service broadcasting that it seeks to be 'popular', but with real class and superior craft whatever the genre of programme, for if it is not popular, i.e. providing a quality service to large numbers of people, consistently and across a range of programmes, in what sense can it claim to be *public* service broadcasting? The garnering of a large audience or collection of audiences is thus not only, or primarily, a functional necessity for survival, important though that is, it is an expression of the very nature, the central philosophical tenet, of the institution of public broadcasting. Many public broadcasters continue to believe that their rightful place is not at the edge but at the heart of their society, central to all its forms of life. The question which is, however, often asked is whether maintaining such centrality is now, or will be in the future, feasible.

Something of the real intractability of this issue of language is captured in the debates around children's television. The debate about the future of television, and in particular the very real struggle which is taking place between the public and private spheres, is clearly of considerable significance. It is a debate which goes to the very heart of how we define ourselves as societies and individuals, of what we feel the axial principles should be to govern the evolution of society and culture at a time of massive amplification of the physical capacity to communicate. Children's TV is an especially sharp and contentious element within that discussion. Internationally, there is a significant debate emerging about the character of the programmes provided for children; a realization that the rapid evolution of technologies of distribution has thrown into even sharper relief the question of the future of children's TV and a widespread belief that of all the areas of broadcasting that are undertaken around the planet, the litmus test for the social and cultural worth of broadcasting is children's television. If we cannot get it right for children, chances are we cannot get it right for anyone.

The notion of 'getting it right' is, however, inevitably loaded with unstated meaning. In whose terms are we talking? What does 'right' look like? What are the objective and subjective categories which we need to employ to give substance to the assertion? What evidence do we require in order to know what a programme is like? Do we do well by younger generations? Do we serve and nurture or merely gratify? Are we manufacturing a culture for them of which we can be properly proud or are we merely expanding the boundaries of the wasteland? Can we claim to know what children need with the same facility with which we appear to grasp what they want? What are the peaks and troughs of children's television and how might we learn to achieve the former and avoid the latter? And just what precisely are we providing for children by way of television? And who decides whose values and preferences should prevail?

Testifying before the Senate Judiciary Committee, Dr William Dietz, a member of the communications committee of the American Academy of Pediatrics, asserted that 'television in the United States constitutes a major health hazard for children'.[7] The journalist Les Brown, decrying that, even in a multi-channel society, 'range' remains limited, described deregulated television as

television without a soul, without a charter except to make money, without concern for social responsibility . . . worst of all is the offense against children, since they are (as opposed to the elderly and the poor) addressed as a market. Even to think of five-year-olds as consumers, with the ability to exercise judgment on what to buy, is indecent—I would go so far as to say immoral. And this extends beyond the products pitched at the young to the very programmes that are designed to capture their attention for the benefit of the advertiser. When commerce is the issue, programmes can be cynically conceived . . . virtually all of it is animated fluff—at best nicely diverting but without any sort of intellectual or moral nourishment, at worst charged with mindless violence.[8]

Dietz and Brown here reflect a widespread concern among laity and, often, professionals, a sense that children are watching 'too much' of the 'wrong' kind of programmes. The quotation marks are used here not to disqualify or question the intent of the commentator. Rather they are used to signal recognition that there is an inevitable contentiousness to such propositions in which articles of faith, sometimes only loosely wedded to evidence, are

---

[7] Quoted in *Cable and Broadcasting*, 26 July 1993.
[8] Les Brown, 'Who is the Winner in Children's Television: Pubs or Coms?', paper presented to conference, Goethe Institute, Jerusalem, 21–3 Jan. 1993.

espoused as detached analyses. So long as the place of public service values in broadcasting remained unproblematic such faith remained inherently stable. Once those core values became problematic so would other discourses, for example about children's television, emerge, in which the evolution of television is viewed as benign, even liberating, as the 'Nanny-state' of regulated communications is laid waste by the 'democratic' charms of 'consumer choice'.

Such polarities point, if nothing else, to the fact that there is within nations, and at a global level, a fractured discourse about the general condition of all television. It is, however, one in which the idea of the market and the alleged cornucopia of choice offered by cable and satellite have become dominant. Children's television did not go unaffected by this trend, and is marked more often than not by the decline of the public and the rise of the commercial sectors. The scale of the industry provides powerful incentives to assert the primacy of the market in provision for children. In the USA, for example, in 1993 advertisers spent an estimated $800 million on advertisements in children's programmes. *The Lion King* made $250 million for Disney at the box-office; when it was released on video it had revenues of $400 million in two weeks. Children between the ages of 2 and 11 spend or influence the spending of $100 billion annually. Children between 8 and 12—known in the trade as 'the tweens'—account for $50 billion in consumer spending in the USA, and spend $10–15 billion directly.[9] Again in the USA an estimated 60 per cent of the available ratings for children's programmes for 1993 came from cable. The year before the rate was 46 per cent. Recognizing the trend and seeking to nurture it, the cable industry now sees children's television as a major area for investment, particularly in original animation. Another important trend, clearly linked to televised children's programming, is the growth in the use of videocassettes. In 1992 the sale of children's videos in the USA was worth $2.4 billion. Video games are now a $4.5 billion industry and growing. In short, selling things to children via television has become a huge industry.

The pattern of the increasing commercialization of children's television is hardly unique to the United States, though the particular significance of the USA in this area lies in the fact that its products readily and significantly seep into the cultural ecology of the planet. In Germany, for example, commercial stations using much imported material have decimated the children's audience for public television: for all households with or without cable and satellite, among 6–13-year-olds, in October 1992 RTL had 21 per cent of viewing, ARD 15 per cent, Pro-7 15 per cent, ZDF 11 per cent, Tele 5 11 per cent. In TVHH with cable Pro-7 had a market share of 22 per cent, RTL 20 per cent, SAT1 15 per cent, Tele 5 14 per cent, ARD 10 per cent. One German public television producer commented:

---

[9] *New York Times*, 18 Oct. 1993.

What makes [Germany's] up-and-comer Pro-7 as a commercial broadcaster so appealing to children is the fact that Pro-7's afternoon programme consists entirely of action series and cartoons. In our department we have arrived at the conclusion that we have no choice but to participate in this process of commercialization in order to hold our own against increasing competition. Making good programmes alone is no longer sufficient.[10]

In Italy, as commercial stations developed in the 1970s and 1980s, RAI de-emphasized children's programmes in order to concentrate on the adult prime-time schedule. Paolo de Benedetti Gonnelli of RAI observed:

The reduced budget given in the past years to daytime programming has practically made impossible the creation of a national series of fiction for young people, educational documentaries, or Italian cartoons. The result has been a progressive growth in the quantity of imported series and cartoons. In other terms, there is no great difference between the private networks and RAI, although the former certainly spend more money on the acquisition of cartoons.[11]

Naohiro Kato of the Asia-Pacific Broadcasting Union has written: 'TV programmes aired in our region are not always innovative and imaginative enough for the adult-to-be audience, who are inundated by handy, imported programmes.'[12] It has also been estimated that the pan-European TNT and Cartoon Network carries programming which is 97 per cent non-European.

There is within public debates about children's TV a prevailing, perhaps inevitable, evaluative subjectivism. Terms such as 'quality', 'excellence', 'trivial', 'dangerous', 'good', 'bad', hang loose from the limbs of public discourse. But these also constitute the broader language of public broadcasting. And yet that language, writ large or small, general or specific, constitutes the most profound conceptual, even philosophical, difficulties of definition and meaning.

The difficulties of language and justification are compounded by the fact that public policy on television is itself dogged by definitional uncertainty. It is not uninteresting that in the UK, the alma mater of public service and educational programming, definitions of what those terms mean have been almost totally absent. The term 'quality' has never been defined, even when incorporated in the most recent British legislation which demanded that applications for commercial franchises must first pass a 'quality threshold'. Rather the habit has been to exemplify and offer the proof of practice.

One of the crucial difficulties in dealing with television, particularly as a regulator, is the making of judgements about what is or is not appropriate. A tendency is to shift the making of judgements away from the subtlety of what is or is not 'good' to things which are manifestly unacceptable or offensive. It is as if the American constitutional model had been exported

---

[10] Smirnov, quoted in Prix Jeunesse report on condition of children's TV (Munich, 1993), 22.
[11] Paolo de Benedetti Gonnelli, ibid. 40.   [12] Naohiro Kato, ibid. 47.

abroad, a model in which for example there is little or no prior restraint on communications and where *post-hoc* review tends to deal with issues of whether something is or is not offensive to community standards, is obscene, and so on. This approach tends to anchor discussion of programme content to moralistic judgements rather than the far more elusive questions of character, quality, and overall worth.

The agonies of definitional uncertainty, as to what we mean by 'quality', have led those of a more philosophical bent to conclude that it is essentially experiential and beyond abstract linguistic apprehension. More policy-oriented research within public broadcasting organizations has tended to fall back onto the construction of measures of whether people *feel* that a programme is a quality programme. The obvious implausibility here is that *any* system of television can apply the same test. As a methodology, therefore, it means little to any debate taking place between public and commercial television systems. The fact that such evaluations are even engaged in speaks powerfully to the real difficulties confronting the public service community.

Less subjectivist, somewhat more abstract, definitions of a quality service have pointed to the presence within the schedule of certain genres—news, current affairs, drama, children, religion—to which the tag line is added 'of a high quality'.

Other depictions of 'quality' suggest definition through character and consequence. So, for example, one finds reference to programmes which demonstrate excellence, choice, range, variety, balance, flexibility, authenticity, seriousness. Or they point to programming which is non-trivial, non-exploitative, innovative, has integrity, respect for subject-matter and audience, and so on.[13]

One also finds reference to programming which assists in 'cultural self-determination', the ability of a society to ensure that its 'cultural traditions, values and characteristic issue frames, tensions and problems are well represented, with adequate resources to guarantee their expression, within its own media system' or providing 'meaningful cultural' experiences, allowing audiences to reflect 'on the meanings, problematics and implications of issues of identity, human relationships and sociopolitical trends in local, national and international contexts'.[14] Others have come at the issue from the standpoint of a set of defining, contextual conditions: the presence of craft skills, adequate resources, truthfulness, relevance, a teasing of the curious mind, a certain clarity of vision and passion, signs of innovation 'stimulating the imagination/creativity/emotions' of the child, 'broadening the mind', 'responding to need

[13] T. Leggett, 'Identifying the Undefinable: An Essay on Approaches to Assessing Quality in TV in the UK', *Studies of Broadcasting*, special issue, *Quality Assessment of Broadcast Programming*, ed. S. Ishikawa and Y. Muramatsu, 27 (Mar. 1991), 113–32.

[14] J. Blumler, 'In Pursuit of Programme Range and Quality', ibid. 191–206.

and expectation'—all these constitute the grammar of what might be called the 'intent' model.[15]

These are all interesting, even clever, attempts to bring a level of precision to what constitutes a 'quality' service that public broadcasting has as its own. These are however attempts which fail, riddled as they are with a looseness, vagueness, and monumental elasticity which suggest the real impossibility of their being a language *sui generis* of public broadcasting. Such a condition renders the public broadcaster mute in the face of other languages which may articulate a cruder view of the purpose of broadcasting but which within their own terms do maintain a significantly higher level of plausibility.

The story of public broadcasting is thus the *story* of our times, a weave of institutional decay and transformation, emerging powerful technologies and their consequences, shifting sociologies and forms of life. I am not suggesting that the particular, substantive issues which touch and challenge public broadcasting are unimportant, that it remains forever a metaphor. Issues of the character of programming remain significant, even vital, questions in any assessment of contemporary culture. Concepts such as 'quality' and 'standards' are important and troubled at the same moment. And still, in many countries, the public broadcasting organization continues to lie at the heart of the national culture, a significant element in the political, social, and cultural life of the society.

By *story* I mean that any narrative of the contemporary condition of public broadcasting becomes an unfolding of plots within plots, like a Russian Matryoshka doll. One begins with an examination of the organizational practices and programme philosophies, how this or that programme is made and how such processes distinguish public from commercial broadcasting. But practice and institutional philosophy are the children of money. One then, therefore, considers finance, with the always plausible Watergate argument that, if you really want to know how something works, 'follow the money'. Very quickly though one realizes that finance is deeply influenced by the attitudes of governments and policy-makers and the shifting sands of legislation. But then one has to consider the ways in which those policies and governmental attitudes are heavily influenced by the need to modernize the industrial economic order, and by the rise of a new entrepreneurial bourgeoisie very different from the patrician bourgeois who so readily understood the cultural elevation and social cohesion and stability which were the assumed corollary of a national instrument of communication. There is also the technology, which like tragedy and nuclear weapons can neither be wished away nor disinvented. And then one has to deal with the realization that popular culture and the

---

[15] Prix Jeunesse report, 87; Leggett, 'Identifying the Undefinable'; T. Nossiter, 'British Television: A Mixed Economy', in *Research on the Range and Quality of Broadcasting Services* (London: HMSO, 1986).

social uses of new distribution technologies such as cable, satellite, and video would not be possible if there were not harmonies between their nature and the character of the social order within which they are present. One therefore has to deal with the nature of 'the public' that is being served, the changing structure of the audience, the possible dissolution of any idea of the collective, the community.

Along with all that goes the question mark which now hangs over the nation-state, and in many instances today the uncertainty over just what kind of society is desirable. For example, our study makes clear that the impasse in developing coherent policy for broadcasting in the new democracies of Central Europe, such as Poland, Hungary, and the Czech Republic, is not just, or primarily, a consequence of the intransigence of an old order which has not quite died, or of the stalling tactics of the nomenclatura in new guise. The problem is fundamentally one of deciding what kinds of societies, polities, and economies they want to be. If a society has not decided its own preferred character in a broad sense, it will find it exceedingly difficult to determine its character in the particular sense of its broadcasting.

In this vein it is also interesting to look at the dilemmas and contradictions of broadcasting in Asia. From Singapore to Malaysia to China to India to Indonesia governments have sought to 'modernize'. Television is no exception, through, for example, involvements in cable, international satellites, the offerings of Star TV, and the development of their own domestic and regional satellites. At the same time those governments have all sought to *limit* access to new programme services which have not been approved by government authorities. Islamic sensibility is a particularly important issue here, as is the clash over western forms of liberal democracy. Again, what all this suggests is that there is a basic indecisiveness about what kinds of societies they wish to be: secular and consumerist or theocratic and controlled. They cannot be both.

The public broadcaster at his or her best tends to believe—in some manner —in creative and intellectual independence; in serving rather than using the audience; in quality and standards in productions; in seeking to be the best whatever the genre; in avoiding the lowest common denominator. It is a sensibility which necessarily presupposes that the rest of the society has at least a level of understanding and empathy. The sense of real instability which now affects public broadcasting is, of course, a function of technology, and government policy fed by ideology. But it cannot only be that. It is aided and abetted by the growth of huge corporations that dwarf the 'ordinary individual'; a deregulated, commercially driven, multi-mediated world that is fundamentally divisive. It is coarsened further by sheer mediocrity, the flight from excellence, and the enthronement of the trivial, the superficial, the ghoulish in much market-driven television. These factors are all definably part of the condition of modern culture constructed from the ground up. Governments have been receiving succour, a kind of silent applause, from viewers and listeners, consumers, who think from within the self rather than with any developed sense of the collective. A simple law seems to be at work: no market, no value. It is in this context that I would suggest that to speak of diversity may actually play into the hands of the new language of television, which co-opts the diversity notion, and which functions within a set of apparently dominant cultural values that welcome the consumerist philosophy of modern television.

If adjustment is the key motif of the times, the matter is complicated in that the character of the 1990s, its intellectual parameters, is unclear, and certainly much less clear than in, say, the period 1945–75 or the decade of the 1980s. We all know that for good or ill the 1980s were about the market, just as the earlier period was anchored to a more collectivist concept of public culture. The sense of the need for change in public broadcasting rests on assumptions about the failure of the earlier period and the importance of market values in all human affairs, including broadcasting. But the 1980s and their crude use of market forces have at least rhetorically been somewhat discredited, even if the actual practice of public and private life remains in the values of self, consumption, and the market. So public broadcasters find themselves between two worlds, two different sets of expectations, trying to bend with the wind when it is blowing from more than one direction. A certain confusion and uncertainty is perhaps understandable.

The conclusions are obvious, if bleak. Whatever the bravery and wisdom of public broadcasters who articulate serious principles and who keep the faith in difficult circumstances, in the end it is not possible to have a viable social institution which is out of step with the prevailing sociological realities; neither is it feasible to have a philosophy of broadcasting which runs ahead of a larger philosophy of society. And if 'the nation' and 'the public' are dissolved —assuming they ever existed—then what is there left to serve?

It is at this point that the extent of the difficult struggle which today faces *national* public broadcasting begins to become clear, and the analysis has yet again to be refracted through a larger lens. The proposition that public broadcasting should not be marginalized, but rather should seek to continue to address the heartland of a society and its culture, presupposes that there is a heartland to be addressed, let alone that public service broadcasting is in a position to do so. We do not mean 'able' only in some formalistic sense of government acquiescence—important though that is—but also in the sense of whether the nature of the moment, its deep rhythms, will *permit* the public broadcaster to survive. The brute truth is that the sets of choices that have been made, in country after country, over the past decade or more—on geopolitical systems, technological innovations, and economic modernization —allied with other more subterranean socio-cultural tensions, have wreaked havoc with all facets of public culture. There remains a rather optimistic, even noble, sensibility within the planet's public broadcasting community, a will to triumph over circumstances. Public broadcasting, when it is properly true to itself, rests above all else on a heady optimism about ordinary folk. Wherever one looks in the history of public broadcasting one sees the same 'field of dreams' optimism: build the institution as a vehicle for superior entertainment, quality journalism, insight and boldness, excellence in all that is done—construct that architecture—and they will come.

In some ways in the past they did. But then they, the public-as-audience, had no choice. If you are the national public broadcaster with little or no competition having an audience does not require genius. They have nowhere else to go. There has to be an architecture of sensibilities within a society if the architecture of institutions is to gain and sustain plausibility and, therefore, organizational stability. What, however, if one's optimistic faith in the people, and their ability and desire to engage with the productions of public broadcasting, rests on an illusion, dependent on a set of presumptions which are now past, while commercial broadcasting rests on a foundation of socio-cultural realities?

If one maintains a broad focus on the changes in the contours of human and social geography it is not difficult to put a name to all that has been described, to all that is happening and will continue to happen. What we are witnessing is the triumph of populism: it may be intelligent populism or corrupted populism, but it is populism nevertheless. We are accustomed to living in a world of borders, literal and metaphorical delineations of difference. The nation-state has for the past couple of centuries been the most obvious articulation of this social phenomenon. Part of the strength of the idea of the nation is that it provided something which is clearly an important aspect of the social psychology of the species, the need to belong, the need to feel the comforts of friends as well as strangers, to be embedded in ways of seeing and feeling good which are familiar, which feel 'right'. Nationalism and jingoism are obvious expressions of this, but so are the family wedding, the street gang, the conversation around the drinking fountain, the journey to Mecca or home at Thanksgiving or Christmas or Hanukkah. Beneath the articulation of the nation-state were these other ways of belonging defined by kinship, friendship, location, gender, generation, education, and happenstance. In other words, and wherever we are, we remain a sociology, as within our 'self' are lodged these in effect objective characteristics.

This social condition does not go away simply because television has started to flow across borders, nor will it as that flow continues and as the technology amplifies by a power of ten or twenty, or whatever it might eventually be, the amount of communication available. What we can begin to see appearing, however, as the clouds of change break up a little, is the manner in which the technology, working with the social grain, gets ever closer to the details of that social condition. So, for example, the old public broadcasters such as the BBC or NHK worked at one level because they did personify certain broad-based commonalities, expressions of what it was to be British or Japanese. That is why there was truth to the cliché that at moments of national crisis the public would turn to them for 'information'. They were successful because they worked with, not against, the grain of the society. That sharing, nevertheless, was extraordinarily superficial. As the amount and form of television increases, what is happening is that other, perhaps more fundamental, defining characteristics are becoming not only apparent but also serviceable, along those lines of characteristics of which I have spoken. The comforts of the familiar and the parochial are becoming ever more available, and there is nothing anyone can do about it, any more than one can stop a season of tides.

National public broadcasters still, and in spite of everything that has happened to them, tend to believe that the national community is something other than a geopolitical entity, something more than an allegory; that fashioned out of the history and sociology of a given experience the community exists in the consciousness of its members.

Underlying these commitments is a sense that they have of the nationalisms that anchor the national broadcaster. I am not talking here of the rabid, racist nationalisms which have scarred European politics, but the more benign, welcome, sense of belonging that the national has historically provided. However, in broad social terms what we are in fact witnessing is the loss of both a sense and reality of shared public space and community, those places in which, to borrow from Richard Sennett, strangers meet and thus become less strange and which have been such an important part of the life of modern, liberal democratic societies.[16] Perhaps the most profound metaphor for this is the diminution in the sovereignty of the nation-state, and therefore a corrosion in the authority and legitimacy of all those organizations which have the prefix 'nation', including public broadcasters. Equally, interior divisions, bred by historic antagonisms and social rivalries, are amplified by technologies which in the very act of giving everyone a voice create a new muteness, neutralizing the possibility of conversation across the divides.

Mary Ellen and Main Street

There is a debate in the United States about the condition of its political culture. Two troubling and, it was assumed, linked issues are the poverty of political coverage by most broadcasting and the apathy of the American public

---

[16] Richard Sennett, *The Fall of Public Man* (New York: Knopf, 1974).

about the political process, most profoundly expressed through a voter turnout at presidential elections which was hovering at around 50 per cent.

Lloyd Morrisett, President of the Markle Foundation, a major source of funding for media-related projects, decided to use his resources to do something about this situation. Having studied the problem of the broadcast coverage of the 1988 election he decided to pump several million dollars into public broadcasting to allow it more in-depth, analytical coverage of the issues. The likely effectiveness of such an ambition need not concern us here, and anyhow he never got the co-operation of the public broadcasting community. What is particularly interesting about Morrisett's position is the way in which, in making his case, he invoked an image of an America long gone, an elegy to a time of innocence and community and shared belief which broadcasting might recreate. Here is what he said of the visits he made, as a boy, to his cousin Mary Ellen.

On soft summer evenings we would often walk the two or three blocks to Main Street and visit the ice-cream parlour. That was the place to see and be seen, and I was glad to bask in the admiration my cousin received from other boys. The ice-cream parlour was also a gathering place for adults. The movie house and the bowling alley were not far away; and when the carnival came to town, it established itself on some vacant land adjacent to Main Street. During the day, Main Street was the town's business center; during the evening, it was the center of the town's social life. As a young boy, I was taken by my cousin's charm, the taste of a good milkshake, and the beckoning adventures of a summer evening. Yet over the years, I have come to see how important Main Street was to the lives of Jerseyville, Illinois. Main Street brought the town together. When people came to shop, pick up their groceries, or take in their cleaning, they would stop here and there to chat. In the evening, the movies, the ice-cream parlor, and the bowling alley drew people together. Sunday school and church meant still more trips to Main Street and more opportunity to greet friends and neighbors. In Jerseyville, as in small towns and cities all across the country, Main Street was a powerful contributor to a sense of community.[17]

As Morrisett observed, the binding together of Main Street began to diminish after the Second World War; and 'though often mourned, it seems impossible to recreate'. The yearning for some form of community, he seems to be suggesting, remains, only now it is fashioned not on the concrete pavements of Main Street or round the ice-cream parlour but through a common cerebral not physical experience: 'Television has, in effect, become America's Main Street.' The essence of Main Street Jerseyville was that the community was physical, whereas the essence of Main Street Televille is that it is mediated.

There is a certain plausibility to the argument that the sense of community of Jerseyville, expressed on its Main Street, rested on a set of shared

---

[17] Lloyd Morrisett, presidential essay, annual report of the Markle Foundation (New York, 1990), 7.

assumptions, beliefs, and a sensibility which not only defined it but also linked the town to a myriad other such communities. And together they defined the national community, suggesting what it is to be American.

Morrisett's laudable desire is to use broadcasting to serve better the national community, which lives on through broadcasting. That it lives on, he suggests, is most profoundly demonstrated in the importance of sport in broadcasting. Ways, he says, 'must be found to use TV to raise the level of political discourse, to inform and educate the public, and to contribute to what John Dewey called "a collective intelligence" '. He adds: 'we need to designate part of broadcasting as the place Americans can turn to see Presidential candidates, learn about the issues, and follow the events and direction of campaigns. The public broadcasting system has a unique opportunity to become that place, the nation's political Main Street for all citizens.'[18]

Here then is a central and common part of the lexicon of justification for public broadcasting, *the power of the shared moment*. The argument points to the extraordinary potential of television—it used to be radio—to lead large numbers of people to engage in a singular experience at the same time and thus somehow to be united and existentially strengthened. JFK's funeral, the coronation of Queen Elizabeth, the last episodes of *MASH* and *Roots*, Princess Di's wedding, the *Challenger* disaster, the first night of Desert Storm—all are grist to the mill.

The question is whether quite as much significance attaches to this as we suggest. It is only partly facetious to point out that millions of people have coffee or tea or beer or supper at more or less the same time and no one suggests that those singularities are expressive and defining of community. In this vein I was much struck by the events in Canada in 1993 surrounding the Toronto Blue Jays who had won the baseball World Series. There was much cheering and waving of flags, crowds lined the street, CBC covered live the triumphant return of the first Canadian team ever to win the USA's national game. The very next day the Canadian public voted overwhelmingly in a national referendum to reject a policy which had been massively touted as the only way to keep Canada unified. How to interpret these two discordant events? One possibility is that the symbolic interpretation of the BJs' return is sharply out of focus. The pleasure of successful sportsmanship is something most people can understand, but clearly in real terms individual Canadians did not define themselves through sport and remained within sociologically fragmented clusterings, new versions of old formations, calcified linguistic difference and historic rivalry.

Or consider what was really going on with JFK's funeral. There is one apparently universal human characteristic: when people see a hearse passing, they

[18] Ibid.

stare. Quite often they stop, stand in pained silence, and stare. We watch, how-ever fleetingly, because we have compassion but also because we see there intimations of our own mortality. It is a gaze which speaks to an ultimate sense of self, not community. If the dominant characteristic of the modern age is 'the self' articulated through private lives, where does that leave public broadcasting? What constitutes a public we can communicate with? Indeed, is there an 'it', a grouping of people defined by their individual uniqueness *and* their commonality? If a problem faced by public broadcasters is one of increasing marginality as the share of viewing diminishes, then that raises the question of what it is to be central. Centrality could be taken to mean an embodiment of ideas, sensibilities, values which are common within a society and which allow the broadcaster to have a purchase on the audience through programme strategies which incorporate those commonalities. In a simpler sense centrality may involve no more than a numbers game—the more people that attend to the service offered the more central the institution is, the fewer, the more marginal.

The Question of Governance

The title of this chapter is drawn from lines in which Yeats suggested that the modern condition was dysfunctional and fragmented. The bureaucratization of modern industrial society was alienating. The human response to this pro-cess was to seek meaning and sanctuary in the primary institution which might provide it, the family. Krishan Kumar describes the modern family as

the only remaining institution capable of giving a sense of identity and belonging in a world of shifting impersonal ties and contractual relationships. As against the tend-encies towards specificity, instrumentality, impersonality, and ephemerality in the roles people play in the wider society, the family stresses diffuse obligations, a wider con-ception of tasks beyond the purely calculative, emotional and expressive relationships, and lasting loyalty and commitment.[19]

If the public sphere became a place where one found comfort in strangers, the private sphere of the family was where one increasingly found sanctuary from the disappointment of strangers, and the ravages of an economic order which was forming the public sphere in the first place: 'As the family became a refuge from the terrors of society, it gradually became also a moral yard-stick with which to measure the public realm of the capital city'—the city, the most profound expression of the public sphere, coming to be seen as 'morally inferior'.[20] The family in the twentieth century reconstituted itself

[19] Kumar, *Prophecy and Progress*, 315.   [20] Sennett, *The Fall of Public Man*, 20.

in the suburbs and housing estates which spread like a geographical Rorschach blot, decentralized and animated by the ganglia of an infrastructure of power, the telephone, the automobile, and roads, and amused and informed by broadcasting which is inherently decentralized and home-centred.

In other words, the more efficient we were in creating the technical infrastructure of a dispersed urban life, the more efficient we were at destroying the possibility of community: 'the replacement of city streets and squares as social centres by suburban living rooms might have something to do with an increased absorption with self.'[21]

There is, however, another turn of the screw. If it is the case that people turned to the family for the creation of meaning and the provision of emotional support, then clearly the family, for many people, also failed. The traditional family is now in a minority. Single-parent and single-person homes are now more prevalent—a function of divorce, personal choice, and an ageing population. If the family is no longer a safe haven, then the only way forward is a further retreat into self or new associations which offer new meaning —God, political movements, street gangs, drugs, cults, with people like 'me' rather than the 'other' who is different. Colouring the whole process is a rampant consumerism, fundamentally private in its character, in which I buy things for me. Elmer Johnson, in a wonderful essay on the place of the car in US society, notes: 'the heavy impingement of the market in every arena of our lives tends to blind us to the public interest—that complex of common goods that lies beyond our private, utilitarian goals.'[22] He adds that the culture of the market, of which the car is a profound expression, 'has led to the automization of urban life and has tended to stunt the development of our capacities to nurture and value shared forms of life: family, community and civic life'.[23]

If this analysis is in any way accurate, public broadcasting has been shaving against the grain: it speaks a language of 'us' when common discourse is of 'me'; it commits itself to that which is excellent when common practice commits to what is buyable. And every development in the institutions of broadcasting will encourage those tendencies—ever more channels, providing slivers of programming, for slices of audience. Thus if one considers the phrase 'national public broadcasting' it begins to appear that each element—the nation, the public, the broadcast—has become problematic.

The immediate question is, does it matter if entertainment is corrupted, programming for the young debased, drama diminished, journalism trivialized? The fact of the matter is that these things do matter if we believe that a certain level of communal civility, caring, and excellence are important to the

[21] Ibid.

[22] Elmer Johnson, 'Taming the Car and its User: Should We Do Both?', *Aspen Quarterly* (Autumn 1992), 112.

[23] Ibid.

well-being of the democratic polity; if we think it important to be concerned with the character of civic culture and the well-being of the public mind.

The fundamental argument for public broadcasting borrows from a rather more broadly drawn argument for the role of governance in human affairs, particularly within the confines of a coherent entity, the nation, imbued with a civic ethic. The mix of ideology and technology in the past decade or so has done much to shred that ethic, dismantle the concept of public space, diminish the idea of national community, inject a certain coarseness into cultural practice, and question the very idea of governance. Margaret Thatcher declared that there is no such thing as society, Ronald Reagan offered that government was the problem not the solution, and his appointed Chairman of the Federal Communications Commission, Mark Fowler, defined the public interest as that in which the public is interested.

In the 1850s Lincoln wrote that 'the legitimate object of government is to do for the people what needs to be done, but which they cannot, by individual effort, do at all, or do so well, for themselves'.[24] Striner notes that Lincoln's respect for the liberating power of egalitarian principles 'was nonetheless balanced by a grim understanding of the ugly side of human nature, of the human lusts that can lead with such appalling speed to unfreedom'.[25] For Lincoln slavery was the most searing evidence of 'the selfishness of man's nature', opposition to it an invocation of 'his love of justice'. He referred to these polarities as 'an eternal antagonism . . . that politics can alter and rearrange, but can never terminate'. But, as Striner notes in this commentary on Lincoln, you 'cannot repeal the oppressive side of human nature, but you can govern it'.[26] In his autobiography Theodore Roosevelt observed that a 'simple and poor society can exist as a democracy on the basis of sheer individuals. But a rich and complex industrial society cannot so exist; for some individuals, and especially those artificial individuals called corporations, become so very big that the ordinary individual is utterly dwarfed beside them, and cannot deal with them on terms of equality. It therefore becomes necessary for these ordinary individuals to combine in their turn . . . through the biggest of all combinations called the government.'[27]

Whatever the objective difficulties which face public broadcasting its canon must be constantly asserted: that it sets its face against the mediocre and the debased and asserts the necessity to nurture quality in the life of the public mind through ensuring that the population of the polity can be properly informed, properly educated, and provided with a sense of coherence and belonging; that the national public broadcaster is the most powerful centripetal

[24] Richard Striner, 'Reviving the Legacy of Lincoln and the Two Roosevelts', *Aspen Quarterly*, 4/3 (summer 1992), 73.

[25] Ibid. 88.   [26] Ibid. 90.   [27] Ibid. 89.

force in societies with dangerous centrifugal tendencies. In these arguments lies the fact that the social forces which so challenge the public broadcaster also provide the most powerful argument for his or her existence; that the modern, democratic nation-state *needs* a national public broadcasting service, because it needs a quality of life, social and cultured coherence, and to quarantine the tendency to division, degradation, and domination.

There will be nothing easy about this, but there is something crucially important. Yeats wrote, 'we who care deeply about the arts find ourselves the priesthood of an almost forgotten faith'. One might substitute public broadcasting for arts. He also wrote however of 'poets who rouse and trouble and . . . poets who hush and console'. Those concerned with the future, through rousing and troublemaking, speak not just to the condition of public broadcasting but to the vastly more important question of what we are and will be as a social species.

Bibliography

BALFOUR, MICHAEL, *West Germany* (London: Ernest Benn Ltd., 1968).

BENEDICT, RUTH, *The Chrysanthemum and the Sword: Patterns of Japanese Culture* (Boston: Houghton Mifflin Co., 1946).

Broadcasting Research Unit, *The Public Service Idea in British Broadcasting* (London: BRN, 1985).

BURNS, TOM, *The BBC: Public Institution Private World* (London: Macmillan, 1977).

BYFORD-JONES, W., *Berlin Twilight* (London: Hutchinson, 1948).

CRAWLEY, AIDAN, *The Rise of West Germany 1945–1972* (London: Collins, 1973).

CURRAN, CHARLES, *A Seamless Robe* (London: Macmillan, 1977).

DICKENS, A. G., *Lübeck Diary* (London: Gollancz, 1947).

FARNSWORTH, JOHN, 'Two-Channel New Zealand Television: Ambiguities of Organization, Profession and Culture' (Ph.D., University of Canterbury, 1989).

FRIENDLY, F. W., *Due to Circumstances beyond our Control* (New York: Random House, 1967).

GRISEWOOD, HARMAN, *One Thing at a Time* (London: Hutchinson, 1968).

HECHT, BEN, *Letters from Bohemia* (New York: Doubleday, 1964).

HOGGART, RICHARD, *Only Connect: On Culture and Communication* (London: Chatto & Windus, 1972).

HOLLINS, TIM, *Beyond Broadcasting: Into the Cable Age* (London: BRU/BFI, 1984).

Home Office, *Report of the Committee on the Future of Broadcasting*, Cmnd 6753 (London: HMSO, 1977) [Annan Report].

—— *Report of the Committee on Financing the BBC*, Cmnd 9824 (London: HMSO, July 1986) [Peacock Report].

ITAP, *Cable Systems: A Report by the Information Technology Advisory Panel* (London: HMSO, 1982).

KIRKPATRICK, IVONE, *The Inner Circle* (London: Macmillan, 1959).

KITAHARA, YASUSADA, *Information Network System: Telecommunications in the 21st Century* (London: Hutchinson, 1983).

KUMAR, KRISHAN, *Prophecy and Progress: The Sociology of Industrial and Post-Industrial Society* (London: Allen Lane, 1978).

MILNE, ALASDAIR, *DG: The Memoirs of a British Broadcaster* (London: Hodder & Stoughton, 1988).

Morrison, David, *Invisible Citizens* (London: BRN/Libbey 1986).

Postman, Neil, *Conscientious Objections: Stirring of Trouble about Language, Technology and Education* (New York: Knopf, 1988).

Postmaster-General, *Report of the Committee on Broadcasting, 1960*, Cmnd. 1753 (London: HMSO, 1962) [Pilkington Report].

Sennett, Richard, *The Fall of Public Man* (New York: Knopf, 1976).

Spender, Stephen, *European Witness* (London: Hamish Hamilton, 1946).

Steiner, George, *Language and Silence* (London: Faber, 1985).

Tracey, Michael, *A Variety of Lives: A Biography of Sir Hugh Greene* (London: Bodley Head, 1983).

Trethowan, Ian, *Split Screen* (London: Hamish Hamilton, 1984).

The Working Party Report on New Technologies (London: Broadcasting Research Unit, 1983).

Index

DATE DUE

FEB 23 REC'D			
MAR 2 7 2002			
APR 1 8 2002		DISCARDED	
MAY 1 1			
MAY 0 8 REC'D			
MAR 2 4 REC'D			
OhioLINK			
MAR 2 8 REC'D			
MAY 0 4 2007			
MAY 0 3 REC'D			
GAYLORD			PRINTED IN U.S.A.

HE 8689.7 .P82 T7 1998

Tracey, Michael.

The decline and fall of
 public service broadcasting